Mathematica®
By Example

REVISED EDITION

Mathematica®
By Example

REVISED EDITION

Martha L. Abell
James P. Braselton
Department of Mathematics and Computer Science
Georgia Southern University
Statesboro, Georgia

AP PROFESSIONAL

Boston   San Diego   New York
London   Sydney   Tokyo   Toronto

Mathematica is a registered trademark of Wolfram Research, Inc.
Macintosh is a trademark of Apple Computer, Inc.
Windows is a trademark of Microsoft Corporation.

All cover graphics produced with *Mathematica*.
Graphics credits (from right to left, front to back cover):
1. Theodore W. Gray (Courtesy Wolfram Research, Inc.)
2. Jerry Keiper (Courtesy Wolfram Research, Inc.)
3. Tom Whickham-Jones (Courtesy Wolfram Research, Inc.)
4. Cameron Smith (Courtesy Wolfram Research, Inc.)
5. Cameron Smith (Courtesy Wolfram Research, Inc.)
6. Jerry Keiper (Courtesy Wolfram Research, Inc.)
7. Andrew J. Hanson (original *Mathematica* code) and Stewart Dickson

AP PROFESSIONAL
1300 Boylston St., Chestnut Hill, MA 02167

An Imprint of ACADEMIC PRESS, INC.
A Division of HARCOURT BRACE & COMPANY

United Kingdom Edition published by
ACADEMIC PRESS LIMITED
24–28 Oval Road, London NW1 7DX

Library of Congress Cataloging-in-Publication Data
Abell, Martha L., date–
      · Mathematica by example / Martha L. Abell, James P. Braselton. —
   Rev. ed.
         p.   cm.
      Includes bibliographical references and index.
      ISBN 0-12-041530-5
         1. Mathematica (Computer file) 2. Mathematics—Data processing.
   I. Braselton, James P., date– .   II. Title
   QA76.95.A214   1993
   515'.1'028553—dc20   93-34930
                                                            CIP

Printed in the United States of America
      95   96   97   98   ML   9   8   7   6   5   4   3   2

Contents

Preface

Mathematica By Example bridges the gap which exists between the very elementary handbooks available on Mathematica and those reference books written for the advanced Mathematica users. This book is an extension of a manuscript which was developed to quickly introduce enough Mathematica commands to a group of students at Georgia Southern University so that they could apply Mathematica towards the solution of nonlinear ordinary differential equations. In addition to these most basic commands, these students were exposed to the vast uses of lists in Mathematica. Having worked through this material, these students were successfully able to take advantage of the capabilities of Mathematica in solving problems of interest to the class.

Mathematica By Example is an appropriate reference book for all users of Mathematica and, in particular, for beginning users like students, instructors, engineers, business people, and other professionals first learning to use Mathematica. *Mathematica By Example* introduces the very basic commands and includes typical examples of applications of these commands. In addition, the text also includes commands useful in areas such as calculus, linear algebra, business mathematics, ordinary and partial differential equations, and graphics. In all cases, however, examples follow the introduction of new commands. Readers from the most elementary to advanced levels will find that the range of topics covered will address their needs.

Some of the changes in the revised edition include:

1. Table of contents. The table of contents includes all chapters, section headings, and sub-section headings. Along with the index, we hope that users will be able to locate information quickly and easily.
2. Additional examples. We have considerably expanded the topics in Chapters 1 through 6. The results should be more useful to instructors, students, business people, engineers, and other professionals using Mathematica on a variety of platforms. In addition, several sections have been added to help make locating information easier for the user.

3. Index. The index to the text is substantially more comprehensive than that in the first edition. Consequently, mathematical examples of commands and elementary sequences of commands will be easier to locate. In addition, commands listed in the index are cross-referenced with frequently used options. Functions contained in packages are cross-referenced both by package and alphabetically.

Of course, appreciation must be expressed to those who assisted in this project. Most importantly, we would like to thank our assistant, Lori Braselton, for typing, running, and verifying a substantial portion of the code that appears in the text in addition to proof-reading a large portion of the text. We would also like to thank Professor William F. Ames for suggesting that we publish our work and for helping to contact the appropriate people at Academic Press. We would like to express appreciation to our editor, Charles B. Glaser, and our production manager, Brian Miller, for providing a pleasant environment in which to work. Finally, we would like to thank those close to us for enduring with us the pressures of meeting a deadline and for graciously accepting our demanding work schedules. We certainly could not have completed this task without their care and understanding.

M. L. Abell

J. P. Braselton

Statesboro, Georgia

CHAPTER 1

Getting Started

1.1 Introduction to Mathematica

Mathematica, first released in 1988 by Wolfram Research, Inc., is a system for doing mathematics on a computer. It combines symbolic manipulation, numerical mathematics, outstanding graphics, and a sophisticated programming language. Because of its versatility, Mathematica has established itself as the computer algebra system of choice for many computer users. Among the over 100,000 users of Mathematica, 28% are engineers, 21% are computer scientists, 20% are physical scientists, 12% are mathematical scientists, and 12% are business, social, and life scientists. Two-thirds of the users are in industry and government with a small (8%) but growing number of student users. However, due to its special nature and sophistication, beginning users need to be aware of the special syntax required to make Mathematica perform in the way intended.

The purpose of this text is to serve as a guide to beginning users of Mathematica and users who do not intend to take advantage of the more specialized applications of Mathematica. The reader will find that calculations and sequences of calculations most frequently used by beginning users are discussed in detail along with many typical examples. In addition, the comprehensive index not only lists a variety of topics but also cross-references commands with frequently used options. We hope that *Mathematica By Example* will serve as a valuable tool to the beginning user of Mathematica.

A Note Regarding Different Versions of Mathematica

For the most part, *Mathematica By Example* was created with Version 2.2 of Mathematica. With the release of Version 2.0 of Mathematica, several commands from earlier versions of Mathematica have been made obsolete. In addition, Version 2.0 incorporates many features not available in Version 1.2. Version 2.2 contains even more features than Version 2.0. If you are using an earlier or later version of Mathematica, your results may not appear in a form identical to those in this text. Similarly, the physical appearance of results may not be identical on all computer platforms.

You can determine the version of Mathematica you are using during a given Mathematica session by entering either the command $Version or the command $VersionNumber.

1.2 Getting Started with Mathematica

After the Mathematica program has been properly installed, a user can access Mathematica. If you are using a text-based interface (like UNIX), Mathematica is started with the operating system command **math**. If you are using a notebook interface (like Macintosh, Windows, or NeXT), Mathematica is started by selecting the Mathematica icon and double-clicking or selecting the Mathematica icon and selecting **Open** from the **File** menu.

Once Mathematica has been started, computations can be carried out immediately. Mathematica commands are typed to the right of the prompt and then evaluated by pressing **ENTER**. Generally, when a semicolon is placed at the end of the command, the resulting output is not displayed. Note that pressing **ENTER** evaluates commands and pressing **RETURN** yields a new line. Output is displayed below input. We illustrate some of the typical steps involved in working with Mathematica in the calculations below. In each case, we type the command and press **ENTER**. Mathematica evaluates the command, displays the result, and inserts a new prompt. For example, entering

```
N[Pi,50]
```

```
3.1415926535897932384626433832795028841971693993751l
```

returns a 50-digit approximation of π.

The next calculation can then be typed and entered in the same manner as the first. For example, entering

```
Solve [x^3-2x+1==0]
```

$$\{\{x \rightarrow 1\}, \{x \rightarrow \frac{-1 - Sqrt[5]}{2}\}, \{x \rightarrow \frac{-1 + Sqrt[5]}{2}\}\}$$

solves the equation $x^3 - 2x + 1 = 0$ for x. Subsequent calculations are entered in the same way. For example, entering

```
Plot [{Sin[x],2 Cos[2x]},{x,0,3Pi}]
```

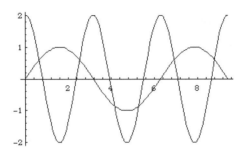

graphs the functions $\sin x$ and $2 \cos 2x$ on the interval $[0, 3\pi]$. Similarly, entering

```
Plot3D [Sin[x+Cos[y]],{x,0,4Pi},{y,0,4Pi},Ticks->None,Boxed->False,
        Axes->None,PlotPoints->25]
```

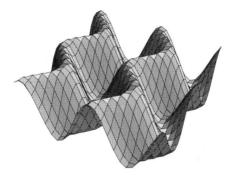

graphs the function $\sin(x + \cos y)$ on the rectangle $[0, 4\pi] \times [0, 4\pi]$.

Notice that **every** Mathematica command begins with **capital letters** and the argument is enclosed by **square brackets** "[. . .]".

Mathematica sessions are terminated by entering Quit[]. On several platforms with notebook interfaces (like Macintosh, Windows, and NeXT), Mathematica sessions are ended by selecting **Quit** from the **File** menu, or by using the keyboard shortcut ⌘**Q**, as with other applications. They can be saved by referring to ⌘**S** from the **File** menu.

On these platforms, input and text regions in notebook interfaces can be edited. Editing input can create a notebook in which the mathematical output does not make sense in the sequence it appears. It is also possible to simply go into a notebook and alter input without doing any recalculation. This also creates misleading notebooks. Hence, common sense and caution should be used when editing the input regions of notebooks. Recalculating all commands in the notebook will clarify any confusion.

Preview

In order for the Mathematica user to take full advantage of the capabilities of this software, an understanding of its syntax is imperative. The goal of *Mathematica By Example* is to introduce the reader to the Mathematica commands and sequences of commands most frequently used by beginning users. Although all of the rules of Mathematica syntax are far too numerous to list here, knowledge of the following five rules equips the beginner with the necessary tools to start using the Mathematica program with little trouble.

Five Basic Rules of Mathematica Syntax

1. The arguments of functions are given in brackets [...] parentheses (...) are used for grouping operations; vectors, matrices, and lists are given in braces { ... }; and double square brackets [[...]] are used for indexing lists and tables.
2. The names of built-in functions have their first letters capitalized; if a name consists of two or more words, the first letter of each word is capitalized.
3. Multiplication is represented by a space or *.
4. Powers are denoted by a ^.
5. If you get no response or an incorrect response, you may have entered or executed the command incorrectly. In some cases, the amount of memory allocated to Mathematica can cause a crash; like people, Mathematica is not perfect and some errors can occur.

1.3 Loading Packages

Although Mathematica contains many built-in functions, some other functions are contained in **packages** which must be loaded separately. A tremendous number of additional commands are available in various packages which are shipped with each version of Mathematica. Experienced users can create their own packages; other packages are available from user groups and MathSource, which electronically distributes Mathematica-related products. For information about MathSource, send the message "help" to mathsource@wri.com. On a computer with a notebook interface, the folder containing the packages shipped with Mathematica is shown below. Descriptions of the various packages shipped with Mathematica are contained in the *Technical Report: Guide to Standard Mathematica Packages* published by and available from Wolfram Research, Inc.

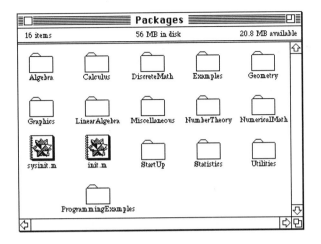

Packages are loaded by entering the command `<<directory`packagename`` where `directory` is the location of the package `packagename`. Entering the command `<<directory`Master`` makes all the functions contained in all the packages in `directory` available. In this case, each package need not be loaded individually. For example, to load the package **SymbolicSum** contained in the **Algebra** folder (or directory), we enter

```
<<Algebra`SymbolicSum`
```

In addition to defining the function `SymbolicSum`, this package enhances the capabilities of the built-in `Sum` function. For example, after the package **SymbolicSum** has been loaded, entering

```
Sum[k^3,{k,1,n}]
```

```
 2       2
n  (1 + n)
-----------
     4
```

computes a closed form of the sum $\displaystyle\sum_{k=1}^{n} k^3$. The same results are obtained by entering

```
SymbolicSum[k^3,{k,1,n}]
```

```
 2       2
n  (1 + n)
-----------
     4
```

After loading the package **SymbolicSum** we are able to compute the partial sums of a geometric series like $\sum_{n=1}^{k}\frac{1}{3^n}$ and $\sum_{n=1}^{\infty}\frac{1}{3^n}$ as illustrated below. `Infinity` represents ∞.

```
Sum[(1/3)^n,{n,1,k}]
```

$$\frac{1-(\frac{1}{3})^k}{2}$$

```
Sum[(1/3)^n,{n,1,  Infinity }]
```

$$\frac{1}{2}$$

Exact values of many series studied in standard calculus courses can be computed explicitly like $\sum_{k=0}^{\infty}\frac{1}{k!}$, as shown below. The symbol `E` in the resulting output represents the mathematical constant $e \approx 2.71828$. The symbol `!`, also represented by `Factorial`, represents the **factorial** function: $n! = n \bullet (n-1) \bullet (n-2) \bullet ... 3 \bullet 2 \bullet 1$.

```
Sum[1/k!  ,{k,0,Infinity}]
```

```
E
```

Two Words of Caution

When users take advantage of packages frequently, they often encounter the error messages discussed here. For example, suppose we have loaded the package **Trigonometry** contained in the **Algebra** folder by entering

```
<<Algebra`Trigonometry`
```

We can then use the command `TrigReduce` contained in the **Trigonometry** package which applied multiple angle identities (like $\sin(x \pm y) = \sin x \cos y \pm \sin y \cos x$ and $\cos(x \pm y) = \cos x \cos y \mp \sin x \sin y$) to an expression to simplify an expression like $\cos(2x - y)$, as illustrated below.

```
TrigReduce [Cos[2x-y]]
```

$$(-1 + 2 \, Cos[x]^2 \,) \, Cos[y] + 2 \, Cos[x] \, Sin[x] \, Sin[y]$$

If, during the same Mathematica work session, we attempt to reload the **Trigonometry** package, we obtain several error messages as shown below.

```
<<Algebra`Trigonometry`
```

```
SetDelayed::write:
   Tag TrigCanonical in TrigCanonical[e_] is Protected.
SetDelayed::write: Tag TrigExpand in TrigExpand[___] is Protected.
SetDelayed::write: Tag TrigExpand in TrigExpand[e_] is Protected.
General::stop:
   Further output of SetDelayed::write
     will be suppressed during this calculation.
Set::wrsym: Symbol TrigFactorRel is Protected.
Set::wrsym: Symbol TrigFactorRel is Protected.
```

These error messages may be ignored as the functions contained in the package **Trigonometry** work in the same way as they did before reloading the package. For example, below we use **TrigFactor** to write $\sin 3x - \sin x$ as a product of trigonometric functions.

```
TrigFactor [Sin[3x]-Sin[x]]
```

```
2 Cos[2 x] Sin[x]
```

Another error message that occurs frequently is when a command is entered before the package is loaded. For example, the command `GramSchmidt[{v1,v2,...,vn}]` returns an orthonormal set of vectors with the same span as the vectors $v_1, v_2, ..., v_n$. Below, we attempt to use the command `GramSchmidt`, contained in the **Orthogon–alization** package located in the **LinearAlgebra** folder before the package has been loaded. Since Mathematica does now know the meaning of `GramSchmidt`, our input is returned.

```
GramSchmidt[{{1,1,0},{0,2,1},{1,0,3}}]
```

```
GramSchmidt[{{1, 1, 0}, {0, 2, 1}, {1, 0, 3}}]
```

At this point, we load the **Orthogonalization** package, which contains the `GramSchmidt` command, located in the **LinearAlgebra** folder. Several error messages result.

```
<<LinearAlgebra`Orthogonalization`
```

```
GramSchmidt::shdw:
   Warning: Symbol GramSchmidt appears in multiple contexts
     {LinearAlgebra`Orthogonalization`, Global`}; definitions in
       context LinearAlgebra`Orthogonalization`
     may shadow or be shadowed by other definitions.
```

In fact, when we reenter the command, we obtain the same result as obtained above.

```
GramSchmidt[{{1,1,0},{0,2,1},{1,0,3}}]
```

```
GramSchmidt[{{1, 1, 0}, {0, 2, 1}, {1, 0, 3}}]
```

However, after using the command `Remove`, the command `GramSchmidt` works as expected. Alternatively, we can quit Mathematica, restart, load the package, and then execute the command.

```
Remove[GramSchmidt]
GramSchmidt
```

$$
\{\{\frac{1}{Sqrt[2]},\ \frac{1}{Sqrt[2]},\ 0\},\ \{-(\frac{1}{Sqrt[3]}),\ \frac{1}{Sqrt[3]},\ \frac{1}{Sqrt[3]}\},
$$

$$
\{\frac{1}{Sqrt[6]},\ -(\frac{1}{Sqrt[6]}),\ Sqrt[\frac{2}{3}]\}\}
$$

Similarly, we can take advantage of other commands contained in the **Orthogonalization**
package like `Normalize` which normalizes a given vector.

```
Normalize[{1,2,3}]
```

$$
\{\frac{1}{Sqrt[14]},\ Sqrt[\frac{2}{7}],\ \frac{3}{Sqrt[14]}\}
$$

1.4 Getting Help from Mathematica

Help Commands

Becoming competent with Mathematica can take a serious investment of time. Hopefully,
messages that result from syntax errors are viewed lightheartedly. Ideally, instead of
becoming frustrated, beginning Mathematica users will find it challenging and fun to
locate the source of errors. Frequently, Mathematica's error messages indicate where the
error(s) has (have) occurred. In this process, it is natural that one will become more
proficient with Mathematica .

 One way to obtain information about commands and functions, including user-defined
functions, is the command `?`. `?object` gives information on the Mathematica object
`object`.

EXAMPLE: Use ? to obtain information about the command
`PolynomialDivision`.

SOLUTION:

```
?PolynomialDivision

    PolynomialDivision[p, q, x] gives a list of
       the quotient and remainder obtained by
       division of the polynomials p and q in x.
```

Below, we illustrate `PolynomialDivision` by computing the quotient and remainder obtained by dividing $x^3 + 1$ by $x - 1$.

```
PolynomialDivision   [x^3+1,x-1,x]
```

```
              2
{1 + x + x  , 2}
```

The result means that $(x-1)(x^2 + x + 1) + 2 = x^3 + 1$ which is verified below with Expand.

```
Expand [(1+x+x^2)(x-1)+2]
```

```
        3
1 + x
```

■

Another way to obtain information on Mathematica commands is the command `Options`. `Options[object]` returns a list of the available options associated with `object` along with their current settings. This is quite useful when working with a Mathematica command such as `ParametricPlot` which has many options. Notice that the default value (the value automatically assumed by Mathematica) for each option is given in the output.

> **EXAMPLE:** Use `Options` to obtain a list of the options and their current settings for the command `ParametricPlot`.

SOLUTION: The command `Options[ParametricPlot]` lists all the options and their current settings for the command `ParametricPlot`.

```
Options[ParametricPlot]
```

```
                           1
{AspectRatio -> -----------, Axes -> Automatic,
                GoldenRatio
 AxesLabel -> None, AxesOrigin -> Automatic,
 AxesStyle -> Automatic, Background -> Automatic,
 ColorOutput -> Automatic, Compiled -> True,
 DefaultColor -> Automatic, Epilog -> {},
 Frame -> False, FrameLabel -> None,
 FrameStyle -> Automatic, FrameTicks -> Automatic,
 GridLines -> None, MaxBend -> 10.,
 PlotDivision -> 20., PlotLabel -> None,
 PlotPoints -> 25, PlotRange -> Automatic,
 PlotRegion -> Automatic, PlotStyle -> Automatic,
 Prolog -> {}, RotateLabel -> True,
 Ticks -> Automatic, DefaultFont :> $DefaultFont,
 DisplayFunction :> $DisplayFunction}
```

■

??object or, equivalently, Information[object] yields the information on the Mathematica object object returned by both ?object and Options[object] in addition to a list of attributes of object. Note that object may either be a user-defined object or a built-in Mathematica object.

EXAMPLE: Use ?? to obtain information about the command Map. Use Information to obtain information about the command PolynomialLCM.

SOLUTION: Below we use ?? to obtain information about the commands Solve and Map, including a list of options and their current settings.

```
??Solve
```

```
Solve[eqns, vars] attempts to solve an equation or
  set of equations for the variables vars. Any
  variable in eqns but not vars is regarded as a
  parameter. Solve[eqns] treats all variables
  encountered as vars above. Solve[eqns, vars,
  elims] attempts to solve the equations for vars,
  eliminating the variables elims.
Attributes[Solve] = {Protected}

Options[Solve] =
 {InverseFunctions -> Automatic,
  MakeRules -> False, Method -> 3, Mode -> Generic,
  Sort -> True, VerifySolutions -> Automatic,
  WorkingPrecision -> Infinity}
```

```
??Map
```

```
Map[f, expr] or f /@ expr applies f to each element
  on the first level in expr. Map[f, expr,
  levelspec] applies f to parts of expr specified
  by levelspec.
Attributes[Map] = {Protected}

Options[Map] = {Heads -> False}
```

Similarly, we use Information to obtain information about the command PolynomialLCM including a list of options and their current settings.

```
Information[PolynomialLCM]
```

```
PolynomialLCM[poly1, poly2, ...] gives the
  least common multiple of the polynomials
  poly1, poly2, ... . PolynomialLCM[poly1,
  poly2, ..., Modulus->p] gives the LCM
  modulo the prime p.
```

```
Attributes[PolynomialLCM] =
 {Listable, Protected}

Options[PolynomialLCM] =
 {Modulus -> 0, Trig -> False}
```

■

The command `Names["form"]` lists all objects which match the pattern defined in form. For example, `Names["Plot"]` returns `Plot`, `Names["*Plot"]` returns all objects that end with the string `Plot`, and `Names["Plot*"]` lists all objects that begin with the string `Plot`, and `Names["*Plot*"]` lists all objects which contain the string `Plot`. `Names["form",SpellingCorrection->True]` finds those symbols which match the pattern defined in form after a spelling correction.

EXAMPLE: Create a list of all built-in functions beginning with the string `Plot`.

SOLUTION: Below, we use `Names` to find all object which match the pattern `Plot`.

```
Names["Plot"]
```

{Plot}

Next, we use `Names` to create a list of all built-in functions beginning with the string `Plot`.

```
Names["Plot*"]
```

{Plot, PlotColor, PlotDivision, PlotJoined,

PlotLabel, PlotPoints, PlotRange, PlotRegion,

PlotStyle, Plot3D, Plot3Matrix}

■

The command `?` can be used in several other ways. Entering

`?letters*` gives all Mathematica commands which begin with the string `letters`;
`?*letters*` gives all Mathematica commands that contain the string `letters`; and
`?*letters` gives all Mathematica commands which end in the string `letters`.

EXAMPLE: What are the Mathematica functions that (a) end in the string Cos; (b) contain the string Sin; and (c) begin with the string Polynomial?

SOLUTION: Entering

    ?*Cos

        ArcCos Cos

yields all functions that end with the string Cos, entering

    ?*Sin*

        ArcSin   SingularValues
        ArcSinh   Sinh
        IncludeSingularTerm   SinhIntegral
        Sin   SinIntegral
        SingularityDepth

returns all functions containing the string Sin, and entering

    ?Polynomial*

        PolynomialDivision   PolynomialQ
        PolynomialGCD   PolynomialQuotient
        PolynomialLCM   PolynomialRemainder
        PolynomialMod

returns all functions that begin with the string Polynomial.

■

Mathematica Help

On some platforms with a notebook interface (like Macintosh, Windows, and NeXT), additional help features are accessed from the Mathmematica Menu. For example, if the user wishes to use a command which begins with Polynomial, but does not remember the rest of the command, help can be obtained in the following manner.

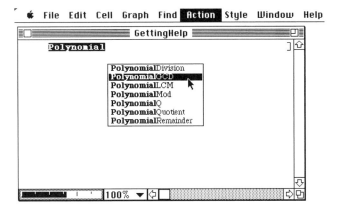

1. Type the word `Poly-nomial`,
2. Move the cursor to the **Action** heading and use the mouse to obtain the **Action** submenu,
3. Choose **Complete Selection** from the submenu (This causes a list of commands which begin with `Polynomial` to be displayed),
4. Move the cursor to the desired command in the list and click. In this particular case, we select `PolynomialDivision`. The selected command is then completed on the screen.

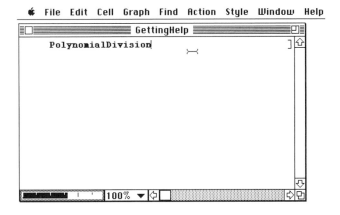

In addition to helping you complete commands, Mathematica can also complete a given command with its typical syntax. For example, to find the typical syntax of the command `PolynomialDivision`,

(1) Type the command `PolynomialDivision`, (2) Move the cursor to the **Action** heading and use the mouse to obtain the **Action** submenu, and (3) Choose **Make Template** from the submenu. The results are shown below. At this point, you can select each argument and replace them with the values you wish.

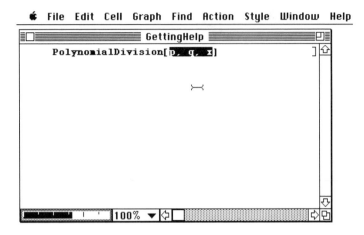

Additional features available to those working with notebook interfaces include the
Help heading of the Mathematica menu. Under the **Help** heading of the Mathematica
menu, we have **Open Function Browser...**, **Find in Function Browser...**, **Why
the Beep?...**, **Getting Started...**, **Shortcuts...**, and **Help Pointer**.

Moving the cursor to the **Help** heading and using the mouse to select **Getting
Started** yields the following window.

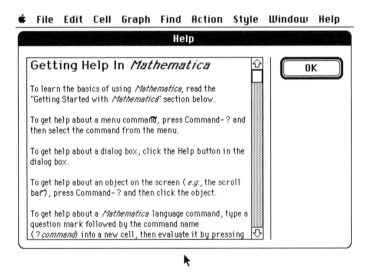

This document provides a variety of basic information about Mathematica.

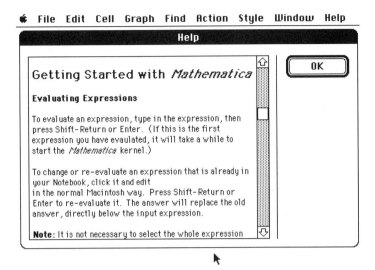

Moving the cursor to the **Help** heading and using the mouse to select **Shortcuts** yields the following window which describes keyboard shortcuts to several of the commands available from the Mathematica menu.

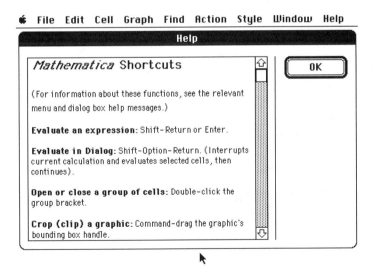

The selection **Help Pointer** can be used to obtain information about particular regions in a notebook. In the following example, we use Help Pointer to obtain information about a graphics cell.

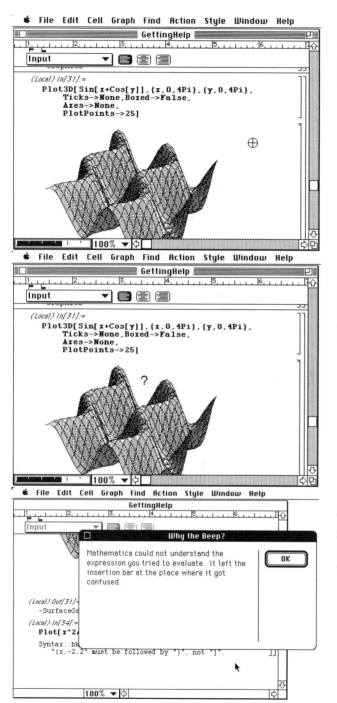

In this case, we have used the `Plot3D` command to graph $\sin(x+\cos y)$ on the rectangle $[0,4\pi]\times[0,4\pi]$.

We then move the cursor to the **Help** heading and use the mouse to select **Help Pointer**. Note that the cursor becomes a question mark.

We then move the cursor to the **Help** heading and use the mouse to select **Why the Beep?**. Mathematica displays the following window.

Why the Beep?... can help explain why Mathematica "beeps" at certain times or under certain conditions.

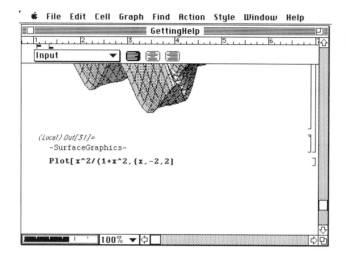

This plot command contains two errors.

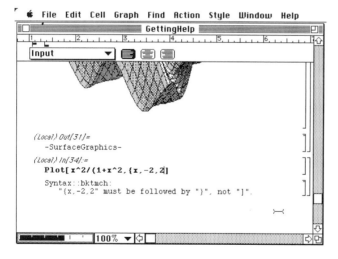

When we press **ENTER**, Mathematica "beeps" and displays an error message.

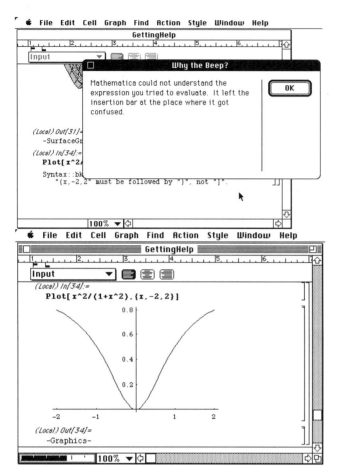

We then move the cursor to the **Help** heading and use the mouse to select **Why the Beep?**. Mathematica displays the following window.

Correcting the command and pressing **ENTER** results in the graph of $\dfrac{x^2}{1+x^2}$ on the interval $[-2,2]$.

Open Function Browser... contains descriptions of all Mathematica commands. As the commands are arranged by topic, the **Function Browser** is an excellent way to become familiar with Mathematica commands. Moving the cursor to **Help** and selecting **Open Function Browser...** yields the following window.

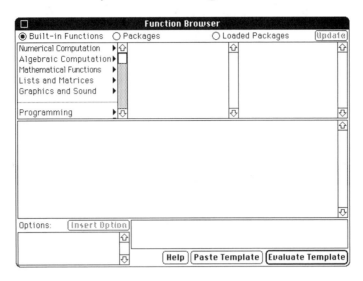

In this case, we select Lists and Matrices, then List Construction, and DiagonalMatrix. Mathematica displays a brief description of the command DiagonalMatrix as shown below.

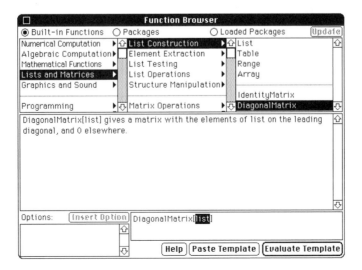

If we then replace list with a list of numbers and press **Evaluate Template**, Mathematica inserts the command into the active notebook and evaluates the command.

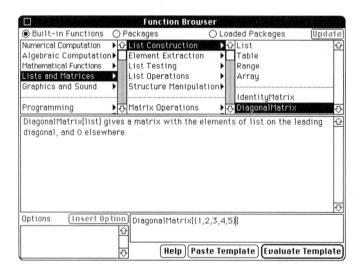

We can also use the **Function Browser** to obtain information about commands contained in a notebook. For example, in the following notebook, we highlight the command ParametricPlot3D

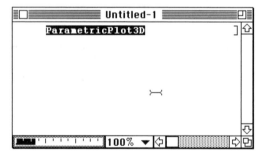

and then move the cursor to **Help** and select **Find in Function Browser...** . The
result is displayed below.

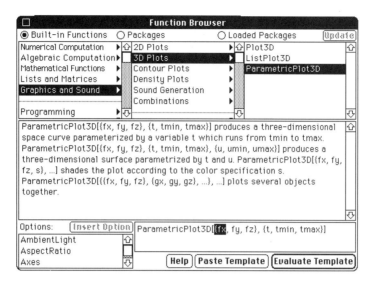

Mathematical Operations on Numbers, Expressions, and Functions

Chapter 2 introduces the essential commands of Mathematica. Basic operations on numbers, expressions, and functions are introduced and discussed.

2.1 Numerical Calculations and Built-in Functions

Numerical Calculations

The basic arithmetic operations (addition, subtraction, multiplication, and division) are performed in the natural way with Mathematica . Whenever possible, Mathematica gives an exact answer and reduces fractions:

"a plus b" is entered as a+b;

"a minus b" is entered as a−b;

"a times b" is entered as either a*b or a b (note the space between a and b); and

"a divided by b" is entered as a/b. Executing the command a/b results in a reduced fraction.

EXAMPLE: Compute (a) $121 + 542$; (b) $3231 - 9876$; (c) $-23 \bullet 76$; (d) $22361 \bullet 832748 \bullet 387281$; and (e) $\dfrac{467}{31}$.

SOLUTION: In each case, we use Mathematica to perform the indicated operation. To execute a command, press **ENTER** or, equivalently, **Shift-RETURN**. In general, the **RETURN** key gives a new line; the **ENTER** key evaluates a Mathematica command.

(a)

```
121+452

    573
```

(b)

```
3231-9876

   -6645
```

(d) Note that a * represents multiplication. However, a space between two expressions on the same line of input also denotes multiplication as shown in (e).

```
-23*76

   -1748

22361 832748 387281

   7211589719761868
```

(f) The symbol / denotes division. Generally, Mathematica expresses fractions in reduced form and not in decimal form, unless a decimal form is requested.

```
467/31

   467
   ---
   31
```

∎

In the same manner as arithmetic operations are entered,

a^b, "a raised to the bth power," is entered as a^b.
$\sqrt{a} = a^{1/2}$ is computed by entering either a^(1/2) or Sqrt[a]; $\sqrt[3]{a} = a^{1/3}$ is computed by entering a^(1/3).

In each of these cases, note that the exponent is included in parentheses. In cases where the exponent consists of more than one symbol, be sure to include the entire exponent in parentheses to avoid possible errors.

Whenever possible, Mathematica returns exact values. To obtain approximations of exact values, use N. N[expression] returns an approximation of expression; N[expression,n] returns an approximation of expression accurate to n digits, if possible. Notice that the arguments of the commands Sqrt and N are contained in brackets ([...]). In fact, arguments of **all** functions are **always** contained in brackets ([...]).

EXAMPLE: Calculate (a) $(-5)^{121}$ and (b) $5^{1/9}$.

SOLUTION: For (a), we enter the command (-5)^121. Note that the symbol \ is used to indicate that the resulting output continues onto the next line.

```
(-5)^121
```

```
       -3761581922631320025499956919111118616\
          9019729781670680068828005460090935\
          230255126953125
```

On the other hand, using N to evaluate this expression yields the result in scientific notation.

```
N[(-5)^121]
```

```
                84
      -3.76158 10
```

For (b), we see that Mathematica returns $5^{1/9}$ as the exact simplified form of $5^{1/9}$ is $5^{1/9}$.

```
5^(1/9)
```

```
     1/9
    5
```

However, we may approximate $5^{1/9}$ using N.

```
N[5^(1/9)]
```

```
    1.19581
```

∎

EXAMPLE: Calculate $\sqrt{233}$.

SOLUTION: We use the command `Sqrt` to calculate $\sqrt{233}$. However, since $\sqrt{233}$ is the simplified form of $\sqrt{233}$, the result returned is `Sqrt[233]`.

> `Sqrt[233]`

>> `Sqrt[233]`

However, including `//N` after the command yields an approximation of $\sqrt{233}$. The same results are obtained with `N[Sqrt[233]]`.

> `Sqrt[233]//N`

>> `15.2643`

■

When computing odd roots of negative numbers, Mathematica results are surprising to the novice. Namely, Mathematica returns a complex number. We will see that this has important consequence when graphing certain functions.

EXAMPLE: Calculate $\sqrt[3]{-3} = (-3)^{1/3}$.

SOLUTION: When entering `(-3)^(1/3)`, Mathematica returns an exact value of $\sqrt[3]{-3} = (-3)^{1/3}$

> `(-3)^(1/3)`

>> `(-1)`$^{1/3}$ `3`$^{1/3}$

When we include `//N` at the end of the command, an approximation is returned. We see that the resulting expression contains a term with an `I`. The symbol `I` represents the imaginary number $i = \sqrt{-1}$.

> `(-3)^(1/3)//N`

>> `0.721125 + 1.24902 I`

Note that in order to calculate $\sqrt[3]{-3} = (-3)^{1/3}$, we must be sure to include the parentheses around the term $1/3$. If we don't, Mathematica computes $\dfrac{(-3)^1}{3} = -1$.

> `(-3)^1/3`

>> `-1`

■

Built-in Constants

Mathematica has built-in definitions of many commonly used constants. Frequently used constants include $\pi \approx 3.14159$, denoted by `Pi`, $e \approx 2.71828$, denoted by `E`, and $i = \sqrt{-1}$, denoted by `I`. Other built-in constants include ∞, denoted by `Infinity`, Euler's constant, $\gamma \approx 0.577216$, denoted by `EulerGamma`, Catalan's constant, approximately 0.915966, denoted by `Catalan`, and the golden ratio, $\frac{1}{2}\left(1+\sqrt{5}\right) \approx 1.61803$, denoted by `GoldenRatio`.

In the previous examples, we see that Mathematica gives an exact answer whenever possible. For a variety of reasons, however, numerical approximations of results are often either more meaningful or more desirable. The command used to obtain a numerical approximation of the number a, is `N[a]` or, equivalently, `a // N`. The command to obtain a numerical approximation of a to n digits of precision is `N[a,n]`.
For example, entering

        N[E,50]

            2.7182818284590452353360287471\
             3526624977572470937

produces a 50-digit approximation of e. Entering

        E^(-5)

             -5
            E

computes $e^{-5} = \dfrac{1}{e^5}$ while entering

        E^(-5)//N

            0.00673795

computes an approximation of $e^{-5} = \dfrac{1}{e^5}$. Entering

        N[Pi,25]

            3.141592653589793238462643 4

computes a 25-digit approximation of π. Entering

        Sqrt[-9]

            3 I

computes $\sqrt{-9} = i\sqrt{9} = 3i$. Entering

        (1-I)^4

            -4

expands $(1-i)^4$ and entering

```
(3+I)/(4-I)
```

$$\frac{11}{17} + \frac{7\,I}{17}$$

simplifies $\dfrac{3+i}{4-i}$.

Built-in Functions

Mathematica recognizes numerous built-in functions. These include the exponential function, `Exp[x]`; the absolute value function, `Abs[x]`; the trigonometric functions `Sin[x]`, `Cos[x]`, `Tan[x]`, `Sec[x]`, `Csc[x]`, and `Cot[x]`; and the inverse trigonometric functions `ArcCos[x]`, `ArcSin[x]`, `ArcTan[x]`, `ArcSec[x]`, `ArcCsc[x]`, and `ArcCot[x]`. Notice that each of these functions is capitalized and uses square brackets. Entering `Exp[x]` produces the same results as entering `E^x`. Entering `Log[x]` returns the natural logarithm of x; entering `Log[n,x]` returns the logarithm of x to base n.

(Note that the inverse trigonometric functions include two capital letters! If both of these requirements are not met, then Mathematica will not recognize the built-in function and undesirable results will be obtained.)

The Absolute Value, Exponential and Logarithmic Functions

Calculations involving the functions `Abs[x]`, `Exp[x]`, and `Log[x]` appear in the following examples. Notice that in order to obtain a numerical value of `Exp[x]`, a numerical approximation must be requested by either the command `N[Exp[x]]` or `Exp[x]//N`. Otherwise, the exact value is given which, in many cases, is not as useful as the numerical approximation.

EXAMPLE: Approximate $e^{-5} = \dfrac{1}{e^5}$ and graph e^x on the interval $[-2,2]$.

SOLUTION: We see that entering

```
Exp[-5]
```

$$E^{-5}$$

yields the exact value of $e^{-5} = \dfrac{1}{e^5}$ while entering

```
Exp[-5]//N
```

```
0.00673795
```

yields an approximation. The same result would have been obtained if N[Exp[-5]] had been entered. Plot is used to graph e^x on the interval [–2,2].

Plot[Exp[x],{x,-2,2}]

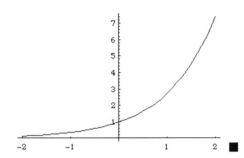

In addition to real numbers, the function Abs[x] can be used to find the absolute value of the complex number a+bI, where Abs[a+bI]=Sqrt[a^2+b^2]. For example, entering

Abs[-5]

5

computes $|-5| = 5$ and entering

Abs[14]

14

returns $|14| = 14$ while entering

Abs[3-4I]

5

computes $|3 - 4i| = \sqrt{3^2 + 4^2} = 5$ and entering

Abs[(3+2I)/(2-9I)]

```
        13
  Sqrt[--]
        85
```

returns $\left|\dfrac{3+2i}{2-9i}\right| = \sqrt{\dfrac{13}{85}}$.

EXAMPLE: Graph |x| on the interval [–5,5].

SOLUTION: `Plot` is used to graph the function `Abs[x]`.

`Plot[Abs[x],{x,-5,5}]`

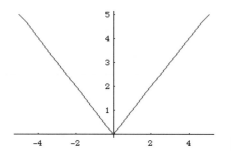

`Log[x]` computes the natural logarithm of x, which is usually denoted by ln x or $\log_e x$. Thus, entering

`Log[E]`

1

returns 1; entering

`Log[E^3]`

3

returns 3; and entering

`Exp[Log[Pi]]`

Pi

returns π.

The `Log` function is also used to calculate logarithms with base other than e. `Log[a,b]` computes $\log_a b = \dfrac{\ln b}{\ln a}$. Therefore, entering

`Log[3,9]`

2

returns 2 and entering

`Log[2,10]`

```
Log[10]
-------
Log[2]
```

returns $\dfrac{\ln 10}{\ln 2}$. An approximation to 10 digits of accuracy is obtained below with N.

```
N[Log[2,10],10]
```

>   3.321928095

EXAMPLE: Graph $\ln x$ on the interval [0.001,5].

SOLUTION: Below we use `Plot` to graph $\ln x$ on the interval [0.001,5].

```
Plot[Log[x],{x,.001,5}]
```

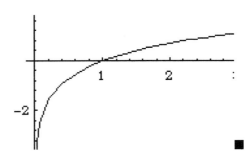

■

Trigonometric Functions

Examples of typical operations involving the trigonometric functions `Sin[x]`, `Cos[x]`, and `Tan[x]` are given below. (Although not illustrated in the following examples, the functions `Sec[x]`, `Csc[x]`, and `Cot[x]` are used similarly.) Notice that Mathematica yields the exact value for trigonometric functions of some angles, while a numerical approximation must be requested for others.

EXAMPLE: Calculate $\cos\left(\dfrac{\pi}{4}\right)$, $\sin\left(\dfrac{\pi}{3}\right)$, $\tan\left(\dfrac{3\pi}{4}\right)$, $\cos\left(\dfrac{\pi}{12}\right)$, $\cos\left(\dfrac{\pi}{5}\right)$, and $\sin\left(-\dfrac{9\pi}{8}\right)$.

SOLUTION:

```
Cos[Pi/4]
```

>   1
>   -------
>   Sqrt[2]

```
Sin[Pi/3]

    Sqrt[3]
    -------
       2

Tan[3 Pi/4]

    -1

Cos[Pi/12]

    1 + Sqrt[3]
    -----------
     2 Sqrt[2]
```

Even though Mathematica returns the exact value of $\cos\left(\dfrac{\pi}{12}\right)$, N can be used to obtain an approximation as shown below.

```
N[Cos[Pi/12]]

    0.965926
```

However, Mathematica does not return a numerical value for $\cos\left(\dfrac{\pi}{5}\right)$

```
Cos[Pi/5]

          Pi
    Cos[--]
          5
```

so we use N to obtain an approximation.

```
N[Cos[Pi/5]]

    0.809017
```

Similarly, we use N to compute an approximation of $\sin\left(-\dfrac{9\pi}{8}\right)$.

```
Sin[-9 Pi/8]

         9 Pi
    -Sin[----]
          8

    0.382683
```

EXAMPLE: Graph $\sin x$, $\cos x$, and $\tan x$.

SOLUTION: In each case, we use `Plot` to graph the indicated function.

`Plot[Cos[x],{x,-2Pi,2Pi}]`

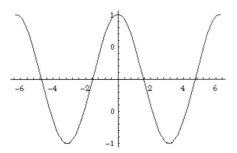

`Plot[Sin[x],{x,-2Pi,2Pi}]`

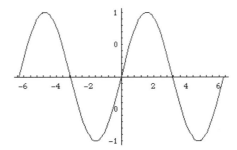

`Plot[Tan[x],{x,-Pi,Pi}]`

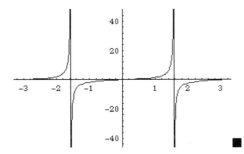

Inverse Trigonometric Functions

Commands involving the inverse trigonometric functions are similar to those demonstrated in the earlier section on trigonometric functions. Again, note the two capital letters in each of the inverse trigonometric functions. The (built-in) inverse trigonometric functions are:

```
ArcCos[x]         ArcCoth[x]        ArcSec[x]         ArcSinh[x]
ArcCosh[x]        ArcCsc[x]         ArcSech[x]        ArcTan[x]
ArcCot[x]         ArcCsch[x]        ArcSin[x]         ArcTanh[x]
```

When particular values are well-known, Mathematica returns them. For example, entering

```
ArcCos[1/2]
```

```
Pi
--
3
```

returns $\cos^{-1}\dfrac{1}{2}=\dfrac{\pi}{3}$; entering

```
ArcSin[-1]
```

```
-Pi
---
2
```

returns $\sin^{-1}(-1)=-\dfrac{\pi}{2}$; and entering

```
ArcTan[1]
```

```
Pi
--
4
```

returns $\tan^{-1}1=\dfrac{\pi}{4}$. In most instances, however, approximation must be computed with N. For example, entering

```
ArcSin[1/3]//N
```

```
0.339837
```

returns an approximation of $\sin^{-1}\dfrac{1}{3}$; entering

```
N[ArcCos[2/3]]
```

```
0.841069
```

returns an approximation of $\cos^{-1}\dfrac{2}{3}$; and entering

```
ArcTan[100]//N
```

```
1.5608
```

returns an approximation of $\tan^{-1}100$.

> **EXAMPLE:** Graph $\sin^{-1}x$, $\cos^{-1}x$, and $\tan^{-1}x$.

SOLUTION: In each case, we use `Plot` to graph the indicated function.

`Plot[ArcSin[x],{x,-1,1}]`

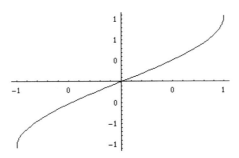

`Plot[ArcCos[x],{x,-1,1}]`

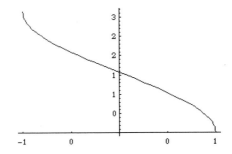

`Plot[ArcTan[x],{x,-25,25}]`

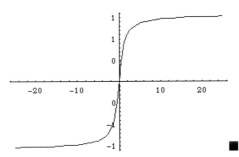

The hyperbolic trigonometric functions and their inverses are computed in the same way as those above. `N` is used to obtain an approximation, when necessary.

> **EXAMPLE:** Compute $\sinh 0$, $\sinh 5$, $\cosh(\ln 4)$, $\cosh(-5)$, $\tanh(\ln 5)$, and $\tanh 1$. Graph each of the functions $\sinh x$, $\cosh x$, and $\tanh x$.

SOLUTION: We first compute the indicated values.

```
Sinh[0]
```

    0

```
Sinh[5]
```

    Sinh[5]

```
Sinh[5]//N
```

    74.2032

```
Cosh[0]
```

    1

```
Cosh[Log[4]]
```

    17
    --
    8

```
Cosh[-5]
```

    Cosh[5]

```
N[Cosh[-5]]
```

    74.2099

```
Tanh[Log[5]]
```

    12
    --
    13

```
Tanh[1]
```

    Tanh[1]

```
Tanh[1]//N
```

    0.761594

Next, we use `Plot` to graph each function.

```
Plot[Sinh[x],{x,-10,10}]
```

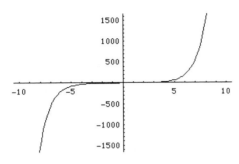

```
Plot[Cosh[x],{x,-10,10}]
```

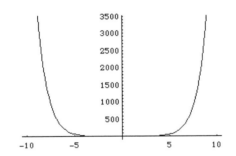

```
Plot[Tanh[x],{x,-10,10}]
```

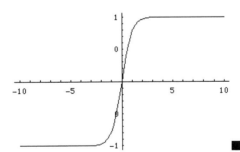

The next example illustrates the inverse hyperbolic trigonometric functions.

EXAMPLE: Calculate $\sinh^{-1}5$, $\cosh^{-1}6$, and $\tanh^{-1}\left(-\dfrac{1}{2}\right)$. Graph each of the functions $\sinh^{-1}x$, $\cosh^{-1}x$, and $\tanh^{-1}x$.

SOLUTION: We proceed as in the previous example: first we compute the indicated values and then graph each function.

```
ArcSinh[5]
```

```
    ArcSinh[5]
```

```
ArcSinh[5]//N
```

```
    2.31244
```

```
ArcCosh[6]
```

```
    ArcCosh[6]
```

```
N[ArcCosh[6]]
```

```
    2.47789
```

```
ArcTanh[-1/2]
```

```
          1
    -ArcTanh[-]
          2
```

```
ArcTanh[-1/2]//N
```

```
    -0.54925
```

```
Plot[ArcSinh[x],{x, -10,10}]
```

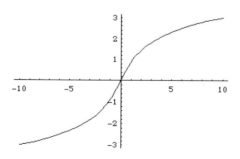

```
Plot[ArcCosh[x],{x,1,10}]
```

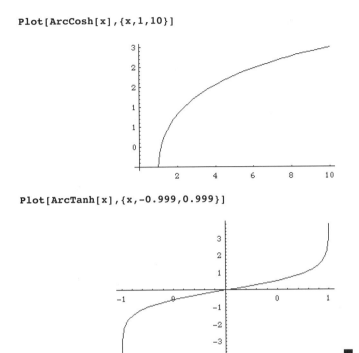

```
Plot[ArcTanh[x],{x,-0.999,0.999}]
```

A Word of Caution

As stated above, every built-in Mathematica object begins with a capital letter and arguments of functions are always contained in brackets. If capital letters are not used or brackets are omitted, errors result. For example, entering

```
sin(pi/2)
```

```
General::spell1:
    Possible spelling error: new symbol name "sin"
        is similar to existing symbol "Sin".
```

```
pi sin
------
   2
```

returns nonsense as parentheses are used instead of brackets, `sin` is used instead of `Sin`, and `pi` is used instead of `Pi`.

2.2 *Expressions and Functions*

Basic Algebraic Operations on Expressions

Expressions involving unknowns are entered in the same way as numbers. Mathematica performs standard algebraic operations on mathematical expressions. For example, the command

> Factor[expression] factors expression;
> Expand[expression] multiplies expression; and
> Together[expression] writes expression as a single fraction.

When entering expressions, be sure to include a space or * between variables to denote multiplication.

EXAMPLE: (a) Factor the polynomial $12x^2 + 27xy - 84y^2$. (b) Expand the expression $(x+y)^2(3x-y)^3$. (c) Write the sum $\dfrac{2}{x^2} - \dfrac{x^2}{2}$ as a single fraction.

SOLUTION: The first command below, with Factor, indicates that

$$12x^2 + 27xy - 84y^2 = 3(x+4y)(4x-7y).$$

When entering the Factor command, be sure to include a space, or *, between the x and y terms to denote multiplication. xy represents an expression while x y or x*y denotes x multiplied by y. The second, with Expand, computes the product $(x+y)^2(3x-y)^3$, and the third, with Together, expresses $\dfrac{2}{x^2} - \dfrac{x^2}{2}$ as a single fraction.

```
Factor[12x^2+27 x y-84y^2]

   3 (-x - 4 y) (-4 x + 7 y)

Expand[ (x+y)^2 (3x-y)^3]

      5         4          3 2        2 3        4     5
   27 x  + 27 x  y - 18 x  y  - 10 x  y  + 7 x y  - y

Together[2/x^2 - x^2/2]

         4
   4 - x
   ------
      2
   2 x
```

In general, a space is not needed between a number and a symbol to denote multiplication. That is, 3dog means "3 times variable dog□"; Mathematica interprets 3 dog the same way. However, when denoting multiplication of two variables, either include a space or *:

> cat dog means "variable cat times variable dog",
> cat*dog means "variable cat times variable dog", but
> catdog is interpreted as a variable catdog.

The command Apart[expression] computes the partial fraction decomposition of expression; Cancel[expression] factors the numerator and denominator of expression then reduces expression to lowest terms.

EXAMPLE: (a) Determine the partial fraction decomposition of the rational function $\dfrac{1}{(x-3)(x-1)}$. (b) Simplify the expression $\dfrac{x^2-1}{x^2-2x+1}$.

SOLUTION: Apart is used below to show that

$$\frac{1}{(x-3)(x-1)} = \frac{1}{2(x-3)} - \frac{1}{2(x-1)}.$$

Then, Cancel is used to find that

$$\frac{x^2-1}{x^2-2x+1} = \frac{(x-1)(x+1)}{(x-1)^2} = \frac{x+1}{x-1}.$$

```
Apart[1/((x-3)(x-1))]

      1            1
 ----------- - -----------
 2 (-3 + x)    2 (-1 + x)

Cancel[(x^2-1)/(x^2-2x+1)]

  1 + x
 ------
 -1 + x
```

■

Naming and Evaluating Expressions

In Mathematica, mathematical objects can be named. Naming objects is convenient: we can avoid typing the same mathematical expression repeatedly and named expressions can be referenced throughout a notebook or Mathematica session.

Since every built-in Mathematica function begins with a capital letter, we will adopt the convention that **every** mathematical object **we** name will begin with a **lower case** letter. Consequently, we will be certain to avoid any possible ambiguity with a built-in Mathematica object. An expression is named by using a single equals sign (=).

Be aware that Mathematica **does not** remember anything defined in a previous Mathematica session. That is, if you define certain symbols during a Mathematica session, quit the Mathematica session, and then continue later, the previous symbols must be redefined to be used.

Expressions can be evaluated easily. To evaluate an expression, we introduce the command /. . The command /. means "replace by". For example, entering the command

```
x^2 /. x -> 3
```

returns the value of the expression x^2 when $x = 3$. Note, however, this does not assign the symbol x the value 3. The symbol "->" is obtained by typing a minus sign (–) followed by a greater than sign (>).

The following example illustrates how to name an expression. In addition, Mathematica has several built-in functions for manipulating fractions:

> Numerator[`fraction`] yields the numerator of a `fraction`;
> ExpandNumerator[`fraction`] expands the numerator of `fraction`;
> Denominator[`fraction`] yields the denominator of a `fraction`;
> ExpandDenominator[`fraction`] expands the denominator of `fraction`; and
> ExpandAll[`fraction`] expands both the numerator and denominator of `fraction`.

The naming of expressions makes the numerator and denominator easier to use in the following examples.

EXAMPLE: Given the rational expression $\dfrac{x^3+2x^2-x-2}{x^3+x^2-4x-4}$, (a) factor both the numerator and denominator; (b) evaluate the numerator when x=2, evaluate the denominator when x=3; (c) reduce $\dfrac{x^3+2x^2-x-2}{x^3+x^2-4x-4}$ to lowest terms; (d) evaluate $\dfrac{x^3+2x^2-x-2}{x^3+x^2-4x-4}$ when x=4 and when x=−3; and (e) find the partial fraction decomposition of $\dfrac{x^3+2x^2-x-2}{x^3+x^2-4x-4}$.

SOLUTION: To avoid retyping (x^3+2x^2-x-2)/(x^3+x^2-4x-4), we define fraction to be

$$\frac{x^3+2x^2-x-2}{x^3+x^2-4x-4}.$$

```
fraction=(x^3+2x^2-x-2)/(x^3+x^2-4x-4)

            2    3
 -2 - x + 2 x  + x
 ------------------
            2    3
 -4 - 4 x + x  + x
```

The numerator of fraction is extracted with Numerator and named num for later use. We then use Factor to factor num and use /. to evaluate num when x=2.

```
num=Numerator[fraction]

            2    3
 -2 - x + 2 x  + x

Factor[num]

 (-1 + x) (1 + x) (2 + x)

num /. x->2

 12
```

Similarly, we use Denominator to extract the denominator of fraction and name the resulting output den for later use. Again, Factor is used to factor den and /. is used to evaluate den when x=3.

```
den=Denominator[fraction]

           2     3
 -4 - 4 x + x   + x

Factor[den]

   (-2 + x) (1 + x) (2 + x)

den /. x->3

   20
```

Mathematica can also evaluate and perform standard algebraic operations on named expressions. Cancel is used to reduce fraction to lowest terms.

```
Cancel[fraction]

   -1 + x
   ------
   -2 + x
```

/. is used to evaluate fraction when x=4 and when x=-3.

```
fraction /. x->4

   3
   -
   2

fraction /. x->-3

   4
   -
   5
```

Finally, Apart is used to find the partial fraction decomposition of fraction.

```
Apart[fraction]

        1
   1 + ------
       -2 + x
```

■

Every Mathematica object can be named; even graphics and functions can be named with Mathematica.

A Word of Caution

When you assign a name to an object that is similar to a previously defined or built-in function, Mathematica issues an error message like that shown below.

```
function=x^2
```

```
General::spell1:
   Possible spelling error: new symbol name "function"
      is similar to existing symbol "Function".
 2
x
```

Since we have adopted the convention that every user-defined function begin with a lower case letter, we know that we have not made an error and the message can be ignored. Sometimes, however, the message can occur frequently and become annoying. If desired, the message

General::spell1:

can be suppressed by entering

Off[General::spell1].

Generally, Off[s::tag] switches off the message s::tag so that it is not printed. On is used to switch on warning or error messages. Specific messages may be permanently turned off by inserting the desired Off commands in the **init.m** file which is contained in the **Packages** folder (or directory).

Defining and Evaluating Functions

It is important to remember that functions, expressions, and graphics can be named anything that is not the name of a built-in Mathematica function or command. Since every built-in Mathematica function begins with a capital letter, every user-defined function or expression in this text will be defined using lower case letters. This way, the possibility of conflicting with a built-in Mathematica command or function is completely eliminated. Also, since definitions of functions are frequently modified, we introduce the command Clear. Clear[expression] clears all definitions of expression. You can see if a particular symbol has a definition by entering ?symbol. Consequently, we are certain to avoid any ambiguity when we create a new definition of a function. When you **first** define a function, you must **always** enclose the argument in square brackets ([. . .]) and place an underline (or blank) "_" after the argument on the left-hand side of the equals sign in the definition of the function.

EXAMPLE: Define $f(x) = x^2$, $g(x) = \sqrt{x}$, and $h(x) = x + \sin x$.

SOLUTION: We first use `Clear` to clear all prior definitions of f, g, and h, if any, and then enter the definition of each function. Entering `f[x_]=x^2` defines and computes $f(x) = x^2$.

```
Clear[f,g,h]

f[x_]=x^2
```
```
     2
    x
```

Similarly, entering `g[x_]=Sqrt[x]` defines and computes $g(x) = \sqrt{x}$.

```
g[x_]=Sqrt[x]
```
```
    Sqrt[x]
```

However, entering `h[x_]:=x+Sin[x]` simply defines $h(x) = x + \sin x$; `h[x]` is not computed so Mathematica does not return any output.

```
h[x_]:=x+Sin[x]
```

We may see the definition of h, however, by entering ?h.

```
?h
```
```
    Global`h
    h[x_] := x + Sin[x]
```

In each of the above cases, don't forget to include the underline (_) on the left-hand side of the equals sign in the definition of each function. Remember to **always** include arguments of functions in square brackets. ∎

    In the preceding examples, functions were defined using each of the forms `f[x_]:=...` and `f[x_]=...`. As a practical matter, when defining "routine" functions with domains consisting of sets of real numbers and ranges consisting of sets of real numbers, either form can be used. Defining a function using the form `f[x_]=...` instructs Mathematica to define f and then compute and return `f[x]` (immediate assignment); defining a function using the form `f[x_]:=...` instructs Mathematica to define f. In this case, `f[x]` is not computed and, thus, Mathematica returns no output (delayed assignment). The form `f[x_]:=...` should be used when `f[x]` does not make sense unless x is a particular value.

    Generally, if attempting to define a function using the form `f[x_]=...` produces one or more error messages, use the form `f[x_]:=...` instead.

    When you evaluate a function, type `functionname[point]` **ENTER**. Notice that functions can be evaluated for any real number (in the function's domain).

> **EXAMPLE:** Using the definitions of f, g, and h, from above, compute f(2), g(4), and h(π/2).

SOLUTION:

```
f[2]

     4

g[4]

     2

h[Pi/2]

          Pi
   1 + --
          2
```

■

Moreover, Mathematica can symbolically evaluate and manipulate many functions.

> **EXAMPLE:** Using the definitions of f, from above, (a) calculate $f(a-b^2)$; (b) calculate and expand $f(a-b^2)$; (c) compute $\dfrac{f(x+h)-f(x)}{h}$; and (d) compute and simplify $\dfrac{f(x+h)-f(x)}{h}$.

SOLUTION: We evaluate functions when the argument consists of symbols other than numbers in the same way as we evaluate functions when the argument consists of numbers in the functions' domain. Note that when evaluating functions when the argument consists of symbols other than numbers, errors are returned if the function does not make sense for non-numerical arguments.
Entering

```
f[a-b^2]

          2 2
   (a - b )
```

calculates $f(a-b^2)$; entering

```
Expand[f[a-b^2]]

      2       2    4
   a   - 2 a b  + b
```

computes and expands $f(a-b^2)$; entering

```
(f[x+h]-f[x])/h
```

```
    2         2
-x   + (h + x)
--------------
      h
```

computes, but does not simplify, $\dfrac{f(x+h)-f(x)}{h}$; and entering

```
Simplify[(f[x+h]-f[x])/h]
```

```
h + 2 x
```

computes and simplifies $\dfrac{f(x+h)-f(x)}{h}$. ■

Many different types of functions can be defined using Mathematica. Examples illustrating how to define a function of two variables and vector-valued functions are illustrated below. Additional ways of defining functions will be discussed, as needed, throughout the text.

EXAMPLE: Define $f(x,y)=1-\sin(x^2+y^2)$. Calculate $f(1,2)$, $f\!\left(2\sqrt{\pi},\dfrac{3}{2}\sqrt{\pi}\right)$, $f(0,a)$, and $f(a^2-b^2,b^2-a^2)$.

SOLUTION: After clearing all prior definitions of f, we define f. Note that since f is a function of two variables, an underline (or blank) "_" is placed after each argument on the left-hand side (but not on the right-hand side) of the definition of the function. Thus, entering `f[x_,y_]=1-Sin[x^2+y^2]` defines $f(x,y)=1-\sin(x^2+y^2)$ and then computes and returns $f(x,y)$.

```
Clear[f]
```

```
f[x_,y_]=1-Sin[x^2+y^2]
```

```
        2    2
1 - Sin[x  + y ]
```

We then evaluate $f(1,2)$ by entering:

```
f[1,2]
```

```
    1 - Sin[5]
```

Note that `/.` can also be used to evaluate $f(1,2)$. Namely, entering

$$f[x,y] \ /. \ x->1 \ /. \ y->2$$

or

$$f[x,y] \ /. \ \{x->1,y->2\}$$

both produce the same result. Similarly, entering

```
f[2 Sqrt[Pi],3/2 Sqrt[Pi]]
```

```
            1
    1 - -------
        Sqrt[2]
```

computes $f\left(2\sqrt{\pi},\dfrac{3}{2}\sqrt{\pi}\right)$. In the same manner as above, entering

$$f[x,y] \ /. \ \{x->2Sqrt[Pi],y->3/2 \ Sqrt[Pi]\}$$

yields the same result. In this case, we can evaluate f for non-numerical arguments. Entering

```
f[0,a]
```

```
             2
    1 - Sin[a ]
```

computes $f(0,a)$ and entering

```
f[a^2-b^2,b^2-a^2]
```

```
             2    2 2     2     2 2
    1 - Sin[(a  - b )  + (-a  + b ) ]
```

computes $f(a^2-b^2,b^2-a^2)$. ∎

EXAMPLE: Define g to be the vector-valued function $g(x)=\langle x^2,1-x^2\rangle$. Calculate $g(1)$ and $g(\sin b)$.

SOLUTION: We remark that Mathematica uses braces "{ . . . }" to denote vectors, lists, and sets. These topics are discussed in more detail in Chapters 4 and 5. Since g is a function of a single variable, we define g in the same manner as defining functions of a single variable, discussed above. As before, be sure to place an underline (or blank) "_" after the argument on the left-hand side of the definition of the function (but not on the right-hand side). Thus, entering `g[x_]={x^2,1-x^2}` defines $g(x) = \langle x^2, 1-x^2 \rangle$ and then computes and returns g(x).

```
Clear[g]
```

```
g[x_]={x^2,1-x^2}
```

```
      2       2
    {x , 1 - x }
```

We then compute $g(1)$ and $g(\sin b)$.

```
g[1]
```

```
    {1, 0}
```

```
g[Sin[b]]
```

```
         2            2
    {Sin[b] , 1 - Sin[b] }
```

In each case, note that entering `g[x] /. x->1` and `g[x] /. x->Sin[b]` produce the same result. ∎

Our last example illustrates how to define a vector-valued function of two variables.

EXAMPLE: Define h to be the vector-valued function of two variables $h(x,y) = \langle \cos(x^2 - y^2), \sin(x^2 - y^2) \rangle$.

Calculate $h(1,2)$, $h(\pi,-\pi)$, and $h(\cos(a^2), \cos(1-a^2))$.

SOLUTION: Proceeding as in the previous example, we first clear all prior definitions of h and then define h. Note that Mathematica returns h(x,y).

```
Clear[h]
```

```
h[x_,y_]={Cos[x^2-y^2],Sin[y^2-x^2]}
```

```
        2    2        2    2
    {Cos[x  - y ], -Sin[x  - y ]}
```

Next, we calculate $h(1,2)$, $h(\pi,-\pi)$, and $h(\cos(a^2), \cos(1-a^2))$.

```
h[1,2]
```

```
    {Cos[3], Sin[3]}
```

```
h[Pi,-Pi]

   {1, 0}

h[Cos[a^2],Cos[1-a^2]]

                2 2
    {Cos[Cos[a ]  -

                  2 2
         Cos[1 - a ] ],

                 2 2
      -Sin[Cos[a ]  -

                  2 2
         Cos[1 - a ] ]}
```

■

Additional Ways to Evaluate Functions and Expressions

Once `f` has been properly defined, not only can a function `f[x]` be evaluated by computing `f[a]` where `a` is either a real number in the domain of `f` or an expression, functions and expressions can be evaluated using the command `/..` In general, to evaluate the function `f[x]` when `x` is replaced by `expression`, the following two commands are equivalent and yield the same output:

1. `f[expression]` replaces each variable in `f` by `expression`; and
2. `f[x] /. x-> expression` replaces each variable `x` in `f[x]` by `expression`.

This is illustrated in the following example.

EXAMPLE: Evaluate $f(1)$ and $g(1,2)$ if

$f(x) = x^2$ and

$g(x,y) = \langle \sin(x^2 - y^2), \cos(y^2 - x^2) \rangle$.

SOLUTION: After clearing all prior definitions of f and g, we define f and g. Note that since we use `:=` to define the functions, f(x) and g(x,y) are not computed and returned.

```
Clear[f,g]

f[x_]:=x^2

g[x_,y_]:={Sin[x^2-y^2],Cos[y^2-x^2]}
```

We note that entering

```
f[1]
```

> 1

and

```
g[1,2]
```

> {-Sin[3], Cos[3]}

produces the same results as entering each of the following commands.

```
f[x] /. x->1
```

> 1

```
g[x,y] /. x->1 /. y->2
```

> {-Sin[3], Cos[3]}

```
g[x,y] /. {x->1,y->2}
```

> {-Sin[3], Cos[3]}

■

Composition of Functions

Mathematica can easily perform the calculation `f[g[x]]`. However, when composing several different functions or repeatedly composing a function with itself, two additional commands are provided.

> `Composition[f1, f2, f3, . . . ,fn][x]` computes the composition $\left(f_1 \circ f_2 \circ \ldots \circ f_n\right)(x) = f_1\left(f_2 \cdots \left(f_n(x)\right)\right)$.
>
> `Nest[f, x, n]` computes the composition $\underbrace{\left(f \circ f \circ \ldots \circ f\right)(x)}_{n\ times} = \underbrace{f\left(f \cdots f(x)\right)}_{n\ times}$, where f is a function, n is a positive integer, and x is an expression.

Mathematica displays output for **EACH** command as it is generated unless a semi colon (;) is included at the end of the command. Thus, in the following example, the formulas for `f[x]`, `g[x]`, and `h[x]` are not displayed since a semi colon is placed at the end of each command.

EXAMPLE: Let $f(x) = x^2 + x$, $g(x) = x^3 + 1$, and $k(x) = \sin x + \cos x$. Compute
(a) $(f \circ g)(x) = f(g(x))$; (b) $(g \circ f)(x - 1) = (g(f(x - 1)))$; (c) $(f \circ k)\left(\dfrac{\pi}{3}\right) = f\left(k\left(\dfrac{\pi}{3}\right)\right)$;
(d) $f(\sin x)$; (e) $(f \circ k)(x) = f(k(x))$; and (f) $f(\sin(x + iy))$;

SOLUTION: We begin by clearing all prior definitions of f, g, and k, if any, and then defining f, g, and k.

```
Clear[f,g,h]
f[x_]=x^2+x;
g[x_]=x^3+1;
k[x_]=Sin[x]+Cos[x];
```

For (a), we note that entering `f[g[x]]` and `Composition[f,g][x]` produce the same result. The results are not simplified.

```
f[g[x]]
```

```
        3        3 2
   1 + x   + (1 + x )
```

```
Composition[f,g][x]
```

```
        3        3 2
   1 + x   + (1 + x )
```

For (b), we use `Composition` to compute $(g \circ f)(x - 1) = (g(f(x - 1)))$. The same results would be obtained with `g[f[x-1]]`.

```
Composition[g,f][x-1]
```

```
                    2       3
   1 + (-1 + (-1 + x)  + x)
```

For (c), we use `Composition` along with `Simplify` to compute $(f \circ k)\left(\dfrac{\pi}{3}\right) = f\left(k\left(\dfrac{\pi}{3}\right)\right)$.

```
Composition[f,k][Pi/3]//Simplify
```

```
   3
   - + Sqrt[3]
   2
```

For (d), we use the built-in function `Sin` to compute $f(\sin x)$.

```
Composition[f,Sin][x]
```

```
                 2
   Sin[x] + Sin[x]
```

For (e), we use `Composition` to compute $(f \circ k)(x) = f(k(x))$ and name the resulting output `exp1`. To simplify `exp1`, we use `Expand` along with the option `Trig->True`. The effect of the option `Trig->True` is to eliminate powers of sines and cosines in trigonometric expressions.

```
exp1=Composition[f,k][x]
```

$$\text{Cos[x] + Sin[x] + (Cos[x] + Sin[x])}^2$$

```
Expand[exp1,Trig->True]
```

```
1 + Cos[x] + Sin[x] + Sin[2 x]
```

For (f), we use `Composition` to compute $f(\sin(x + iy))$ and name the resulting output `exp2`. We then rewrite `exp1` in terms of its real and imaginary parts with `ComplexExpand`. If `expression` is a Mathematica expression in terms of x+I y, the command `ComplexExpand[expression]` rewrites `expression` in terms of its real and imaginary components, assuming that x and y are both real.

```
exp2=Composition[f,Sin][x+I y]
```

$$\text{Sin[x + I y] + Sin[x + I y]}^2$$

```
ComplexExpand[exp2]
```

$$\text{Cosh[y] Sin[x] + Cosh[y]}^2 \text{ Sin[x]}^2 - \text{Cos[x]}^2 \text{ Sinh[y]}^2 +$$

$$\text{I (Cos[x] Sinh[y] + 2 Cos[x] Cosh[y] Sin[x] Sinh[y])}$$

■

The next example illustrates the use of `Nest`.

EXAMPLE: Let $f(x) = x^2 + x$ as in the previous example. Compute:

(a) $(f \circ f \circ f)(x) = f(f(f(x)))$; and (b) $t(x) = \sin\left(\sin\left(\sin\left(\sin(\sin x)\right)\right)\right)$.

SOLUTION: For (a), we use `Nest` and name the resulting output exp3. Entering `f[f[f[x]]]` produces the same results. Since `exp3` is not simplified, we use `Expand` to simplify exp3.

```
exp3=Nest[f,x,3]
```

$$x + x^2 + (x + x^2)^2 + (x + x^2 + (x + x^2)^2)^2$$

```
Expand[exp3]
```

$$x + 3 x^2 + 6 x^3 + 9 x^4 + 10 x^5 + 8 x^6 + 4 x^7 + x^8$$

We define the function $t(x) = \sin\left(\sin\left(\sin\left(\sin(\sin(\sin x))\right)\right)\right)$ with `Nest`.

```
t[x_]=Nest[Sin,x,6]
```

```
Sin[Sin[Sin[Sin[Sin[Sin[x]]]]]]
```

We can compare the graphs of t(x) and $\sin x$ by graphing them on the same axes. Below, we use `Plot` to graph each function. The graph of $\sin x$ is dashed. Graphing functions and expressions is discussed in more detail in the next section.

```
Plot[{Sin[x],t[x]},{x,0,4Pi},PlotStyle->{Dashing[{.01}],GrayLevel[0]}]
```

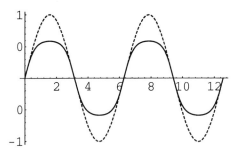

■

A Word of Caution

As stated above, we have adopted the convention that the name of every user-defined object will begin with lower case letters. If you don't follow this convention and accidentally attempt to define a function that has the same name as a built-in function, errors result as indicated below. If you use capital letters when defining functions, be careful!

```
Sin[x_]:=Cos[x]
```

```
SetDelayed::write: Tag Sin in Sin[x_] is Protected.
$Failed
```

2.3 *Graphing Functions, Expressions, and Equations*

One of the best features of Mathematica is its graphics capabilities. In this section, we discuss methods of graphing functions, expressions and equations and several of the options available to help graph functions.

Graphing Functions of a Single Variable

The command used to graph real-valued functions of a single variable is `Plot`. The form of the command to graph the function `f[x]` on the domain [a,b] is

$$\text{Plot[f[x],\{x,a,b\}].}$$

Mathematica returns information about the basic syntax of the `Plot` command with `?Plot`.

> `?Plot`
>
> ```
> Plot[f, {x, xmin, xmax}] generates a plot of f as a function of x
>     from xmin to xmax. Plot[{f1, f2, ...}, {x, xmin, xmax}] plots
>     several functions fi.
> ```

In the following examples, we illustrate the `Plot` function.

EXAMPLE: Let $f(x) = 4x^3 + 6x^2 - 9x + 2$, $g(x) = 12x^2 + 12x - 9$, and $h(x) = 24x + 12$. Graph f(x) on the interval $[-3, 2]$.

SOLUTION: After clearing all prior definitions of f, g, and h, if any, we define f, g, and h, and then use `Plot` to graph f on the interval $[-3, 2]$.

```
Clear[f,g,h]
f[x_]=4x^3+6x^2-9x+2;
g[x_]=12x^2+12x-9;
h[x_]=24x+12;
Plot[f[x],{x,-3,2}]
```

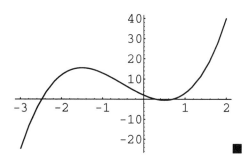

To plot the graph of f[x] in various shades of gray or colors, the command is

```
Plot[f[x],{x,a,b},PlotStyle->GrayLevel[w]],
```

where w is a number between 0 and 1. `PlotStyle->GrayLevel[0]` represents black; `PlotStyle->GrayLevel[1]` represents a white graph. If a color monitor is being used, the command is

```
Plot[f[x],{x,a,b},PlotStyle->RGBColor[r,g,b]],
```

where r, g, and b are numbers between 0 and 1. `RGBColor[1,0,0]` represents red, `RGBColor[0,1,0]` represents green, and `RGBColor[0,0,1]` represents blue. Remember that the results of entering a `Plot` command are Mathematica objects and, consequently, can be named for later use. A dashed graph can be generated by using the option

```
PlotStyle->Dashing[{n1,n2,...}],
```

where n1, n2, ... are numbers.

Graphs of functions, like expressions, can be named. This is particularly useful when one needs to refer to the graph of particular functions repeatedly or to display several graphs on the same axes.

The command used to display several graphs on the same axes is `Show`. To show two graphs named `graph1` and `graph2`, the command entered is `Show[graph1, graph2]`.

> **EXAMPLE:** Show the graphs of f, g, and h, defined in the previous example, on the same axes.

SOLUTION: Below, we graph g on the interval [−3,2]. We use `PlotStyle` and `Dashing` so that the graph of g is dashed. The resulting output is named `plotg`.

`plotg=Plot[g[x],{x,-3,2},PlotStyle->Dashing[{.01}]]`

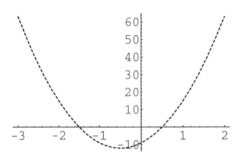

Next, we graph f and h, in gray, on the interval $[-3,2]$, naming the results `plotf` and `ploth`. In each case, the option

```
DisplayFunction->Identity
```

is used to indicate that the graphics objects generated are not displayed. These graphs, along with `plotg`, are shown simultaneously by using the `Show` command together with the option

```
DisplayFunction->$DisplayFunction
```

which instructs Mathematica to display the resulting graphics objects. Note that no graphs would be displayed if the `DisplayFunction->$DisplayFunction` option were omitted from the following `Show` command:

```
plotf=Plot[f[x],{x,-3,2},DisplayFunction->Identity];
ploth=Plot[h[x],{x,-3,2},PlotStyle->GrayLevel[.3],
        DisplayFunction->Identity];
Show[plotf,plotg,ploth,DisplayFunction->$DisplayFunction]
```

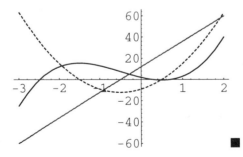

A complete list of the available options along with their current settings is obtained by entering the command `Options[Plot]` as indicated below. The commands `Plot` and `Show` have many options. To implement the various options, the form of the command `Plot` is

```
                          Plot[f[x],{x,a,b},options];
```

the form of the command `Show` is

```
                          Show[graphs, options].
```

Several of these options are discussed below.

```
Options [Plot]

                                 1
    {AspectRatio -> -----------, Axes -> Automatic, AxesLabel -> None,
                     GoldenRatio
      AxesOrigin -> Automatic, AxesStyle -> Automatic,
      Background -> Automatic, ColorOutput -> Automatic,
      Compiled -> True, DefaultColor -> Automatic, Epilog -> {},
      Frame -> False, FrameLabel -> None, FrameStyle -> Automatic,
      FrameTicks -> Automatic, GridLines -> None, MaxBend -> 10.,
      PlotDivision -> 20., PlotLabel -> None, PlotPoints -> 25,
      PlotRange -> Automatic, PlotRegion -> Automatic,
      PlotStyle -> Automatic, Prolog -> {}, RotateLabel -> True,
      Ticks -> Automatic, DefaultFont :> $DefaultFont,
      DisplayFunction :> $DisplayFunction}
```

Other Available Options

Additional `Plot` options include:

1. `AspectRatio->number`
   This makes the ratio of the length of the x-axis to the y-axis number. The default value is $1/$`GoldenRatio`. `GoldenRatio` is a built-in Mathematica constant (like `E` and `Pi`) which represents the golden ratio, $\left(1+\sqrt{5}\right)/2 \approx 1.61803$.

2. `Frame->True`
   This draws a frame around the graph; the default value is `False`—no frame is drawn.

3. `Ticks->None` or `Ticks->{{x-axis ticks},{y-axis ticks}}`
   This specifies that either no tick marks be placed on either axis **or** tick marks be placed on the x-axis at `x-axis ticks` and on the y-axis at `y-axis ticks`.

4. `AxesLabel->{"x-axis label","y-axis label"}`
   This labels the x-axis `x-axis label` and the y-axis `y-axis label`. For example, the command
   `Plot[f[x],{x,xmin,xmax,AxesLabel->{"jane","mary"}]`
   graphs the function `f[x]` on the interval [xmin,xmax]; and labels the x-axis `jane` and the y-axis `mary`. The default for the option is that no labels are shown.

5. `PlotLabel->{"name"}`
   This centers name above the graph. The default for the option is that the graph is not labeled.
6. `AxesOrigin->{x-coordinate,y-coordinate}`
   This option specifies that the x-axis and y-axis intersect at the point (xcoordinate,ycoordinate). The option `Axes->False` specifies that the graph is to be drawn without axes.
7. `PlotRange->{y-minimum,y-maximum}`
   This option specifies the range displayed on the final graph to be the interval `[y-minimum,y-maximum]`; `PlotRange->All` attempts to show the entire graph. `PlotRange->{{xmin,xmax},{ymin,ymax}}` shows the graph on the rectangle `[xmin,xmax]` ¥ `[ymin,ymax]`.
8. `GridLines`
   `GridLines->Automatic` specifies that grid lines on the resulting graph are drawn automatically, `GridLines->{None,Automatic}` specifies that only horizontal gridlines be displayed, and `GridLines->{{1,2,3},None}` gives vertical gridlines at x =1, 2, and 3.

Graphing Several Functions

The `Plot` command can also be used to graph several functions simultaneously. To display the graphs of the functions `f[x]`, `g[x]`, and `h[x]` on the domain [a,b] on the same axes, enter commands of the form `Plot[{f[x],g[x],h[x]},{x,a,b},options]`. This command can be generalized to include more than three functions.

EXAMPLE: Graph the functions $\sin x$, $\sin 2x$, and $\sin \dfrac{x}{2}$ on the interval $[0, 4\pi]$. Display all three graphs on the same axes.

SOLUTION: We use `Plot` to graph the functions on the interval $[0, 4\pi]$. The option `PlotStyle` is used to display the graph of $\sin x$ in black, $\sin 2x$ in gray, and $\sin \dfrac{x}{2}$ dashed; `PlotRange` is used to specify that the y-values displayed correspond to the interval $\left[-\dfrac{3}{2}, \dfrac{3}{2}\right]$; and `Ticks` is used to specify that the tick marks placed on the x-axis are chosen automatically while those placed on the y-axis are placed at −1 and 1.

```
Plot[{Sin[x],Sin[2x],Sin[x/2]},{x,0,4Pi},
     PlotStyle->{GrayLevel[0],GrayLevel[.3],Dashing[{.01}]},
     PlotRange->{-3/2,3/2},Ticks->{Automatic,{-1,1}}]
```

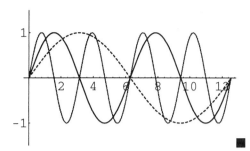

Instead of plotting several graphs simultaneously with `Plot`, each graph may be generated individually and named and then the resulting graphs can be displayed together with `Show`.

EXAMPLE: Sketch the graph of the circle $x^2 - 4x + y^2 - 2y = 4$.

SOLUTION: We find the center and radius of the circle $x^2 - 4x + y^2 - 2y = 4$ by completing the square and obtain the equation $(x-2)^2 + (y-1)^2 = 3^2$. Thus, the center is $(2,1)$ and the radius is 3. Solving this equation for y results in $y = 1 \pm \sqrt{9 - (x-2)^2}$.

Thus, a function describing the top half of the circle is given by $y_1(x) = 1 + \sqrt{9 - (x-2)^2}$, while a function describing the bottom half is given by $y_2(x) = 1 - \sqrt{9 - (x-2)^2}$. Below, we define `y1` and `y2` to be the functions describing the top and bottom half of the circle, respectively. We then use `Plot` to graph `y1` and `y2` on the interval [–1,5], naming the resulting graphs `p1` and `p2`, respectively. Neither graph is displayed since the option `DisplayFunction->Identity` is included. We then use `Show` to display both graphs together. Since Mathematica's default `AspectRatio` is `1/GoldenRatio`, the resulting displayed graphics object does not look like a circle.

```
Clear[y1,y2]
y1=1+Sqrt[9-(x-2)^2];
y2=1-Sqrt[9-(x-2)^2];
p1=Plot[y1,{x,-1,5},DisplayFunction->Identity];
p2=Plot[y2,{x,-1,5},DisplayFunction->Identity];
Show[p1,p2,DisplayFunction->$DisplayFunction]
```

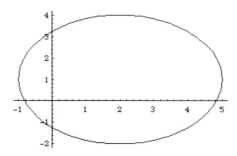

However, when we include the option `AspectRatio->1`, the resulting graph looks like a circle.

```
Show[p1,p2,AspectRatio->1,DisplayFunction->$DisplayFunction]
```

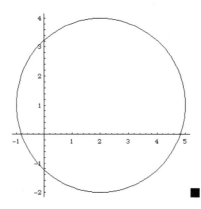

Piecewise-Defined Functions

Piecewise-defined functions may also be defined and graphed with Mathematica. In the following example, f(x) is defined in two "pieces". Notice that `Condition` (`/;`) designates the definition of f(x) for different domain values.

Note that <= represents a ≤ symbol; >= represents a ≥ symbol.

EXAMPLE: If $f(x) = \begin{cases} x^2 + 1 \text{ if } x \geq 0 \\ -x^2 - 1 \text{ if } x < 0 \end{cases}$, graph f on the interval $[-2,2]$.

SOLUTION: Entering f[x_]:=x^2+1 /; x>=0 defines $f(x) = x^2 + 1$ if $x \geq 0$ and entering f[x_]:=-x^2-1 /; x<0 defines $f(x) = -x^2 - 1$ if $x < 0$. In this case, we must use := when defining f, because f[x] does not make sense unless x is a particular number. After defining f, we use Plot to graph f on the interval $[-2, 2]$.

```
Clear[f]
f[x_]:=x^2+1 /; x>=0
f[x_]:=-x^2-1 /; x<0
Plot[f[x],{x,-2,2}]
```

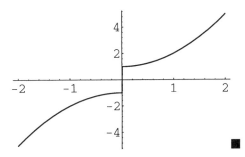

Functions can be defined recursively. For example, if the function f[x] is defined on the interval [a,b], then f can be defined for x > b with f[x_]:=f[x-(b-a)] /; x>b. Functions of this type are useful in the study of Fourier series.

EXAMPLE: Let g(x) be the periodic extension of the function $f(x) = \begin{cases} x \ if \ 0 \leq x < 1 \\ 1 \ if \ 1 \leq x < 2 \\ 3 - x \ if \ 2 \leq x < 3 \end{cases}$.

Graph g on the interval $[0, 12]$.

SOLUTION: We proceed as in the previous example. Entering g[x_]:=x /; 0<=x<1 defines $g(x) = x$ if $0 \leq x < 1$, entering g[x_]:=1 /; 1<=x<2 defines $g(x) = 1$ if $1 \leq x < 2$, and entering g[x_]:=3-x /; 2<=x<3 defines $g(x) = 3 - x$ if $2 \leq x < 3$. For x>3, we define $g(x) = g(x-3)$. We then use Plot along with the PlotRange and Ticks option to graph g on the interval $[0, 12]$. As in the previous example, we must use := when defining g as g[x] does not make sense unless x is a particular number.

```
Clear[g]
g[x_]:=x /; 0<=x<1
g[x_]:=1 /; 1<=x<2
g[x_]:=3-x /; 2<=x<3
g[x_]:=g[x-3] /; x>=3
Plot[g[x],{x,0,12},PlotRange->{0,2},Ticks->{Automatic,{1,2}}]
```

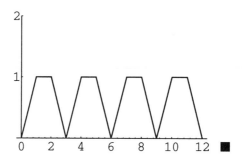

Graphs of Parametric Functions in Two Dimensions

The function `ParametricPlot` is used to graph parametric curves in two dimensions. The command

`ParametricPlot[{x[t],y[t]},{t,tmin,tmax}]`

plots the curve given by `x=x[t]` and `y=y[t]` from `t=tmin` to `t=tmax`. `ParametricPlot` has the same options as `Plot`.

EXAMPLE: Use `ParametricPlot` to graph the circle $x^2 - 4x + y^2 - 2y = 4$.

SOLUTION: In the previous example, we saw the equation $x^2 - 4x + y^2 - 2y = 4$ is equivalent to the equation $(x-2)^2 + (y-1)^2 = 3^2$. Thus, the center of the circle $x^2 - 4x + y^2 - 2y = 4$ is $(2,1)$ and the radius is 3. Parametric equations of the circle are given by $\begin{cases} x = 2 + 3\cos t \\ y = 1 + 3\sin t \end{cases}$, $0 \le t \le 2\pi$. Below, we use `ParametricPlot` along with the option `AspectRatio->1` to graph the circle.

```
ParametricPlot[{2+3Cos[t],1+3Sin[t]},{t,0,2Pi},AspectRatio->1]
```

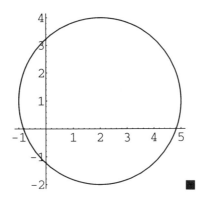

Arrays of graphics objects can be displayed with the command `GraphicsArray` as illustrated in the following example.

EXAMPLE: For a<b, the **Prolate Cycloid** is the graph of the parametric equations

$\begin{cases} x = at - b\sin t \\ y = a - b\cos t \end{cases}$. The **Folium of Descartes** has parametrization $\begin{cases} x = \dfrac{3at}{1+t^3} \\ y = \dfrac{3at^2}{1+t^3} \end{cases}$. Graph the

Prolate Cycloid and the Folium of Descartes for a=1 and b=2.

SOLUTION: After clearing all prior definitions of x and y, if any, we define x and y and then use `ParametricPlot` to graph the Prolate Cycloid, naming the resulting graphics object pp1. Note that pp1 is not displayed since the option `DisplayFunction->Identity` is included.

```
Clear[x,y]
x[t_]=t-2Sin[t];
y[t_]=1-2Cos[t];
pp1=ParametricPlot[{x[t],y[t]},{t,0,8Pi},
        PlotRange->{-3/2,5},DisplayFunction->Identity];
```

Similarly, we use `ParametricPlot` to graph the Folium of Descartes, naming the resulting graphics object pp2.

```
Clear[x,y]
x[t_]=3t/(1+t^3);
y[t_]=3t^2/(1+t^3);
pp2=ParametricPlot[{x[t],y[t]},{t,-10,10},PlotRange->{{-4,5},{-4,5}},
        AspectRatio->1,DisplayFunction->Identity];
```

The set of graphics {pp1,pp2} can be displayed together, but not on the same axes, with the command `GraphicsArray` as shown below.

```
Show[GraphicsArray[{pp1,pp2}]]
```

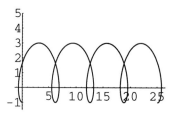 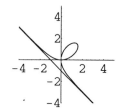

Three-Dimensional Graphics

As was mentioned in Chapter 1, functions of more than one variable can be defined with Mathematica . Of particular interest are functions of two variables. The command which plots the graph of the function f(x,y) on the rectangle [xmin,xmax] × [ymin,ymax] is

```
Plot3D[f[x,y],{x,xmin,xmax},{y,ymin,ymax}]
```

EXAMPLE: Let $f(x,y) = x^2 - 4x + y^2 - 2y + 5$. Graph f on the rectangle $[0,4] \times [-1,3]$.

SOLUTION: After clearing all prior definitions of f, if any, we define f and then use Plot3D to graph f on the rectangle $[0,4] \times [-1,3]$.

```
Clear[f]
f[x_,y_]=x^2-4x+y^2-2y+5;
Plot3D[f[x,y],{x,0,4},{y,-1,3}]
```

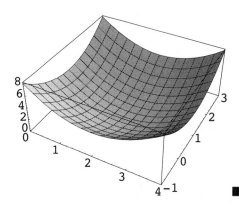

Information about the Plot3D command, including a brief explanation of the syntax along with a list of the associated options and their current settings is obtained with ??Plot3D or, equivalently, Information[Plot3D].

```
??Plot3D

    Plot3D[f, {x, xmin, xmax}, {y, ymin, ymax}] generates a
        three-dimensional plot of f as a function of x and y. Plot3D[{f,
        s}, {x, xmin, xmax}, {y, ymin, ymax}] generates a
        three-dimensional plot in which the height of the surface is
        specified by f, and the shading is specified by s.
    Attributes[Plot3D] = {HoldAll, Protected}

    Options[Plot3D] =
      {AmbientLight -> GrayLevel[0], AspectRatio -> Automatic,
      Axes -> True, AxesEdge -> Automatic, AxesLabel -> None,
      AxesStyle -> Automatic, Background -> Automatic, Boxed -> True,
      BoxRatios -> {1, 1, 0.4}, BoxStyle -> Automatic,
      ClipFill -> Automatic, ColorFunction -> Automatic,
      ColorOutput -> Automatic, Compiled -> True,
      DefaultColor -> Automatic, Epilog -> {}, FaceGrids -> None,
      HiddenSurface -> True, Lighting -> True,
      LightSources ->
       {{{1., 0., 1.}, RGBColor[1, 0, 0]},
         {{1., 1., 1.}, RGBColor[0, 1, 0]},
         {{0., 1., 1.}, RGBColor[0, 0, 1]}}, Mesh -> True,
      MeshStyle -> Automatic, PlotLabel -> None, PlotPoints -> 15,
      PlotRange -> Automatic, PlotRegion -> Automatic,
      Plot3Matrix -> Automatic, Prolog -> {}, Shading -> True,
      SphericalRegion -> False, Ticks -> Automatic,
      ViewCenter -> Automatic, ViewPoint -> {1.3, -2.4, 2.},
      ViewVertical -> {0., 0., 1.}, DefaultFont :> $DefaultFont,
      DisplayFunction :> $DisplayFunction}
```

On several platforms, the option ViewPoint can be changed by going to the Mathematica menu, selecting **Action**, then **Prepare Input**, and then **3D ViewPoint Selector...** at which point the following window appears.

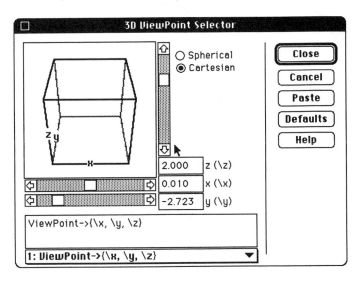

Various perspectives can be adjusted by scrolling as indicated above. When a satisfactory `ViewPoint` is found, select **Paste** and the `ViewPoint` will be pasted into the Mathematica notebook at the location of the cursor.

Several of these options are illustrated in the following examples.

EXAMPLE: Graph $f(x,y) = x^2 - 4x + y^2 - 2y + 5$ on the rectangle $[0,4] \times [-1,3]$.

SOLUTION: Unlike the previous example, we take advantage of `ViewPoint` and `BoxRatios` to adjust the point from which the graphics object is viewed and the ratios of the side lengths of the bounding box in the resulting graph.

```
Clear[f]
f[x_,y_]=x^2-4x+y^2-2y+5;
Plot3D[f[x,y],{x,0,4},{y,-1,3},BoxRatios->{1,1,3},
      ViewPoint->{3.752, 2.219, 1.137}]
```

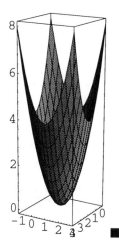

In the following example, we illustrate the `PlotPoints` and `Shading` options.

EXAMPLE: If $g(x,y) = x \sin y + y \sin x$, graph g on the rectangle $[0,5\pi] \times [0,5\pi]$.

SOLUTION: We first use `Plot3D` to graph g. The resulting graph appears "choppy."

```
Clear[g]
g[x_,y_]=x Sin[y]+y Sin[x];
Plot3D[g[x,y],{x,0,5Pi},{y,0,5Pi}]
```

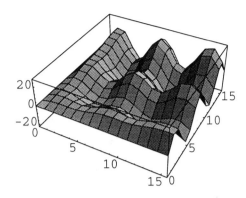

The option `PlotPoints->n` causes Mathematica to evaluate the function at n^2 points when plotting the graph. These n^2 points are called **sample points**. In the command
`Plot3D[f[x,y],{x,xmin,xmax},{y,ymin,ymax}, PlotPoints->n]`, the sample points are obtained by dividing each interval [xmin,xmax] and [ymin,ymax] into n subintervals. If different numbers are to be used in the two directions, then

`PlotPoints->{nx,ny}`

is used. Hence, a larger value of n (or nx and ny) yields a smoother graph. The option

`Shading->False`

causes Mathematica to **not** shade squares in the graph. Below, we use the options `PlotPoints->30` and `Shading->False` to indicate that 30 points be selected in the direction of both the x and the y-coordinates, for a total of 900 sample points, and that the resulting graph is not shaded. The resulting graph is smoother than the first.

`Plot3D[g[x,y],{x,0,5Pi},{y,0,5Pi},PlotPoints->30,Shading->False]`

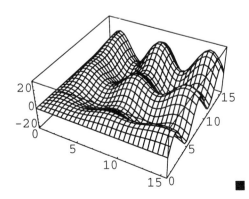

Graphing Level Curves of Functions of Two Variables

The **level curves** of the function f(x,y) are curves in the xy-plane which satisfy the equation f(x,y)=c where c is a constant. Mathematica graphs several of the level curves of the function f(x,y) with the command

$$\texttt{ContourPlot[f[x,y],\{x,xmin,xmax\},\{y,ymin,ymax\}].}$$

`Information[ContourPlot]` or `??ContourPlot` yields the basic syntax of the `ContourPlot` command along with a list of the options for `ContourPlot` and their current settings.

```
??ContourPlot

ContourPlot[f, {x, xmin, xmax}, {y, ymin, ymax}] generates a contour
    plot of f as a function of x and y.
Attributes[ContourPlot] = {HoldAll, Protected}

Options[ContourPlot] =
  {AspectRatio -> 1, Axes -> False, AxesLabel -> None,
   AxesOrigin -> Automatic, AxesStyle -> Automatic,
   Background -> Automatic, ColorFunction -> Automatic,
   ColorOutput -> Automatic, Compiled -> True, ContourLines -> True,
   Contours -> 10, ContourShading -> True, ContourSmoothing -> True,
   ContourStyle -> Automatic, DefaultColor -> Automatic,
   Epilog -> {}, Frame -> True, FrameLabel -> None,
   FrameStyle -> Automatic, FrameTicks -> Automatic,
   PlotLabel -> None, PlotPoints -> 15, PlotRange -> Automatic,
   PlotRegion -> Automatic, Prolog -> {}, RotateLabel -> True,
   Ticks -> Automatic, DefaultFont :> $DefaultFont,
   DisplayFunction :> $DisplayFunction}
```

All contour plots are shaded unless the `ContourShading->False` option is employed. The option `Contours->k` instructs Mathematica to use k contour levels.

EXAMPLE: Sketch several level curves of $g(x,y)=x\sin y+y\sin x$ on the rectangle $[0,5\pi]\times[0,5\pi]$.

SOLUTION: The three-dimensional plot of this function was given in the previous example. Contour levels represent intersections of planes of the form g(x,y) = constant with the surface shown in the previous example. Below we use `ContourPlot` to generate various level curves of g. The option `PlotPoints->30` is included so that 30 sample points in the x and y directions are used to create the plot.

```
Clear[g]
g[x_,y_]=x Sin[y]+y Sin[x];
ContourPlot[g[x,y],{x,0,5Pi},{y,0,5Pi},PlotPoints->30]
```

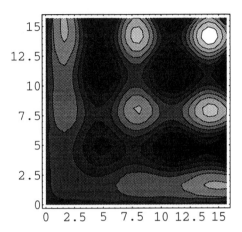

Next, we generate a similar graph except that the option `Contours->20` specifies that 20 contours be included in the contour plot, `ContourShading->False` specifies that the resulting contour plot not be shaded, `Axes->Automatic` specifies that the resulting graph have axes, `Frame->False` specifies that the resulting contour plot not be enclosed in a frame, `AxesOrigin->{0,0}` specifies that the axes intersect at the point (0,0), and the option `PlotPoints->60` specifies that 60 sample points in the x and y directions are used to create the plot.

```
ContourPlot[g[x,y],{x,0,5Pi},{y,0,5Pi},Contours->20,
        ContourShading->False,Axes->Automatic,Frame->False,
        AxesOrigin->{0,0},PlotPoints->60]
```

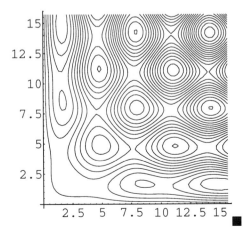

In the previous examples, Mathematica has selected the contour levels. However, these values can be chosen by the user with the `Contours->valuelist` option. This particular feature is helpful in graphing equations.

EXAMPLE: (a) Graph several level curves of $f(x,y) = x^2 - 4x + y^2 - 2y + 5$ on the rectangle $[-2,6] \times [-3,5]$. (b) Graph the circle $x^2 - 4x + y^2 - 2y + 5 = 9$.

SOLUTION: After defining f, we use `ContourPlot` along with the option `ContourShading` to graph several level curves of f on the rectangle $[-2,6] \times [-3,5]$.

```
Clear[f]
f[x_,y_]=x^2-4x+y^2-2y+5;
ContourPlot[f[x,y],{x,-2,6},{y,-3,5},ContourShading->False]
```

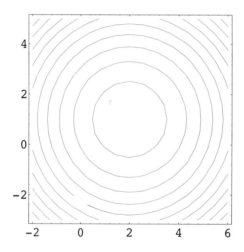

To graph the circle $x^2 - 4x + y^2 - 2y + 5 = 9$, which is the same as the circle $(x-2)^2 + (y-1)^2 = 3^2$ considered in previous examples, we note that the graph of $x^2 - 4x + y^2 - 2y + 5 = 9$ is the level curve of f(x,y) corresponding to 9. Below, we use `ContourPlot` to graph this particular curve by including the option `Contours->{9}` which specifies that the contour corresponding to 9 be graphed. If, for example, the option `Contours->{4,9,16,25}` had been included, then the contours corresponding to 4, 9, 16, and 25 would be graphed.

```
ContourPlot[f[x,y],{x,-2,6},{y,-3,5},Contours->{9},
        Frame->False,Axes->Automatic,AxesOrigin->{0,0},
        PlotPoints->30,ContourShading->False]
```

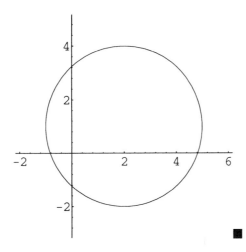

ContourPlot can also help us investigate the behavior of some functions near particular points.

EXAMPLE: Graph h and several level curves of h on the rectangle $[-2,2]\times[-2,2]$ if $h(x,y)=\dfrac{x^2-y^2}{x^2+y^2}$.

SOLUTION: In the following graphs, Mathematica does not compute h[0,0] and thus no error messages are generated even though h is undefined when x=0 and y=0. In the following code, we use Plot3D to graph h, naming the resulting graph ploth, and ContourPlot to graph several level curves of h, naming the resulting graph cph. Neither graph is displayed since the option DisplayFunction->Identity is included in each command. We then use GraphicsArray to display the set of graphs {ploth,cph}.

```
Clear[h]
h[x_,y_]=(x^2-y^2)/(x^2+y^2);
ploth=Plot3D[h[x,y],{x,-2,2},{y,-2,2},PlotPoints->25,
        Shading->False,DisplayFunction->Identity];
cph=ContourPlot[h[x,y],{x,-2,2},{y,-2,2},Frame->False,
        Axes->Automatic,AxesOrigin->{0,0},PlotRange->{-1,1},
        ContourShading->False,DisplayFunction->Identity];
Show[GraphicsArray[{ploth,cph}]]
```

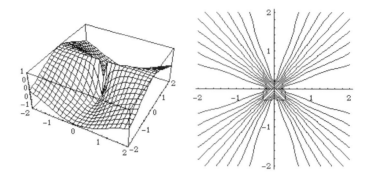

From the graph on the left, we see that h behaves strangely near (0,0). In fact, if h had been graphed on a different rectangle, Mathematica may have sampled (0,0) and subsequently displayed an error message. In any case, the resulting graph would be sufficiently accurate for our purposes. From the graph on the right, we see that all contours are approaching (0,0). In fact, near (0,0), h attains every value between –1 and 1 and in calculus we show that $\lim\limits_{(x,y)\to(0,0)} h(x,y)$ does not exist. ∎

Graphing Parametric Curves and Surfaces in Space

`ParametricPlot3D` is used to graph parametric curves and surfaces in space. The command

$$\text{ParametricPlot3D[\{x[t],y[t],z[t]\},\{t,tmin,tmax\}]}$$

generates the three-dimensional curve defined by `x=x[t]`, `y=y[t]`, and `z=z[t]` for `t=tmin` to `t=tmax` and the command

$$\text{ParametricPlot3D[\{x[u,v],y[u,v],z[u,v]\},}$$
$$\text{\{u,umin,umax\},\{v,vmin,vmax\}]}$$

plots the surface defined by `x=x[u,v]`, `y=y[u,v]`, and `z=z[u,v]` for $\text{umin}\le u\le\text{umax}$ and $\text{vmin}\le v\le\text{vmax}$.

The command `Information[ParametricPlot3D]` or `??ParametricPlot3D` returns a description of the `ParametricPlot3D` command along with a list of options and their current settings.

```
ParametricPlot3D[{fx, fy, fz}, {t, tmin, tmax}] produces a
   three-dimensional space curve parameterized by a variable t which
   runs from tmin to tmax. ParametricPlot3D[{fx, fy, fz}, {t, tmin,
   tmax}, {u, umin, umax}] produces a three-dimensional surface
   parametrized by t and u. ParametricPlot3D[{fx, fy, fz, s}, ...]
   shades the plot according to the color specification s.
   ParametricPlot3D[{{fx, fy, fz}, {gx, gy, gz}, ...}, ...] plots
   several objects together.
Attributes[ParametricPlot3D] = {HoldAll, Protected}

Options[ParametricPlot3D] =
  {AmbientLight -> GrayLevel[0.], AspectRatio -> Automatic,
   Axes -> True, AxesEdge -> Automatic, AxesLabel -> None,
   AxesStyle -> Automatic, Background -> Automatic, Boxed -> True,
   BoxRatios -> Automatic, BoxStyle -> Automatic,
   ColorOutput -> Automatic, Compiled -> True,
   DefaultColor -> Automatic, Epilog -> {}, FaceGrids -> None,
   Lighting -> True, LightSources ->
    {{{1., 0., 1.}, RGBColor[1, 0, 0]},
     {{1., 1., 1.}, RGBColor[0, 1, 0]},
     {{0., 1., 1.}, RGBColor[0, 0, 1]}}, PlotLabel -> None,
   PlotPoints -> Automatic, PlotRange -> Automatic,
   PlotRegion -> Automatic, Plot3Matrix -> Automatic,
   PolygonIntersections -> True, Prolog -> {}, RenderAll -> True,
   Shading -> True, SphericalRegion -> False, Ticks -> Automatic,
   ViewCenter -> Automatic, ViewPoint -> {1.3, -2.4, 2.},
   ViewVertical -> {0., 0., 1.}, DefaultFont :> $DefaultFont,
   DisplayFunction :> $DisplayFunction}
```

The following examples illustrate the `ParametricPlot3D` command along with several frequently used options.

EXAMPLE: Compare the graphs of $\begin{cases} x = \cos 2t \\ y = \sin 2t, 0 \leq t \leq 8\pi \\ z = t/5 \end{cases}$ and $\begin{cases} x = t\cos 2t \\ y = t\sin 2t, 0 \leq t \leq 8\pi. \\ z = t/5 \end{cases}$

SOLUTION: In pp1 we graph

$$\begin{cases} x = \cos 2t \\ y = \sin 2t, 0 \leq t \leq 8\pi \\ z = t/5 \end{cases}$$

and in pp2 we graph

$$\begin{cases} x = t\cos 2t \\ y = t\sin 2t, \; 0 \le t \le 8\pi \, . \\ z = t/5 \end{cases}$$

In each case, the option `PlotPoints->120` is used to increase the number of sample points to assure smooth graphs and the option `Ticks->None` specifies that the resulting graphs are to be displayed without tick marks. Neither graph is displayed since the option `DisplayFunction->Identity` is included. The set of graphs {pp1,pp2} is displayed side-by-side with `GraphicsArray`.

```
pp1=ParametricPlot3D[{Cos[2t],Sin[2t],t/5},{t,0,8Pi},
        PlotPoints->120,Ticks->None,DisplayFunction->Identity];
pp2=ParametricPlot3D[{t Cos[2t],t Sin[2t],t/5},{t,0,8Pi},
        PlotPoints->120,Ticks->None,DisplayFunction->Identity];
Show[GraphicsArray[{pp1,pp2}]]
```

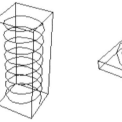
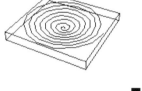

The intersection of a plane and a surface is called the **trace** of the surface. We can use `ParametricPlot3D` to help us visualize the traces of some surfaces.

EXAMPLE: Let $g(x,y) = \cos(x + \sin y)$. Sketch a graph of the intersection of the graph of g with the plane (a) $x = 5$; (b) $y = 6$; (c) $x = y$; and (d) $y = 4\pi - x$.

SOLUTION: We begin by using `Plot3D` to graph g on the rectangle $[0, 4\pi] \times [0, 4\pi]$.

```
Clear[g]
g[x_,y_]=Cos[x+Sin[y]];
Plot3D[g[x,y],{x,0,4Pi},{y,0,4Pi},PlotPoints->25]
```

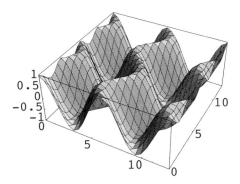

For (a), the intersection of the plane $x = 5$ and the xy-plane is the line $x = 5$ which has parametrization

$$\begin{cases} x = 5 \\ y = t \\ z = 0 \end{cases}.$$

The intersection of the plane $x = 5$ and the graph of g is the set of points on the graph of g above the line $x = 5$ which has parametrization

$$\begin{cases} x = 5 \\ y = t \\ z = g(5,t) \end{cases}.$$

The lines

$$\begin{cases} x = 5 \\ y = t \\ z = 0 \end{cases} \text{ and } \begin{cases} x = 5 \\ y = t \\ z = g(5,t) \end{cases}$$

are graphed below using `ParametricPlot3D` for $0 \le t \le 4\pi$ in `pp1` and `pp2`, respectively. Similarly, for (b), the intersection of the plane $y = 6$ and the xy-plane is the line $y = 6$ with parametrization

$$\begin{cases} x = t \\ y = 6 \\ z = 0 \end{cases}$$

and the intersection of the plane $y = 6$ and the graph of g is the set of points on the graph of g above the line $y = 6$ which has parametrization

$$\begin{cases} x = t \\ y = 6 \\ z = g(t,6) \end{cases}.$$

These two curves are graphed in pp3 and pp4. Finally, Show is used to display the graphs of pp1, pp2, pp3, and pp4.

```
pp1=ParametricPlot3D[{5,t,0},{t,0,4Pi},DisplayFunction->Identity];
pp2=ParametricPlot3D[{5,t,g[5,t]},{t,0,4Pi},DisplayFunction->Identity];
pp3=ParametricPlot3D[{t,5,0},{t,0,4Pi},DisplayFunction->Identity];
pp4=ParametricPlot3D[{t,6,g[t,6]},{t,0,4Pi},DisplayFunction->Identity];
Show[pp1,pp2,pp3,pp4,DisplayFunction->$DisplayFunction]
```

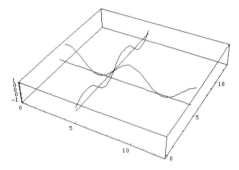

For (c) and (d) we proceed in the same manner as in (a) and (b). The line of intersection of the plane $x = y$ with the xy-plane is the line $x = y$ with parametrization

$$\begin{cases} x = t \\ y = t ; \\ z = 0 \end{cases}$$

the intersection of the plane $x = y$ with g has parametrization

$$\begin{cases} x = t \\ y = t \\ z = g(t,t) \end{cases}.$$

ParametricPlot3D is used to graph these two curves in pp5 and pp6. Similarly, the line of intersection of the plane $y = 4\pi - x$ with the xy-plane is the line $y = 4\pi - x$ with parametrization

$$\begin{cases} x = t \\ y = 4\pi - t\,; \\ z = 0 \end{cases}$$

the intersection of the plane $y = 4\pi - x$ with g has parametrization

$$\begin{cases} x = t \\ y = 4\pi - t \\ z = g(t, 4\pi - t) \end{cases}.$$

These two curves are graphed with `ParametricPlot3D` in pp7 and pp8. `Show` is used to display all four graphs.

```
pp5=ParametricPlot3D[{t,t,0},{t,0,4Pi},DisplayFunction->Identity];
pp6=ParametricPlot3D[{t,t,g[t,t]},{t,0,4Pi},DisplayFunction->Identity];
pp7=ParametricPlot3D[{t,4Pi-t,0},{t,0,4Pi},
        DisplayFunction->Identity];
pp8=ParametricPlot3D[{t,4Pi-t,g[t,4Pi-t]},{t,0,4Pi},
        DisplayFunction->Identity];
Show[pp5,pp6,pp7,pp8,DisplayFunction->$DisplayFunction]
```

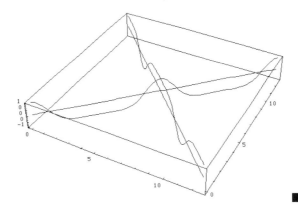

In Chapter 3, we will use the **Method of Lagrange Multipliers** to solve some problems of the form "find the minimum and maximum values of f(x,y) subject to the constraint $g(x,y) = c$. To see that the maximum and minimum values subject to the constraint exist, we can graph f(x,y) for points (x,y) on the graph of $g(x,y) = c$ if we know a parametrization of the equation $g(x,y) = c$ with `ParametricPlot3D`.

EXAMPLE: Sketch the graph of f(x,y) for points (x,y) on the circle $x^2 + y^2 = 1$ if $f(x,y) = x^3 \sin 4y + y^2 \cos 3x$.

SOLUTION: A parametrization of the circle $x^2 + y^2 = 1$ is given by

$$\begin{cases} x = \cos t \\ y = \sin t, 0 \le t \le 2\pi \; . \\ z = 0 \end{cases}$$

Thus, a graph of f(x,y) for points (x,y) on the circle is obtained by graphing

$$\begin{cases} x = \cos t \\ y = \sin t \qquad , 0 \le t \le 2\pi \; . \\ z = f(\cos t, \sin t) \end{cases}$$

We use `ParametricPlot3D` to graph each of these curves in pp3 and pp4. We use `Show` to show the graphs pp3 and pp4 together, naming the resulting graph pp5. Note that the results of the `Show` command are not displayed since pp3 is not displayed and the option `DisplayFunction->$DisplayFunction` is not included in the `Show` command. We also use `Plot3D` to graph $f(x,y) = x^3 \sin 4y + y^2 \cos 3x$ on the rectangle $[-1.5, 1.5] \times [-1.5, 1.5]$, naming the resulting graph pp6. Finally, we use `GraphicsArray` to display the set of graphs pp5 and pp6.

```
Clear[f]
f[x_,y_]=x^3 Sin[4y]+y^2 Cos[3x];
pp3=ParametricPlot3D[{Cos[t],Sin[t],0},{t,0,2Pi},
        DisplayFunction->Identity];
pp4=ParametricPlot3D[{Cos[t],Sin[t],f[Cos[t],Sin[t]]},
        {t,0,2Pi},DisplayFunction->Identity];
pp5=Show[pp3,pp4];
pp6=Plot3D[f[x,y],{x,-1.5,1.5},{y,-1.5,1.5},
        PlotPoints->20,DisplayFunction->Identity];
Show[GraphicsArray[{pp5,pp6}]]
```

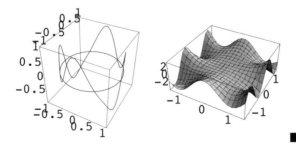

■

`ParametricPlot3D` can also be used to graph parametric equations of surfaces..

EXAMPLE: The quadric surfaces are the three-dimensional objects corresponding to the conic sections in two dimensions. A **quadric surface** is a graph of

$$A x^2 + B y^2 + C z^2 + D x y + E x z + F y z + G x + H y + I z + J = 0.$$

The intersection of a plane and a quadric surface is a conic section. Several of the basic quadric surfaces, in standard form, and a parametrization of the surface are listed in the following table.

Use `ParametricPlot3D` to graph the ellipsoid with equation $\dfrac{x^2}{16} + \dfrac{y^2}{4} + z^2 = 1$ and the hyperboloid of one sheet with equation $\dfrac{x^2}{16} + \dfrac{y^2}{4} - z^2 = 1$.

Name	**Parametric Equations**
Ellipsoid $$\frac{x^2}{a^2} + \frac{y^2}{b^2} + \frac{z^2}{c^2} = 1$$	$\begin{cases} x = a\cos(t)\cos(r) \\ y = b\cos(t)\sin(r), \\ \quad z = c\sin(t) \end{cases}$ $$-\frac{\pi}{2} \leq t \leq \frac{\pi}{2} \ and -\pi \leq r \leq \pi.$$
Hyperboloid of One Sheet $$\frac{x^2}{a^2} + \frac{y^2}{b^2} - \frac{z^2}{c^2} = 1$$	$\begin{cases} x = a\sec(t)\cos(r) \\ y = b\sec(t)\sin(r), \\ \quad z = c\tan(t) \end{cases}$ $$-\frac{\pi}{2} < t < \frac{\pi}{2} \ and -\pi \leq r \leq \pi.$$
Hyperboloid of Two Sheets $$\frac{x^2}{a^2} - \frac{y^2}{b^2} - \frac{z^2}{c^2} = 1$$	$\begin{cases} \quad x = a\sec(t) \\ y = b\tan(t)\cos(r), \\ z = c\tan(t)\sin(r) \end{cases}$ $$-\frac{\pi}{2} < t < \frac{\pi}{2} \ and -\pi \leq r \leq \pi \ or \ \frac{\pi}{2} < t < \frac{3\pi}{2}.$$

SOLUTION: A parametrization of the ellipsoid with equation $\dfrac{x^2}{16}+\dfrac{y^2}{4}+z^2=1$ is given by

$$\begin{cases} x = 4\cos t\cos r \\ y = 2\cos t\sin r\,, \\ \quad z = \sin t \end{cases} \quad -\frac{\pi}{2}\le t\le\frac{\pi}{2} \ \text{and} \ -\pi\le r\le\pi\,,$$

which is graphed below with `ParametricPlot3D`.

```
Clear[x,y,z]
x[t_,r_]=4Cos[t]Cos[r];
y[t_,r_]=2Cos[t]Sin[r];
z[t_,r_]=Sin[t];
ParametricPlot3D[{x[t,r],y[t,r],z[t,r]},{t,-Pi/2,Pi/2},{r,-Pi,Pi}]
```

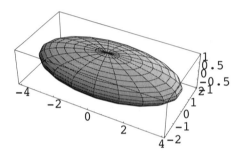

A parametrization of the hyperboloid of one sheet with equation $\dfrac{x^2}{16}+\dfrac{y^2}{4}-z^2=1$ is given by

$$\begin{cases} x = 4\sec t\cos r \\ y = 2\sec t\sin r\,, \\ \quad z = \tan t \end{cases} \quad -\frac{\pi}{2}< t<\frac{\pi}{2} \ \text{and} \ -\pi\le r\le\pi\,.$$

Since $\sec t$ and $\tan t$ are undefined when $t=\pm\dfrac{\pi}{2}$, we use `ParametricPlot3D` to graph these parametric equations on a subinterval of $\left[-\dfrac{\pi}{2},\dfrac{\pi}{2}\right]$, $\left[-\dfrac{\pi}{3},\dfrac{\pi}{3}\right]$.

```
Clear[x,y,z]
x[t_,r_]=4Sec[t]Cos[r];
y[t_,r_]=2Sec[t]Sin[r];
z[t_,r_]=Tan[t];
ParametricPlot3D[{x[t,r],y[t,r],z[t,r]},{t,-Pi/3,Pi/3},{r,-Pi,Pi}]
```

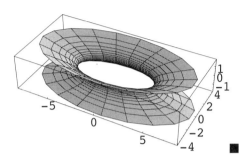

A Word of Caution

If we enter a `Plot` command before defining a function as in the following, errors result

```
Plot[g[x],{x,0,1}]
```

```
Plot::plnr: CompiledFunction[{x}, <<1>>, -CompiledCode-][x]
        is not a machine-size real number at x = 0..
Plot::plnr: CompiledFunction[{x}, <<1>>, -CompiledCode-][x]
        is not a machine-size real number at x = 0.0416667.
Plot::plnr: CompiledFunction[{x}, <<1>>, -CompiledCode-][x]
        is not a machine-size real number at x = 0.0833333.
General::stop:
    Further output of Plot::plnr
        will be suppressed during this calculation.
```

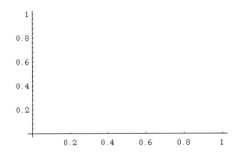

In this case, g has not been defined. Defining g to be a real-valued function defined on the interval [0,1] and reentering the command eliminates the error messages.

2.4 Exact and Approximate Solutions of Equations

Exact Solutions of Equations

Mathematica can find exact solutions of many equations. For example, Mathematica can find exact solutions to systems of equations and exact solutions to polynomial equations of degree four or less. Since a single equals sign "=" is used to name objects and assign values in Mathematica, equations in Mathematica are of the form

left-hand side==right-hand side.

The double equals sign "==" between the left-hand side and right-hand side specifies that the object is an equation. For example, to represent the equation 3x+7=4 in Mathematica, type 3x+7==4. The command Solve[lhs==rhs,x] solves the equation lhs=rhs for x. If the only unknown in the equation lhs=rhs is x and Mathematica does not need to use inverse functions to solve for x, then the command Solve[lhs==rhs] solves the equation lhs=rhs for x. Hence, to solve the equation 3x+7=4, both the command Solve[3x+7==4] and Solve[3x+7==4,x] produce the same result.

EXAMPLE: Solve the equations $3x + 7 = 4$, $\dfrac{x^2 - 1}{x - 1} = 0$, and $x^3 + x^2 + x + 1 = 0$.

SOLUTION: In each case, we use Solve to solve the indicated equation. Be sure to include the double equals sign "==" between the left- and right-hand sides of each equation. Thus, the result of entering

```
Solve[3x+7==4]
```

```
{{x -> -1}}
```

means that the solution of $3x + 7 = 4$ is $x = -1$ and the result of entering

```
Solve[(x^2-1)/(x-1)==0]
```

```
{{x -> -1}}
```

means that the solution of $\dfrac{x^2 - 1}{x - 1} = 0$ is $x = -1$. On the other hand, the equation $x^3 + x^2 + x + 1 = 0$ has two imaginary roots. We see that entering

```
Solve[x^3+x^2+x+1==0]
```

```
{{x -> -1}, {x -> -I}, {x -> I}}
```

yields all three solutions. Thus, the solutions of $x^3 + x^2 + x + 1 = 0$ are $x = -1$ and $x = \pm i$. Remember that the Mathematica symbol I represents the complex number $i = \sqrt{-1}$. In general, Mathematica will find the exact roots of any polynomial equation of degree four or less. ∎

As stated above, the exception to the above rule is when using the command `Solve` to find solutions of equations where inverse functions must be used.

EXAMPLE: Find a solution of $\sin^2 x - 2\sin x - 3 = 0$.

SOLUTION: When the command `Solve[Sin[x]^2-2Sin[x]-3==0]` is entered, Mathematica solves the equation for `Sin[x]`. However, when the command

$$\texttt{Solve[Sin[x]\^2-2Sin[x]-3==0,x]}$$

is entered, Mathematica attempts to solve the equation for x. In this case, Mathematica succeeds in finding one solution.

```
Solve[Sin[x]^2-2Sin[x]-3==0]

    {{Sin[x] -> -1}, {Sin[x] -> 3}}

Solve[Sin[x]^2-2Sin[x]-3==0,x]

    Solve::ifun:
       Warning: Inverse functions
         are being used by Solve,
         so some solutions may not
         be found.
           -Pi
    {{x -> ---}, {x -> ArcSin[3]}}
           2
```
∎

We can also use `Solve` to find the solutions, if any, of various types of systems of equations. Entering

$$\texttt{Solve[\{lhs1=rhs1,lhs2==rhs2\},\{x,y\}]}$$

solves a system of two equations for x and y, while entering

$$\texttt{Solve[\{lhs1==rhs1,lhs2==rhs2\}]}$$

attempts to solve the system of equations for all unknowns. In general, `Solve` can find the solutions to a system of linear equations. In fact, if the systems to be solved are inconsistent or dependent, Mathematica 's output will tell you so.

EXAMPLE: Solve each system: (a) $\begin{cases} 3x - y = 4 \\ x + y = 2 \end{cases}$; and (b) $\begin{cases} 2x - 3y + 4z = 2 \\ 3x - 2y + z = 0 \\ x + y - z = 1 \end{cases}$.

SOLUTION: In each case we use `Solve` to solve the given system. For (a), the result of entering

```
Solve[{3x-y==4,x+y==2},{x,y}]
```

$$\{\{x \;\text{->}\; \frac{3}{2}, \; y \;\text{->}\; \frac{1}{2}\}\}$$

means that the solution of

$$\begin{cases} 3x - y = 4 \\ x + y = 2 \end{cases} \text{ is } (x, y) = \left(\frac{3}{2}, \frac{1}{2}\right).$$

For (b), the result of entering

```
Solve[{2x-3y+4z==2,3x-2y+z==0,x+y-z==1},{x,y,z}]
```

$$\{\{x \;\text{->}\; \frac{7}{10}, \; y \;\text{->}\; \frac{9}{5}, \; z \;\text{->}\; \frac{3}{2}\}\}$$

means that the solution of

$$\begin{cases} 2x - 3y + 4z = 2 \\ 3x - 2y + z = 0 \\ x + y - z = 1 \end{cases} \text{ is } (x, y, z) = \left(\frac{7}{10}, \frac{9}{5}, \frac{3}{2}\right).$$

■

Our next example illustrates how to use `Solve` to find the solutions of a nonlinear system of equations.

EXAMPLE: Solve the systems (a) $\begin{cases} 4x^2 + y^2 = 4 \\ x^2 + 4y^2 = 4 \end{cases}$ and (b) $\begin{cases} \dfrac{x^2}{a^2} + \dfrac{y^2}{b^2} = 1 \\ y = mx \end{cases}$ (a, b greater than zero) for x and y.

SOLUTION: We note that the graphs of the equations $4x^2 + y^2 = 4$ and $x^2 + 4y^2 = 4$ are both ellipses. We use `ContourPlot` to graph each equation, naming the results `cp1` and `cp2`, respectively, and then use `Show` to show both graphs simultaneously. The solutions of the system

$$\begin{cases} 4x^2 + y^2 = 4 \\ x^2 + 4y^2 = 4 \end{cases}$$

correspond to the intersection points of the two graphs.

```
cp1=ContourPlot[4x^2+y^2-4,{x,-3,3},{y,-3,3},Contours->{0},
       ContourShading->False,PlotPoints->50,DisplayFunction->Identity];
cp2=ContourPlot[x^2+4y^2-4,{x,-3,3},{y,-3,3},Contours->{0},
       ContourShading->False,PlotPoints->50,DisplayFunction->Identity];
Show[cp1,cp2,Frame->False,Axes->Automatic,AxesOrigin->{0,0},
       DisplayFunction->$DisplayFunction]
```

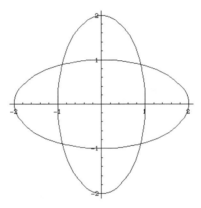

Finally, we use `Solve` to find the solutions of the system.

```
Solve[{4x^2+y^2==4,x^2+4y^2==4}]
```

```
          -2             -2
{{x -> -------, y -> -------},
         Sqrt[5]        Sqrt[5]


          -2              2
 {x -> -------, y -> -------},
         Sqrt[5]        Sqrt[5]


           2             -2
 {x -> -------, y -> -------},
         Sqrt[5]        Sqrt[5]


           2              2
 {x -> -------, y -> -------}}
         Sqrt[5]        Sqrt[5]
```

For (b), we also use `Solve` to find the solutions of the system. However, since the unknowns in the equations are a, b, m, x, and y, we must specify that we want to solve for x and y in the `Solve` command.

```
Solve[{x^2/a^2+y^2/b^2==1,y==m x},{x,y}]
                  a b m
      {{y -> -(---------------),
                2    2 2
             Sqrt[b  + a  m ]

                 a b
         x -> -(---------------)},
                2    2 2
             Sqrt[b  + a  m ]

                 a b m
      {y -> -----------------,
              2    2 2
           Sqrt[b  + a  m ]

                a b
        x -> ----------------}}
              2    2 2
           Sqrt[b  + a  m ]
```

■

Although Mathematica can find the exact solution to every polynomial equation of degree four or less, exact solutions to some equations that Mathematica can solve may not be meaningful. In those cases, Mathematica can provide approximations of the exact solutions using either the `N[expression]` or the `expression // N` command.

EXAMPLE: Approximate the solutions of the equations (a) $x^4 - 2x^2 = 1 - x$; and (b) $1 - x^2 = x^3$.

SOLUTION: Since each of these is a polynomial equation with degree less than five, `Solve` will find the exact solution of each equation. However, since the solutions are quite complicated, we use `N` to obtain approximate solutions of each equation.

For (a), entering

```
N[Solve[x^4-2x^2==1-x]]

    {{x ->

        0.182777 - 0.633397 I},
```

```
{x ->

    0.182777 + 0.633397 I},

{x -> -1.71064},

{x -> 1.34509}}
```

first finds the exact solutions of the equation $x^4 - 2x^2 = 1 - x$ and then computes approximations of those solutions. The resulting output is the list of approximate solutions.

For (b), entering

```
Solve[1-x^2==x^3,x]//N

    {{x -> 0.754878},

    {x ->

        -0.877439 + 0.744862 I},

    {x ->

        -0.877439 - 0.744862 I}}
```

first finds the exact solutions of the equation $1 - x^2 = x^3$ and then computes approximations of those solutions. The resulting output is the list of approximate solutions. ∎

Mathematica can also solve equations involving more than one variable for one variable in terms of other unknowns.

EXAMPLE: (a) Solve the equation $v = \dfrac{\pi r^2}{h}$ for h. (b) Solve the equation $a^2 + b^2 = c^2$ for c.

SOLUTION: Since these equations involve more than one unknown, we must specify the variable for which we are solving. Thus, entering

```
Solve[v==Pi r^2/h,h]

                2
             Pi r
    {{h -> -----}}
               v
```

solves the equation $v = \dfrac{\pi r^2}{h}$ for h. Note that if we had wanted to solve for r instead, then we would have entered `Solve[v==Pi r^2h,r]`. Similarly, entering

```
Solve[a^2+b^2==c^2,a]
```

$$\{\{a\ \text{->}\ -\text{Sqrt}[-b^2 + c^2]\},$$

$$\{a\ \text{->}\ \text{Sqrt}[-b^2 + c^2]\}\}$$

solves the equation $a^2 + b^2 = c^2$ for a. ∎

Numerical Approximation of Solutions of Equations

When solving an equation is either impractical or impossible, Mathematica provides several functions to approximate roots of equations. Some of these commands include `FindRoot` and `NRoots`.

`NRoots` numerically approximates the roots of any **polynomial** equation. The command `NRoots[poly1==poly2,x]` approximates the solutions of the polynomial equation `poly1==poly2`, where both `poly1` and `poly2` are polynomials in x.

`FindRoot` attempts to approximate a root to an equation provided that a "reasonable" guess of the root is given. The command `FindRoot[lhs==rhs,{x,firstguess}]` searches for a numerical solution to the equation `lhs==rhs`, starting with `x=firstguess`. One way of obtaining `firstguess` is to graph both `lhs` and `rhs` with `Plot`, find the point(s) of intersection, and estimate the x-coordinates of the point(s) of intersection. Thus, `FindRoot` works on functions other than polynomials. Moreover, to locate more than one root, `FindRoot` must be used several times. `NRoots` is easier to use when trying to approximate the roots of a polynomial.

EXAMPLE: Approximate the solutions of $x^5 + x^4 - 4x^3 + 2x^2 - 3x - 7 = 0$.

SOLUTION: Since $x^5 + x^4 - 4x^3 + 2x^2 - 3x - 7 = 0$ is a polynomial equation, we may use `NRoots` to approximate the solutions of the equation. Thus, entering

```
NRoots[x^5+x^4-4x^3+2x^2-3x-7==0,x]
```

```
x == -2.74463 ||

  x == -0.880858 ||

  x == 0.41452 - 1.19996 I ||
```

```
x == 0.41452 + 1.19996 I ||

x == 1.79645
```

approximates the solutions of $x^5 + x^4 - 4x^3 + 2x^2 - 3x - 7 = 0$.

`FindRoot` may also be used to approximate each root of the equation. However, to use `FindRoot`, we must supply an approximation of the solution. Note that the solutions of $x^5 + x^4 - 4x^3 + 2x^2 - 3x - 7 = 0$ correspond to the values of x where the graph of $x^5 + x^4 - 4x^3 + 2x^2 - 3x - 7$ intersects the x-axis. Below we use `Plot` to graph $x^5 + x^4 - 4x^3 + 2x^2 - 3x - 7$.

```
Plot[x^5+x^4-4x^3+2x^2-3x-7,{x,-3,2}]
```

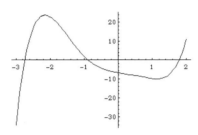

Note that the graph intersects the x-axis when $x \approx -2.5$, $x \approx -1$, and when $x \approx 1.5$. We use these values as initial approximations of each solution. Thus, entering

```
FindRoot[x^5+x^4-4x^3+2x^2-3x-7,{x,-2.5}]

    {x -> -2.74463}
```

approximates the solution near −2.5, entering

```
FindRoot[x^5+x^4-4x^3+2x^2-3x-7,{x,-1}]

    {x -> -0.880858}
```

approximates the solution near −1, and entering

```
FindRoot[x^5+x^4-4x^3+2x^2-3x-7,{x,2}]

    {x -> 1.79645}
```

approximates the solution near 1.5.

Note that `FindRoot` may be used to approximate complex solutions as well. Thus, entering

```
FindRoot[x^5+x^4-4x^3+2x^2-3x-7,{x,.5+I}]

    {x -> 0.41452 + 1.19996 I}
```

approximates the solution near 0.5+i. Of course, finding an initial estimation of a complex root may be difficult. ∎

> **EXAMPLE:** Approximate the positive solutions of the equation $\cos x - x = 0$.

SOLUTION: In order to approximate the roots of the equation $\cos x - x = 0$, FindRoot must be used since $\cos x - x = 0$ is not a polynomial equation. Note that since $\cos x \leq 1$ for all values of x, $\cos x < x$ when $x > 1$. Thus, all positive solutions of the equation $\cos x - x = 0$, if any, must be contained in the interval [0,1]. Therefore, to obtain initial approximations of the solution(s) of $\cos x - x = 0$, we graph $\cos x - x$ on the interval [0,1].

```
Clear[f]
f[x_]=Cos[x]-x
Plot[f[x],{x,0,1}]
```

     -x + Cos[x]

Notice that $\cos x - x = 0$ near 0.7. Thus, we use 0.7 as our initial approximation in the FindRoot command below.

```
FindRoot[f[x]==0,{x,.7}]
```

     {x -> 0.739085}

∎

FindRoot can also be used to approximate solutions to systems of equations. Although NRoots can solve a polynomial equation, NRoots cannot be used to solve a system of polynomial equations. When approximations of solutions of systems of equations are desired, use either Solve and N together, when possible, or FindRoot.

> **EXAMPLE:** Approximate the solutions to the system of equations
> $$\begin{cases} x^2 + 4xy + y^2 = 4 \\ 5x^2 - 4xy + 2y^2 = 8 \end{cases}.$$

SOLUTION: We begin by using `ContourPlot` to graph each equation. From the resulting graph, we see that $x^2 + 4xy + y^2 = 4$ is a hyperbola, $5x^2 - 4xy + 2y^2 = 8$ is an ellipse, and there are four solutions to the system of equations.

```
cp1=ContourPlot[x^2+4x y+y^2-4,{x,-4,4},{y,-4,4},
        Contours->{0},PlotPoints->50,
        ContourShading->False,DisplayFunction->Identity];
cp2=ContourPlot[5x^2-4x y+2y^2-8,{x,-4,4},{y,-4,4},
        Contours->{0},PlotPoints->50,
        ContourShading->False,DisplayFunction->Identity];
Show[cp1,cp2,Frame->False,Axes->Automatic,
        AxesOrigin->{0,0},DisplayFunction->$DisplayFunction]
```

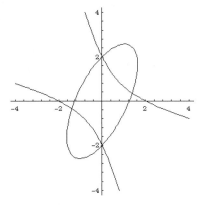

From the graph we see that possible solutions are (0,2) and (0,–2). In fact, substituting x=0 and y=–2 and x=0 and y=2 into each equation verifies that these points are both exact solutions of the equation. The remaining two solutions are estimated with `FindRoot`.

```
FindRoot[{x^2+4x y+y^2==4,5x^2-4x y+2y^2==8},{x,1},{y,.25}]

    {x -> 1.39262, y -> 0.348155}

FindRoot[{x^2+4x y+y^2==4,5x^2-4x y+2y^2==8},{x,-1},{y,-.25}]

    {x -> -1.39262, y -> -0.348155}
```

■

In addition to the commands `FindRoot` and `NRoots`, `NSolve` can also be used to approximate roots of some equations.

EXAMPLE: If $h(x) = x^3 - 8x^2 + 19x - 12$ and $k(x) = \dfrac{1}{2}x^2 - x - \dfrac{1}{8}$, approximate the solutions of the equation $h(x) = k(x)$ using `NRoots` and `NSolve`.

SOLUTION: After clearing all prior definitions of h and k, if any, we use `NRoots` to approximate the solutions of the equation.

```
Clear[h,k]
h[x_]=x^3-8x^2+19x-12
k[x_]=1/2x^2-x-1/8
NRoots[h[x]==k[x],x]
```

$$-12 + 19\ x - 8\ x^2 + x^3$$

$$-\left(\frac{1}{8}\right) - x + \frac{x^2}{2}$$

```
x == 0.904363 ||

  x == 2.66088 || x == 4.93476
```

As expected, the same results are obtained with `NSolve`.

```
NSolve[h[x]==k[x],x]

   {{x -> 0.904363},

    {x -> 2.66088},

    {x -> 4.93476}}  ∎
```

Application: Intersection Points of Graphs of Functions

In several later examples, we will need to locate the intersection points of graphs of functions. Here we discuss several methods to locate the intersection points of graphs of functions.

> **EXAMPLE:** If $h(x) = x^3 - 8x^2 + 19x - 12$ and $k(x) = \frac{1}{2}x^2 - x - \frac{1}{8}$, find the x-coordinates of the points where the graphs of h and k intersect.

SOLUTION: Notice that the x-coordinates of the intersection points satisfy the equation h(x)=k(x). Consequently, to locate the intersection points, it is sufficient to solve the equation h(x)=k(x). Although this step is not necessary to solve the problem, we first graph h and k and notice that h and k intersect three times.

```
Clear[h,k]
h[x_]=x^3-8x^2+19x-12;
k[x_]=1/2x^2-x-1/8;
Plot[{h[x],k[x]},{x,0,7},PlotStyle->{GrayLevel[0],GrayLevel[.5]}]
```

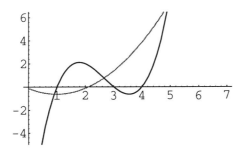

Since h(x)=k(x) is a polynomial equation of degree three, Mathematica can compute exact values of all three roots. However, the roots are complicated so we approximate the solutions. Moreover, since h(x)=k(x) is a polynomial equation we use the command NRoots[h[x]==k[x],x]. Using NSolve[h[x]==k[x],x], instead, produces the same result.

```
NRoots[h[x]==k[x],x]
```

```
x == 0.904363 ||

x == 2.66088 || x == 4.93476
```

In the following example, the exact solutions of the equation h(x)=k(x) are computed with the command Solve[h[x]==k[x]] and named exactsols. Note that since a semicolon ";" is included at the end of the command, Mathematica suppresses the resulting output (it is very long!). However, an abbreviated three-line portion of exactsols is displayed using Short.

```
exactsols=Solve[h[x]==k[x]];
Short[exactsols,3]
```

```
                                  1/3
           17                 98 2
   {{x ->  -- +  ------------------------------- +
           6                               1/3
               3 (9664 + 192 I Sqrt[49755])

                                  1/3
           (9664 + 192 I Sqrt[49755])
           -----------------------------}, {<<1>>},
                        1/3
                   24 2

           17                (1 + I Sqrt[3]) <<1>>
   {x ->  -- + <<1>> -  ----------------------}}
           6                       1/3
                               48 2
```

Notice that the resulting solution is expressed as a list. Lists are discussed in detail in Chapters 4 and 5. We can obtain particular solutions using Part "[[...]]". In

general, the command `Solve[lhs==rhs][[1]]` (as illustrated below) yields the
first element of the list of solutions, `Solve[lhs==rhs][[2]]` yields the second
element of the list of solutions, and `Solve[lhs==rhs][[j]]` yields the jth
element of the list of solutions.

```
Solve[h[x]==k[x]][[1]]

          17              1/3
  {x -> -- + (98 2   ) /
          6

       (3 Power[9664 +

          192 I Sqrt[49755],

          1/3]) +

        Power[9664 +

          192 I Sqrt[49755], 1/3]

                 1/3
        / (24 2    )}
```

■

In other cases, when exact solutions cannot be obtained and the equation to be solved is
not a polynomial equation, we use `FindRoot` to estimate the intersection points.

EXAMPLE: Locate the points where the graphs of $f(x) = e^{-(x/4)^2} \cos\left(\dfrac{x}{\pi}\right)$ and
$g(x) = \dfrac{5}{4} + \sin x^{3/2}$ intersect.

SOLUTION: Notice that the x-coordinates of the intersection points satisfy the
equation f(x)=g(x). Consequently, to locate the intersection points, it is sufficient to
solve the equation f(x)=g(x). Since this problem does not involve polynomials, we
must first graph f and g and notice that they intersect twice. On a color monitor,
the graph of f would be in red and the graph of g would be in blue.

```
Clear[f,g]
f[x_]=Exp[-(x/4)^2] Cos[(x/Pi)];
g[x_]=Sin[x^(3/2)]+5/4;
Plot[{f[x],g[x]},{x,0,5},PlotStyle->{RGBColor[1,0,0],RGBColor[0,0,1]}]
```

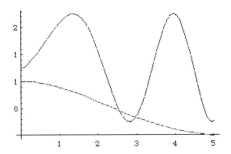

Mathematica cannot solve f(x)=g(x) exactly. Since f(x)=g(x) is not a polynomial equation, the command NRoots cannot be used to numerically approximate the roots. However, we can use the command FindRoot to approximate each root provided we have a "good" initial approximation of the root. To obtain a "good" initial approximation of each root on a computer with a notebook interface we proceed as follows.

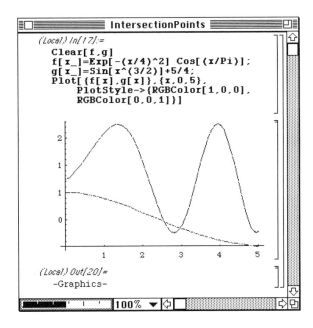

1. The result of defining and then graphing f and g is shown to the left on a computer with a notebook interface.

To approximate the points of intersection, first move the cursor within the graphics cell and click once. Notice that a box appears around the graph as shown in the figure below.

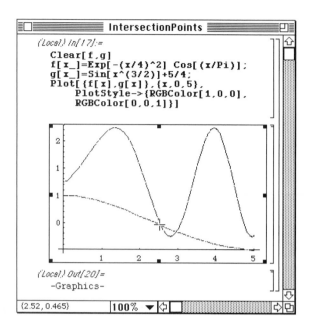

2. Next, press and hold down the ⌘-key; as you move the cursor within the graphics cell, notice that the thermometer at the bottom of the screen has changed to ordered pairs approximating the location of the cursor within the graphics cell.

When the cursor is placed over the point of intersection, the corresponding coordinates are displayed in the lower left-hand corner of the screen.

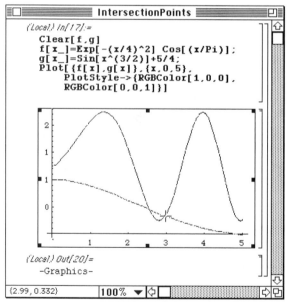

3. Similarly, an approximation of the second intersection point is obtained by placing the cursor over the point of intersection.

We then use FindRoot twice to compute an approximation of each solution:

```
FindRoot[f[x]==g[x],{x,2.52}]

  {x -> 2.54105}
```

```
f[2.54105]//N
```

```
    0.461103
```

```
FindRoot[f[x]==g[x],{x,2.99}]
```

```
    {x -> 2.9746}
```

```
f[2.9746]//N
```

```
    0.336066
```

We conclude that one intersection point is approximately $(2.54105, 0.461103)$ and the other intersection point is approximately $(2.9746, 0.336066)$. ∎

CHAPTER 3

Calculus

Chapter 3 introduces Mathematica's built-in calculus commands. The examples used to illustrate the various commands are similar to examples routinely done in first-year calculus courses.

3.1 Computing Limits

One of the first topics discussed in calculus is that of limits. Mathematica can be used to investigate limits graphically and numerically. In addition, Mathematica uses the command

```
Limit[expression,x->a]
```

to find the limit of `expression` as x approaches the value a, where a can be a finite number, positive infinity (`Infinity`), or negative infinity (`-Infinity`). The "->" is obtained by typing a minus sign "-" followed by a greater than sign ">".

EXAMPLE: Use a graph and table of values to investigate $\lim\limits_{x \to 0} \dfrac{\sin 3x}{x}$.

SOLUTION: Below, we use `Clear` to clear all prior definitions of f, define $f(x) = \dfrac{\sin 3x}{x}$, and then graph f on the interval $[-\pi,\pi]$.

```
Clear[f]
f[x_]=Sin[3x]/x;
Plot[f[x],{x,-Pi,Pi}]
```

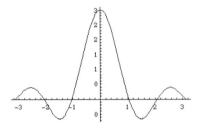

From the graph, we might, correctly, conclude that $\lim\limits_{x\to 0} \dfrac{\sin 3x}{x} = 3$. Further evidence that $\lim\limits_{x\to 0} \dfrac{\sin 3x}{x} = 3$ can be obtained by computing the values of f(x) for values of x "near" 0. In the following we define `xvals` to be a table of 5 "random" real numbers. Note that the first number in `xvals` is between −1 and 1, the second between $-\dfrac{1}{10}$ and $\dfrac{1}{10}$, and so on.

```
xvals=Table[Random[Real,{-10^(-n),10^(-n)}],{n,0,5}]
```

```
{0.371263, 0.0587702, -0.00452615, 0.0000945869,

                      -6
 0.0000788866, -5.81236 10   }
```

We then use `Map` to compute the value of f(x) for each x in `xvals`:

```
fvals=Map[f,xvals]
```

```
{2.41709, 2.98448, 2.99991, 3., 3., 3.}
```

The x-values along with the corresponding y-values are shown in `TableForm`, below:

```
pairs=Table[{xvals[[i]],fvals[[i]]},{i,1,6}];
TableForm[pairs]
```

```
   0.371263         2.41709
   0.0587702        2.98448
   -0.00452615      2.99991
   0.0000945869     3.
   0.0000788866     3.
              -6
   -5.81236 10      3.
```

From the table of values, above, we might again correctly deduce that $\lim_{x\to 0}\frac{\sin 3x}{x}=3$. Of course, these results do not prove that $\lim_{x\to 0}\frac{\sin 3x}{x}=3$ but they are helpful in convincing us that $\lim_{x\to 0}\frac{\sin 3x}{x}=3$. ∎

Computing Limits

Some limits involving rational functions can be computed by factoring the numerator and denominator.

> **EXAMPLE:** Compute $\lim_{x\to -9/2}\dfrac{2x^2+25x+72}{72-47x-14x^2}$.

SOLUTION: Below we define `frac1` to be the rational expression $\dfrac{2x^2+25x+72}{72-47x-14x^2}$. We then attempt to compute the value of $\dfrac{2x^2+25x+72}{72-47x-14x^2}$ when $x=-\dfrac{9}{2}$ but this value is undefined.

```
frac1=(2x^2+25x+72)/(72-47x-14x^2)

                 2
    72 + 25 x + 2 x
    -----------------
                 2
    72 - 47 x - 14 x

frac1 /. x->-9/2

                           1
    Power::infy: Infinite expression - encountered.
                           0
    Infinity::indet:
       Indeterminate expression 0 ComplexInfinity
          encountered.
    Indeterminate
```

Factoring the numerator and denominator below with `Factor`, `Numerator`, and `Denominator`, we see that

$$\lim_{x\to -9/2}\frac{2x^2+25x+72}{72-47x-14x^2}=\lim_{x\to -9/2}\frac{(x+8)(2x+9)}{(8-7x)(2x+9)}=\lim_{x\to -9/2}\frac{x+8}{8-7x}.$$

The fraction $\dfrac{x+8}{8-7x}$ is named `frac2` and the limit is evaluated by computing the value of `frac2` when $x=-\dfrac{9}{2}$.

```
Factor[Numerator[frac1]]
Factor[Denominator[frac1]]

    (8 + x) (9 + 2 x)
    (8 - 7 x) (9 + 2 x)

frac2=Factor[frac1]

     8 + x
    -------
    8 - 7 x

frac2/. x->-9/2

    7
    --
    79
```

We conclude that $\displaystyle\lim_{x\to-9/2}\dfrac{2x^2+25x+72}{72-47x-14x^2}=\dfrac{7}{79}$. ■

We can also use the command `Limit` to evaluate frequently encountered limits as illustrated in the following example.

EXAMPLE: Calculate the indicated limits.

(a) $\displaystyle\lim_{x\to-5/3}\dfrac{3x^2-7x-20}{21x^2+14x-35}$; (b) $\displaystyle\lim_{x\to0}\dfrac{\sin x}{x}$;

(c) $\displaystyle\lim_{x\to+\infty}\dfrac{50x^2+95x+24}{20x^2+77x+72}$; and (d) $\displaystyle\lim_{x\to-\infty}\dfrac{1+4x-16x^2-64x^3}{20x^2+13x+2}$.

SOLUTION: In each case, we use `Limit` to evaluate the indicated limit. Entering

```
Limit[(3x^2-7x-20)/(21x^2+14x-35),x->-5/3]

    17
    --
    56
```

computes $\displaystyle\lim_{x\to-5/3}\dfrac{3x^2-7x-20}{21x^2+14x-35}=\dfrac{17}{56}$; entering

```
Limit[Sin[x]/x,x->0]

    1
```

computes $\lim\limits_{x\to 0}\dfrac{\sin x}{x}=1$; entering

```
Limit[(50x^2+95x+24)/(20x^2+77x+72),x->Infinity]
```

$$\dfrac{5}{2}$$

computes $\lim\limits_{x\to +\infty}\dfrac{50x^2+95x+24}{20x^2+77x+72}=\dfrac{5}{2}$; and entering

```
Limit[(1+4x-16x^2-64x^3)/(20x^2+13x+2),x->-Infinity]
```

```
Infinity
```

computes $\lim\limits_{x\to -\infty}\dfrac{1+4x-16x^2-64x^3}{20x^2+13x+2}=+\infty$. ■

In differential calculus, we learn that the **derivative** of f at x is given by

$$f'(x)=\lim_{h\to 0}\frac{f(x+h)-f(x)}{h},$$

provided the limit exists. The `Limit` command can also be used along with `Simplify` to assist in determining the derivative of a function by using the definition of the derivative. This is illustrated in the following example. (This example also shows that an expression can be assigned any name, as long as that name is not a built-in Mathematica function or constant. Remember: Since every built-in Mathematica object begins with a capital letter, we have adopted the convention that all user-defined objects will be named using lowercase letters.)

EXAMPLE: Compute and simplify (a) $\dfrac{g(x+h)-g(x)}{h}$ and (b) $\lim\limits_{h\to 0}\dfrac{g(x+h)-g(x)}{h}$ if $g(x)=x^3-3x^2+x+1$.

SOLUTION: After defining g, we compute and simplify $\dfrac{g(x+h)-g(x)}{h}$, naming the result quog.

```
Clear[g]
g[x_]=x^3-3x^2+x+1
```

```
            2     3
1 + x - 3 x  + x
```

```
quog=Simplify[(g[x+h]-g[x])/h]
```

$$1 - 3\ h + h^2 - 6\ x + 3\ h\ x + 3\ x^2$$

Next, we use `Limit` to compute $\lim\limits_{h\to 0}\dfrac{g(x+h)-g(x)}{h}$. The result, $g'(x)$, is named dg.

```
dg=Limit[quog,h->0]
```

$$1 - 6\ x + 3\ x^2$$

Last, we use `Plot` to graph g(x) and $g'(x)$. The graph of dg ($g'(x)$) is dashed; the graph of g(x) is in black.

```
Plot[{g[x],dg},{x,-1,3},PlotStyle->{GrayLevel[0],Dashing[{.01,.01}]}]
```

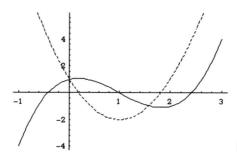

The next example illustrates how several Mathematica commands can be combined in a single statement to obtain the desired result.

EXAMPLE: Compute and simplify (a) $\dfrac{f(x+h)-f(x)}{h}$ and (b) $\lim\limits_{h\to 0}\dfrac{f(x+h)-f(x)}{h}$ if $f(x)=\dfrac{1}{\sqrt{x}}+\sqrt{x}$.

SOLUTION: Below we define f. In this case, we define f by entering `f[x_]=1/Sqrt[x]+Sqrt[x]`. However, entering `f[x_]=x^(-1/2)+x^(1/2)` would yield the same result, but in this case we must be particularly careful to enclose parentheses around the exponents. For example, entering `x^-1/2` returns $\dfrac{1}{2}x^{-1}=\dfrac{1}{2x}\neq x^{-1/2}=\dfrac{1}{\sqrt{x}}$.

```
f[x_]=1/Sqrt[x]+Sqrt[x]
```

```
   1
------- + Sqrt[x]
Sqrt[x]
```

Then, proceeding in the same manner as in the previous example, we define `quof` to be $\dfrac{f(x+h)-f(x)}{h}$. `Together` is used to express the result as a combined fraction.

```
quof=Together[(f[x+h]-f[x])/h]
```

```
                          3/2
(Sqrt[x] + h Sqrt[x] + x      - Sqrt[h + x] -

   x Sqrt[h + x]) / (h Sqrt[x] Sqrt[h + x])
```

`Limit` is used to compute $f'(x)=\lim\limits_{h\to 0}\dfrac{f(x+h)-f(x)}{h}$ and the result is named `df`.

```
df=Limit[quof,h->0]
```

```
-1 + x
------
   3/2
2 x
```

Note that the square brackets must be properly nested in order to correctly perform the combined operations.

Last, we use `Plot` to graph f(x) and $f'(x)$(`df`). To see that f has a minimum when x=1, we use the option `PlotRange->{-8,8}` to indicate that the range displayed corresponds to the interval [–8,8].

Since division by 0 is undefined, Mathematica produces several error messages because the `Plot` command instructs Mathematica to graph the functions on an interval containing 0. We do not display all the error messages generated here. Nevertheless, the resulting graphs are displayed correctly. The graph of f(x) is in black and the graph of $f'(x)$(`df`) is dashed.

```
Plot[{f[x],df},{x,0,3},PlotRange->{-8,8},
     PlotStyle->{GrayLevel[0],Dashing[{.01,.01}]}]
```

```
                                      1
Power::infy: Infinite expression -------- encountered.
                                  Sqrt[0.]
                                      1
Power::infy: Infinite expression -------- encountered.
                                  Sqrt[0.]
```

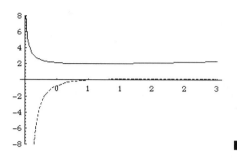

One-Sided Limits

In some cases, Mathematica can compute certain one-sided limits. The command

$$\texttt{Limit[f[x],x->a,Direction->1]}$$

attempts to compute $\lim\limits_{x\to a^-} f(x)$ while

$$\texttt{Limit[f[x],x->a,Direction->-1]}$$

attempts to compute $\lim\limits_{x\to a^+} f(x)$.

EXAMPLE: Compute (a) $\lim\limits_{x\to 0^-}\dfrac{1}{x}$ and (b) $\lim\limits_{x\to 0^+}\dfrac{1}{x}$.

SOLUTION: Entering

```
Limit[1/x,x->0,Direction->1]
```

```
    -Infinity
```

computes $\lim\limits_{x\to 0^-}\dfrac{1}{x}=-\infty$ and entering

```
Limit[1/x,x->0,Direction->-1]
```

```
    Infinity
```

computes $\lim\limits_{x\to 0^+}\dfrac{1}{x}=+\infty$. ∎

However, even with this option, Mathematica cannot compute many familiar one-sided limits. For example, $\lim\limits_{x\to 0^+}\dfrac{|x|}{x}=1$ and $\lim\limits_{x\to 0^-}\dfrac{|x|}{x}=-1$. But, Mathematica is unable to compute either of these limits:

```
Limit[Abs[x]/x,x->0,Direction->1]
Limit[Abs[x]/x,x->0,Direction->-1]

        Abs[x]
  Limit[------, x -> 0, Direction -> 1]
          x
        Abs[x]
  Limit[------, x -> 0, Direction -> -1]
          x
```

A Word of Caution

Results obtained with `Limit` should be questioned. In some cases, Mathematica returns surprising, or even incorrect, results. For example, Mathematica can compute $\lim\limits_{x \to +\infty} xe^{-x} = 0$

```
Limit[x Exp[-x],x->Infinity]

  0
```

but cannot compute $\lim\limits_{x \to +\infty} x^5 e^{-x} = 0$.

```
Limit[x^5 Exp[-x],x->Infinity]

         5
        x
  Limit[--, x -> Infinity]
         x
        E
```

Similarly, Mathematica cannot compute more difficult limits like $\lim\limits_{x \to +\infty} \dfrac{e^x}{x!} = 0$.

```
Limit[Exp[x]/x!,x->Infinity]

     Series::esss:
        Essential singularity encountered in
               1        3
          Gamma[- + 1 + O[x] ].
               x
            x
           E
     Limit[--, x -> Infinity]
           x!
```

In these particular cases, the command `NLimit` contained in the package **NLimit** which is located in the **NumericalMath** folder (or directory) can be used to compute the limits. After loading the **NLimit** package, we use `NLimit` to calculate each limit. In each case, we interpret the results to mean that the value of each limit is 0.

```
<<NumericalMath`NLimit`
NLimit[Exp[x]/x!,x->Infinity]
```

```
   0.
```

```
NLimit[x^5 Exp[-x],x->Infinity]
```

```
                -19
      1.35525 10
```

3.2 Differential Calculus

Calculating Derivatives of Functions and Expressions

If we are given a differentiable function f(x), Mathematica can compute the derivative of f(x) in at least two ways once f(x) has been properly defined using Mathematica.

1. The command f'[x] computes the derivative of f[x] with respect to x.
2. The command D[f[x],x] computes the derivative of f[x] with respect to x.
3. The command D[f[x],{x,n}] computes the nth derivative of f[x] with respect to x.
4. The command D[expression, variable] computes the derivative of expression with respect to variable.
5. The command D[expression,{variable,n}] computes the nth derivative of expression with respect to variable.

Other ways Mathematica can compute derivatives of functions and expressions are discussed in Section 3.6.

EXAMPLE: Calculate the indicated derivatives:

(a) $\dfrac{d}{dx}(2x^2-7x-4)$;   (b) $\dfrac{d}{dx}(\sin x)$;

(c) $\dfrac{d}{dx}\left((3x+4)^2(x+5)^2\right)$;   (d) $\dfrac{d}{dx}\left(\dfrac{x^2+2x+1}{x^2+3x}\right)$;

(e) $f'(x)$ if $f(x)=x^3e^{-2x}$; and

(f) $g'(x)$ if $g(x)=x\tan^{-1}x$

SOLUTION: For (a)-(d), we use D to compute the derivative of the indicated expression. Generally, the results from D are not expressed in simplified form.

(a)

```
D[2x^2-7x-4,x]

   -7 + 4 x
```

(b)

```
D[Sin[x],x]

   Cos[x]
```

(c)

```
D[(3x+4)^2(x+5)^2,x]

            2                            2
   6 (5 + x)  (4 + 3 x) + 2 (5 + x) (4 + 3 x)
```

(d)

```
D[(x^2+2x+1)/(x^2+3x),x]

                        2
     (3 + 2 x) (1 + 2 x + x )    2 + 2 x
   -(-------------------------) + --------
               2 2                      2
         (3 x + x )              3 x + x
```

For (e) and (f), we first clear all prior definitions of f and g, define f and g, and then compute the indicated derivatives.

```
Clear[f,g]
f[x_]=x^3 Exp[-2x];
g[x_]=x ArcTan[x];
f'[x]

      2      3
   3 x    2 x
   ---- - ----
    2 x    2 x
   E      E


D[f[x],x]

      2      3
   3 x    2 x
   ---- - ----
    2 x    2 x
   E      E


g'[x]

       x
   ------ + ArcTan[x]
        2

   1 + x
```

```
D[g[x],x]

    x
   ------  + ArcTan[x]
      2
   1 + x
```

Note that the results using D and ' are the same, as should be expected. ∎

Mathematica knows the familiar rules of differentiation like the product rule, quotient rule, and chain rule. After clearing all prior definitions of f and g, below, we compute the derivative of f(x)g(x), f(x)/g(x), and f(g(x)). Note that we use **Together** to see the familiar form of the quotient rule.

```
Clear[f,g]
D[f[x] g[x],x]

    g[x] f'[x] + f[x] g'[x]

Together[D[f[x]/g[x],x]]

    g[x] f'[x] - f[x] g'[x]
    -----------------------
                2
              g[x]

D[f[g[x]],x]

    f'[g[x]] g'[x]
```

The next example illustrates how to compute higher order derivatives.

EXAMPLE: Compute the indicated derivatives.

(a) $\dfrac{d^2}{dx^2}\left(x^4 - 2x^3 - 36x^2 + 162x + 24\right)$;

(b) $\dfrac{d^3}{dx^3}\left(x^2 + 2\cos x\right)$;

(c) $h''(x)$ if $h(x) = (2x+1)(3x^2 - 4x + 2)$; and

(d) $f'''(x)$ if $f(x) = \dfrac{\sin^{-1} x}{x^2 - 1}$.

SOLUTION: For (a) and (b) we use D to compute the desired derivative.

(a)

```
D[x^4-2x^3-36x^2+162x+24,{x,2}]
```

$$-72 - 12\ x + 12\ x^2$$

(b)

```
D[x^2+2Cos[x],{x,3}]
```

$$2\ Sin[x]$$

For (c) and (d), we first clear all prior definition of h and f and then use ' ' and ' ' ', respectively, to compute the desired derivatives.

```
Clear[h,f]
h[x_]=(2x+1)(3x^2-4x+2);
f[x_]=ArcSin[x]/(x^2-1);
h''[x]
```

$$6\ (1 + 2\ x) + 4\ (-4 + 6\ x)$$

We use Together to simplify $f'''(x)$ as the output obtained when entering f'''[x] is very long.

```
Together[f'''[x]]
```

$$(-7 - 19\ x^2 + 26\ x^4 - 24\ x\ Sqrt[1 - x^2]\ ArcSin[x] -$$
$$24\ x^3\ Sqrt[1 - x^2]\ ArcSin[x])\ /$$
$$(Sqrt[1 - x^2]\ (-1 + x^2)^4\ )$$

Note that using D in the same manner as in (a) and (b) would have produced the same results. ∎

Tangent Lines

If f is a function for which $f'(x_0)$ exists, then $f'(x_0)$ is the slope of the line tangent to the graph of f at the point $(x_0, f(x_0))$. An equation of the line tangent to the graph of f at the point $(x_0, f(x_0))$, in point-slope form, is given by

$$y - f(x_0) = f'(x_0)(x - x_0),$$

while a function of x, which can be graphed by Mathematica, is given by

$$y = f'(x_0)(x - x_0) + f(x_0).$$

EXAMPLE: Find an equation of the line tangent to the graph of $f(x) = 2x^3 + 3x^2 - 12x + 7$ when $x = -1$.

SOLUTION: After clearing all prior definitions of f, we define f and then compute $f'(x)$.

```
Clear[f]
f[x_]=2x^3+3x^2-12x+7;
f'[x]
```

```
                    2
    -12 + 6 x + 6 x
```

The slope of the line tangent to the graph of f when $x = -1$ is $f'(-1)$.

```
f'[-1]
```

```
    -12
```

Finally, to find an equation of the desired tangent line, we must compute the value of $f(-1)$.

```
f[-1]
```

```
    20
```

Thus, in point-slope form, an equation of the line tangent to the graph of f when $x = -1$ is

$$y - 20 = -12(x - (-1)).$$

We graph f along with the tangent line below.

```
plotf=Plot[f[x],{x,-4,3},DisplayFunction->Identity];
plotl=Plot[f'[-1](x+1)+20,{x,-4,3},DisplayFunction->Identity];
Show[plotf,plotl,DisplayFunction->$DisplayFunction]
```

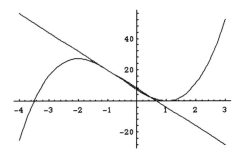

Note that the option `DisplayFunction->Identity` is used to prevent `plotf`, the graph of f, and `plotl`, the graph of the tangent line, from being displayed immediately while in the `Show` command, `DisplayFunction->$DisplayFunction` is used so that the graphs are displayed. ■

We can also use Mathematica to locate the values of x for which the line tangent to the graph of a particular function has certain properties. For example, the values of x for which the line tangent to the graph of f at the point (x,f(x)) is horizontal are the solutions of the equation $f'(x) = 0$.

EXAMPLE: Find the values of x for which the line tangent to the graph of $h(x) = \dfrac{x^2 - x + 4}{x - 1}$ is horizontal.

SOLUTION: As in the previous examples, we begin by clearing all prior definitions of h and then define h and compute h'. `Together` is used so that h' is expressed as a single fraction.

```
Clear[h]
h[x_]=(x^2-x+4)/(x-1);
Together[h'[x]]
```

$$\frac{-3 - 2x + x^2}{(-1 + x)^2}$$

The values of x for which the tangent line is horizontal are the solutions of the equation $h'(x) = 0$. We can compute these numbers by either factoring the numerator of h' or using `Solve`.

```
Factor[h'[x]]

   (-3 + x) (1 + x)
   ----------------
          2
      (-1 + x)

Solve[h'[x]==0]

   {{x -> -1}, {x -> 3}}
```

We conclude that the line tangent to the graph of h is horizontal when $x = -1$ and $x = 3$. These results are confirmed by examining the graph of h shown below.

```
Plot[h[x],{x,-4,6}]
```

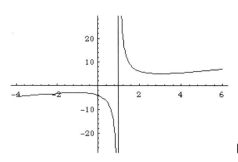

Locating Critical Points and Inflection Points

Since derivatives of functions are expressions, algebraic procedures can be performed on them. Hence, in addition to finding the zeros of a function, f, Mathematica can also be used to locate the **critical points** and **inflection points** of f. The critical points correspond to those points on the graph of f where the tangent line is horizontal or vertical; the inflection points correspond to those points on the graph of f where the graph of f is neither concave up nor concave down.

EXAMPLE: Find the critical points and inflection points of f(x) if

(a) $f(x) = (1 + 5x - 3x^2)(x^2 + x - 2)$ and (b) $f(x) = \dfrac{x+2}{(x+5)^2}$.

SOLUTION: For (a), we first clear all prior definitions of f, define f, and then compute f' and f'', naming the results **df** and **ddf**, respectively.

```
Clear[f]
f[x_]=(1+5x-3x^2)(x^2+x-2);
df=f'[x]
ddf=f''[x]
```

$$
\begin{array}{c}
2 \qquad\qquad\qquad\qquad 2 \\
(1\ +\ 2\ x)\ (1\ +\ 5\ x\ -\ 3\ x\ )\ +\ (5\ -\ 6\ x)\ (-2\ +\ x\ +\ x\ ) \\
2 \\
2\ (5\ -\ 6\ x)\ (1\ +\ 2\ x)\ +\ 2\ (1\ +\ 5\ x\ -\ 3\ x\ )\ - \\
2 \\
6\ (-2\ +\ x\ +\ x\ )
\end{array}
$$

Next, we must solve the equations $f'(x)=0$ and $f''(x)=0$. We first try to factor f' and f''.

```
Factor[df]
Factor[ddf]
```

$$
\begin{array}{c}
2 \\
3\ (-3\ +\ 2\ x)\ (1\ -\ 2\ x\ -\ 2\ x\ ) \\
12\ (1\ -\ x)\ (2\ +\ 3\ x)
\end{array}
$$

From the above, we see that one solution of $f'(x)=0$ is $x=\dfrac{3}{2}$, while the other two solutions are the two solutions of the equation $1-2x-2x^2=0$. On the other hand, we see that the two solutions of $f''(x)=0$ are $x=1$ and $x=-\dfrac{2}{3}$. To obtain the exact solutions of the equation $f'(x)=0$, we use Solve. When representing an equation with Mathematica, be sure to include the double equals (==) between the left- and right-hand side of the equation. The resulting list is named critnums, and approximations of the solutions are obtained with N.

```
critnums=Solve[df==0]

N[critnums]
```

$$
\begin{array}{c}
3 \qquad\qquad -2\ -\ 2\ \text{Sqrt}[3] \qquad\quad -2\ +\ 2\ \text{Sqrt}[3] \\
\{\{x\ \to\ -\},\ \{x\ \to\ \text{-------------}\},\ \{x\ \to\ \text{-------------}\}\} \\
2 \qquad\qquad\qquad 4 \qquad\qquad\qquad\qquad 4 \\
\{\{x\ \to\ 1.5\},\ \{x\ \to\ -1.36603\},\ \{x\ \to\ 0.366025\}\}
\end{array}
$$

The critical points and inflection points are then obtained by evaluating f when $x=\dfrac{3}{2}$, $x=\dfrac{-2-2\sqrt{3}}{4}$, and $x=\dfrac{-2+2\sqrt{3}}{4}$ and when $x=1$ and $x=-\dfrac{2}{3}$, respectively.

```
{3/2,f[3/2]}
{(-2-2Sqrt[3])/4,Simplify[f[(-2-2Sqrt[3])/4]]}
{(-2+2Sqrt[3])/4,Simplify[f[(-2+2Sqrt[3])/4]]}
{1,f[1]}
{-2/3,f[-2/3]}
```

```
  3   49
{-,  --}
  2   16
 -2 - 2 Sqrt[3]   27
{-------------, -- + 6 Sqrt[3]}
       4         4
 -2 + 2 Sqrt[3]   27
{-------------, -- - 6 Sqrt[3]}
       4         4
{1, 0}
   2    220
{-(-),  ---}
   3     27
```

Thus, the critical points are

$$\left(\frac{3}{2},\frac{49}{16}\right),\left(\frac{-2-2\sqrt{3}}{4},\frac{27}{4}+6\sqrt{3}\right), and \left(\frac{-2+2\sqrt{3}}{4},\frac{27}{4}-6\sqrt{3}\right),$$

while the inflection points are

$$(1,0) \, and \left(-\frac{2}{3},\frac{220}{27}\right).$$

For (b), we again first clear all prior definitions of f, define f, and then compute and simplify f' and f''.

```
Clear[f]
f[x_]=(x+2)/(x+5)^2;
Together[f'[x]]
Together[f''[x]]
```

```
  1 - x
--------
        3
 (5 + x)
 2 (-4 + x)
----------
         4
  (5 + x)
```

In each case, we can see that the solution of $f'(x)=0$ is x=1 while the solution of $f''(x)=0$ is x=4. Below, we calculate f(1) and f(4).

```
f[1]
f[4]
```

```
 1
--
12
 2
--
27
```

We conclude that the only critical point of f is $\left(1, \dfrac{1}{12}\right)$ and the only inflection point

is $\left(4, \dfrac{2}{27}\right)$. ■

Using Derivatives to Graph Functions

Mathematica is of great use in graphing functions. Unfortunately, if we have no idea of how the graph of a function ought to look or desire to see particular features of the graph, "randomly" choosing an interval on which to graph a particular function yields unsatisfactory results. In these cases, information supplied by the derivative can help us locate an interval on which the graph of f will show the features we wish to see. In particular, the first and second derivatives of a function give us the following information:

   a. The values of x for which f is **increasing** are the same as the values of x for which f' is positive.
   b. The values of x for which f is **decreasing** are the same as the values of x for which f' is negative.
   c. The values of x for which f is **concave up** are the same as the values of x for which f'' is positive.
   d. The values of x for which f is **concave down** are the same as the values of x for which f'' is negative.

EXAMPLE: Graph $f(x) = x^4 + 2x^3 - 72x^2 + 70x + 24$.

SOLUTION: We proceed by clearing all prior definition of f, defining f, and computing f' and f''.

```
Clear[f]
f[x_]=x^4+2x^3-72x^2+70x+24;
f'[x]
f''[x]
                        2       3
      70 - 144 x + 6 x   + 4 x
                      2
      -144 + 12 x + 12 x
```

To solve the equations $f'(x) = 0$ and $f''(x) = 0$, we use Solve.

```
Solve[f'[x]==0]
Solve[f''[x]==0]
```

$$\{\{x \to -7\}, \{x \to -\frac{1}{2}\}, \{x \to 5\}\}$$
$$\{\{x \to -4\}, \{x \to 3\}\}$$

Since the solutions of these polynomial equations are rational numbers, we could have used Factor to factor f' and f'' and, consequently, determine the solutions of the equations $f'(x) = 0$ and $f''(x) = 0$. Below, we graph f' on an interval containing -7, $1/2$, and 5, and graph f'' on an interval containing -4 and 3. The results are displayed as a graphics array.

```
pdf=Plot[f'[x],{x,-8,6},DisplayFunction->Identity];
pddf=Plot[f''[x],{x,-5,4},DisplayFunction->Identity];
Show[GraphicsArray[{pdf,pddf}]]
```

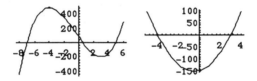

From the graphs, we see that f' is positive when $-7 < x < \frac{1}{2}$ or $x > 5$ and f' is negative when $x < -7$ or $\frac{1}{2} < x < 5$, while f'' is positive when $x < -4$ or $x > 3$ and f'' is negative when $-4 < x < 3$. Thus, f is decreasing and concave up when $x < -7$, f is increasing and concave down when $-7 < x < -4$, f is increasing and concave down when $-4 < x < \frac{1}{2}$, f is decreasing and concave down when $\frac{1}{2} < x < 3$, f is decreasing and concave up when $3 < x < 5$, and f is increasing and concave up when $x > 5$. Below, we graph f.

```
Plot[f[x],{x,-9,7}]
```

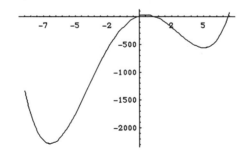

Since f is a polynomial of degree 4, we know that for "large" values of x, the graph of f looks like the graph of x^4 because.

$$f(x) = x^4\left(1 + \frac{2}{x} - \frac{72}{x^2} + \frac{70}{x^3} + \frac{24}{x^4}\right),$$

and for "large" values of x, $1 + \frac{2}{x} - \frac{72}{x^2} + \frac{70}{x^3} + \frac{24}{x^4}$ is close to 1. However, when we graph f on a large interval, we do not see the subintervals on which f is increasing or decreasing and concave up or concave down.

```
Plot[f[x],{x,-100,100}]
```

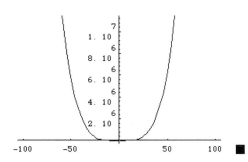

In our next example, we graph a function with a vertical tangent.

EXAMPLE: Graph $h(x) = (x-7)\sqrt[3]{x-3}$.

SOLUTION: As in the previous examples, we first clear all prior definitions of h, define h, and then compute $h'(x)$. Be particularly careful when defining h to include the parentheses around the exponent. Entering $h[x\_]=(x-7)(x-3)^1/3$ defines h(x) to be $\frac{(x-7)(x-3)}{3} \neq (x-7)\sqrt[3]{x-3}$.

```
Clear[h]
h[x_]=(x-7)(x-3)^(1/3)
h'[x]
Together[h'[x]]
```

```
                    1/3
  (-7 + x) (-3 + x)


    -7 + x                 1/3
  ------------- + (-3 + x)
            2/3
  3 (-3 + x)


   4 (-4 + x)
  -------------
            2/3
  3 (-3 + x)
```

From the simplified form of h′(x), we see that the critical numbers are x=4 and x=3. Note that x=3 is a critical number, because h(3) exists and $h'(x)$ is not defined when x=3. Thus, h has a vertical tangent when x=3. We compute the values of x for which $h''(x) = 0$ in the same manner.

```
Together[h''[x]]

      4 (-1 + x)
    -------------
                5/3
      9 (-3 + x)
```

We see that $h''(x) = 0$ when x=1. Of course, since $h'(x)$ does not exist when x=3, neither does $h''(x)$. Constructing a sign chart for both $h'(x)$ and $h''(x)$, or using an equivalent method, we see that $h'(x)$ is positive when $x > 4$ and is negative when $x < 4$ as long as $x \neq 3$, while $h''(x)$ is positive when $x < 1\, or\, x > 3$ and negative when $1 < x < 3$. Thus, h is decreasing and concave up when $x < 1$, decreasing and concave down when $1 < x < 3$, decreasing and concave up when $3 < x < 4$, and increasing and concave up when $x > 4$.

Graphing h with Mathematica requires several steps. To understand why, we note that if x is negative, then Mathematica does not return a real number when computing $\sqrt[3]{x}$. We illustrate this below with −1.

```
(-1)^(1/3)

        1/3
    (-1)
```

```
N[(-1)^(1/3)]

    0.5 + 0.866025 I
```

The symbol I represents the (complex) number $i = \sqrt{-1}$. Because Mathematica does not return real numbers, we are unable to graph h in the usual manner. Instead, we note that when x<3, the unique real number $\sqrt[3]{x-3}$ satisfying $\left(\sqrt[3]{x-3}\right)^3 = x-3$ also satisfies $\sqrt[3]{x-3} = -\sqrt[3]{|x-3|}$. Thus, we redefine h as a piecewise-defined function and graph h as indicated below.

```
Clear[h]
h[x_]:=(x-7)(x-3)^(1/3) /; x>=3
h[x_]:=-(x-7)Abs[x-3]^(1/3) /; x<3
Plot[h[x],{x,-3,8}]
```

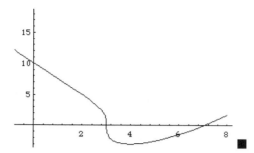

Graphing Functions and Derivatives

Because $f'(x)$ is a function of x, $f'(x)$ can be graphed. The following example shows how to compute the derivative of a function and then plot the original function and its derivative simultaneously.

EXAMPLE: Graph f and f' if $f(x) = \dfrac{x}{x^2+1}$.

SOLUTION: After clearing all prior definitions of f and defining $f(x) = \dfrac{x}{x^2+1}$, we compute f'.

```
Clear[f]
f[x_]=x/(x^2+1);
Together[f'[x]]
```

```
        2
  1 - x
  ---------
        2 2
  (1 + x )
```

By examining the result, we can see that $f'(x) = 0$ when $x = 1$ and when $x = -1$. Thus, we graph f and f' on an interval containing these values, so we see the maximum and minimum values of f. Below, we use Plot to graph f and f' on the interval [–5,5]. The graph of f is in black; the graph of f' is dashed.

```
Plot[{f[x],f'[x]},{x,-5,5},PlotStyle->{GrayLevel[0],Dashing[{.01,.01}]}]
```

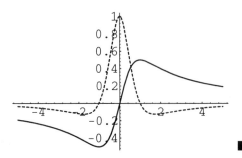

Instead of graphing f and f' simultaneously, we can also graph each separately and then show the results together with Show or as a graphics array with GraphicsArray.

EXAMPLE: Graph f and f' if $f(x) = (x-3)\sqrt[3]{(x-8)^2}$.

SOLUTION: Proceeding in the same manner as in the previous example, we first clear all prior definitions of f, define f, and then compute f'.

```
Clear[f]
f[x_]=(x-3)(x-8)^(2/3);
f'[x]
```

$$
(-8 + x)^{2/3} + \frac{2\ (-3 + x)}{3\ (-8 + x)^{1/3}}
$$

To identify the zeros of f', we use Together to express the above results as a single fraction. We could also use Solve to solve the equation $f'(x) = 0$.

```
Together[f'[x]]
```

$$
\frac{5\ (-6 + x)}{3\ (-8 + x)^{1/3}}
$$

From the above, we see that $f'(x) = 0$ when x=6. Thus, we will graph both f and f' on an interval containing 6.

We have seen that when x is negative, Mathematica does not return a real number when entering x^(1/3). However,

$$
f(x) = (x-3)\sqrt[3]{(x-8)^2} = (x-3)|x-8|^{2/3}
$$

and

$$f'(x) = \frac{5(x-6)}{3\sqrt[3]{x-8}} = \begin{cases} \frac{5}{3}(x-6)(x-8)^{-1/3} \ \text{for } x>8 \\ -\frac{5}{3}(x-6)|x-8|^{-1/3} \ \text{for } x<8 \end{cases}.$$

Thus, to graph f and f', we redefine them as follows. Note that df corresponds to f'.

```
Clear[f]
f[x_]=(x-3)Abs[x-8]^(2/3);
df[x_]:=5/3(x-6)(x-8)^(-1/3) /; x>8
df[x_]:=-5/3(x-6)Abs[x-8]^(-1/3) /; x<8
```

Next, we graph f and f', naming the results pf and pdf, respectively. In each case, the option DisplayFunction->Identity is included so that the resulting graphics are not displayed. If this option had not been included, both results would have been displayed.

```
pf=Plot[f[x],{x,0,13},PlotRange->{-15,15},DisplayFunction->Identity];
pdf=Plot[df[x],{x,0,13},PlotRange->{-15,15},
        PlotStyle->Dashing[{.01,.01}],DisplayFunction->Identity];
```

The results can be displayed simultaneously with Show:

```
Show[pf,pdf,DisplayFunction->$DisplayFunction]
```

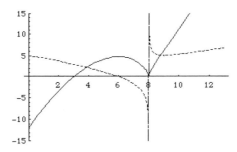

or, they can be displayed separately, but as a single graphics object, with GraphicsArray.

```
Show[GraphicsArray[{pf,pdf}]]
```

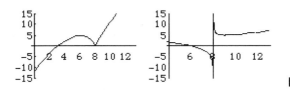

Approximations with `FindRoot`

In many cases, finding exact values of the zeros of the derivative of a function may be difficult. However, we may use `FindRoot` to approximate the zeros of the derivative of many functions.

EXAMPLE: Let $w(x) = 2\sin^2 2x + \dfrac{5}{2}x\cos^2\left(\dfrac{x}{2}\right)$ on $(0,\pi)$. Approximate the values of x for which the line tangent to the graph of w is horizontal.

SOLUTION: We begin by clearing all prior definitions of w, defining w, and then graphing w on the interval $[0,\pi]$. From the graph, we see that the tangent line is horizontal at three points.

```
Clear[w]
w[x_]=2Sin[2x]^2+5/2x Cos[x/2]^2;
Plot[w[x],{x,0,Pi}]
```

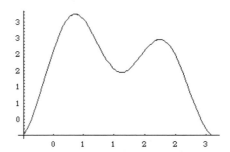

To approximate the values of x for which the tangent line is horizontal, we will use `FindRoot` which requires an initial approximation. To obtain reasonable approximations to use in the `FindRoot` commands later, we graph $w'(x)$.

```
Plot[w'[x],{x,0,Pi}]
```

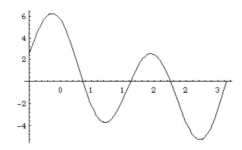

After using the graph of w'(x) to find the initial guesses, the x-values such that $w'(x) = 0$ can be approximated using FindRoot. These three calculations are given below using initial guesses x=0.863, x=1.63, x=2.25, the values where $w'(x)$ appears to cross the x-axis.

```
FindRoot[w'[x]==0,{x,0.863}]
FindRoot[w'[x]==0,{x,1.63}]
FindRoot[w'[x]==0,{x,2.25}]

    {x -> 0.864194}
    {x -> 1.62391}
    {x -> 2.24489}
```

■

When dealing with polynomial equations, NRoots can be used to solve polynomial equations.

EXAMPLE: Approximate the values of x for which the line tangent to the graph of $$p(x) = \frac{1}{2}x^6 - 2x^5 - \frac{25}{2}x^4 + 60x^3 - 150x^2 - 180x - 25$$ is horizontal.

SOLUTION: For this example, we begin by clearing all prior definitions of p, defining p, and then graphing p and p' on the interval [–6,6]. The graph of p' is dashed.

```
Clear[p]
p[x_]=1/2x^6-2x^5-25/2x^4+60x^3-150x^2-180x-25;
Plot[{p[x],p'[x]},{x,-6,6},PlotStyle->{GrayLevel[0],Dashing[{.01}]}]
```

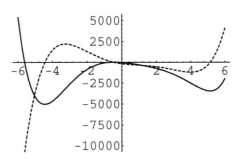

Next, we use NRoots to find the values of x for which $p'(x) = 0$. Those values that contain I are imaginary values which we ignore.

```
NRoots[p'[x]==0,x]
```

> x == -4.44315 || x == -0.459096 ||
>
> x == 1.55293 - 1.82277 I ||
>
> x == 1.55293 + 1.82277 I || x == 5.12971

Thus, we conclude that approximations of the values of x for which the line tangent to the graph of p at the point (x,f(x)) is horizontal are –4.44315, –0.459096, and 5.12971. ■

Application: Rolle's Theorem and The Mean-Value Theorem

Let f be a continuous function on [a,b] and differentiable on (a,b).

> **Rolle's Theorem** says that if f(a)=f(b)=0, then there is at least one value of c in (a,b) satisfying $f'(c) = 0$.

> **The Mean-Value Theorem** says that there is at least one value of c in (a,b) satisfying $f'(c) = \dfrac{f(b) - f(a)}{b - a}$.

EXAMPLE: Verify that f(x) satisfies the hypotheses of Rolle's Theorem on the interval $[-3,2]$ if $f(x) = x^3 - 7x + 6$ and find all values of c on the interval $[-3,2]$ that satisfy the conclusion of the theorem.

SOLUTION: Since f is a polynomial function, f is differentiable for all real numbers and, in particular, on the interval (–3,2). We first define f and compute f(–3) and f(2).

```
Clear[f]
f[x_]=x^3-7x+6
f[-3]
f[2]
```

$$6 - 7 x + x^3$$
$$0$$
$$0$$

Since both values are 0, we know that there is at least one value of c in the interval $[-3,2]$ for which $f'(c) = 0$. Next, we graph f on an interval containing the interval $[-3,2]$. From the graph, we see that we should be able to find at least two values of c for which $f'(c) = 0$.

```
Plot[f[x],{x,-4,3}]
```

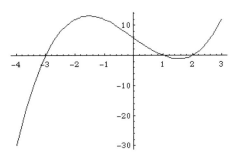

Computing $f'(x)$ and solving the equation $f'(x) = 0$ yields the desired values.

```
f'[x]
```

$$-7 + 3\ x^2$$

```
Solve[f'[x]==0]
```

$$\{\{x\ ->\ -Sqrt[\tfrac{7}{3}]\},\ \{x\ ->\ Sqrt[\tfrac{7}{3}]\}\}$$

We conclude that the values of c for which $f'(c) = 0$ are $c = \pm\sqrt{\dfrac{7}{3}}$. ■

Generally, verifying Rolle's Theorem and the Mean-Value Theorem for particular functions is difficult, as the resulting equations that need to be solved are either very difficult or even impossible to solve. In these cases, FindRoot can be helpful in approximating solutions of equations; NRoots can be used when dealing with polynomial equations.

EXAMPLE: Approximate the values of c that satisfy the conclusion of the Mean-Value Theorem for $f(x) = \dfrac{\cos 3x}{x^2 + 1}$ on the interval $[0, \pi]$.

SOLUTION: We begin by defining and graphing f on the interval $[0,\pi]$. We name the graph of f plotf for later use.

```
Clear[f]
f[x_]=Cos[3x]/(x^2+1);
plotf=Plot[f[x],{x,0,Pi}]
```

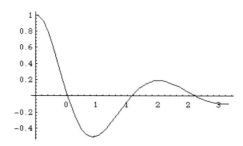

We must find the values of c in $(0,\pi)$ that satisfy the equation $f'(c) = \dfrac{f(\pi) - f(0)}{\pi - 0}$.

Below we compute $\dfrac{f(\pi) - f(0)}{\pi - 0}$ and name the number avg.

```
avg=(f[Pi]-f[0])/(Pi-0)//N
```

    -0.347594

Solve cannot be used to solve the equation $f'(c) = \dfrac{f(\pi) - f(0)}{\pi - 0}$. But, graphing $f'(x)$ and avg on the interval $[0,\pi]$ shows that there are 4 values of c satisfying the conclusion of the Mean-Value Theorem. We use FindRoot to approximate these values and name the results c1, c2, c3, and c4, respectively.

```
Plot[{f'[x],avg},{x,0,Pi}]
```

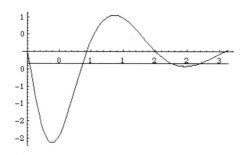

```
c1=FindRoot[f'[x]==avg,{x,.03}]
```

    {x -> 0.0317021}

```
c2=FindRoot[f'[x]==avg,{x,.869}]
```

    {x -> 0.875621}

```
c3=FindRoot[f'[x]==avg,{x,2.25}]
```

    {x -> 2.26848}

```
c4=FindRoot[f'[x]==avg,{x,2.71}]
```

    {x -> 2.67683}

These numbers represent the values of c for which the slope of the line tangent to the graph of f at (c,f(c)) is the same as the slope of the line passing through (0,f(0)) and (π,f(π)). Below, we define `secline` to be the line segment with endpoints (0,f(0)) and (π,f(π)), `p1` to be a graph of the line tangent to the graph of f at the point (.8756,f(.8756)), and `p2` to be a graph of the line tangent to the graph of f at the point (2.6768,f(2.6768)). All three graphs along with `plotf` are shown together. Note that all three lines are parallel.

```
secline=Graphics[Line[{{0,f[0]},{Pi,f[Pi]}}]];
p1=Plot[f'[.8756](x-.8756)+f[.8756],{x,0,Pi},DisplayFunction->Identity];
p2=Plot[f'[2.6768](x-2.6768)+f[2.6768],{x,0,Pi},
        DisplayFunction->Identity];
Show[plotf,secline,p1,p2,DisplayFunction->$DisplayFunction]
```

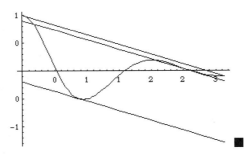

Application: Graphing Functions and Tangent Lines

If f is a differentiable function, then the graph of the function $y = f'(x_0)(x - x_0) + f(x_0)$ is the line tangent to the graph of f at the point $(x_0, f(x_0))$. Often, we wish to graph both f and the line tangent to the graph of f at the point $(x_0, f(x_0))$ for many values of x_0. Mathematica's animation capabilities can be used to animate the resulting set of graphics.

EXAMPLE: Let $f(x) = x \sin x$. Graph f along with various tangent lines on the interval $[0, 4\pi]$.

SOLUTION: We begin by clearing all prior definitions of f, defining f, and then graphing f on the interval $[0, 4\pi]$. The graph of f, named `plotf`, is not displayed because the option `DisplayFunction->Identity` is included. Also, the option `PlotRange->{-12,12}` is included to assure that the coordinates on the y-axis correspond to $[-12, 12]$. We can use `Show` to display `plotf`.

```
Clear[f]
f[x_]=x Sin[x];
plotf=Plot[f[x],{x,0,4Pi},PlotRange->{-12,12},
        DisplayFunction->Identity];
Show[plotf,DisplayFunction->$DisplayFunction]
```

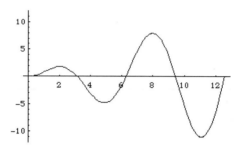

Since we will be graphing the tangent line for various values of x, we define the
function t1 below. The function t1 is defined using Module because t1 performs
several operations. First, the variables 1 and p1 are declared local to the procedure
t1. This means that if 1 and p1 have other (global) values, changes in the value of
1 and p1 within the procedure t1 do not affect their (global) values. Then, for a
given value of x0, t1 first defines 1 to be the function f'[x0](x-x0)+f[x0],
corresponding to the function with graph tangent to the graph of f at the point
$(x_0, f(x_0))$, and p1 to be the graph of 1 on the interval $[0,4\pi]$. Note that p1 is not
displayed since the option DisplayFunction->Identity is included.
Moreover, including the option PlotRange->{-12,12} assures that the y-range
displayed is the same as the y-range displayed in plotf. Finally, t1 shows the
graph of plotf and p1. Note that the graphs are not actually displayed because
the option DisplayFunction->$DisplayFunction is not included in the
Show command.

```
t1[x0_]:=Module[{1,p1},
        1=f'[x0](x-x0)+f[x0];
        p1=Plot[1,{x,0,4Pi},PlotRange->{-12,12},
                DisplayFunction->Identity];
        Show[plotf,p1]
                                    ]
```

However, if we do include DisplayFunction->$DisplayFunction, the
resulting graph is displayed. Below, we display a graph of f along with the line
tangent to the graph of f at the point (5,f(5)).

```
Show[tl[5],DisplayFunction->$DisplayFunction]
```

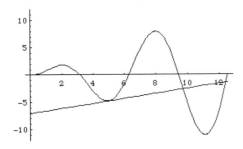

We may use a Do loop to generate several graphs. The results can then be animated. The following shows the resulting animation on a computer with a notebook interface.

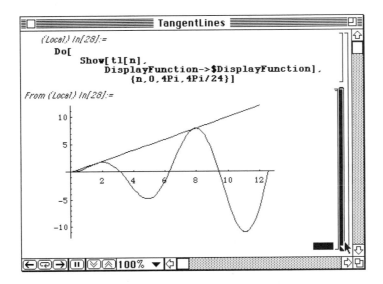

Alternatively, we can use Table to create a table of several graphs and display the result as a graphics array. In the following commands, graphs is defined to be a table consisting of tl[n] for 8 equally spaced values of n between 0 and 4π. graphs is a set consisting of eight graphics objects. Then, Partition is used to partition graphs into a set consisting of two sets each containing four graphics objects. The result is a 2×4 array of graphics cells named toshow displayed with GraphicsArray. Note that the option Ticks->None is included so that the axes are shown without tick marks.

```
graphs=Table[Show[tl[n],Ticks->None],{n,0,4Pi,4Pi/7}];
toshow=Partition[graphs,4];
Show[GraphicsArray[toshow]]
```

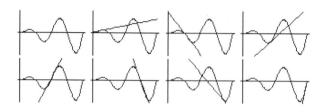

Remember that each time Mathematica generates a plot, unless otherwise instructed to do so, Mathematica selects a range for the displayed graphics object. Consequently, when generating graphics for an animation, be sure to specify the range displayed with `PlotRange`. Otherwise, the resulting animation may appear "choppy."

Application: Maxima and Minima

Mathematica can be used to solve maximization/minimization problems. An example of this type of problem is as follows :

EXAMPLE: A farmer has 100 feet of fencing to construct four dog kennels by first constructing a fence around a rectangular region, and then dividing that region into four smaller regions by placing fences parallel to one of the sides. What dimensions will maximize the total area?

SOLUTION: First, let y denote the length across the top and bottom of the rectangular region and let x denote the vertical length. A figure describing this situation is shown below.

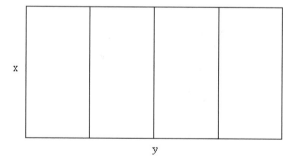

Then, since 100 feet of fencing are used, a relationship between x and y is given by the equation: $2y + 5x = 100$.

Solving this equation for y, we obtain $y = \dfrac{100 - 5x}{2}$ which is shown below.

```
Solve[2y+5x==100,y]
```

$$\{\{y \rightarrow \frac{5\ (20\ -\ x)}{2}\}\}$$

Since the area of a rectangle is $area = xy$, the function to be maximized is

$$area(x) = x \bullet \frac{100 - 5x}{2}, \quad 0 \le x \le 20.$$

After defining `area`, the value of x which maximizes the area is found by finding the critical value and observing the graph of `area[x]`.

```
area[x_]=x(100-5x)/2;
Plot[area[x],{x,0,20}]
```

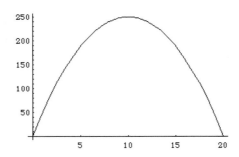

```
Solve[area'[x]==0]
```

$$\{\{x \rightarrow 10\}\}$$

Thus, we see the value of x that maximizes area is 10. To find the other dimension, we evaluate $y = \frac{100 - 5x}{2}$ when x=10.

```
(100-5x)/2 /. x->10
```

```
25
```

Thus, dimensions that maximize the area are 10×25. ∎

The next problem is slightly different.

EXAMPLE: A woman is located on one side of a body of water 4 miles wide. Her position is directly across from a point on the other side of the body of water 16 miles from her house. If she can move across land at a rate of 10 miles per hour and move over water at a rate of 6 miles per hour, find the least amount of time for her to reach her house.

SOLUTION: The figure below illustrates the situation described in the problem.

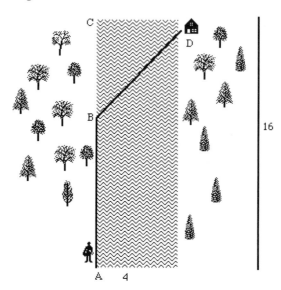

From the figure, we see that the woman will travel from A to B by land and then from B to D by water. We wish to find the least time for her to complete the trip.

Let x denote the distance BC, where $0 \le x \le 16$. Then, the distance AB is given by $16 - x$ and, by the Pythagorean theorem, the distance BD is given by $\sqrt{x^2 + 4^2} = \sqrt{x^2 + 16}$. Since $\text{rate} \times \text{time} = \text{distance}$, $\text{time} = \dfrac{\text{distance}}{\text{rate}}$. Thus, the time to travel from A to B is $\dfrac{16 - x}{10}$, the time to travel from B to D is $\dfrac{\sqrt{x^2 + 16}}{6}$, and the total time to complete the trip, as a function of x, is

$$time(x) = \frac{16 - x}{10} + \frac{\sqrt{x^2 + 16}}{6}, \quad 0 \le x \le 16.$$

We must minimize the function time. Below, we use Mathematica to define `time`. To verify that `time` has a minimum, we graph `time` on the interval [0,16].

```
Clear[time]
time[x_]=(16-x)/10+Sqrt[x^2+16]/6;
Plot[time[x],{x,0,16},PlotRange->{{0,16},{2,3}}]
```

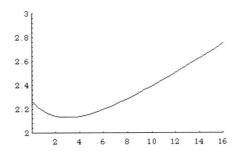

Next, we compute the derivative of `time` and find the values of x for which the derivative is 0 with `Solve`. The resulting output is named `critnums`.

```
Together[time'[x]]
```

$$\frac{5\ x\ -\ 3\ Sqrt[16\ +\ x^2]}{30\ Sqrt[16\ +\ x^2]}$$

```
critnums=Solve[time'[x]==0]
```

```
{{x -> 3}}
```

At this point, we can calculate the minimum time by calculating `time[3]`. Alternatively, we also demonstrate how to find the value of `time[x]` for the value(s) listed in `critnums`.

```
time[3]
time[x] /. critnums[[1]]
```

$$\frac{32}{15}$$

$$\frac{32}{15}$$

Thus, we see that the minimum time to complete the trip is 32/15 hours.

∎

Our final two examples illustrates Mathematica's ability to symbolically manipulate algebraic expressions.

EXAMPLE: Let $f(x) = mx + b$ and (x_0, y_0) be any point not on the graph of f. Find the value of x for which the distance from (x_0, y_0) to (x, f(x)) is a minimum.

SOLUTION: The distance between two points (x_1, y_1) and (x_2, y_2) is given by

$$\text{distance}\big((x_1, y_1), (x_2, y_2)\big)(x_2, y_2) = \sqrt{(x_2 - x_1)^2 + (y_2 - y_1)^2}\,.$$

In order to determine the value of x which minimizes the distance between (x_0, y_0) and $(x, f(x))$, a function which determines this distance must first be defined. This is accomplished by defining the function `distance` by entering

```
distance[{x1_,y1_},{x2_,y2_}]
```

which gives the distance between any two points (x_1, y_1) and (x_2, y_2). Then the particular distance function for this problem is obtained by substituting the appropriate points (x_0, y_0) and (x,f(x)) into `distance` and naming the resulting output `tominimize`. Note that minimizing the square of `tominimize` produces the same results as minimizing `tominimize`. The value of x that minimizes this function is obtained in the usual manner. (Notice how naming the distance function expression simplifies the solution of the problem.)

```
Clear[f,a,m,b,x0,y0,x1,y1,x2,y2]
distance[{x1_,y1_},{x2_,y2_}]=Sqrt[(x2-x1)^2+(y2-y1)^2]
f[x_]=m x+b
                2            2
   Sqrt[(-x1 + x2)  + (-y1 + y2) ]
   b + m x

tominimize=distance[{x0,y0},{x,f[x]}]
              2                  2
   Sqrt[(x - x0)  + (b + m x - y0) ]
```

To find the minimum, we first compute the derivative of `tominimize`, name the result `dtm`, and then use `Solve` to find the values of x for which the derivative is 0.

```
dtm=D[tominimize,x]//Simplify
                 2
      b m + x + m  x - x0 - m y0
   ----------------------------------
              2                  2
   Sqrt[(x - x0)  + (b + m x - y0) ]

val=Solve[Numerator[dtm]==0,x]
              b m - x0 - m y0
   {{x -> -(---------------)}}
                    2
                1 + m
```

The value of x that minimizes `dtm` is extracted from `val` below and named `xcoord`.

```
xcoord=val[[1,1,2]]
```

```
 b  m  -  x0  -  m  y0
-(---------------)
          2
       1 + m
```

We then compute and simplify the value of f(x) for the number `xcoord` and name the result `ycoord`. Thus, (`xcoord`,`ycoord`) is the point on the graph of f closest to (x_0, y_0). The minimum distance is then computed using `distance`.

```
ycoord=f[xcoord] // Simplify
```

```
             2
 b + m  x0 + m  y0
 ----------------
          2
       1 + m
```

```
distance[{x0,y0},{xcoord,ycoord}]//Simplify
```

```
                   2
       (-b - m x0 + y0)
 Sqrt[------------------]
               2
            1 + m
```

Thus, the point on the graph of $f(x) = mx + b$ closest to (x_0, y_0) is

$$\left(\frac{my_0 + x_0 - bm}{m^2 + 1}, \frac{m^2 y_0 + mx_0 + b}{m^2 + 1} \right)$$

and the minimum distance is

$$\sqrt{\frac{\left(y_0 - mx_0 - b\right)^2}{m^2 + 1}} = \frac{\left|y_0 - mx_0 - b\right|}{\sqrt{m^2 + 1}}. \quad \blacksquare$$

The next example is a familiar exercise to students in introductory differential calculus courses.

EXAMPLE: Find the dimensions of the cone of minimum volume that can be inscribed about a sphere of radius R.

SOLUTION: Let r and h denote the radius and height, respectively, of the right circular cone of base radius r and height h circumscribed about the sphere of radius R. Then a cross section of the solid containing a diameter of the base of the cone is shown in the figure below.

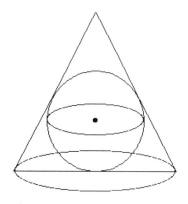

Right circular cone circumscribed
about a sphere.

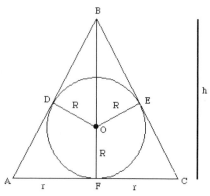

Cross section of a right circular cone
circumscribed about a sphere

From the figure, notice that triangle BOD is similar to triangle BAF. Moreover,
BO=h–R, OD=R, and AF=r and, by the Pythagorean Theorem, $r^2 + h^2 = BA^2$ so that
$BA = \sqrt{r^2 + h^2}$. Consequently, $\dfrac{h-R}{R} = \dfrac{\sqrt{r^2 + h^2}}{r}$. Below, we use Mathematica to solve
this equation for h in terms of r. Note our convention to use `capr` to represent R
in the equation.

```
Clear[h,capr,r]
Solve[(h-capr)/capr==Sqrt[r^2+h^2]/r,h]


                         2
                -2 capr r
  {{h -> 0}, {h ->  ----------}}
                      2    2
                  capr  - r
```

The volume of the cone is given by $V = \dfrac{1}{3}\pi r^2 h$ and substituting $h = \dfrac{2r^2 R}{r^2 - R^2}$ yields V,
as a function of r,

$$V(r) = \frac{2\pi R r^4}{3(r^2 - R^2)} .$$

Below we define `capv` to be $V(r) = \dfrac{2\pi R r^4}{3(r^2 - R^2)}$. Then, we differentiate `capv` and find
the values of r for which `capv` equals 0. Note that r can be neither 0 nor $-R\sqrt{2}$.

```
capv[r_]=2 Pi capr r^4/(3(r^2-capr^2))
```

```
               4
    2 capr Pi r
    ---------------
            2    2
    3 (-capr  + r )
```

```
capv'[r]//Together
```

```
          3      3            5
    4 (-2 capr  Pi r  + capr Pi r )
    -------------------------------
                  2     2 2
            3 (capr  - r )
```

```
critnums=Solve[capv'[r]==0,r]
```

```
    {{r -> 0}, {r -> 0}, {r -> 0}, {r -> -(Sqrt[2] capr)},

     {r -> Sqrt[2] capr}}
```

The value $R\sqrt{2}$ is extracted from `critnums` with `critnums[[5,1,2]]`. Extracting data from lists is discussed in more detail in Chapters 4 and 5.

```
critnums[[5,1,2]]
```

```
    Sqrt[2] capr
```

To see that $r = R\sqrt{2}$ yields the desired minimum, we evaluate $V''(r)$ when $r = R\sqrt{2}$.

```
capv''[capr Sqrt[2]]
```

```
    32 capr Pi
    ----------
        3
```

Since the value of $V''(r)$ when $r = R\sqrt{2}$ is positive, we conclude that $r = R\sqrt{2}$ yields the minimum volume, computed below.

```
capv[capr Sqrt[2]]
```

```
         3
    8 capr  Pi
    ----------
        3
```

We conclude that the minimum volume is $V\left(R\sqrt{2}\right)=\dfrac{8}{3}\pi R^3$ and the cone has radius

$r = R\sqrt{2}$ and height $h = \dfrac{2r^2R}{r^2 - R^2} = 4R$. ∎

3.3 Implicit Differentiation

Computing Derivatives of Implicit Functions

If `equation` is an equation with variables x and y, Mathematica computes the implicit derivative of `equation` with the command `Dt[equation,x]`, where `equation` is differentiated with respect to the variable x.

The expression `Dt[y,x]` encountered when using implicit differentiation represents the derivative of y with respect to x, dy/dx . (Hence, `Dt[x,y]` represents dx/dy.)

The built-in command `Dt` is versatile. Although here `Dt` is used to perform implicit differentiation, `Dt[expression,variable]` computes the total derivative: $\frac{d(\text{expresssion})}{d\text{variable}}$; and `Dt[expression]` computes the total differential d(`expression`).

The following examples demonstrate the use of the implicit differentiation command, `Dt[equation,x]` and show how this command can be used with `Solve` to obtain the desired derivative in a single command.

EXAMPLE: Find an equation of the line tangent to the graph of

$$2x^2 - 2xy + y^2 + x + 2y + 1 = 0$$

at the points $\left(-\frac{3}{2}, -1\right)$ and $\left(-\frac{3}{2}, -4\right)$.

S O L U T I O N :   The slope of the lines tangent to the graph of $2x^2 - 2xy + y^2 + x + 2y + 1 = 0$ at the points $\left(-\frac{3}{2}, -1\right)$ and $\left(-\frac{3}{2}, -4\right)$ is obtained by evaluating the derivative of this equation at each of these points. To find the derivative, we use implicit differentiation.

After clearing all prior definitions of eq, we define eq to be the equation

$$2x^2 - 2xy + y^2 + x + 2y + 1 = 0 \, .$$

Don't forget to include the space between the x and y to denote multiplication and the double equals sign (==) between the left- and right-hand sides of the equation. Note that the left-hand side of eq is extracted from eq with eq[[1]].

```
eq=2x^2-2x y+y^2+x+2y+1==0

                2                    2
    1 + x + 2 x   + 2 y - 2 x y + y    == 0
```

```
eq[[1]]
```

$$1 + x + 2 x^2 + 2 y - 2 x y + y^2$$

The graph of `eq` corresponds to the level curve of $2x^2 - 2xy + y^2 + x + 2y + 1$ with $2x^2 - 2xy + y^2 + x + 2y + 1 = 0$. Thus, we can use `ContourPlot` to generate this particular level curve.

In the following command, `eq[[1]]` is enclosed in `Evaluate`. This ensures that Mathematica computes `eq[[1]]` **before** sampling points. This is important: if `Evaluate` is not included, error messages occur. The option `Contours->{0}` is included so that Mathematica only graphs the level curve of $2x^2 - 2xy + y^2 + x + 2y + 1$ with $2x^2 - 2xy + y^2 + x + 2y + 1 = 0$; `ContourShading->False` specifies that the resulting graph not be shaded; `PlotPoints->50` helps assure that the resulting graph is smooth; `Frame->False` specifies that no frame is to be displayed around the resulting graphics object; `Axes->Automatic` specifies that the resulting graphics object be displayed with axes; and `AxesOrigin->{0,0}` specifies that the axes intersect at the point (0,0).

```
grapheq=ContourPlot[Evaluate[eq[[1]]],{x,-6,1},{y,-6,1},
        Contours->{0},ContourShading->False,PlotPoints->50,
        Frame->False,Axes->Automatic,AxesOrigin->{0,0}]
```

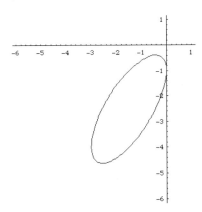

We see that the graph of $2x^2 - 2xy + y^2 + x + 2y + 1 = 0$ is an ellipse. Next, we use Dt to implicitly differentiate the equation with respect to x. The result is named `deriv`. We then use `Solve` to solve the equation `deriv` for `Dt[y,x]` and name the result `imderiv`.

```
deriv=Dt[eq,x]
```

```
1 + 4 x - 2 y + 2 Dt[y, x] -

    2 x Dt[y, x] + 2 y Dt[y, x] == 0
```

```
imderiv=Solve[deriv,Dt[y,x]]
```

```
               -(1 + 4 x - 2 y)
    {{Dt[y, x] -> ----------------}}
                 2 (1 - x + y)
```

The derivative of $2x^2 - 2xy + y^2 + x + 2y + 1 = 0$ is $\dfrac{dy}{dx} = -\dfrac{1+4x-2y}{2(1-x+y)}$. This expression is extracted from `imderiv` with `imderiv[[1,1,2]]`. Extracting data from lists is discussed in more detail in Chapters 4 and 5.

```
imderiv[[1,1,2]]
```

```
    -(1 + 4 x - 2 y)
    ----------------
    2 (1 - x + y)
```

To find the slope of each tangent line, we evaluate $\dfrac{dy}{dx} = -\dfrac{1+4x-2y}{2(1-x+y)}$ at each point.

Below, we calculate the value of `imderiv[[1,1,2]]` at the points $\left(-\dfrac{3}{2}, -1\right)$ and $\left(-\dfrac{3}{2}, -4\right)$, naming the results `m1` and `m2`, respectively. Note that in each case, the slope of the tangent line is 1.

```
m1=imderiv[[1,1,2]] /. {x->-3/2,y->-1}
m2=imderiv[[1,1,2]] /. {x->-3/2,y->-4}
```

```
    1
    1
```

To visualize the tangent line at these points, we graph the tangent lines simultaneously and name the result `plotlines`. Note that `plotlines` is not displayed since we include the option `DisplayFunction->Identity`. To see each particular point, we use `Graphics`, `Point`, and `PointSize` to represent the points $\left(-\dfrac{3}{2}, -1\right)$ and $\left(-\dfrac{3}{2}, -4\right)$ as graphics objects. Finally, `Show` is used to show `grapheq`, generated above, `plotlines`, and `points`, simultaneously.

```
plotlines=Plot[{m1(x+3/2)-1,m2(x+3/2)-4},{x,-6,1},
        DisplayFunction->Identity];
points=Graphics[{PointSize[.03],Point[{-3/2,-1}],Point[{-3/2,-4}]}];
Show[grapheq,points,plotlines,PlotRange->{{-6,1},{-6,1}}]
```

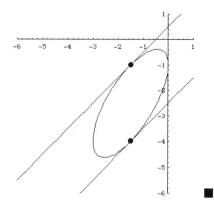

In the next example, we implicitly differentiate an equation in which the right-hand side is not zero.

EXAMPLE: Find $y' = \dfrac{dy}{dx}$ if $\cos(x + \sin y) = \sin y$.

SOLUTION: As in the preceding example, we begin by clearing all prior definitions of eq and defining eq to be the equation $\cos(x + \sin y) = \sin y$.

```
Clear[eq]
eq=Cos[x+Sin[y]]==Sin[y]
```

```
Cos[x + Sin[y]] == Sin[y]
```

Next, we use Dt to compute the derivative of eq with respect to x. The result is named deriv. Remember that the symbol Dt[y,x] represents $y' = \dfrac{dy}{dx}$.

```
deriv=Dt[eq,x]
```

```
-((1 + Cos[y] Dt[y, x])

     Sin[x + Sin[y]]) == Cos[y] Dt[y, x]
```

Finally, we use Solve to solve deriv for Dt[y,x]. The result means that

$$y' = \frac{dy}{dx} = \frac{\sin(x + \sin y)}{-\cos y - \cos y \sin(x + \sin y)}.$$

```
Solve[deriv,Dt[y,x]]

   {{Dt[y, x] ->

                Sin[x + Sin[y]]
        --------------------------------}}
        -Cos[y] - Cos[y] Sin[x + Sin[y]]
```

Finally, we use `ContourPlot` to graph the equation $\cos(x+\sin y)=\sin y$. First, we rewrite this equation in the form $\cos(x+\sin y)-\sin y=0$. The graph of $\cos(x+\sin y)-\sin y=0$ is the same as the level curve of $\cos(x+\sin y)-\sin y$ corresponding to 0. Thus, we proceed in the exact same manner as in the previous example. The displayed graph corresponds to the graph of $\cos(x+\sin y)=\sin y$ on the interval $[-4\pi, 4\pi]$.

```
ContourPlot[Cos[x+Sin[y]]-Sin[y],{x,-4Pi,4Pi},{y,-4Pi,4Pi},
        Contours->{0},PlotPoints->70,ContourShading->False,
        Frame->False,Axes->Automatic,AxesOrigin->{0,0}]
```

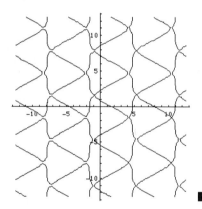

Other Methods to Compute Derivatives of Implicit Functions

Implicit derivatives can also be computed with `D` if `y` is declared to be a function of `x`. For example, to implicitly differentiate $(x^2+y^2)^2=a^2(x^2-y^2)$ (the **Lemniscate of Bernoulli**), where a is a constant, we define `eq` to be

```
Clear[a,x,y,eq]
eq=(x^2+y[x]^2)^2==a^2(x^2-y[x]^2)

         2       2 2      2    2        2
    (x  + y[x] )   == a  (x  - y[x] )
```

and then use `D` to differentiate `eq` with respect to x, naming the result `deriv`.

```
deriv=D[eq,x]
```

```
     2      2
2 (x  + y[x] ) (2 x + 2 y[x] y'[x]) ==

     2
    a  (2 x - 2 y[x] y'[x])
```

Finally, we use `Solve` to solve `deriv` for `y'[x]`.

```
Solve[deriv,y'[x]]
```

```
{{y'[x] ->

              2       3          2
        -(a  x) + 2 x  + 2 x y[x]
     -(---------------------------)}}
         2         2           3
        a  y[x] + 2 x  y[x] + 2 y[x]
```

Other Methods to Graph Equations

As we have seen, `ContourPlot` can be used to graph many equations by including the appropriate options in the `ContourPlot` command. Some equations may also be graphed with the command `ImplicitPlot`. `ImplicitPlot` is not a built-in Mathematica function and is contained in the package **ImplicitPlot** located in the **Graphics** folder (or directory).

The most basic form of the syntax for the command `ImplicitPlot` is

$$\texttt{ImplicitPlot[equation,\{x,xmin,xmax\}].}$$

The set of y-values displayed can also be specified by entering the command in the form

$$\texttt{ImplicitPlot[equation,\{x,xmin,xmax\},\{y,ymin,ymax\}].}$$

Be sure to always include the double-equals sign between the right- and left-hand side of equations.

EXAMPLE: Graph $\left(x^2 + y^2\right)^2 = a^2\left(x^2 - y^2\right)$ when a=2.

SOLUTION: In this case, we first load the package **ImplicitPlot**. After the package is loaded, we may use the command `ImplicitPlot`.

```
<<Graphics`ImplicitPlot`
```

Next, we define a=2 and use `ImplicitPlot` to graph the equation for x-values in [−3,3]. Note that the actual interval displayed corresponds to [−2,2].

```
a=2;
ImplicitPlot[(x^2+y^2)^2==a^2(x^2-y^2),{x,-3,3}]
```

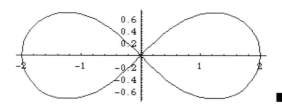

The command `ImplicitPlot` works best with equations that are (easily) solvable. Notice that the command

```
ImplicitPlot[y^2==x Cos[x y],{x,-3Pi,3Pi}]
```

```
        Solve::tdep:
           The equations appear to involve transcendental functions
              of the variables in an essentially non-algebraic way.
        Solve::tdep:
           The equations appear to involve transcendental functions
              of the variables in an essentially non-algebraic way.
        ImplicitPlot::epfail:
                      2
           Equation y   == x Cos[x y]
              could not be solved for points to plot.
                      2
        ImplicitPlot[y   == x Cos[x y], {x, -3 Pi, 3 Pi}]
```

produces several error messages and cannot graph the equation $y^2 = x\cos(xy)$. On the other hand, entering

```
ImplicitPlot[y^2==x Cos[x y],{x,-3Pi,3Pi},{y,-Pi,Pi},PlotPoints->50]
```

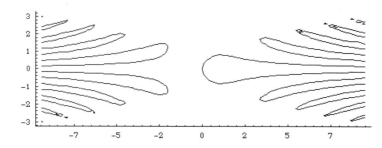

produces the desired graph. `ContourPlot` is used with equal success to generate the same graph.

```
ContourPlot[y^2-x Cos[x y],{x,-3Pi,3Pi},{y,-Pi,Pi},
       PlotPoints->50,Contours->{0},ContourShading->False,
       Frame->False,Axes->Automatic,AxesOrigin->{0,0}]
```

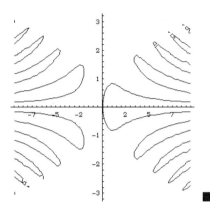

3.4 Integral Calculus

Estimating Areas

In integral calculus courses, the definite integral is frequently motivated by investigating the area under the graph of a positive continuous function on a closed interval.

Let $y = f(x)$ be a positive continuous function on an interval $[a,b]$ and let n be a positive integer. If we divide $[a,b]$ into n equal subintervals and let $\left[x_{k-1}, x_k\right]$ denote the kth subinterval, $x_k = a + k\dfrac{b-a}{n}$ and the width of each subinterval is $\dfrac{b-a}{n}$. Then, the area bounded by the graphs of $y = f(x)$, $x = a$, $x = b$, and the y-axis can be approximated with the sums

$$S_{left} = \frac{b-a}{n}\sum_{k=1}^{n} f(x_{k-1}) \text{ and } S_{right} = \frac{b-a}{n}\sum_{k=1}^{n} f(x_k).$$

In the case when f is **increasing** on $[a,b]$, S_{left} is an under approximation and S_{right} is an upper approximation. S_{left} corresponds to an approximation of the area using n inscribed rectangles; S_{right} corresponds to an approximation of the area using n circumscribed rectangles. When f is **decreasing** on $[a,b]$, S_{right} is an under approximation and S_{left} an upper approximation. S_{right} corresponds to an approximation of the area using n inscribed rectangles; S_{left} corresponds to an approximation of the area using n circumscribed rectangles.

Our first example illustrates the case when f is increasing.

> **EXAMPLE:** Let $f(x) = 1 + 12x - x^2$. Approximate the area bounded by the graph of f(x), the y-axis, $x = 2$, and $x = 5$ using (a) 100 inscribed and (b) 100 circumscribed rectangles. (c) What is the exact value of the area?

SOLUTION: We begin by defining and graphing f.

```
Clear[f]
f[x_]=1+12x-x^2;
Plot[f[x],{x,-1,13}]
```

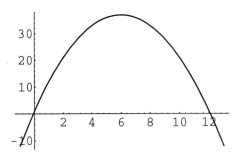

Since $f'(x) = 2(6 - x)$ is positive on the interval $[2,5]$, f is increasing on $[2,5]$. Thus, an approximation of the area using 100 inscribed rectangles is given by $\dfrac{3}{100}\sum\limits_{k=0}^{99} f\left(2 + k\dfrac{3}{100}\right)$, while an approximation of the area using 100 circumscribed rectangles is given by $\dfrac{3}{100}\sum\limits_{k=1}^{100} f\left(2 + k\dfrac{3}{100}\right)$. Each of these numbers, along with a corresponding approximation, is computed below with Sum. The symbol % represents Out. N[%] returns a numerical approximation of the previous output.

```
3/100 Sum[f[2+k 3/100],{k,0,99}]
```

$$\frac{1795491}{20000}$$

```
N[%]
```

$$89.7745$$

```
3/100 Sum[f[2+i 3/100],{i,1,100}]
```

$$\frac{1804491}{20000}$$

```
N[%]
```

```
90.2245
```

More generally, below we define the functions `la` and `ra`, which compute the

sums $S_{left} = \dfrac{b-a}{n}\sum_{k=1}^{n} f(x_{k-1})$ and $S_{right} = \dfrac{b-a}{n}\sum_{k=1}^{n} f(x_k)$, respectively.

```
la[f_,{a_,b_},n_]:=(b-a)/n Sum[f[a+k (b-a)/n],{k,0,n-1}]//N;
ra[f_,{a_,b_},n_]:=(b-a)/n Sum[f[a+k (b-a)/n],{k,1,n}]//N;
```

We then use `la` and `ra` to compute $\dfrac{3}{n}\sum_{k=0}^{n-1} f\left(2+k\dfrac{3}{100}\right)$ and $\dfrac{3}{n}\sum_{k=1}^{n} f\left(2+k\dfrac{3}{100}\right)$ for

$n = 2, 4, 8, 2^4, ..., 2^9 = 512$. Note that the under approximations computed with `la` and the over approximations computed with `ra` appear to be getting closer together.

```
approxes=Table[{2^n,la[f,{2,5},2^n],ra[f,{2,5},2^n]},{n,1,9}];
TableForm[approxes,TableHeadings->{None,{"n","Lower","Upper"}}]
```

n	Lower	Upper
2	77.625	100.125
4	84.0937	95.3437
8	87.1172	92.7422
16	88.5762	91.3887
32	89.2925	90.6987
64	89.6473	90.3505
128	89.8239	90.1755
256	89.912	90.0878
512	89.956	90.0439

In fact, $\lim_{n\to\infty}\dfrac{3}{n}\sum_{k=0}^{n-1} f(x_k) = \lim_{n\to\infty}\dfrac{3}{n}\sum_{k=1}^{n} f(x_{k-1})$, and this number is the exact value of the area bounded by the graphs of $y = f(x)$, the y-axis, $x = 2$, and $x = 5$. To help us see why this is true, we define the function `rleft` which, given f, a, b, and n, graphs f on the interval $[a,b]$ and then shows the graph of f along with n rectangles, where the kth rectangle has vertices $(x_{k-1},0)$, $(x_{k-1},f(x_{k-1}))$, $(x_k,f(x_{k-1}))$, and $(x_k,0)$. Since the function $f(x) = 1+12x - x^2$ on the interval $[2,5]$ is increasing, in this case, these rectangles are inscribed rectangles. The commands used in defining the function `rleft` are discussed in later chapters.

```
rleft[f_,{a_,b_},n_]:=Module[{recs,plotf,x,pts},
    x[k_]=a+k (b-a)/n;
    recs=Table[Rectangle[{x[k],0},{x[k-1],f[x[k-1]]}],
        {k,1,n}];
    pts=Table[Point[{x[k],f[x[k]]}],{k,0,n-1}];
```

```
plotf=Plot[f[x],{x,a,b},DisplayFunction->Identity];
g1=Show[Graphics[{GrayLevel[.8],recs}],
        DisplayFunction->Identity];
g2=Show[Graphics[{PointSize[.02],pts}],
        DisplayFunction->Identity];
Show[g1,g2,plotf,Axes->Automatic]
        ]
```

We then use `rleft` to show the graph of f on the interval $[2,5]$ with $2 \bullet 2^i$ inscribed rectangles for $i = 0, 1, 2, 3$. First, we use `Table` to generate the graphs.

```
graphs=Table[rleft[f,{2,5},2*2^i],{i,0,3}]
```

```
{-Graphics-, -Graphics-, -Graphics-, -Graphics-}
```

We then partition the set of four graphics objects, `graphs`, into two element subsets with `Partition`.

```
toshow=Partition[graphs,2]
```

```
{{-Graphics-, -Graphics-}, {-Graphics-, -Graphics-}}
```

Finally, we display the 2×2 array of graphics objects, `toshow`, with `Show` and `GraphicsArray`.

```
Show[GraphicsArray[toshow]]
```

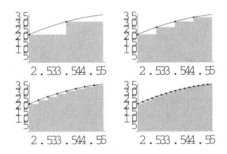

Similarly, we define `rright`, which, given f, a, b, and n, graphs f on the interval $[a,b]$ and then shows the graph of f along with n rectangles, where the kth rectangle has vertices $(x_{k-1},0)$, $(x_{k-1},f(x_k))$, $(x_k,f(x_k))$, and $(x_k,0)$. Since the function $f(x) = 1 + 12x - x^2$ on the interval $[2,5]$ is increasing, in this case, these rectangles are circumscribed rectangles. Note that `rleft` and `rright` could be combined into a single function by using an `If` statement.

```
rright[f_,{a_,b_},n_]:=Module[{recs,plotf,x,pts},
    x[k_]=a+k (b-a)/n;
    recs=Table[Rectangle[{x[k-1],0},{x[k],f[x[k]]}],
        {k,1,n}];
    pts=Table[Point[{x[k],f[x[k]]}],{k,1,n}];
    plotf=Plot[f[x],{x,a,b},DisplayFunction->Identity];
    g1=Show[Graphics[{GrayLevel[.8],recs}],
        DisplayFunction->Identity];
    g2=Show[Graphics[{PointSize[.02],pts}],
        DisplayFunction->Identity];
    Show[g1,g2,plotf,Axes->Automatic]
    ]
```

Then, in the exact same manner as with rleft above, we use rright to show the graph of f on the interval $[2,5]$ with $2 \cdot 2^i$ circumscribed rectangles for $i = 0, 1, 2, 3$.

```
graphs=Table[rright[f,{2,5},2*2^i],{i,0,3}];
toshow=Partition[graphs,2];
Show[GraphicsArray[toshow]]
```

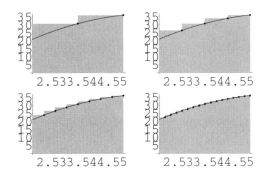

The graphs above help convince us that the limit of the sum of the areas of the inscribed and circumscribed rectangles is the same. In fact, for any positive integer n, the sum of the areas of the inscribed rectangles is given by $\dfrac{3}{n}\sum_{k=0}^{n-1} f\left(2+k\dfrac{3}{n}\right)$ and the sum of the areas of the circumscribed rectangles is given by $\dfrac{3}{n}\sum_{k=1}^{n} f\left(2+k\dfrac{3}{n}\right)$.

Closed forms of these sums can be computed with Sum after the **SymbolicSum** package, located in the **Algebra** folder (or directory), is loaded. Below, we load the **SymbolicSum** package and then use Sum to calculate closed forms for each of these sums, naming the resulting output left and right, respectively.

```
<<Algebra`SymbolicSum`
left=3/n Sum[f[2+3k/n],{k,0,n-1}]//Simplify
```

$$\frac{9\,(-1-5\,n+20\,n^2)}{2\,n^2}$$

```
right=3/n Sum[f[2+3k/n],{k,1,n}]//Simplify
```

$$\frac{9\,(-1+5\,n+20\,n^2)}{2\,n^2}$$

We then use Limit to compute the limit as $n \to \infty$ of both left and right. The results, as expected, are the same.

```
Limit[left,n->Infinity]
Limit[right,n->Infinity]

   90
   90
```

We conclude that the area is 90. ∎

In our next example we examine a function that is decreasing on the interval under consideration. Be sure the functions la, ra, rright, and rleft from the previous example have been defined and the package **SymbolicSum** has been loaded before carrying out the subsequent calculations.

EXAMPLE: Approximate the area bounded by the graphs of $y = f(x)$, the y-axis, $x = 1$, and $x = 3$ using 2, 4, 8, 16, 32, 64, 128, 256, and 512 (a) circumscribed and (b) inscribed rectangles if $f(x) = 2x^3 - 9x^2 + 30$. (c) What is the exact value of the area?

SOLUTION: As in the previous example, we begin by defining and graphing f.

```
Clear[f]
f[x_]=2x^3-9x^2+30;
Plot[f[x],{x,-1,4}]
```

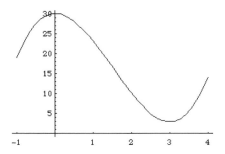

Then, we use the functions la and ra to approximate the area for the indicated numbers of circumscribed and inscribed rectangles. In this case, because f is decreasing on the interval $[1,3]$, la yields an upper approximation, while ra yields a lower approximation.

```
approxes=Table[{2^n,la[f,{1,3},2^n],ra[f,{1,3},2^n]},{n,1,9}];
TableForm[approxes,TableHeadings->{None,{"n","Upper","Lower"}}]
```

n	Upper	Lower
2	33.	13.
4	27.25	17.25
8	24.5625	19.5625
16	23.2656	20.7656
32	22.6289	21.3789
64	22.3135	21.6885
128	22.1565	21.844
256	22.0782	21.9219
512	22.0391	21.961

We also use the functions rleft and rright, defined in the previous example, to visualize various circumscribed and inscribed rectangles.

```
toshow=Partition[graphs,2];
Show[GraphicsArray[toshow]]
```

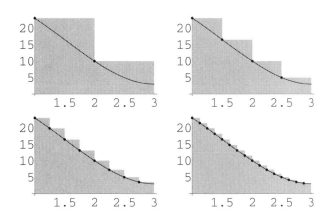

```
graphs=Table[rright[f,{1,3},2*2^i],{i,0,3}];
toshow=Partition[graphs,2];
Show[GraphicsArray[toshow]]
```

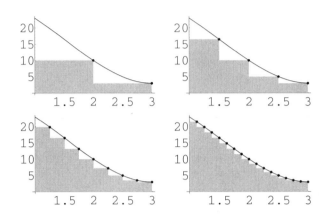

For any positive integer n, the sum of the areas of the circumscribed rectangles is given by $\dfrac{2}{n}\sum_{k=0}^{n-1} f\left(1+k\dfrac{2}{n}\right)$ and the sum of the areas of the inscribed rectangles is given by $\dfrac{2}{n}\sum_{k=1}^{n} f\left(1+k\dfrac{2}{n}\right)$. Closed forms of these sums can be computed with Sum after the **SymbolicSum** package, located in the **Algebra** folder (or directory), has been loaded.

```
left=2/n Sum[f[1+2k/n],{k,0,n-1}]//Simplify
```

$$22 + \frac{4}{n^2} + \frac{20}{n}$$

```
right=2/n Sum[f[1+2k/n],{k,1,n}]//Simplify
```

$$22 + \frac{4}{n^2} - \frac{20}{n}$$

To find the exact area, we use Limit to compute the limit as $n \to \infty$ of both left and right. The area is 22.

```
Limit[left,n->Infinity]
Limit[right,n->Infinity]
```

```
22
22
```

∎

Computing Definite and Indefinite Integrals

The built-in command `Integrate` can be used to find antiderivatives of some functions and evaluate some definite integrals.

The command `Integrate[f[x],x]` attempts to compute $\int f(x)dx$, while the command `Integrate[f[x],{x,a,b}]` attempts to compute the definite integral $\int_a^b f(x)dx$. The command `Integrate[expression,variable]` instructs Mathematica to try to integrate `expression` with respect to `variable`. Each of the following examples illustrates typical commands used to compute indefinite integrals.

EXAMPLE: Compute each of the following indefinite integrals.

(a) $\int x^2(1-x^3)^5 dx$;   (b) $\int e^{-2x}\sin 3x\, dx$;

(c) $\int x^2\tan^{-1}x$;   (d) $\int f(x)dx$ if $f(x)=\dfrac{x^2-4x}{x^2-2x-3}$; and

(e) $\int g(y)dy$ if $g(y)=y^3(\ln y)^2$.

SOLUTION: For (a), (b), and (c), we use `Integrate` directly. Entering

```
Integrate[x^2(1-x^3)^5,x]

       3        6         9        12       15      18
      x      5 x      10 x      5 x        x       x
      -- - ----- + ------ - ------ + --- - ---
       3      6        9        6        3      18
```

computes $\int x^2(1-x^3)^5 dx$; entering

```
Integrate[Exp[-2x]Sin[3x],x]

        -3 Cos[3 x]     2 Sin[3 x]
        ----------- - ----------
           2 x             2 x
          E               E
        -------------------------
                    13
```

computes $\int e^{-2x}\sin 3x\, dx$; and entering

```
Integrate[x^2 ArcTan[x],x]

        2      3                        2
      -x      x  ArcTan[x]     Log[1 + x ]
      --- + ------------ + -----------
       6          3                6
```

computes $\int x^2\tan^{-1}x$.

For (d) and (e), we first define f and g and then use `Integrate`.

```
Clear[f]
f[x_]=(x^2-4x)/(x^2-2x-3);
Integrate[f[x],x]

          3 Log[-3 + x]    5 Log[1 + x]
    x - ------------- - ------------
               4                 4
```

```
Clear[g]
g[y_]=y^3 Log[y]^2;
Integrate[g[y],y]

     4     4              4        2
    y     y  Log[y]    y  Log[y]
    -- - --------- + ----------
    32        8            4
```

Generally, Mathematica can compute antiderivatives of most functions encountered in an introductory integral calculus course. ∎

Since integration is a difficult procedure, it is relatively easy to make up integrals that Mathematica cannot calculate. Nevertheless, Mathematica can calculate a wide variety of integrals.

EXAMPLE: Calculate (a) $\int \sin x \ln x \, dx$; (b) $\int \frac{1}{\sin^2 x + 2} dx$; and (c) $\int \frac{x}{\sin x + 2} dx$.

SOLUTION: Mathematica can compute (a) and (b), but not (c).

```
Integrate[Sin[x] Log[x],x]

    CosIntegral[x] - Cos[x] Log[x]
```

The function `CosIntegral[x]`, appearing in the result above, represents the **cosine integral function**, Ci(z), where

$$Ci(z) = -\int_z^\infty \frac{\cos t}{t} dt = \gamma + \ln z + \int_0^z \frac{\cos t - 1}{t} dt .$$

Here, γ represents Euler's constant which is approximately 0.577216. Note that Mathematica has a built-in definition of Euler's constant, `EulerGamma`.

```
Integrate[1/(Sin[x]^2+2),x]

                  3
    ArcTan[Sqrt[-] Tan[x]]
                  2
    ----------------------
             Sqrt[6]
```

```
Integrate[x/(Sin[x]+2),x]

                  x
  Integrate[----------, x]
              2 + Sin[x]
```

∎

Definite integrals are also computed with `Integrate`. In general, the command

```
Integrate[expression,{variable,lowerlimit,upperlimit}]
```

integrates `expression` with respect to `variable` and evaluates from `lowerlimit` to `upperlimit` as illustrated in the following example.

EXAMPLE: Calculate each definite integral.

(a) $\int_0^1 (x-x^2)dx$; (b) $\int_0^\pi \sin x\, dx$;

(c) $\int_1^2 \sqrt{4-x^2}\,dx$; (d) $\int_1^2 f(x)dx$, if $f(x)=x^3 e^{-4x}$; and

(e) $\int_{-\pi}^{2\pi} g(x)dx$, if $g(x)=e^{2x}\sin^2 2x$.

SOLUTION: For (a), (b), and (c), we use `Integrate` to evaluate each definite integral.

```
Integrate[x-x^2,{x,0,1}]

  1
  -
  6

Integrate[Sin[x],{x,0,Pi}]

  2

Integrate[Sqrt[4-x^2],{x,1,2}]

  -Sqrt[3]    2 Pi
  -------- +  ----
     2         3
```

On the other hand, for (d) and (e), we clear all prior definitions of f and g, define f and g, and then use `Integrate` to compute the indicated definite integral.

```
Clear[f]
f[x_]=x^3 Exp[-4x];
Integrate[f[x],{x,1,2}]
```

```
       -379        71
      ------  +  ------
         8          4
      128 E       128 E
```

```
Clear[g]
g[x_]=Exp[2x] Sin[2x]^2;
Integrate[g[x],{x,-Pi,2Pi}]
```

```
                    4 Pi
        -1        E
      -------  +  -----
         2 Pi       5
      5 E
```

∎

When the command `Integrate[f[x],{x,xmin,xmax}]` is entered, Mathematica computes an antiderivative F of f, when possible, and computes `F[xmax]-F[xmin]`. Nevertheless, Mathematica does not apply the Fundamental Theorem of Calculus since Mathematica does not verify that f is continuous on the interval [xmin,xmax]. In cases when f is not continuous on [xmin,xmax], errors often occur. Consequently, before believing the results presented by Mathematica, be sure the results that Mathematica gives you are reasonable.

EXAMPLE: Calculate $\int_{-1}^{1} \frac{1}{x}dx$,

SOLUTION: Below we use `Integrate` to attempt to calculate the definite integral.

```
Integrate[1/x,{x,-1,1}]
```

```
    -I Pi
```

```
-Log[-1]
```

```
    -I Pi
```

Since the function $\frac{1}{x}$ is not continuous when x=0, we cannot use the Fundamental Theorem of Calculus to calculate this integral. In fact, the integral $\int_{-1}^{1} \frac{1}{x}dx$ does not exist. ∎

Approximating Definite Integrals

When an exact value of a definite integral is either unnecessary or impossible to compute, Mathematica can frequently compute approximations of definite integrals with `NIntegrate`,

```
NIntegrate[expression,{variable,lowerlimit,upperlimit}],
```

which numerically integrates `expression` with respect to `variable` and evaluates from `lowerlimit` to `upperlimit`.

The command `NIntegrate` is useful when an anti-derivative of `expression` cannot be (easily) found and `expression` is fairly smooth on the interval [`lowerlimit, upperlimit`] Also, in those cases in which an anti-derivative can be determined, the value of the definite integral can usually be computed more quickly by an approximation with `NIntegrate` rather than `Integrate`.

EXAMPLE: Compute both exact and approximate values of $\displaystyle\int_{4}^{10}\frac{\sqrt{4x^2-9}}{x^3}\,dx$,

---

SOLUTION: `Integrate` is used to compute the exact value of the integral; `NIntegrate` is used to compute an approximation of the integral.

```
Integrate[Sqrt[4x^2-9]/x^3,{x,4,10}]

    Sqrt[55]    Sqrt[391]
    --------  - ---------  +
       32          200

                   3                      3
      2 ArcTan[--------]   2 ArcTan[---------]
               Sqrt[55]             Sqrt[391]
    ------------------- - -------------------
              3                      3

NIntegrate[Sqrt[4x^2-9]/x^3,{x,4,10}]

    0.288773
```

The approximation obtained with `NIntegrate` is computed much more quickly than the exact value computed with `Integrate`. ■

In many cases, Mathematica can compute approximate values of definite integrals it cannot compute exactly.

EXAMPLE: Approximate $\displaystyle\int_0^{\sqrt[3]{\pi}} e^{-x^2}\cos x^3 dx$.

SOLUTION: We first graph $e^{-x^2}\cos x^3$ on the interval $[0,\pi]$. Note that the graph is relatively smooth so that the chances of `NIntegrate` producing a reasonable approximation of the integral are good.

```
Plot[Exp[-x^2] Cos[x^3],{x,0,Pi},PlotRange->All]
```

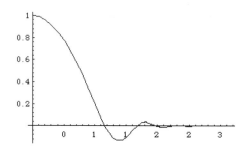

Next, we try to use `Integrate` to evaluate the integral but are unsuccessful. In this particular case, the Mathematica kernel ran out of memory and quit.

```
Integrate[Exp[-x^2] Cos[x^3],{x,0,Pi^(1/3)}]
```

```
    General::intinit: Loading integration packages -- please wait.
```

Finally, we use `NIntegrate` to approximate the integral.

```
NIntegrate[Exp[-x^2] Cos[x^3],{x,0,Pi^(1/3)}]
```

```
    0.701566
```

Application: Area Between Curves

A type of problem which incorporates the commands `Integrate` and `NIntegrate` is that of finding the area between curves. These problems also use several other Mathematica commands (`Plot`, `NRoots`, `FindRoot`, `Solve`,...) which were introduced earlier in the text.

EXAMPLE: Find the area between the graphs of $y=\sin x$ and $y=\cos x$ on the interval $[0,2\pi]$.

SOLUTION: Below, we graph $y = \sin x$ and $y = \cos x$ on the interval $[0, 2\pi]$. The graph of $y = \cos x$ is dashed.

```
Plot[{Sin[x],Cos[x]},{x,0,2Pi},PlotStyle->{GrayLevel[0],Dashing[{.01}]}]
```

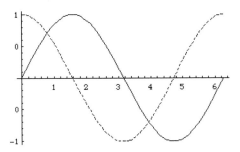

To find the upper and lower limits of integration, we must solve the equation $\sin x = \cos x$ for x. We see that `Solve` is unable to solve this equation. However, we see that $\sin x = \cos x$ on the interval $[0, 2\pi]$ when $x = \dfrac{\pi}{4}$ and when $x = \dfrac{5\pi}{4}$. Note that `FindRoot` can be used to approximate these numbers, but the resulting area computed would not be exact.

```
Solve[Sin[x]==Cos[x],x]
```

```
    Solve::tdep:
        The equations appear to involve
           transcendental functions of the
           variables in an essentially
           non-algebraic way.
    Solve[Sin[x] == Cos[x], x]
```

```
Sin[Pi/4]==Cos[Pi/4]
Sin[5Pi/4]==Cos[5Pi/4]
```

```
    True
    True
```

Thus, the desired area is given by

$$Area = \int_{0}^{\pi/4}(\cos x - \sin x)dx + \int_{\pi/4}^{5\pi/4}(\sin x - \cos x)dx + \int_{5\pi/4}^{2\pi}(\cos x - \sin x)dx$$

which is computed below.

```
Integrate[Cos[x]-Sin[x],{x,0,Pi/4}]+
        Integrate[Sin[x]-Cos[x],{x,Pi/4,5Pi/4}]+
                Integrate[Cos[x]-Sin[x],{x,5Pi/4,2Pi}]
```

```
    4 Sqrt[2]
```

Thus, the desired area is $4\sqrt{2}$. ■

In cases when we cannot calculate the points of intersection of two graphs exactly, we can frequently use NRoots or FindRoot to estimate the points of intersection.

EXAMPLE: Let

$$p(x)=\frac{3}{10}x^5-3x^4+11x^3-18x^2+12x+1$$

and

$$q(x)=-4x^3+28x^2-56x+32.$$

Approximate the area of the region bounded by the graphs of p and q.

SOLUTION: Mathematica is quite helpful in problems of this type. We can observe the region whose area we are seeking using the Plot command, and we can locate the points of intersection with one of the commands used in solving equations (NRoots, FindRoot, Solve, or NSolve). These steps are carried out below. After defining p and q, we graph p and q (the graph of q is dashed) and then use NRoots to find the x-coordinates of the points of intersection, naming the resulting output intpts.

```
Clear[p,q]
p[x_]=3/10x^5-3x^4+11x^3-18x^2+12x+1;
q[x_]=-4x^3+28x^2-56x+32;
Plot[{p[x],q[x]},{x,-1,5},PlotStyle->{GrayLevel[0],Dashing[{.01}]}]
```

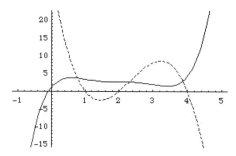

```
intpts=NRoots[p[x]==q[x],x]
```

    x == 0.772058 || x == 1.5355 - 3.57094 I ||

        x == 1.5355 + 3.57094 I || x == 2.29182 ||

        x == 3.86513

Two of the solutions listed contain an imaginary part. We can ignore these solutions. The real solutions are extracted from intpts and named x1, x2, and x3, respectively.

```
x1=intpts[[1,2]]
x2=intpts[[4,2]]
x3=intpts[[5,2]]

    0.772058
    2.29182
    3.86513
```

Using the roots to the equation p(x) = q(x) found above, the graph shows that p(x) > q(x) between x=0.772058 and x=2.29182 ; and q(x) > p(x) between x=2.29182 and x=3.86513.

Hence, an approximation of the area bounded by p(x) and q(x) is given by the integral

$$\int_{0.772058}^{2.29182} \left(p(x) - q(x)\right)dx + \int_{2.29182}^{3.86513} \left(q(x) - p(x)\right)dx \ .$$

This integral is computed below with both `Integrate` and `NIntegrate`. In either case, the result is the same.

```
    12.1951

NIntegrate[p[x]-q[x],{x,x1,x2}]+NIntegrate[q[x]-p[x],{x,x2,x3}]

    12.1951
```

■

Next, consider a problem which involves functions which are not polynomials.

EXAMPLE: Let

$$f(x) = e^{-(x-2)^2 \cos \pi x} \ \text{and} \ \ g(x) = 4\cos(x-2)$$

on the interval [0,4]. Approximate the area of the region bounded by the graphs of f and g.

SOLUTION: Since these functions are not polynomials, `FindRoot` must be used to approximate the x-coordinates of the points of intersection. Recall that `FindRoot` depends on an initial guess of the root. Therefore, the first step towards solving this problem is to graph the functions f and g and estimate the x-coordinates of the points of intersection.

```
Clear[f,g]
f[x_]=Exp[-(x-2)^2Cos[Pi x]];
g[x_]=4Cos[x-2];
Plot[{f[x],g[x]},{x,0,4},PlotStyle->{GrayLevel[0],Dashing[{.01}]}]
```

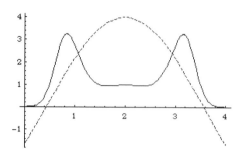

Once the initial guesses have been determined, `FindRoot` is used to approximate the solutions to the equation f(x) = g(x), and the area is approximated with `NIntegrate`. Below, we use `FindRoot` to approximate the x-coordinate of each intersection point. The results are named `fr1` and `fr2`, respectively. The values are then extracted from `fr1` and `fr2` and named `x1` and `x2`, respectively.

```
fr1=FindRoot[f[x]==g[x],{x,1.06}]
fr2=FindRoot[f[x]==g[x],{x,2.93}]
```

```
{x -> 1.06258}
{x -> 2.93742}
```

```
x1=fr1[[1,2]]
x2=fr2[[1,2]]
```

```
1.06258
2.93742
```

Thus, the area is approximated by the integral $\int_{1.023}^{2.937}(g(x)-f(x))dx$ which is computed below with `NIntegrate`.

```
NIntegrate[g[x]-f[x],{x,x1,x2}]
```

```
4.17413
```

■

Application: Arc Length

Let f(x) be a function for which $f'(x)$ is continuous on an interval [a,b]. Then the **arc length** of the graph of f from (a,f(a)) to (b,f(b)) is given by

$$Length = \int_{a}^{b} \sqrt{1+\left(f'(x)\right)^2}\ dx\ .$$

The resulting definite integrals used for determining arc length are usually difficult to compute since they involve a radical. Because the built-in command `NIntegrate[f[x],{x,a,b}]` numerically approximates the integral $\int_a^b f(x)dx$, Mathematica is very helpful with approximating solutions to these types of problems.

EXAMPLE: Let $f(x) = \sin(x + x\sin x)$. Approximate the arc length of the graph of f from (0,f(0)) to (2π,f(2π)).

SOLUTION: We begin by defining and graphing f on the interval $[0,2\pi]$.

```
Clear[f]
f[x_]=Sin[x+x Sin[x]];
Plot[f[x],{x,0,2Pi}]
```

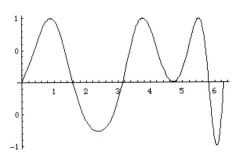

In order to evaluate the arc length formula, we first compute the derivative of f(x) and then approximate $\int_0^{2\pi} \sqrt{1+\left(f'(x)\right)^2}\, dx$ with `NIntegrate`.

```
f'[x]
```

```
Cos[x + x Sin[x]] (1 + x Cos[x] + Sin[x])
```

```
NIntegrate[Sqrt[1+f'[x]^2],{x,0,2Pi}]
```

```
12.0564
```

Thus, an approximation of the arc length is 12.0564. ∎

Application: Volume of Solids of Revolution

Mathematica can be used to solve volume problems as well. Let f be a non-negative continuous function on [a,b] where both a and b are greater than zero. Then the **volume of**

the solid of revolution obtained by revolving the region bounded by the graphs of y=f(x), x=a,x=b, and the x-axis about the x-axis is given by

$$V = \int_a^b \pi(f(x))^2 \, dx .$$

The **volume of the solid of revolution** obtained by revolving the region bounded by the graphs of y=f(x), x=a, x=b, and the x-axis about the y-axis is given by

$$V = \int_a^b 2\pi x f(x) dx .$$

EXAMPLE: Let $g(x) = x\sin^2(x)$. Find the volume of the solid obtained by revolving the region bounded by the graphs of y=g(x), x=0, x=π, and the x-axis about (a) the x-axis; and (b) the y-axis.

SOLUTION: In this case, after defining g, we graph g on the interval [0,π] and then use `Integrate` to compute the volume of each solid. The volume of the solid obtained by revolving the region about the x-axis is given by $V = \int_0^\pi \pi(g(x))^2 dx$, while the volume of the solid obtained by revolving the region about the y-axis is given by $V = \int_0^\pi 2\pi x g(x) dx$. These integrals are computed below and named `xvol` and `yvol`, respectively. `N` is used to approximate each volume.

```
Clear[g]
g[x_]=x Sin[x]^2;
Plot[g[x],{x,0,Pi}]
```

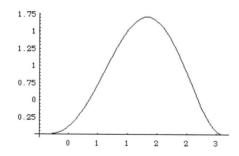

```
xvol=Integrate[Pi g[x]^2,{x,0,Pi}]
```

$$\frac{-60 \ Pi^2 + 32 \ Pi^4}{256}$$

```
N[xvol]
```

> 9.86295

```
yvol=Integrate[2 Pi x g[x],{x,0,Pi}]
```

$$\frac{-6 \ Pi^2 + 4 \ Pi^4}{12}$$

```
N[yvol]
```

> 27.5349

We can use `ParametricPlot3D` to visualize the resulting solids by parametrically graphing the equations given by $\begin{cases} x = r\cos(t) \\ y = r\sin(t) \\ z = g(r) \end{cases}$ for r between 0 and π

and t between $-\pi$ and π to visualize the graph of the solid obtained by revolving the region about the y-axis, or by parametrically graphing the equations given by

$\begin{cases} x = r \\ y = g(r)\cos(t) \\ z = g(r)\sin(t) \end{cases}$ for r between 0 and π and t between $-\pi$ and π to visualize the graph

of the solid obtained by revolving the region about the x-axis. In this case, we identify the z-axis as the y-axis. Notice that we are simply using polar coordinates for the x- and y-coordinates, and the height above the x,y-plane is given by g(r) since r is replacing x in the new coordinate system. .

```
x[r_,t_]=r Cos[t];
y[r_,t_]=r Sin[t];
z[r_,t_]=g[r];
ParametricPlot3D[{x[r,t],y[r,t],z[r,t]},{r,0,Pi},{t,-Pi,Pi}]
```

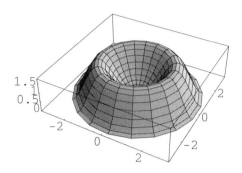

```
Clear[x,y,z]
x[r_,t_]=r;
y[r_,t_]=g[r] Cos[t];
z[r_,t_]=g[r] Sin[t];
ParametricPlot3D[{x[r,t],y[r,t],z[r,t]},{r,0,Pi},{t,-Pi,Pi}]
```

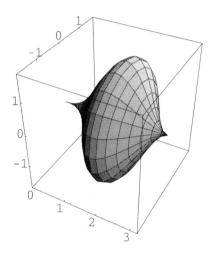

We now demonstrate a volume problem for which we cannot use `Integrate` to calculate an exact value of the volume. Instead, we use `NIntegrate` to approximate the volume.

EXAMPLE: Let $f(x)=e^{-(x-3)^2\cos(4(x-3))}$. Approximate the volume of the solid obtained by revolving the region bounded by the graphs of y=f(x), x=1, x=5, and the x-axis about the y-axis.

SOLUTION: Proceeding as in the previous example, we first define and graph f on the interval [1,5].

```
Clear[f]
f[x_]=Exp[-(x-3)^2 Cos[4(x-3)]];
Plot[f[x],{x,1,5}]
```

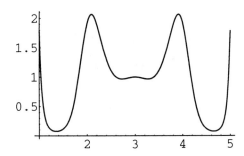

In this case, an approximation is desired so we use NIntegrate to approximate the integral $V = \int_1^5 \pi(f(x))^2 dx$.

```
NIntegrate[Pi f[x]^2,{x,1,5}]
```

    16.0762

In the same manner as before, ParametricPlot3D can be used to visualize the resulting solid by graphing the set of equations given parametrically by

$$\begin{cases} x = r \\ y = f(r)\cos(t) \\ z = f(r)\sin(t) \end{cases}$$

for r between 1 and 5 and t between 0 and 2π. In this case, polar coordinates are used in the y,z-plane with the distance from the x-axis given by f(x). Because r replaces x in the new coordinate system, f(x) becomes f(r) in the equations given above.

```
Clear[x,y,z]
x[r_,t_]=r;
y[r_,t_]=f[r] Cos[t];
z[r_,t_]=f[r] Sin[t];
ParametricPlot3D[{x[r,t],y[r,t],z[r,t]},{r,1,5},{t,-Pi,Pi}]
```

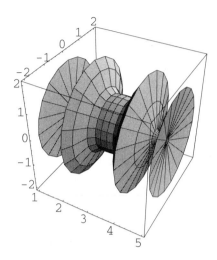

Application: The Mean-Value Theorem for Integrals

Another application of integrals involves the Mean-Value Theorem for Integrals. The **Mean-Value Theorem for Integrals** states that if f is continuous on [a,b] then there is at least one number c between a and b satisfying $\int_a^b f(x)dx = f(c)(b-a)$.

EXAMPLE: Find all values of c satisfying the conclusion of the Mean-Value theorem for integrals for the function $f(x) = x^2 - 3x + 4$ on the interval [2,6].

SOLUTION: After defining f, we compute $\int_2^6 f(x)dx$ and name the resulting output

`val`. We then solve the equation $\int_2^6 f(x)dx = f(x)$ (6-2) for x and name the resulting output `exvals`. To determine which of the numbers in the list `exvals` is contained in the interval [2,6] we use N to compute an approximation of each number in `exvals`. We conclude that the only value of c satisfying the conclusion of the Mean-Value theorem is $\frac{3}{2} + \frac{\sqrt{3 \bullet 91}}{6}$

```
Clear[f]
f[x_]=x^2-3x+4;
val=Integrate[f[x],{x,2,6}]

   112
   ---
    3
```

```
exvals=Solve[val==f[x](6-2)]

        9 - Sqrt[273]         9 + Sqrt[273]
{{x -> -------------}, {x -> -------------}}
              6                     6
```

```
N[exvals]

{{x -> -1.25379}, {x -> 4.25379}}
```

∎

A Word of Caution

When using commands like Integrate and D, be sure to include the correct number of arguments. For example, entering

```
Integrate[Sin[x]+Cos[x]]

Integrate::argmu:
    Integrate called with 1 argument; 2
      or more arguments are expected.
Integrate[Cos[x] + Sin[x]]
```

results in an error message because there are not enough arguments in the command. Entering the command Integrate[Sin[x]+Cos[x],x] computes $\int (\sin x + \cos x)\,dx$.

3.5 Series

Introduction to Series

Sequences and series are usually discussed in the third quarter or second semester of introductory calculus courses. The first topic addressed in these courses usually is determining whether a sequence or series converges or diverges. Mathematica can help determine the answer to these questions in some problems either graphically or explicitly.

EXAMPLE: Find the sum of each of the following series: (a) $\displaystyle\sum_{n=1}^{\infty}\frac{1}{4n^2+8n+3}$;

(b) $\displaystyle\sum_{k=1}^{\infty}x^{3k}$; and (c) $\displaystyle\sum_{n=1}^{\infty}\frac{3^{n/2}}{5^n}$.

SOLUTION: Since we will be computing infinite sums, we begin by loading the package **SymbolicSum** contained in the **Algebra** folder (or directory). We compute $\displaystyle\sum_{n=1}^{\infty}\frac{1}{4n^2+8n+3}$ by entering `Sum[1/(4n^2+8n+3), {n,1,Infinity}]`. The same results are obtained by entering `SymbolicSum[1/(4n^2+8n+3), {n,1,Infinity}]`.

```
<<Algebra`SymbolicSum`
Sum[1/(4n^2+8n+3),{n,1,Infinity}]

    1
    -
    6
```

Similarly, we use `Sum`, or `SymbolicSum`, to compute $\displaystyle\sum_{k=1}^{\infty}x^{3k}$. The result is valid for $|x|<1$.

```
Sum[x^(3k),{k,1,Infinity}]

      3
      x
    ------
        3
    1 - x
```

In the same manner as in the previous two examples, `Sum` calculates $\displaystyle\sum_{n=1}^{\infty}\frac{3^{n/2}}{5^n}$.

```
Sum[3^(n/2)/5^n,{n,1,Infinity}]

      Sqrt[3]
    -----------
    5 - Sqrt[3]
```

■

EXAMPLE: Determine whether or not the series $\displaystyle\sum_{k=1}^{\infty}\frac{k}{2^k}$ converges.

SOLUTION: We use the Integral test to determine whether or not the series $\sum_{k=1}^{\infty} \dfrac{k^2}{2^k}$ converges.

We begin by calculating the integral $\displaystyle\int_1^n \dfrac{k}{2^k}\,dk$ with `Integrate` and naming the resulting output exp1. We then use `Simplify` to simplify exp1 and name the resulting output exp2.

```
exp1=Integrate[k/2^k,{k,1,n}]
```

$$\frac{\mathrm{Log}[2]^{-2} + \dfrac{1}{\mathrm{Log}[2]}}{2} + \frac{-\mathrm{Log}[2]^{-2} - \dfrac{n}{\mathrm{Log}[2]}}{2^n}$$

```
exp2=Simplify[exp1]
```

$$\frac{-2 + 2^n + 2^n\,\mathrm{Log}[2] - 2\,n\,\mathrm{Log}[2]}{2\cdot 2^n\,\mathrm{Log}[2]^2}$$

Next, we must calculate $\displaystyle\lim_{n\to\infty}\int_1^n \dfrac{k}{2^k}\,dk$. We first try using `Limit` but are unsuccessful.

```
Limit[exp2,n->Infinity]
```

```
        Infinity::indet:
           Indeterminate expression -2 + -Infinity + Infinity + Infinity
              encountered.
        Infinity::indet:
           Indeterminate expression -2 + -Infinity + Infinity + Infinity
              encountered.
        Infinity::indet:
           Indeterminate expression -2 + -Infinity + Infinity + Infinity
              encountered.
        General::stop:
           Further output of Infinity::indet
              will be suppressed during this calculation.
                     n     n
              -2 + 2   + 2   Log[2] - 2 n Log[2]
        Limit[-----------------------------------, n -> Infinity]
                          n     2
                       2 2   Log[2]
```

Since we are unsuccessful with `Limit`, we load the package **NLimit** contained in the **NumericalMath** folder (or directory) and then attempt to use the command `NLimit` but are again unsuccessful.

```
<<NumericalMath`NLimit`
NLimit[exp2,n->Infinity]
```

```
NLimit::noise:
   Cannot recognize a limiting value.  This may be due to  noise
      resulting from roundoff errors in which case higher
      WorkingPrecision,  fewer Terms, or a different Scale might help.
            n    n
      -2 + 2  + 2  Log[2] - 2 n Log[2]
NLimit[---------------------------------, n -> Infinity]
                   n    2
              2 2  Log[2]
```

However, we are able to use `Integrate` to calculate the improper integral $\int_1^\infty \frac{k}{2^k} dk$ as shown below. Thus, by the Integral test, we conclude that the series $\sum_{k=1}^\infty \frac{k}{2^k}$ converges.

```
Integrate[k/2^k,{k,1,Infinity}]

        -2     1
   Log[2]   + ------
              Log[2]
   ------------------
          2
```

Since the series converges, we know that the limit of the partial sums is the value of the series. Below, we use `Sum` to approximate the value of the series by computing $\sum_{k=1}^{1000} \frac{k}{2^k}$.

```
Sum[k/2^k,{k,1,1000}]//N
   2.
```

In fact, after loading the **SymbolicSum** package contained in the **Algebra** folder (or directory), we are able to compute the exact value of $\sum_{k=1}^\infty \frac{k}{2^k}$.

```
<<Algebra`SymbolicSum`
Sum[k/2^k,{k,1,Infinity}]

   2
```

■

EXAMPLE: Determine whether or not the series $\sum_{n=1}^\infty \frac{10^n}{n!}$ converges.

SOLUTION: After clearing all prior definitions of a, if any, we define $a_n = \dfrac{10^n}{n!}$ and then use `Table` to calculate $a_1, a_2, \ldots, a_{24}, a_{25}$, naming the resulting set of numbers vals. These numbers are then graphs with `ListPlot`.

```
Clear[a]
a[n_]=10^n/n!;
vals=Table[a[n],{n,1,25}];
ListPlot[vals]
```

To determine whether or not the series converges, we use the Ratio test. First, we compute $\dfrac{a_{n+1}}{a_n}$ and then attempt to use `Limit` to calculate $\lim\limits_{n \to \infty} \dfrac{a_{n+1}}{a_n}$ but are unsuccessful.

```
a[n+1]/a[n]

    10 n!
   --------
   (1 + n)!

Limit[a[n+1]/a[n],n->Infinity]

    Series::esss:
                                        1          3
       Essential singularity encountered in Gamma[- + 1 + O[n] ].
                                        n
    Series::esss:
                                        1          3
       Essential singularity encountered in Gamma[- + 2 + O[n] ].
                                        n
    Series::esss:
                                        1          3
       Essential singularity encountered in Gamma[- + 1 + O[n] ].
                                        n
    General::stop:
       Further output of Series::esss
         will be suppressed during this calculation.
            10 n!
    Limit[--------, n -> Infinity]
          (1 + n)!
```

Since `Limit` is unsuccessful, we load the package **NLimit**, as in the preceding example, and then attempt to use `NLimit` to calculate $\lim_{n\to\infty} \frac{a_{n+1}}{a_n}$. In this case, we interpret the result to be the same as 0. Thus, by the Ratio test, we conclude that the series $\sum_{n=1}^{\infty} \frac{10^n}{n!}$ converges.

```
<<NumericalMath`NLimit`
NLimit[a[n+1]/a[n],n->Infinity]
```
$$-1.59203 \ 10^{-6}$$

Alternatively, we load the package **CombinatorialSimplification** contained in the **DiscreteMath** folder (or directory) which contains elementary rules for simplifying expressions involving factorials and similar expressions. After loading the package, the expression $\frac{a_{n+1}}{a_n} = \frac{10 n!}{(n+1)!}$ is simplified to $\frac{10}{n+1}$ and we see that

$$\lim_{n\to\infty} \frac{a_{n+1}}{a_n} = \lim_{n\to\infty} \frac{10 n!}{(n+1)!} = \lim_{n\to\infty} \frac{10}{n+1} = 0 \ .$$

Thus, by the Ratio test, the series converges.

```
<<DiscreteMath`CombinatorialSimplification`
a[n+1]/a[n]
```
```
  10
-----
1 + n
```

In fact, after loading the **SymbolicSum**, Mathematica can compute the exact value of the series with `Sum`, or `SymbolicSum`, as shown below.

```
<<Algebra`SymbolicSum`
Sum[10^n/n!,{n,1,Infinity}]
```
$$-1 + E^{10}$$

■

   In addition to the above examples, which are similar to those discussed in introductory calculus courses, Mathematica can also help determine the solution of more difficult problems.

EXAMPLE: Determine whether or not the series $\displaystyle\sum_{k=1}^{\infty}\frac{\sin k}{k}$.

SOLUTION: We begin by defining $a_k = \dfrac{\sin k}{k}$ and then using `Table` to compute a list of the values $a_1, a_2, a_3, \ldots, a_{999}, a_{1000}$, naming the resulting list of numbers nums. We then use `ListPlot` to graph the list of numbers nums.

```
Clear[a]
a[k_]=Sin[k]/k;
nums=Table[a[k],{k,1,1000}];
ListPlot[nums,Axes->None,Frame->True]
```

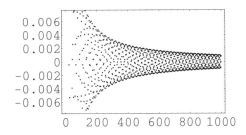

Although the graph is not helpful in determining whether or not the series $\displaystyle\sum_{k=1}^{\infty}\frac{\sin k}{k}$ converges, we compute $\displaystyle\sum_{k=1}^{1000}\frac{\sin k}{k}$ with `Sum`. At this point, we might conclude that the series converges. However, we must be careful about any conclusions, as the partial sums, $\displaystyle\sum_{k=1}^{n}\frac{1}{k}$, of the series $\displaystyle\sum_{k=1}^{\infty}\frac{1}{k}$ are relatively small for "large" values of n, like $n = 1000$, even though the series $\displaystyle\sum_{k=1}^{\infty}\frac{1}{k}$ diverges.

```
Sum[Sin[k]/k,{k,1,1000}]//N
```

```
1.07069
```

However, after loading the package **SymbolicSum**, we are able to compute the exact value of the series.

```
<<Algebra`SymbolicSum`
val=Sum[Sin[k]/k,{k,1,Infinity}]
```

```
  I              -I            I
- (-Log[1 - E   ] + Log[1 - E ])
2
```

To see that this is a real number, we use `ComplexExpand` and `?ArcTan`.

```
val2=ComplexExpand[val]

   -ArcTan[1 - Cos[1], -Sin[1]] + ArcTan[1 - Cos[1], Sin[1]]
   ---------------------------------------------------------
                             2
```

```
?ArcTan

   ArcTan[z] gives the inverse tangent of z. ArcTan[x, y] gives the
      inverse tangent of y/x where x and y are real, taking into
      account which quadrant the point (x, y) is in.
```

A numerical approximation of the result given above is obtained with `N`.

```
N[val2]

   1.0708
```

∎

Determining the Interval of Convergence of a Power Series

After discussing sequences and series, the next topic addressed in these courses is usually power series. Given a power series $\sum_{n=0}^{\infty} a_n x^n$, a fundamental problem is finding the interval of convergence of the given power series.

EXAMPLE: Find the interval of convergence of each series: (a) $\sum_{n=0}^{\infty} \frac{1}{(-5)^n} x^{2n+1}$; and

(b) $\sum_{n=0}^{\infty} \frac{4^{2n}}{n+2}(x-3)^n$.

SOLUTION: For (a), we proceed using the Root test. The Root test says that if $\sum a_n$ is a series with positive terms and $\ell = \lim_{n\to\infty} \sqrt[n]{a_n}$, then

i.   the series converges if $\ell < 1$;
ii. diverges if $\ell > 1$; and
iii. no conclusion can be drawn if $\ell = 1$.

We begin by defining a_n to be $\dfrac{1}{(-5)^n}x^{2n+1}$ and then computing and simplifying

$\sqrt[n]{\dfrac{1}{(-5)^n}x^{2n+1}}$. Note that `Simplify` does not simplify the expression $\sqrt[n]{\dfrac{1}{(-5)^n}x^{2n+1}}$ as

desired so we use `PowerExpand` to simplify the resulting powers. We name the resulting output `stepone`.

```
Clear[a]
a[n_]=x^(2n+1)/(-5)^n;
a[n]^(1/n)//Simplify
```

```
   1 + 2 n
  x          1/n
 (--------)
      n
   (-5)
```

```
stepone=PowerExpand[a[n]^(1/n)]//Simplify
```

```
   2 + 1/n
 -x    .
 ---------
     5
```

We then compute the limit of `stepone` as n approaches infinity. This is the same as computing

$$\lim_{n\to\infty}\sqrt[n]{\dfrac{1}{(-5)^n}x^{2n+1}} = \lim_{n\to\infty}\dfrac{-1}{5}x^2x^{1/n}.$$

```
Limit[stepone,n->Infinity]
```

```
   2
 -x
 ---
  5
```

The result means that $\displaystyle\sum_{n=0}^{\infty}\dfrac{1}{(-5)^n}x^{2n+1}$ converges absolutely when $\left|\dfrac{-1}{5}x^2\right|<1$. We solve

this inequality below:

```
Solve[x^2/5==1,x]
```

```
   {{x -> -Sqrt[5]}, {x -> Sqrt[5]}}
```

```
Plot[{1,x^2/5},{x,-3,3}]
```

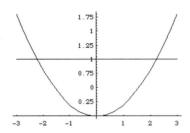

We conclude that $\displaystyle\sum_{n=0}^{\infty}\frac{1}{(-5)^n}x^{2n+1}$ converges absolutely when $-\sqrt{5}<x<\sqrt{5}$. We investigate if $\displaystyle\sum_{n=0}^{\infty}\frac{1}{(-5)^n}x^{2n+1}$ converges when $x=-\sqrt{5}$ and $x=\sqrt{5}$ separately. We first substitute $x=-\sqrt{5}$ in a_n. The resulting alternating series diverges, since the a_n which results does not approach zero as n approaches infinity.

```
PowerExpand[a[n] /. x->-Sqrt[5]]//Simplify

        2 n   1/2 + n
   (-1)     5
  -(---------------)
            n
        (-5)


PowerExpand[a[n] /. x->Sqrt[5]]//Simplify

   1/2 + n
  5
  --------
       n
   (-5)
```

We conclude that the interval of convergence of the series $\displaystyle\sum_{n=0}^{\infty}\frac{1}{(-5)^n}x^{2n+1}$ is the open interval $\left(-\sqrt{5},\sqrt{5}\right)$.

For (b), we use the **Ratio test**. The Ratio test says that if $\sum a_n$ is a series with positive terms and $\ell=\lim\limits_{n\to\infty}\dfrac{a_{n+1}}{a_n}$, then

   i. the series converges if $\ell<1$;

  ii. diverges if $\ell>1$; and

 iii. no conclusion can be drawn if $\ell=1$.

In the same manner as above, we begin by defining a_n to be $\dfrac{4^{2n}}{n+2}(x-3)^n$. We then compute and simplify $\dfrac{a_{n+1}}{a_n}$, naming the resulting output `stepone`,

```
Clear[a]
a[n_]=4^(2n)(x-3)^n/(n+2);
stepone=a[n+1]/a[n]//Simplify
```

```
16 (2 + n) (-3 + x)
-------------------
       3 + n
```

and then compute $\lim\limits_{n\to\infty}16\dfrac{n+2}{n+3}(x-3)$, naming the resulting output `steptwo`.

```
steptwo=Limit[stepone,n->Infinity]
```

```
16 (-3 + x)
```

The result means that $\sum\limits_{n=0}^{\infty}\dfrac{4^{2n}}{n+2}(x-3)^n$ converges absolutely when $|16x-48|<1$. We solve this inequality below and then test to see if the series converges when $x=\dfrac{47}{16}$ and $x=\dfrac{49}{16}$ separately.

```
rp=Solve[steptwo==1,x]
lp=Solve[steptwo==-1,x]
```

```
         49
{{x -> --}}
         16
         47
{{x -> --}}
         16
```

```
a[n] /. rp[[1]]
```

```
  1  n  2 n
(--)   4
  16
----------
   2 + n
```

```
a[n] /. lp[[1]]
```

```
   1   n  2 n
(-(--))   4
   16
-------------
    2 + n
```

Since $\sum_{n=0}^{\infty} \frac{(-1)^n}{n+2}$ converges by the alternating series test and $\sum_{n=0}^{\infty} \frac{1}{n+2}$ diverges by the basic comparison test, we conclude that the interval of convergence of the series $\sum_{n=0}^{\infty} \frac{4^{2n}}{n+2}(x-3)^n$ is $\left[\frac{47}{16}, \frac{49}{16}\right)$. ∎

Computing Power Series

Recall that the power series expansion of a function f(x) about the point x=a is given by the expression

$$\sum_{n=0}^{\infty} \frac{f^{(n)}(a)}{n!}(x-a)^n .$$

Mathematica computes the power series expansion of a function f(x) about the point x = a up to order n with the command

Series[f[x],{x,a,n}].

The symbol O[x-a]^(n+1) appearing in the output that results from the Series[f[x],{x,a,n}] command represents the terms that are omitted from the power series for f expanded about the point x=a. The O-term is removed from the output of the Series command with the Normal command; the result is a polynomial function.

Several familiar power series are computed below using this command.

EXAMPLE: Find the first few terms of the power series for the given function about the indicated point:
(a) $\cos x$ about $x = 0$;   (b) e^x about $x = 0$;
(c) $\sin x$ about $x = \pi$; and   (d) $\ln x$ about $x = 1$.

SOLUTION: Entering

```
Series[Cos[x],{x,0,6}]

         2     4    6
        x     x    x                7
    1 - -- + -- - --- + O[x]
         2    24   720
```

computes the terms of the power series for $\cos x$ about $x = 0$ to order 6; entering

```
Series[Exp[x],{x,0,7}]
```

$$1 + x + \frac{x^2}{2} + \frac{x^3}{6} + \frac{x^4}{24} + \frac{x^5}{120} + \frac{x^6}{720} + \frac{x^7}{5040} + O[x]^8$$

computes the terms of the powers series for e^x about x = 0 to order 7; entering

```
Series[Sin[x],{x,Pi,5}]
```

$$-(-Pi + x) + \frac{(-Pi + x)^3}{6} - \frac{(-Pi + x)^5}{120} +$$

$$O[-Pi + x]^6$$

computes the terms of the power series for $\sin x$ about $x = \pi$ to order 5; and entering

$$(-1 + x) - \frac{(-1 + x)^2}{2} + \frac{(-1 + x)^3}{3} - \frac{(-1 + x)^4}{4} +$$

$$\frac{(-1 + x)^5}{5} - \frac{(-1 + x)^6}{6} + \frac{(-1 + x)^7}{7} -$$

$$\frac{(-1 + x)^8}{8} + O[-1 + x]^9$$

computes the terms of the power series for $\ln x$ about $x = 1$ to order 8. ∎

Mathematica can also compute the general formula for the power series expansion of a function y(x). The results of entering the following commands

```
Series[y[x],{x,0,3}]
```

$$y[0] + y'[0] x + \frac{y''[0] x^2}{2} + \frac{y^{(3)}[0] x^3}{6} + O[x]^4$$

```
Series[y[x],{x,a,3}]
```

$$y[a] + y'[a] (-a + x) + \frac{y''[a] (-a + x)^2}{2} +$$

```
      (3)              3
     y   [a] (-a + x)                  4
     ----------------- + O[-a + x]
              6
```

are the power series for y(x) about x=0 and x=a to order 3, respectively.

Note that the result of entering a `Series` command is not a function that can be evaluated when x is a number. However, we can remove the remainder term of the power series `Series[f[x],{x,a,n}]` with the command `Normal[Series[f[x],{x,a,n}]]` and evaluate the resulting polynomial. Hence, with the `Normal` command, a polynomial is obtained. This polynomial serves as an approximation to the function f(x). These ideas are illustrated below.

EXAMPLE: Find the fifth degree Maclaurin polynomial of $f(x) = \tan^{-1} x$. Compare the graphs of $f(x) = \tan^{-1} x$ and the polynomial.

SOLUTION: If f is a function with n derivatives at 0, then the nth degree Maclaurin polynomial of f is

$$\sum_{k=0}^{n} \frac{f^{(k)}(0)}{k!} x^k .$$

Below, we define `ser1` to be the power series expansion for the function $f(x) = \tan^{-1} x$ about x=0 to order 5. To illustrate that the resulting output is not a function, we attempt to evaluate `ser1` when x=1. Note the error messages that occur.

```
ser1=Series[ArcTan[x],{x,0,5}]

        3    5
       x    x          6
   x - -- + -- + O[x]
        3    5


ser1 /. x->2

     SeriesData::ssdn:
        Attempt to evaluate a series at the number 2;
           returning Indeterminate.
     Indeterminate
```

However, we can use `Normal` to remove the O-term which represents the omitted higher-order terms of the series. Below, we use `Normal` and name the resulting output `poly`. Note that `poly` is an expression which can be evaluated for particular numbers. In fact, `poly` represents the fifth degree Maclaurin polynomial of $f(x) = \tan^{-1} x$.

```
poly=Normal[ser1]

        3    5
       x    x
   x - -- + --
        3    5

poly /. x->2

    86
    --
    15
```

Finally, we use `Plot` to compare the graphs of `poly` and $f(x) = \tan^{-1} x$. The graph of $f(x) = \tan^{-1} x$ is dashed and the graph of `poly` is in black. Note that `poly` appears to approximate f well on an interval containing 0.

```
Plot[{ArcTan[x],poly},{x,-3/2,3/2},
     PlotStyle->{Dashing[{.01}],GrayLevel[0]}]
```

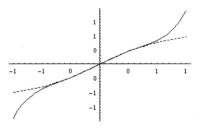

We can also use `Series` to compute Taylor polynomials. If f is a function with n derivatives at x=a, then the **nth degree Taylor polynomial** of f at x=a is

$$\sum_{k=0}^{n} \frac{f^{(k)}(a)}{k!}(x-a)^{k}.$$

EXAMPLE: Find the 8th degree Taylor polynomial of f(x) about x=1 if $f(x) = e^{-(x-1)^2(x+1)^2}$. Compare the graphs of the polynomial and f.

SOLUTION: After clearing all prior definitions of f, we define and graph f naming the result `plotf`. Note that `plotf` is not displayed since the option `DisplayFunction->Identity` is included. The option `AxesOrigin->{0,0}` assures that the axes in the plot intersect at the point (0,0); the option `PlotStyle->Dashing[{.01}]` assures that the resulting displayed graph is dashed.

```
Clear[f]
f[x_]=Exp[-(x-1)^2(x+1)^2];
plotf=Plot[f[x],{x,-1.75,1.75},PlotStyle->Dashing[{.01}],
      AxesOrigin->{0,0},DisplayFunction->Identity];
```

Next, we define `ser` to be the power series of f about x=1 to order 8. We then
remove the O-term from `ser` with `Normal` and name the resulting polynomial
`poly`. `poly` represents the 8th degree Taylor polynomial of f(x) about x=1.

```
ser=Series[f[x],{x,1,8}]
```

$$1 - 4 (-1 + x)^2 - 4 (-1 + x)^3 + 7 (-1 + x)^4 +$$

$$16 (-1 + x)^5 + \frac{4 (-1 + x)^6}{3} - 28 (-1 + x)^7 -$$

$$\frac{173 (-1 + x)^8}{6} + O[-1 + x]^9$$

```
poly=Normal[ser]
```

$$1 - 4 (-1 + x)^2 - 4 (-1 + x)^3 + 7 (-1 + x)^4 +$$

$$16 (-1 + x)^5 + \frac{4 (-1 + x)^6}{3} - 28 (-1 + x)^7 -$$

$$\frac{173 (-1 + x)^8}{6}$$

Next, we graph `poly` and name the resulting graph `plotpoly`. `plotf` and
`plotpoly` are displayed together with `Show`. Note that if the option

```
DisplayFunction->$DisplayFunction
```

had not been included in the `Show` command, the graphs would not have been
displayed.

```
plotpoly=Plot[poly,{x,-1.75,1.75},DisplayFunction->Identity];
Show[plotf,plotpoly,PlotRange->{-2,3/2},
      DisplayFunction->$DisplayFunction]
```

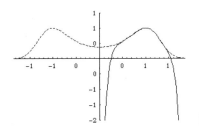

Application: Approximating the Remainder

Let f have (at least) n+1 derivatives in an interval containing a. **Taylor's Theorem** says that if x is any number in the interval, then

$$f(x) = \underbrace{\sum_{k=0}^{n} \frac{f^{(k)}(a)}{k!}(x-a)^k}_{\substack{\text{nth degree Taylor} \\ \text{polynomial of f} \\ \text{at } x=a.}} + \underbrace{\frac{f^{(n+1)}(z)}{(n+1)!}(x-a)^{n+1}}_{\text{nth remainder}},$$

where z is between a and x. We may use Taylor's Theorem to estimate the error involved when using a Taylor polynomial to approximate a given function.

EXAMPLE: Find an upper bound on the error when using the 4th degree Maclaurin polynomial of f(x) to approximate f(x) on the interval $[0,1/2]$ if $f(x) = \dfrac{x}{x^2+1}$. What is an upper bound on the error when using the 10th degree Maclaurin polynomial to approximate f(x) on the interval $[0,1/2]$?

SOLUTION: We proceed by clearing all prior definitions of f, defining f, and then graphing f.

```
Clear[f]
f[x_]=x/(x^2+1);
Plot[f[x],{x,-4,4}]
```

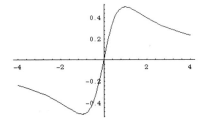

Since we will be computing several Maclaurin polynomials for f, we define `mp` to compute the nth Maclaurin polynomial of f. We then use `mp` to compute the 4th degree Maclaurin polynomial of f.

```
mp[n_]:=Normal[Series[f[x],{x,0,n}]]
mp[4]
```

$$x - x^3$$

Since we will examine the (n+1)st derivative when estimating an upper bound on the error, we next define `d` to compute the (n+1)st derivative of f and then replace the x's by z's. We then compute `d[4]`.

```
d[n_]:=(D[f[x],{x,n+1}] /. x->z)//Simplify
d[4]
```

$$\frac{120\ (1 - 15\ z^2 + 15\ z^4 - z^6)}{(1 + z^2)^6}$$

To estimate the maximum value of `d[4]` on the interval [0,1/2], we graph `d[4]`. We see that the maximum value of `d[4]` on the interval [0,1/2] is 120, which occurs when z=0.

```
Plot[d[4],{z,0,2}]
```

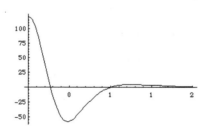

Next, we define `r` to compute the nth remainder and compute `r[4]`.

```
r[n_]:=d[n] x^(n+1)/(n+1)!//Simplify
r[4]
```

$$\frac{x^5\ (1 - 15\ z^2 + 15\ z^4 - z^6)}{(1 + z^2)^6}$$

Since we know that the maximum value of `d[4]` on [1,1/2] is 120, it follows that the maximum possible value of `r[4]` for any value of x in the interval [0,1/2] is

$$\frac{120}{120}\left(\frac{1}{2}\right)^5 = \frac{1}{32} \approx 0.03125.$$

Below, we use `Plot` to graph both f and the 4th degree Maclaurin polynomial on the interval $[0,1/2]$. Be sure to include the command `Evaluate` so that `mp[4]` is computed immediately; otherwise, error messages result.

```
Plot[Evaluate[{f[x],mp[4]}],{x,0,1/2},
      PlotStyle->{Dashing[{.01}],GrayLevel[0]}]
```

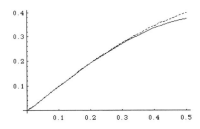

We proceed in the same manner in estimating an upper bound on the error when using the 10th degree Maclaurin polynomial. First, we compute the 11th derivative of f and then graph this function on the interval $[0,1/2]$.

```
d[10]
```

$$
(39916800 \ (-1 + 66 \ z^2 - 495 \ z^4 + 924 \ z^6 - \\
495 \ z^8 + 66 \ z^{10} - z^{12})) \ / \ (1 + z^2)^{12}
$$

```
Plot[d[10],{z,0,1}]
```

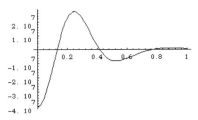

Next, computing the 10th remainder, we have:

```
r[10]
```

$$
(x^{11} \ (-1 + 66 \ z^2 - 495 \ z^4 + 924 \ z^6 - 495 \ z^8 + \\
66 \ z^{10} - z^{12})) \ / \ (1 + z^2)^{12}
$$

Thus, the maximum possible error is $\dfrac{4 \times 10^7}{11!}\left(\dfrac{1}{2}\right)^{11} \approx 0.000489299$.

```
4 10^7/11! (1/2)^11//N
```

```
0.000489299
```

In the graph below, we see that the graphs of f and the 10th Maclaurin polynomial are virtually identical on the interval [0,1/2].

```
Plot[Evaluate[{f[x],mp[10]}],{x,0,1/2},
      PlotStyle->{Dashing[{.01}],GrayLevel[0]}]
```

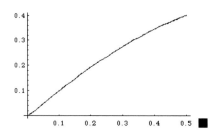

Application: Series Solutions to Differential Equations

Power series can be used to find series solutions of some differential equations. This topic is discussed in further detail in section 7.3.

EXAMPLE: Use power series to approximate a function y(x) that satisfies the differential equation $4y'' + 4y' + 37y = 0$ and the initial conditions $y(0) = y'(0) = 2$.

SOLUTION: Let $y(x) = \displaystyle\sum_{n=0}^{\infty} a_n x^n$ be a function that satisfies the differential equation and initial conditions. Below, after clearing all prior definitions of y, we define sery to be the power series expansion of y about x=0 to order 10.

```
Clear[y]
sery=Series[y[x],{x,0,10}]
```

$$y[0] + y'[0] \ x + \frac{y''[0] \ x^2}{2} + \frac{y^{(3)}[0] \ x^3}{6} +$$

```
    (4)     4    (5)     5    (6)     6
   y   [0] x    y   [0] x    y   [0] x
   ---------- + ---------- + ---------- +
       24          120          720


    (7)     7    (8)     8    (9)     9
   y   [0] x    y   [0] x    y   [0] x
   ---------- + ---------- + ---------- +
      5040        40320        362880


    (10)      10
   y    [0] x             11
   ------------ + O[x]
     3628800
```

Since we must have the condition that $y(0) = y'(0) = 2$, we replace the symbols $y(0)$ and $y'(0)$ by 2 in sery and name the resulting output sersol.

```
sersol=sery /. {y[0]->2,y'[0]->2}
```

```
                     2    (3)     3    (4)     4
           y''[0] x    y   [0] x    y   [0] x
  2 + 2 x + --------- + ---------- + ---------- +
               2            6           24


   (5)     5    (6)     6    (7)     7
  y   [0] x    y   [0] x    y   [0] x
  ---------- + ---------- + ---------- +
     120          720          5040


   (8)     8    (9)     9    (10)     10
  y   [0] x    y   [0] x    y    [0] x             11
  ---------- + ---------- + ------------ + O[x]
     40320        362880        3628800
```

sersol must satisfy the differential equation $4y'' + 4y' + 37y = 0$. Therefore, we substitute sersol into the equation $4y'' + 4y' + 37y = 0$ and name the resulting output eq.

```
eq=4D[sersol,{x,2}]+4D[sersol,x]+37sersol==0
```

```
                                         (3)
     (82 + 4 y''[0]) + (74 + 4 y''[0] + 4 y   [0])


             37 y''[0]      (3)          (4)
     x + (--------- + 2 y   [0] + 2 y   [0])
              2


      2      37 y   [0]    2 y   [0]    2 y   [0]
     x  + (---------- + --------- + ---------)
              6            3            3
```

$$x^3 + \left(\frac{37 \, y^{(4)}[0]}{24} + \frac{y^{(5)}[0]}{6} + \frac{y^{(6)}[0]}{6}\right) x^4 +$$

$$\left(\frac{37 \, y^{(5)}[0]}{120} + \frac{y^{(6)}[0]}{30} + \frac{y^{(7)}[0]}{30}\right) x^5 +$$

$$\left(\frac{37 \, y^{(6)}[0]}{720} + \frac{y^{(7)}[0]}{180} + \frac{y^{(8)}[0]}{180}\right) x^6 +$$

$$\left(\frac{37 \, y^{(7)}[0]}{5040} + \frac{y^{(8)}[0]}{1260} + \frac{y^{(9)}[0]}{1260}\right) x^7 +$$

$$\left(\frac{37 \, y^{(8)}[0]}{40320} + \frac{y^{(9)}[0]}{10080} + \frac{y^{(10)}[0]}{10080}\right) x^8 + O[x]^9 \ \backslash$$

$$== 0$$

At this point, we note that two power series are equal, if and only if all their coefficients are exactly the same. When we equate the coefficients on the left-hand side of eq with those on the right (namely, 0), we obtain a system of linear equations. This system of linear equations is obtained below with LogicalExpand and named lineqs.

```
lineqs=LogicalExpand[eq]
```

$$82 + 4 \, y''[0] == 0 \ \&\&$$

$$74 + 4 \, y''[0] + 4 \, y^{(3)}[0] == 0 \ \&\&$$

$$\frac{37 \, y''[0]}{2} + 2 \, y^{(3)}[0] + 2 \, y^{(4)}[0] == 0 \ \&\&$$

$$\frac{37 \, y^{(3)}[0]}{6} + \frac{2 \, y^{(4)}[0]}{3} + \frac{2 \, y^{(5)}[0]}{3} == 0 \ \&\&$$

$$\frac{37 \, y^{(4)}[0]}{24} + \frac{y^{(5)}[0]}{6} + \frac{y^{(6)}[0]}{6} == 0 \ \&\&$$

```
       (5)         (6)         (7)
   37 y   [0]     y  [0]     y   [0]
   ---------- + ------- + ------- == 0 &&
      120         30          30


       (6)         (7)         (8)
   37 y   [0]     y  [0]     y   [0]
   ---------- + ------- + ------- == 0 &&
      720         180         180


       (7)         (8)         (9)
   37 y   [0]     y  [0]     y   [0]
   ---------- + ------- + ------- == 0 &&
      5040        1260        1260


       (8)         (9)         (10)
   37 y   [0]     y  [0]     y    [0]
   ---------- + ------- + -------- == 0
      40320       10080       10080
```

We then use `Solve` to solve this system for the unknowns and name the resulting output roots.

```
    roots=Solve[lineqs]

         (10)          28969841
     {{y    [0] -> -(--------),
                        512

         (9)           5439299              41
      y    [0] -> -(-------), y''[0] -> -(--),
                     128                   2

         (3)               (4)         1501
      y    [0] -> 2, y    [0] -> ----,
                                   8

         (5)          1649   (6)          48941
      y    [0] -> -(----), y    [0] -> -(-----),
                     8                    32

         (7)         54977   (8)         1371001
      y    [0] -> -----, y    [0] -> -------}}
                    16                   128
```

The values obtained above are then substituted into our series solution, sersol.

```
    sersol /. roots[[1]]

                    2    3        4          5
              41 x    x     1501 x    1649 x
    2 + 2 x - ----- + -- + ------- - ------- -
                4     3       192       960
```

$$
\frac{48941\,x^{6}}{23040} + \frac{54977\,x^{7}}{80640} + \frac{1371001\,x^{8}}{5160960} -
$$

$$
\frac{5439299\,x^{9}}{46448640} - \frac{28969841\,x^{10}}{1857945600} + O[x]^{11}
$$

Since this series cannot be evaluated for real numbers, we remove the O-term with
`Normal` and name the result `poly`. This is our approximate solution of the
equation.

```
poly=Normal[sersol /. roots[[1]]]
```

$$
2 + 2\,x - \frac{41\,x^{2}}{4} + \frac{x^{3}}{3} + \frac{1501\,x^{4}}{192} - \frac{1649\,x^{5}}{960} -
$$

$$
\frac{48941\,x^{6}}{23040} + \frac{54977\,x^{7}}{80640} + \frac{1371001\,x^{8}}{5160960} -
$$

$$
\frac{5439299\,x^{9}}{46448640} - \frac{28969841\,x^{10}}{1857945600}
$$

We then graph `poly` on the interval $[0,\pi]$ and name the resulting graph `papprox`
for later use.

```
papprox=Plot[poly,{x,0,Pi}]
```

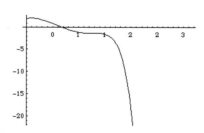

In this case, we can also use `DSolve` to find an exact solution of the equation,
naming the result `sol`. We will discuss this topic in more detail in Chapter 7.

```
Clear[y]
sol=DSolve[{4y''[x]+4y'[x]+37y[x]==0,y[0]==2,y'[0]==2},y[x],x]
```

```
        2 Cos[3 x]     Sin[3 x]
{{y[x] -> ----------  + --------}}
            x/2           x/2
           E             E
```

The exact solution is graphed below and named `pexact`.

pexact=Plot[y[x] /. sol,{x,0,2Pi}]

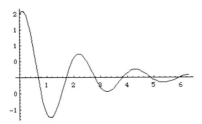

To compare the approximate solution with the exact solution, we use `Show` to show both graphs simultaneously.

Show[pexact,papprox]

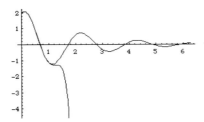

Alternatively, if we let $y(x) = \displaystyle\sum_{n=0}^{\infty} a_n x^n$, computing y' and y'' results in

$$y'(x) = \sum_{n=0}^{\infty} n a_n x^{n-1} = \sum_{n=0}^{\infty} (n+1)a_{n+1}x^n$$

and

$$y''(x) = \sum_{n=0}^{\infty} n(n-1)a_n x^{n-2} = \sum_{n=0}^{\infty} (n+2)(n+1)a_{n+2}x^n .$$

Substituting into the equation $4y'' + 4y' + 37y = 0$ yields

$$4\left(\sum_{n=0}^{\infty}(n+2)(n+1)a_{n+2}x^n\right) + 4\left(\sum_{n=0}^{\infty}(n+1)a_{n+1}x^n\right) + 37\left(\sum_{n=0}^{\infty}a_n x^n\right) = 0 .$$

Simplifying and equating coefficients we obtain

$$a_{n+2} = \frac{-4(n+1)a_{n+1} - 37a_n}{4(n+2)(n+1)} \text{ or, equivalently, } a_n = \frac{-4(n-1)a_{n-1} - 37a_{n-2}}{4n(n-1)} .$$

These coefficients may then be calculated with Mathematica. In the following we define a[0] and a[1] using the initial conditions specified in the problem. We then define a[n] to be the coefficient of x^n in $y(x) = \sum_{n=0}^{\infty} a_n x^n$ using the formula obtained above. Note that a is defined to remember the values it computes. We then compute the values of a[n] for values of n from 0 to 30 in steps of 3. Of course, these are the same as those found previously.

```
a[0]=2;
a[1]=2;
a[n_]:=a[n]=(-4(n-1)a[n-1]-37a[n-2])/(4n (n-1));
Table[{n,a[n]},{n,0,30,3}]
```

```
                  1            48941
     {{0, 2}, {3, -}, {6, -(-----)},
                  3            23040

            5439299             150988501
      {9, -(--------)}, {12, ------------},
            46448640           980995276800

            145836290927
      {15, ----------------},
            5356234211328000

            117187844492359
      {18, --------------------},
            839171926357180416000

            131470113409897
      {21, -(------------------------)},
            1575668699371835228160000

            362762759591677421
      {24, -(------------------------------)},
            273931496124561380364779520000

            78035955515313060037
      {27, -(----------------------------------)},
            456712286913674961413178654720000000

      {30,

             81930307485915574145659
       -----------------------------------------}}
       142406544757979162368320409970933760000000  ■
```

Other Series

In calculus, we show that if $f(x) = \sum_{n=0}^{\infty} c_n x^n$ is a power series with radius of convergence $r > 0$, then f is differentiable and integrable on its interval of convergence. However, if f is not a power series, this result is not true in general. For example, the function $f(x) = \sum_{n=0}^{\infty} \frac{\cos(3^n x)}{2^n}$ is continuous for all values of x but nowhere differentiable. We can use Mathematica to help us see why this function is not differentiable. Let $f_k(x) = \sum_{n=0}^{k} \frac{\cos(3^n x)}{2^n}$. Below, we use Mathematica to recursively define f_k.

```
Clear[f]
f[0]=Cos[x];
f[k_]:=f[k]=f[k-1]+Cos[3^k x]/2^k
```

We define f using the form `f[k_]:=f[k]=...` so that Mathematica "remembers" the values it computes. Thus, to compute `f[5]`, Mathematica uses the previously computed values, namely `f[4]`, to compute `f[5]`.

Note that we can produce the same results by defining f with the command

```
f[k_]:=Sum[Cos[3^n x]/2^n,{n,0,k}].
```

The disadvantage of defining f in this manner is that Mathematica does not "remember" the previously computed values and thus takes longer to compute `f[k]` for larger values of k.

Next, we use `Table` to generate `f[3]`, `f[6]`, `f[9]`, and `f[12]`, naming the result `tograph` and then display tograph, in `TableForm`.

```
tograph=Table[f[n],{n,3,12,3}];
TableForm[tograph]

               Cos[3 x]    Cos[9 x]    Cos[27 x]
     Cos[x] + -------- + -------- + ---------
                  2           4          8
               Cos[3 x]    Cos[9 x]    Cos[27 x]
     Cos[x] + -------- + -------- + --------- +
                  2           4          8

       Cos[81 x]    Cos[243 x]    Cos[729 x]
       --------- + ---------- + ----------
           16           32           64
               Cos[3 x]    Cos[9 x]    Cos[27 x]
     Cos[x] + -------- + -------- + --------- +
                  2           4          8
```

```
Cos[81 x]    Cos[243 x]    Cos[729 x]
--------- + ---------- + ---------- +
    16           32            64

Cos[2187 x]    Cos[6561 x]    Cos[19683 x]
----------- + ----------- + ------------
    128            256             512
          Cos[3 x]    Cos[9 x]    Cos[27 x]
Cos[x] + -------- + -------- + --------- +
             2           4           8

Cos[81 x]    Cos[243 x]    Cos[729 x]
--------- + ---------- + ---------- +
    16           32            64

Cos[2187 x]    Cos[6561 x]    Cos[19683 x]
----------- + ----------- + ------------ +
    128            256             512

Cos[59049 x]    Cos[177147 x]    Cos[531441 x]
------------ + ------------- + -------------
    1024            2048              4096
```

Finally, we use `Table` and `Plot` to graph each of the functions in `tograph` and name the resulting set of four graphs `graphs`. Note that `tograph[[i]]` corresponds to the ith element of `tograph`; `tograph[[1]]` is the first function in `tograph`, corresponding to $\cos x + \frac{1}{2}\cos 3x + \frac{1}{4}\cos 9x + \frac{1}{8}\cos 27x$. Be sure to include the command `Evaluate` within the `Plot` command and be sure to nest square brackets correctly. To compare the graphs we use `Partition` to partition `graphs` into a set consisting of two sets of two graphs and name the result `toshow`. Last, `GraphicsArray` is used to show the set of graphs `toshow`.

```
graphs=Table[Plot[Evaluate[tograph[[i]]],{x,0,3Pi},
       DisplayFunction->Identity],{i,1,4}];
toshow=Partition[graphs,2];
Show[GraphicsArray[toshow]]
```

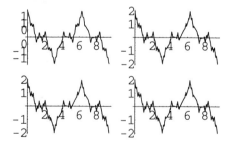

From the graphs above, we see that for large values of k, the graph of $f_k(x)$, although actually smooth, appears "jagged", and thus we might suspect that f(x) is indeed continuous everywhere but nowhere differentiable.

3.6 Multivariable Calculus

Limits of Functions of Two Variables

One of the first topics discussed in mulivariable calculus courses is limits of functions of two variables. Mathematica's graphics and numerical capabilities are helpful in investigating these problems.

EXAMPLE: Show that the limit $\lim\limits_{(x,y)\to(0,0)} \dfrac{xy}{x^2+y^2}$ does not exist.

SOLUTION: We begin by clearing all prior definitions of f, if any, and defining $f(x,y) = \dfrac{xy}{x^2+y^2}$. Next, we use `Plot3D` to graph f on the rectangle $[-2,2]\times[-2,2]$ and `ContourPlot` to graph several level curves on the same rectangle. Note that the point $(0,0)$ is not in the domain of f and if Mathematica computes `f[0,0]` while generating either graph, several error messages will result but the graphs will be displayed correctly.

```
Clear[f]
f[x_,y_]=x y/(x^2+y^2);
p1=Plot3D[f[x,y],{x,-2,2},{y,-2,2},DisplayFunction->Identity]
c1=ContourPlot[f[x,y],{x,-2,2},{y,-2,2},ContourShading->False,
        Axes->Automatic,AxesOrigin->{0,0},DisplayFunction->Identity];
Show[GraphicsArray[{p1,c1}]]
```

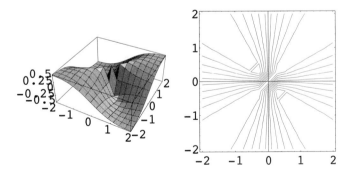

From the graphs above, we see that f behaves strangely near $(0,0)$. In fact, from the graph of the level curves, we see that near $(0,0)$, f attains many different values. We can obtain further evidence that the limit does not exist by computing the value of f for various points chosen randomly near $(0,0)$. Below, we use `Table`, `Random`, and `Real` to generate 10 ordered pairs near $(0,0)$ and name the result pts. Note that since Random is included in the calculation, your results will almost certainly be different from those here. Tables and lists are discussed in more detail in Chapters 4 and 5.

```
pts=Table[Random[Real,{-10^-i,10^-i}],{i,1,10},{2}]
```

$\{\{0.0407686, -0.0753765\}, \{-0.00335464, 0.00237699\},$

$\{0.000961185, 0.000332866\}, \{-0.0000963083, 0.0000547618\},$

$\{4.94446 \times 10^{-6}, -2.24515 \times 10^{-6}\}, \{-3.88716 \times 10^{-7}, 2.84132 \times 10^{-7}\},$

$\{6.52111 \times 10^{-8}, 1.04603 \times 10^{-8}\}, \{5.04186 \times 10^{-9}, 4.23245 \times 10^{-9}\},$

$\{9.69119 \times 10^{-10}, 7.635 \times 10^{-10}\}, \{-5.37026 \times 10^{-11}, -4.85893 \times 10^{-11}\}\}$

Next, we define a function g, which given x and y, returns x, y, and f(x,y). We then use Map to compute the value of g for each point in pts and display the result in TableForm. Note that the first column corresponds to the x-coordinate, the second column the y-coordinate, and the third column the value of f(x,y).

```
g[{x_,y_}]={x,y,f[x,y]}
```

$$\{x, y, \frac{x\ y}{x^2 + y^2}\}$$

```
Map[g,pts]//TableForm
```

0.0407686	-0.0753765	-0.418453
-0.00335464	0.00237699	-0.471728
0.000961185	0.000332866	0.309223
-0.0000963083	0.0000547618	-0.429685
4.94446×10^{-6}	-2.24515×10^{-6}	-0.376455
-3.88716×10^{-7}	2.84132×10^{-7}	-0.47641
6.52111×10^{-8}	1.04603×10^{-8}	0.156383
5.04186×10^{-9}	4.23245×10^{-9}	0.492441
9.69119×10^{-10}	7.635×10^{-10}	0.486112
-5.37026×10^{-11}	-4.85893×10^{-11}	0.497508

From the third column, we see that f does not appear to approach any particular value for points chosen randomly near $(0,0)$. In fact, along the line $y = x$ we see that $f(x,y) = f(x,x) = \frac{1}{2}$, while along the line $y = -x$, $f(x,y) = f(x,-x) = -\frac{1}{2}$. Thus, f does not have a limit as $(x,y) \to (0,0)$.

```
Simplify[f[x,x]]

    1
    -
    2

Simplify[f[x,-x]]

      1
    -(-)
      2
```

■

Partial Differentiation

Partial derivatives can be calculated with Mathematica using the command

$$D[f[x,y],variable],$$

where f[x,y] is differentiated with respect to variable.

Second order derivatives can be found using D[f[x,y],variable1,variable2], where f[x,y] is differentiated first with respect to variable2 and then with respect to variable1.

EXAMPLE: Calculate $\frac{\partial f}{\partial x}$, $\frac{\partial f}{\partial y}$, $\frac{\partial^2 f}{\partial x \partial y}$, $\frac{\partial^2 f}{\partial y \partial x}$, and the value of $\frac{\partial^2 f}{\partial y \partial x}$ when $x = \frac{\pi}{2}$ and y=1 if $f(x,y) = \sin xy$.

SOLUTION: After defining f, we graph f on the rectangle $[-\pi,\pi] \times [-\pi,\pi]$. The option PlotPoints->20 is included in the Plot3D command to help assure that the resulting displayed graph is smooth.

```
Clear[f]
f[x_,y_]=Sin[x y]

    Sin[x y]

Plot3D[f[x,y],{x,-Pi,Pi},{y,-Pi,Pi},PlotPoints->20]
```

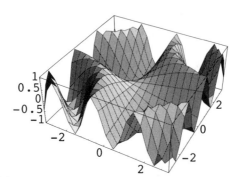

Next, we use D to compute the indicated partial derivatives. Entering

```
D[f[x,y],x]
```

```
    y Cos[x y]
```

computes $\dfrac{\partial f}{\partial x}$, entering

```
D[f[x,y],y]
```

```
    x Cos[x y]
```

computes $\dfrac{\partial f}{\partial y}$, and entering

```
D[f[x,y],x,y]
```

```
    Cos[x y] - x y Sin[x y]
```

computes $\dfrac{\partial^2 f}{\partial x \partial y}$. Similarly, entering

```
dyx=D[f[x,y],y,x]
```

```
    Cos[x y] - x y Sin[x y]
```

computes $\dfrac{\partial^2 f}{\partial y \partial x}$ and names the resulting output **dyx**. Note that $\dfrac{\partial^2 f}{\partial x \partial y} = \dfrac{\partial^2 f}{\partial y \partial x}$.

Below, we calculate the value of $\dfrac{\partial^2 f}{\partial y \partial x}$ when $x = \dfrac{\pi}{2}$ and y=1.

```
dyx /. {x->Pi/2,y->1}
```

```
    -Pi
    ---
     2
```

■

Higher order derivatives with respect to the same variable can be determined with the command `D[f[x,y],{variable,n}]`. This command computes the nth partial derivative of f with respect to `variable`.

EXAMPLE: Calculate $\dfrac{\partial^2 h}{\partial x^2}$ and $\dfrac{\partial^2 h}{\partial y^2}$ if $h(x,y) = \sqrt[3]{x^2 + y^2}$.

SOLUTION: Proceeding as in the previous example, we first define and graph h and then use D to calculate the indicated partial derivatives.

```
Clear[h]
h[x_,y_]=(x^2+y^2)^(1/3);
Plot3D[h[x,y],{x,-2,2},{y,-2,2}]
```

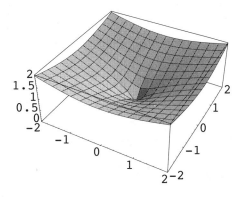

Entering

```
hxx=D[h[x,y],{x,2}]
```

$$\frac{-8\ x^2}{9\ (x^2\ +\ y^2)^{5/3}}\ +\ \frac{2}{3\ (x^2\ +\ y^2)^{2/3}}$$

computes $\dfrac{\partial^2 h}{\partial x^2}$ and names the resulting output `hxx`. We can display `hxx` as a single fraction with `Together`.

```
Together[hxx]
```

$$\frac{2\ (-x^2\ +\ 3\ y^2)}{9\ (x^2\ +\ y^2)^{5/3}}$$

Similarly, entering

```
Together[D[h[x,y],{y,2}]]
```

```
        2     2
   2  (3 x  - y )
   --------------
        2     2 5/3
   9  (x  + y )
```

computes $\dfrac{\partial^2 h}{\partial y^2}$ and combines the result into a single fraction. ∎

Other Methods of Computing Derivatives

The command `Derivative` can also be used to compute derivatives of functions. For example, if `f[x]` is a function of a single variable, the command `Derivative[1][f][a]` computes the derivative of f with respect to x and evaluates the result by replacing x by a; the command

$$Derivative[n][f][a]$$

computes the nth derivative of f with respect to x and evaluates the result by replacing x by a. Similarly, if `f[x,y]` is a function of two variables, the command

$$Derivative[1,0][f][a,b]$$

computes the partial derivative of f with respect to x and evaluates the result by replacing x by a and y by b; the command `Derivative[0,1][f][a,b]` computes the partial derivative of f with respect to y and evaluates the result by replacing x by a and y by b; and the command `Derivative[n,m][f][a,b]` computes the nth partial derivative of f with respect to x and then the mth partial derivative of f with respect to y and evaluates the result by replacing x by a and y by b.

EXAMPLE: If $g(x,y) = e^{-(x^2+y^2)/8}\left(\cos^2 x + \sin^2 y\right)$, calculate $\dfrac{\partial g}{\partial x}(x,y)$, $\dfrac{\partial^2 g}{\partial x \partial y}(x,y)$, and $\dfrac{\partial^3 g}{\partial x \partial y^2}\left(\dfrac{\pi}{3},\dfrac{\pi}{6}\right)$.

SOLUTION: Below, we define and graph g on the rectangle $[-\pi,\pi]\times[-\pi,\pi]$.

```
Clear[g]
g[x_,y_]=Exp[-(x^2+y^2)/8]*(Cos[x]^2+Sin[y]^2);
Plot3D[g[x,y],{x,-Pi,Pi},{y,-Pi,Pi},PlotPoints->25]
```

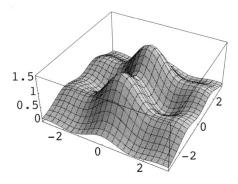

After defining g, we illustrate that `Derivative[1,0][g][x,y]` and `D[g[x,y],x]` both produce the same result.

```
gx=Derivative[1,0][g][x,y]
```

$$-2\,E^{(-x^2-y^2)/8}\,\mathrm{Cos}[x]\,\mathrm{Sin}[x]\;-$$

$$\frac{E^{(-x^2-y^2)/8}\,x\,(\mathrm{Cos}[x]^2+\mathrm{Sin}[y]^2)}{4}$$

```
D[g[x,y],x]
```

$$-2\,E^{(-x^2-y^2)/8}\,\mathrm{Cos}[x]\,\mathrm{Sin}[x]\;-$$

$$\frac{E^{(-x^2-y^2)/8}\,x\,(\mathrm{Cos}[x]^2+\mathrm{Sin}[y]^2)}{4}$$

Similarly `Derivative[1,1][g][x,y]` and `Derivative[g[x,y],x,y]` produce the same result:

```
gxy=Derivative[1,1][g][x,y]
```

$$
\frac{E^{(-x^2 - y^2)/8} \; y \; \text{Cos}[x] \; \text{Sin}[x]}{2} \; -
$$

$$
\frac{E^{(-x^2 - y^2)/8} \; x \; \text{Cos}[y] \; \text{Sin}[y]}{2} \; +
$$

$$
\frac{E^{(-x^2 - y^2)/8} \; x \; y \; (\text{Cos}[x]^2 + \text{Sin}[y]^2)}{16}
$$

```
D[g[x,y],x,y]
```

$$
\frac{E^{(-x^2 - y^2)/8} \; y \; \text{Cos}[x] \; \text{Sin}[x]}{2} \; -
$$

$$
\frac{E^{(-x^2 - y^2)/8} \; x \; \text{Cos}[y] \; \text{Sin}[y]}{2} \; +
$$

$$
\frac{E^{(-x^2 - y^2)/8} \; x \; y \; (\text{Cos}[x]^2 + \text{Sin}[y]^2)}{16}
$$

Last, we compute $\dfrac{\partial^3 g}{\partial x \partial y^2}\left(\dfrac{\pi}{3},\dfrac{\pi}{6}\right)$.

```
Derivative[1,2][g][Pi/3,Pi/6]
```

$$
\frac{\text{Sqrt}[3]}{8 \, E^{(5\,\text{Pi}^2)/288}} \; - \; \frac{7\,\text{Pi}}{96 \, E^{(5\,\text{Pi}^2)/288}} \; +
$$

$$
\frac{\text{Pi}^2}{128 \, \text{Sqrt}[3] \, E^{(5\,\text{Pi}^2)/288}} \; - \; \frac{\text{Pi}^3}{13824 \, E^{(5\,\text{Pi}^2)/288}}
$$

Note that when we can use `Derivative` to evaluate the derivative of a function for a particular number or point in a single command. On the other hand, using `D`, we must first compute the derivative and then evaluate the result at the desired number or point. ∎

Application: Classifying Critical Points

Mathematica can be used to assist in determining certain properties of functions of more than one variable. Just as we found critical points of single variable functions in an earlier example, we can perform a similar task in the case of multivariable functions. We begin with the following. Let f be a real-valued function of two variables with continuous second-order partial derivatives. A **critical point** of f is a point (x_0, y_0) in the interior of the domain of f for which $f_x(x_0, y_0) = \frac{\partial f}{\partial x}(x_0, y_0) = 0$ and $f_y(x_0, y_0) = \frac{\partial f}{\partial y}(x_0, y_0) = 0$. Critical points are classified by the Second Derivatives Test which is stated below. Let $f_x(x, y) = \frac{\partial f}{\partial x}(x, y)$, $f_y(x, y) = \frac{\partial f}{\partial y}(x, y)$, $f_{xx}(x, y) = \frac{\partial^2 f}{\partial x^2}(x, y)$, $f_{yy}(x, y) = \frac{\partial^2 f}{\partial y^2}(x, y)$, and $f_{xy}(x, y) = \frac{\partial^2 f}{\partial x \partial y}(x, y)$.

Second Derivatives Test for Extrema

Let (x_0, y_0) be a critical point of a function f of two variables and let

$$D(f, (x_0, y_0)) = \begin{vmatrix} f_{xx}(x_0, y_0) & f_{xy}(x_0, y_0) \\ f_{xy}(x_0, y_0) & f_{yy}(x_0, y_0) \end{vmatrix} = (f_{xx}(x_0, y_0))(f_{yy}(x_0, y_0)) - (f_{xy}(x_0, y_0))^2 .$$

a. if $D(f, (x_0, y_0)) > 0$ and $f_{xx}(x_0, y_0) > 0$, then f has a relative minimum at (x_0, y_0);

b. if $D(f, (x_0, y_0)) > 0$ and $f_{xx}(x_0, y_0) < 0$, then f has a relative maximum at (x_0, y_0);

c. if $D(f, (x_0, y_0)) < 0$, then f has a saddle at (x_0, y_0); and

d. if $D(f, (x_0, y_0)) = 0$, no conclusion can be drawn and (x_0, y_0) is called a **degenerate critical point**.

We show how Mathematica can be used to locate and classify the critical points of a function of two variables in the following example.

> **EXAMPLE:** Locate and classify all the critical points of the function $f(x,y) = -120x^3 - 30x^4 + 18x^5 + 5x^6 + 30xy^2$.

SOLUTION: After clearing all prior definitions of f, we define f. Be sure to include the space between the x and y^2 to denote multiplication.

```
Clear[f]
f[x_,y_]=-120x^3-30x^4+18x^5+5x^6+30x y^2
```

$$-120 \overset{3}{x} - 30 \overset{4}{x} + 18 \overset{5}{x} + 5 \overset{6}{x} + 30 \overset{2}{x y}$$

The critical points of f correspond to the solutions of the system of equations

$$\begin{cases} \dfrac{\partial f}{\partial x}(x,y) = 0 \\ \dfrac{\partial f}{\partial y}(x,y) = 0 \end{cases}.$$

In order to find the critical points of f(x,y), the partial derivatives $f_x(x,y)$ and $f_y(x,y)$ are calculated and set equal to zero. These steps are shown below. We then locate the critical points by solving the system of equations

$$\begin{cases} f_x(x,y) = 0 \\ f_y(x,y) = 0 \end{cases}$$

with `Solve` and naming the resulting list of numbers `critpts`.

```
dfx=D[f[x,y],x]
dfy=D[f[x,y],y]
```

$$-360 \overset{2}{x} - 120 \overset{3}{x} + 90 \overset{4}{x} + 30 \overset{5}{x} + 30 \overset{2}{y}$$
$$60 \, x \, y$$

```
critpts=Solve[{dfx==0,dfy==0}]
```

```
{{y -> 0, x -> -3}, {y -> 0, x -> -2},

  {y -> 0, x -> 0}, {y -> 0, x -> 0},

  {y -> 0, x -> 0}, {y -> 0, x -> 0},

  {y -> 0, x -> 2}}
```

Next, we define `dfxx`, `dfyy`, and `dfxy` to be $f_{xx}(x,y)$, $f_{yy}(x,y)$, and $f_{xy}(x,y)$, respectively:

```
dfxx=D[f[x,y],{x,2}]
dfyy=D[f[x,y],{y,2}]
dfxy=D[f[x,y],x,y]
```

$$-720\ x\ -\ 360\ x^2\ +\ 360\ x^3\ +\ 150\ x^4$$
$$60\ x$$
$$60\ y$$

and `discriminant` to be $\left(f_{xx}(x,y)\right)\left(f_{yy}(x,y)\right)-\left(f_{xy}(x,y)\right)^2$.

```
discriminant=dfxx dfyy-dfxy^2;
```

In order to classify the critical points, we need to evaluate `dfxx` and `discriminant` for each critical point. Below, we evaluate `dfxx` and `discriminant` when $x = -2$ and $y = 0$.

```
{dfxx,discriminant} /. {x->-2,y->0}
```

```
{-480, 57600}
```

Since `dfxx` is negative and `discriminant` is positive, the f has a relative maximum at $(-2,0)$. Below, we define `data` to be the ordered quadruple `{x,y,dfxx,discriminant}` and evaluate `data` for each set of ordered pairs in `critpts`. In addition, we use `TableForm` and `TableHeadings` to display the result in row-and-column form with columns labeled `x`, `y`, `dfxx`, and `discriminant`.

```
data={x,y,dfxx,discriminant};
TableForm[data /. critpts,
    TableHeadings->{None,{"x","y","dfxx","discriminant"}}]
```

x	y	dfxx	discriminant
-3	0	1350	-243000
-2	0	-480	57600
0	0	0	0
0	0	0	0
0	0	0	0
0	0	0	0
2	0	2400	288000

By the Second Derivatives test we conclude that $(0,0)$ is a degenerate critical point, f has a relative minimum at $(2,0)$, $(-3,0)$ is a saddle, and f has a relative maximum at $(-2,0)$. ∎

Application: Tangent Planes

Mathematica can be used to determine the equation of the plane tangent to a three-dimensional surface at a particular point as well as to graph this plane simultaneously with the surface. Let f be a real-valued function of two variables. If both $f_x(x_0, y_0)$ and $f_y(x_0, y_0)$ exist, then an equation of the plane tangent to the graph of f at the point $(x_0, y_0, f(x_0, y_0))$ is given by

$$f_x(x_0, y_0)(x - x_0) + f_y(x_0, y_0)(y - y_0) - (z - z_0) = 0 .$$

Solving for z yields the function (of two variables)

$$z = f_x(x_0, y_0)(x - x_0) + f_y(x_0, y_0)(y - y_0) + z_0 .$$

We demonstrate the usefulness of Mathematica in finding and graphing the tangent plane in the example below.

EXAMPLE: Find an equation of the plane tangent to the graph of

$$k(x, y) = e^{-(x^2 + y^2)/8}\left(\cos^2 x + \sin^2 y\right)$$

when x=−1 and y=2.

SOLUTION: We begin by defining and graphing k on the rectangle $[-5, 5] \times [-\pi, \pi]$. The resulting graphics object is named `plotk`.

```
Clear[k]
k[x_,y_]=Exp[-(x^2+y^2)/8](Cos[x]^2+Sin[y]^2);
plotk=Plot3D[k[x,y],{x,-5,5},{y,-Pi,Pi},PlotPoints->30]
```

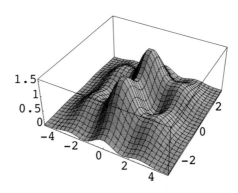

To find an equation of the tangent plane, we must compute the partial derivatives $\dfrac{\partial k}{\partial x}$ and $\dfrac{\partial k}{\partial y}$ and evaluate each when $x = -1$ and $y = 2$. Below, we calculate $\dfrac{\partial k}{\partial x}(-1,2)$ and $\dfrac{\partial k}{\partial y}(-1,2)$, naming the resulting output kx and ky, respectively. In each case, N is used to obtain an approximation of the result.

```
kx=D[k[x,y],x] /. {x->-1,y->2}
N[kx]
ky=D[k[x,y],y] /. {x->-1,y->2}
N[ky]
```

```
                          2         2
    2 Cos[1] Sin[1]   Cos[1]  + Sin[2]
    --------------- + -----------------
          5/8                 5/8
          E                 4 E
    0.636418
                          2         2
    2 Cos[2] Sin[2]   Cos[1]  + Sin[2]
    --------------- - -----------------
          5/8                 5/8
          E                 2 E
    -0.704499
```

Hence, the tangent plane is defined by the function $z = kx(x+1) + ky(y-2) + k(-1,2)$.

Below, we define and graph z on the rectangle $[-5,5] \times [-\pi,\pi]$. Note that plotz is not displayed because the option DisplayFunction->Identity is included. Last, we use Show to display both plotk and plotz.

```
z=kx(x+1)+ky(y-2)+k[-1,2];
plotz=Plot3D[z,{x,-5,5},{y,-Pi,Pi},DisplayFunction->Identity];
Show[plotk,plotz,PlotRange->{0,2},DisplayFunction->$DisplayFunction]
```

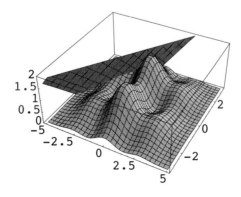

Application: The Method of Lagrange Multipliers

Certain types of optimization problems can be solved using the method of Lagrange multipliers which is based on the following theorem:

> **Lagrange's theorem:** Let f(x,y) and g(x,y) be real-valued functions with continuous partial derivatives and let f have an extreme value at a point (x_0, y_0) on the smooth constraint curve g(x,y)=c. If $g_x(x_0, y_0) \neq 0$ and $g_y(x_0, y_0) \neq 0$, then there is a real number λ satisfying $f_x(x_0, y_0) = \lambda g_x(x_0, y_0)$ and $f_y(x_0, y_0) = \lambda g_y(x_0, y_0)$.

The points (x_0, y_0) at which the extreme values occur correspond to the points where the level curves of f(x,y) are tangent to the graph of g(x,y)=c.

EXAMPLE: Find the maximum and minimum values of $f(x,y) = x^2 + 4y^3$ subject to the constraint $x^2 + 4y^2 = 1$.

SOLUTION: We can graph $f(x,y) = x^2 + 4y^3$ on the ellipse $x^2 + 4y^2 = 1$ using `ParametricPlot3D`. A parametrization of $x^2 + 4y^2 = 1$ is given by

$$\begin{cases} x(t) = \cos t \\ y(t) = \dfrac{\sin t}{2}, 0 \le t \le 2\pi . \end{cases}$$

To graph this equation in space, we set the z-coordinate equal to 0.

```
pp1=ParametricPlot3D[{Cos[t],Sin[t]/2,0},{t,0,2Pi}]
```

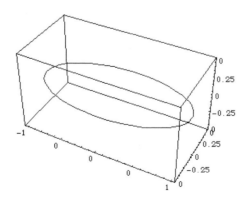

To graph $f(x,y) = x^2 + 4y^3$ on the ellipse $x^2 + 4y^2 = 1$, we first define f and then use ParametricPlot3D to graph the set of points

$$\begin{cases} x(t) = \cos t \\ y(t) = \dfrac{\sin t}{2} \\ z(t) = f\left(\cos t, \dfrac{\sin t}{2}\right) \end{cases}.$$

To see the graph of f on the ellipse, we use Show to display pp1 and pp2 simultaneously.

```
Clear[f]
f[x_,y_]=x^2+4y^3;
pp2=ParametricPlot3D[{Cos[t],Sin[t]/2,f[Cos[t],Sin[t]/2]},{t,0,2Pi},
          DisplayFunction->Identity];
Show[pp1,pp2,BoxRatios->{1,1,1},DisplayFunction->$DisplayFunction]
```

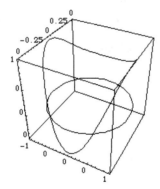

From the graphs above, we see that $f(x,y) = x^2 + 4y^3$ attains a minimum and maximum on the ellipse $x^2 + 4y^2 = 1$. The minimum and maximum values occur at the points where the level curves of f are tangent to the graph of $x^2 + 4y^2 = 1$. We can see these points using ContourPlot. To graph the equation $x^2 + 4y^2 = 1$, we first define $g(x,y) = x^2 + 4y^2 - 1$. Then, the graph of $x^2 + 4y^2 = 1$ is the graph of the level curve of g corresponding to 0. Below, we use ContourPlot to graph this level curve and name the resulting graphics object cp1.

```
g[x_,y_]=x^2+4y^2-1;
cp1=ContourPlot[g[x,y],{x,-2,2},{y,-2,2},
          Contours->{0},PlotPoints->30,ContourShading->False,
          Frame->False,Axes->Automatic,AxesOrigin->{0,0}]
```

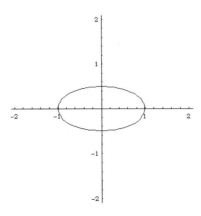

Next, we use `ContourPlot` to graph several level curves of f and name the
resulting graphics object `cp2`. The graphs `cp1` and `cp2` are shown together with
`Show`.

```
cp2=ContourPlot[f[x,y],{x,-2,2},{y,-2,2},
            PlotPoints->30,Contours->10,ContourShading->False,
            PlotRange->{-2,2},Frame->False,Axes->Automatic,
            AxesOrigin->{0,0},DisplayFunction->Identity];
Show[cp1,cp2,DisplayFunction->$DisplayFunction]
```

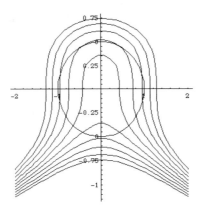

In order to find the points at which the minimum and maximum values are
located, the first order derivatives (with respect to x and y) of f and g are
computed so that Lagrange's Theorem can be applied. We then define `eq1`, `eq2`,
and `eq3` to be the equations representing $\frac{\partial f}{\partial x}=\lambda\frac{\partial g}{\partial x}$, $\frac{\partial f}{\partial y}=\lambda\frac{\partial g}{\partial y}$, and $g(x,y)=0$,
respectively. (The lambda in Lagrange's Theorem is represented in the calculations
below as `lambda`.)

```
dfx=D[f[x,y],x];
dfy=D[f[x,y],y];
dgx=D[g[x,y],x];
dgy=D[g[x,y],y];

eq1=dfx==lambda dgx;
eq2=dfy==lambda dgy;
eq3=g[x,y]==0;
```

The values of x, y, and lambda which satisfy the system of three equations in Lagrange's Theorem are determined using Solve and the resulting output is named extpoints. The solutions of this system are ordered triples (x, y, lambda). The values of x and y in each ordered triple represent the point at which f may have a maximum or minimum value.

```
extpoints=Solve[{eq1,eq2,eq3},{x,y,lambda}]

                3                 1
  {{lambda -> -(-), x -> 0, y -> -(-)},
                4                 2

              3             1
    {lambda -> -, x -> 0, y -> -},
              4             2

    {lambda -> 1, x -> -1, y -> 0},

    {lambda -> 1, x -> 1, y -> 0},

                      -I           2
    {lambda -> 1, x -> -- Sqrt[7], y -> -},
                       3            3

                    I            2
    {lambda -> 1, x -> - Sqrt[7], y -> -}}
                    3            3
```

Thus, the maximum and minimum values of f are found by substituting these points back into the function f(x,y) and comparing the resulting values of f. We may evaluate each point directly as we have done below to compute $f\left(0,-\frac{1}{2}\right)$.

```
f[0,-1/2]

      1
    -(-)
      2
```

However, we may also compute all four values with a singe command. Below, we compute f(x,y) for each value in the table extpoints. We use TableForm and TableHeadings to display the result in row-and-column form. The columns are labeled x, y, and f[x,y].

```
TableForm[{x,y,f[x,y]} /. extpoints,
    TableHeadings->{None,{"x","y","f[x,y]"}}]
```

```
x                y        f[x,y]
                  1          1
                -(-)       -(-)
0                 2          2
                  1          1
                  -          -
0                 2          2
-1                0          1
1                 0          1
-I                2          11
-- Sqrt[7]        -          --
3                 3          27
I                 2          11
- Sqrt[7]         -          --
3                 3          27
```

Thus, we see that maximum values of 1 occur at $(-1,0)$ and $(1,0)$; a minimum value of $-\dfrac{1}{2}$ occurs at $\left(0,-\dfrac{1}{2}\right)$. The imaginary results, containing the symbol I which represents $i = \sqrt{-1}$, are ignored. ∎

Double Integrals

The command `Integrate`, used to compute single integrals, is used to compute iterated integrals. The command which computes the iterated integral

$$\int_{x0}^{x1}\int_{y0}^{y1} f(x,y)\,dy\,dx$$

is

```
Integrate[f[x,y],{x,x0,x1},{y,y0,y1}]
```

and the definite integral $\displaystyle\int_{x0}^{x1}\int_{y0}^{y1} f(x,y)\,dy\,dx$ is numerically evaluated with the command

```
NIntegrate[f[x,y],{x,x0,x1},{y,y0,y1}].
```

The first variable given (in this case, x), corresponds to the **outermost** integral and integration with respect to this variable is done last. Also, the inner limits of integration (in this case, y0 and y1) can be functions of the outermost variable.

EXAMPLE: Evaluate each of the integrals: (a) $\iint xy^2 dx\,dy$; (b) $\int_1^2 \int_{1-y}^{\sqrt{y}} xy^2 dx\,dy$; and (c)

$\int_0^{\pi/6} \int_0^{\pi/2} \big(y\sin(x) - x\sin(y)\big)dy\,dx$.

SOLUTION: In each case we use `Integrate`. Entering

```
Integrate[x y^2,y,x]
```

$$\frac{x^2\,y^3}{6}$$

computes $\iint xy^2 dx\,dy$, entering

```
Integrate[x y^2,{y,1,2},{x,1-y,Sqrt[y]}]
```

$$\frac{163}{120}$$

computes $\int_1^2 \int_{1-y}^{\sqrt{y}} xy^2 dx\,dy$, and entering

```
Integrate[y Sin[x]-x Sin[y],{x,0,Pi/6},{y,0,Pi/2}]
```

$$\frac{Pi^2}{8} + \frac{-\frac{Pi^2}{9} - \frac{Sqrt[3]\ Pi^2}{2}}{8}$$

computes $\int_0^{\pi/6} \int_0^{\pi/2} \big(y\sin(x) - x\sin(y)\big)dy\,dx$. ∎

When `Integrate` produces an exact value of an integral but an approximation is desired, `N` can be used to compute an approximation of the result. On the other hand, in cases when the double integral cannot be computed exactly, or when a numerical approximation is desired instead of an exact result, the command

```
NIntegrate[f[x,y],{x,xmin,xmax},{y,ymin,ymax}]
```

can frequently be used to quickly calculate a numerical approximation of the integral.

EXAMPLE: Find both an exact and approximate value of $\int_0^{\sqrt{\pi}}\int_0^{\sqrt{\pi}}\cos(x^2-y^2)\,dy\,dx$.

SOLUTION: In this case, `Integrate` produces an exact value of the integral which we name `value`.

```
value=Integrate[Cos[x^2-y^2],{x,0,Sqrt[Pi]},{y,0,Sqrt[Pi]}]
```

```
                         2
    (Pi (FresnelC[Sqrt[2]]  +

                       2
         FresnelS[Sqrt[2]] )) / 2
```

The symbols `FresnelC` and `FresnelS` represent the Fresnel integrals C(x) and S(x), respectively.

```
?FresnelC
?FresnelS
```

```
    FresnelC[  x] gives the Fresnel integral C[x]
       = Integrate[Cos[Pi t^2/2], {t, 0, x}].
    FresnelS[x] gives the Fresnel integral S[x]
       = Integrate[Sin[Pi t^2/2], {t, 0, x}].
```

An approximation of `value` is then obtained with `N`. Note that the result is an approximation of π.

```
N[value]
```

```
    3.14159  ∎
```

EXAMPLE: Approximate the value of $\int_0^1\int_0^1\sin(e^{xy})\,dy\,dx$.

SOLUTION: In this case, `Integrate` does not produce a result as indicated below.

```
Integrate[Sin[Exp[x y]],{x,0,1},{y,0,1}]
```

```
    General::intinit:
       Loading integration packages -- please
          wait.
```

However, `NIntegrate` quickly approximates the integral.

```
NIntegrate[Sin[Exp[x y]],{x,0,1},{y,0,1}]
```

```
    0.917402  ∎
```

Application: Volume

A typical application of iterated integrals is determining the volume of a region in three-dimensional space. We illustrate the solution of a problem of this type in the following example.

> **EXAMPLE:** Find the volume of the region between the graphs of $q(x,y) = e^{-x^2} \cos(x^2 + y^2)$ and $w(x,y) = 3 - x^2 - y^2$ on the domain $[-1,1] \times [-1,1]$.

SOLUTION: After defining q and w, the region can be viewed using Mathematica's Plot3D command.

```
Clear[q,w]
q[x_,y_]=Exp[-x^2]Cos[x^2+y^2];
w[x_,y_]=3-x^2-y^2;
pq=Plot3D[q[x,y],{x,-1,1},{y,-1,1},DisplayFunction->Identity];
pw=Plot3D[w[x,y],{x,-1,1},{y,-1,1},DisplayFunction->Identity];
Show[pq,pw,DisplayFunction->$DisplayFunction]
```

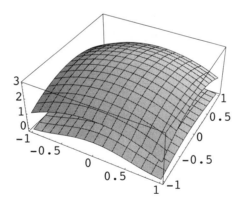

In this case, we see that q and w do not intersect on the rectangle. However, to compute the volume of the region we must know which function is larger on the interval. We proceed by graphing q and w on the interval $[-3,3] \times [-3,3]$ to observe that the graphs do intersect and computing q(0,0) and w(0,0).

```
pq2=Plot3D[q[x,y],{x,-3,3},{y,-3,3},DisplayFunction->Identity];
pw2=Plot3D[w[x,y],{x,-3,3},{y,-3,3},DisplayFunction->Identity];
Show[pq2,pw2,DisplayFunction->$DisplayFunction]
```

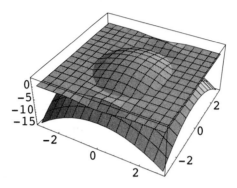

```
w[0,0]
q[0,0]
```

    3
    1

Since w(0,0) is greater than q(0,0), we conclude that w is larger than q on the rectangle $[-1,1] \times [-1,1]$. Thus, the region is bounded above by w(x,y) and below by q(x,y) so that the volume is given by the double integral $\iint\limits_{[-1,1] \times [-1,1]} (w(x,y) - q(x,y))dA$ which is equivalent to the iterated integral $\int_{-1}^{1} \int_{-1}^{1} (w(x,y) - q(x,y))dy\,dx$. We then use NIntegrate to approximate the integral $\int_{-1}^{1} \int_{-1}^{1} (w(x,y) - q(x,y))dy\,dx$.

```
volume=NIntegrate[w[x,y]-q[x,y],{x,-1,1},{y,-1,1}]
```

    7.02707

■

In the example below, the surfaces intersect. Hence, we must determine the region of integration.

EXAMPLE: Find the volume of the solid bounded by the graphs of $f(x,y) = 1 - x - y$ and $g(x,y) = 2 - x^2 - y^2$.

SOLUTION: After defining f and g, we use Plot3D to graph each function and then use Show to observe that the graphs intersect.

```
Clear[f,g]
f[x_,y_]=1-x-y;
g[x_,y_]=2-x^2-y^2;
plotf=Plot3D[f[x,y],{x,-3/2,2},{y,-3/2,2},DisplayFunction->Identity];
plotg=Plot3D[g[x,y],{x,-3/2,2},{y,-3/2,2},DisplayFunction->Identity];
Show[plotf,plotg,ViewPoint->{0.010, -2.723, 2.000},
        DisplayFunction->$DisplayFunction]
```

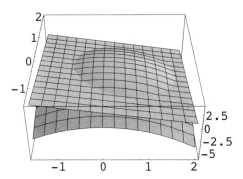

From the graph, we see that the region is bounded above by the paraboloid and below by the plane. In this case, we note that the graphs of $f(x,y)=1-x-y$ and $g(x,y)=2-x^2-y^2$ intersect when $f(x,y)=g(x,y)$, which is equivalent to the equation $1-x-y=2-x^2-y^2$. Simplifying and completing the square yields

$$x^2-x+y^2-y=\left(x-1/2\right)^2+\left(y-1/2\right)^2=\left(\sqrt{3/2}\right)^2$$

so that the graph of the intersection is a circle with center $(1/2,1/2)$ and radius $\sqrt{3/2}$. To graph this equation, we note that the graph of the $f(x,y)=g(x,y)$ is the graph of the level curve of $f(x,y)-g(x,y)$ corresponding to 0. Below, we use ContourPlot to graph the circle $f(x,y)=g(x,y)$.

```
ContourPlot[f[x,y]-g[x,y],{x,-3/2,2},{y,-3/2,2},
        Contours->{0},ContourShading->False,PlotPoints->30,
        Frame->False,Axes->Automatic,AxesOrigin->{0,0}]
```

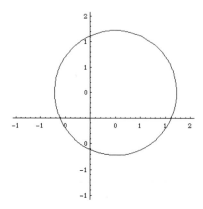

Let R denote the interior and boundary of the circle:

$$R = \left\{(x,y):(x-1/2)^2 + (y-1/2)^2 \le 3/2\right\}.$$

Then the volume of the region bounded by the graphs of f and g is given by the double integral $\iint_R (g(x,y)-f(x,y))\,dA$ since g is the larger of the two functions over R, as shown in the graph above. To rewrite this double integral as an iterated integral, we first use `Solve` to solve the equation $1-x-y = 2-x^2-y^2$ for y and name the resulting output `intpts`. These numbers represent the upper and lower limit of integration with respect to y and are extracted from `intpts` with `y1=intpts[[1,1,2]]` and `y2=intpts[[2,1,2]]`, respectively. Extracting data from lists is discussed in more detail in Chapters 4 and 5. Note that an alternate method of solution can be performed in the same way by solving the equation for x. Note that the result of entering `intpts[[1,1,2]]` and `intpts[[2,1,2]]` corresponds to the equations $y = \dfrac{1+\sqrt{5+4x-4x^2}}{2}$ and $y = \dfrac{1-\sqrt{5+4x-4x^2}}{2}$.

```
intpts=Solve[f[x,y]==g[x,y],y]

        {{y ->
                                2
             1 - Sqrt[1 - 4 (-1 - x + x )]
             -----------------------------},
                          2
          {y ->
                                2
             1 + Sqrt[1 - 4 (-1 - x + x )]
             -----------------------------}}
                          2
```

```
y1=intpts[[1,1,2]]
y2=intpts[[2,1,2]]
```

```
                        2
    1 - Sqrt[1 - 4 (-1 - x + x )]
    -----------------------------
                 2
                        2
    1 + Sqrt[1 - 4 (-1 - x + x )]
    -----------------------------
                 2
```

Then, to find the upper and lower limits of integration with respect to x we solve the equation $5 + 4x - 4x^2 = 0$. We illustrate how the expression $5 + 4x - 4x^2$ is extracted from y2 with [[...]]. We name the resulting solutions xvals. Extracting elements from lists is discussed in more detail in Chapters 4 and 5.

```
y2[[2]]
```

```
                        2
    1 + Sqrt[1 - 4 (-1 - x + x )]
```

```
y2[[2,2]]
```

```
                      2
    Sqrt[1 - 4 (-1 - x + x )]
```

```
y2[[2,2,1]]
```

```
                 2
    1 - 4 (-1 - x + x )
```

```
xvals=Solve[y2[[2,2,1]]==0]
```

```
           4 - 4 Sqrt[6]
    {{x -> -------------},
               8

           4 + 4 Sqrt[6]
     {x -> -------------}}
               8
```

Note that entering xvals[[1,1,2]] yields $\frac{1-\sqrt{6}}{2}$, while xvals[[2,1,2]] yields $\frac{1+\sqrt{6}}{2}$.

```
x1=xvals[[1,1,2]]
x2=xvals[[2,1,2]]

  4 - 4 Sqrt[6]
  -------------
        8
  4 + 4 Sqrt[6]
  -------------
        8
```

Then, the volume is given by the iterated integral

$$\iint_R \big(g(x,y)-f(x,y)\big)dA = \int_{(1-\sqrt{6})/2}^{(1+\sqrt{6})/2} \int_{(1-\sqrt{5+4x-4x^2})/2}^{(1+\sqrt{5+4x-4x^2})/2} \big(g(x,y)-f(x,y)\big)dy\,dx$$

which is evaluated below in volume. Note that we do not need to retype the limits of integration since they have been named x1, x2, c, and y2 in previous calculations. We also obtain an approximation of volume with N.

```
volume=Integrate[g[x,y]-f[x,y],{x,x1,x2},{y,y1,y2}]

  9 Pi
  ----
    8
```

```
N[volume]

  3.53429
```

■

Triple Integrals

Triple iterated integrals are calculated in the same manner as double iterated integrals. The commands

```
Integrate[f[x,y,z],{z,z0,z1},{y,y0,y1},{x,x0,x1}]
```

and

```
NIntegrate[f[x,y,z],{z,z0,z1},{y,y0,y1},{x,x0,x1}]
```

attempt to evaluate and numerically evaluate, respectively, the triple iterated integral $\int_{z_0}^{z_1}\int_{y_0}^{y_1}\int_{x_0}^{x_1} f(x,y,z)dx\,dy\,dz.$

EXAMPLE: Evaluate $\int_0^3 \int_1^x \int_{z-x}^{z+x} e^{2x}(2y-z)dy\,dz\,dx$.

SOLUTION: Entering

```
Integrate[Exp[2x](2y-z),{x,0,3},{z,1,x},{y,z-x,z+x}]
```

```
     6
 1   59 E
 - + -----
 8    8
```

computes $\int_0^3 \int_1^x \int_{z-x}^{z+x} e^{2x}(2y-z)dy\,dz\,dx$. ■

We illustrate how triple integrals can be used to find the volume of a solid when using spherical coordinates.

EXAMPLE: Find the volume of the torus with equation in spherical coordinates $\rho = 5\sin\theta$.

SOLUTION: In general, the volume of the solid region D is given by $\iiint_D 1\,dV$. We proceed by graphing the torus. Since the equation of the torus is given in spherical coordinates we will use the command SphericalPlot3D to graph the torus. The command SphericalPlot3D is not a built-in command but is contained in the package **ParametricPlot3D**. Thus, we first load the package **ParametricPlot3D** located in the **Graphics** folder (or directory) and then use SphericalPlot3D to graph $\rho = 5\sin\theta$.

```
<<Graphics`ParametricPlot3D`
SphericalPlot3D[5 Sin[theta],{theta,0,Pi},{phi,0,2Pi},
      ViewPoint->{4.000, 0.540, 2.000}]
```

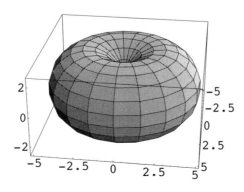

In the graph, we see that the volume of the torus is the volume of the set points with spherical coordinates (ρ, ϕ, θ) satisfying $0 \leq \phi \leq 2\pi$, $0 \leq \theta \leq \pi$, and $0 \leq \rho \leq 5\sin\theta$.

Thus, the volume is given by the triple integral $\iiint\limits_{D} 1\, dV = \int_0^{2\pi} \int_0^{\pi} \int_0^{5\sin\theta} \rho^2 \sin\theta\, d\rho\, d\theta\, d\phi$, evaluated below.

```
Integrate[r^2 Sin[theta],{phi,0,2Pi},{theta,0,Pi},{r,0,5Sin[theta]}]

          2
     125 Pi
     -------
        4
```

Thus, the volume of torus is $\dfrac{125}{4}\pi^2$. ∎

Higher-Order Integrals

Higher order iterated integrals are computed in the same manner as double and triple iterated integrals.

> **EXAMPLE:** Evaluate $\displaystyle\int_0^1 \int_0^x \int_0^{x+y} \int_0^{x+y+z} x\,y\,z\,w\, dw\, dz\, dy\, dx$.

SOLUTION: Entering

```
Integrate[x y z w, {x,0,1},{y,0,x}, {z,0,x+y},{w,0,x+y+z}]

     731
     ----
     1920
```

computes $\displaystyle\int_0^1 \int_0^x \int_0^{x+y} \int_0^{x+y+z} x\,y\,z\,w\, dw\, dz\, dy\, dx$. ∎

CHAPTER 4

Introduction to Lists and Tables

Chapter 4 introduces elementary operations on lists and tables. Chapter 4 is a prerequisite for Chapter 5 which discusses nested lists and tables in detail. The examples used to illustrate the various commands in this chapter are taken from calculus, business, and engineering applications.

4.1 Defining Lists

A **list** is a Mathematica object of the form

```
{element[[1]], element[[2]], . . . ,element[[n-1]], element[[n]]},
```

where `element[[i]]` is the ith element of the list. Elements of a list are separated by commas. Notice that lists are always enclosed in braces `{...}` and each element of a list may be (almost any) Mathematica object; even other lists. Since lists are Mathematica objects, they can be named. For easy reference, we will usually name lists.

Lists may be defined in a variety of ways. Lists may be completely typed in or they may be created with either the `Table` or `Array` commands. Given a function `f` and a number `n`, the command

```
Table[f[i],{i,n}  creates the list consisting of {f[1],...,f[n];
Table[f[i],{i,0,n}]  creates the list consisting of {f[0],...,f[n]};
Table[f[i],{i,n,m}]  creates the list {f[n],f[n+1],...,f[m-1],f[m]};
Table[f[i],{i,imin,imax,istep}]  creates the list
{f[imin],f[imin+istep],f[imin+2step],...,f[imax]};  and
Array[f,n]  creates the list {f[1],...,f[n]}.
```

In addition to the above, lists of numbers can be calculated using `Range`:

```
Range[n]  generates the list {1,2, ... , n};
Range[n1,n2]  generates the list {n1, n1+1, ... , n2-1, n2};  and
Range[n1,n2,nstep]  generates the list
{n1, n1+nstep,n1+2nstep, ... , n2-nstep,n2}.
```

EXAMPLE: Use Mathematica to generate the list {1,2,3,4,5,6,7,8,9,10}.

SOLUTION: Generally, a list can be constructed in several ways. In fact, each of the following five commands generates the list {1,2,3,4,5,6,7,8,9,10}.

```
{1,2,3,4,5,6,7,8,9,10}

      {1, 2, 3, 4, 5, 6, 7, 8, 9, 10}

Table [i,{i,10}]

      {1, 2, 3, 4, 5, 6, 7, 8, 9, 10}

Table[i,{i,1,10}]

      {1, 2, 3, 4, 5, 6, 7, 8, 9, 10}

Table[i/2,{i,2,20,2}]

      {1, 2, 3, 4, 5, 6, 7, 8, 9, 10}

Range[10]

      {1, 2, 3, 4, 5, 6, 7, 8, 9, 10}
```

∎

EXAMPLE: Use Mathematica to define `listone` to be the list of numbers consisting of 1, 3/2, 2, 5/2, 3, 7/2, and 4.

SOLUTION: In this case, we generate a table and name the resulting output `listone`. As in the previous example, we illustrate that `listone` can be created in several ways.

```
listone={1,3/2,2,5/2,3,7/2,4}
```

$$\{1, \ \frac{3}{2}, \ 2, \ \frac{5}{2}, \ 3, \ \frac{7}{2}, \ 4\}$$

```
listone=Table[i,{i,1,4,1/2}]
```

$$\{1, \ \frac{3}{2}, \ 2, \ \frac{5}{2}, \ 3, \ \frac{7}{2}, \ 4\}$$

Last, we define $i(n) = \frac{n}{2} + \frac{1}{2}$ and use **Array** to create the table `listone`.

```
i[n_]=n/2+1/2;
listone=Array[i,7]
```

$$\{1, \ \frac{3}{2}, \ 2, \ \frac{5}{2}, \ 3, \ \frac{7}{2}, \ 4\} \quad \blacksquare$$

In the following example, we define a list consisting of ordered pairs.

EXAMPLE: Create a list of the first 25 prime numbers. What is the fifteenth prime number?

SOLUTION: The built-in function **Prime[n]** yields the nth prime number. Below, we use **Table** to generate a list of the ordered pairs {n,Prime[n]} for n=1, 2, 3, ... , 25.

```
Table[{n,Prime[n]},{n,1,25}]
```

```
{{1, 2}, {2, 3}, {3, 5}, {4, 7}, {5, 11}, {6, 13},

  {7, 17}, {8, 19}, {9, 23}, {10, 29}, {11, 31},

  {12, 37}, {13, 41}, {14, 43}, {15, 47}, {16, 53},

  {17, 59}, {18, 61}, {19, 67}, {20, 71}, {21, 73},

  {22, 79}, {23, 83}, {24, 89}, {25, 97}}
```

From the resulting output, we see that the fifteenth prime number is 47. ∎

EXAMPLE: The **Fibonacci numbers** are defined by the recursive relationship $f(0) = 1$, $f(1) = 1$, and $f(n) = f(n-1) + f(n-2)$.
Create a list, **fiblist**, consisting of the first 10 Fibonacci numbers.

SOLUTION: We begin by defining f. Note that we define f using the form f[n_]:=f[n]=... so that Mathematica remembers the functional values it computes and thus avoids recomputing functional values previously computed. This is particularly advantageous if we were to compute the value of f for large values of n. We then use `Table` to compute a list consisting of the values of f for n=0, 1, ... , 9. The resulting list is a list of the first ten Fibonacci numbers.

```
Clear[f]
f[0]=1;
f[1]=1;
f[n_]:=f[n]=f[n-1]+f[n-2]
Table[f[n],{n,0,9}]
```

> {1, 1, 2, 3, 5, 8, 13, 21, 34, 55} ■

In addition, we can use `Table` to generate lists consisting of the same or similar objects.

EXAMPLE: (a) Generate a list consisting of five copies of the letter a. (b) Generate a table consisting of ten random integers between −10 and 10.

SOLUTION: Entering

```
Table[a,{5}]
```

> {a, a, a, a, a}

generates a table consisting of five copies of the letter a. For (b), we use the command `Random` to generate the desired table.

```
Table[Random[Integer,{-10,10}],{10}]
```

> {0, −5, −8, 6, 2, 0, −3, 7, 9, −7} ■

As indicated above, elements of lists can be numbers, ordered pairs, functions, and even other lists. For example, Mathematica has built-in definitions of many commonly used special functions. Consequently, lists of special functions can be quickly created.

EXAMPLE: The Mathematica function `Cyclotomic[n,x]` produces the cyclotomic polynomial of order n, $C_n(x) = \prod_k (x - e^{2\pi i k/n})$, where the product ranges over integer values of k which are relatively prime to n. The **cyclotomic polynomials** are irreducible over the integers. Create a table of the first ten cyclotomic polynomials and name the resulting table `polys`.

SOLUTION: Mathematica will display a list, like other output, on successive lines which may sometimes be difficult to read or interpret. The commands `TableForm` and `MatrixForm` are used to display lists in traditional row/column form. In the following, we first define `polys` to be a table consisting of the first ten cyclotomic polynomials. Note that the resulting output is not displayed because a semi-colon is included at the end of the command. We then use `TableForm` to display each of the ten polynomials in `polys` on successive lines.

```
polys=Table[Cyclotomic[n,x],{n,1,10}];
TableForm[polys]
```

$$-1 + x$$
$$1 + x$$
$$1 + x + x^2$$
$$1 + x^2$$
$$1 + x + x^2 + x^3 + x^4$$
$$1 - x + x^2$$
$$1 + x + x^2 + x^3 + x^4 + x^5 + x^6$$
$$1 + x^4$$
$$1 + x^3 + x^6$$
$$1 - x + x^2 - x^3 + x^4$$ ■

The following example shows that a variety of operations can be performed on lists. We will discuss other operations that can be performed on lists in the following sections.

EXAMPLE: The **Hermite polynomials**, $H_n(x)$, satisfy the differential equation $y'' - 2xy' + 2ny = 0$. The Mathematica command `HermiteH[n,x]` yields the Hermite polynomial $H_n(x)$. (a) Create a table of the first five Hermite polynomials; (b) evaluate each Hermite polynomial when x=1 and then compute the value of each Hermite polynomial for j=1, 6/5, 7/5, ... , 2; (c) compute the derivative of each Hermite polynomial in the table; and (d) graph the five Hermite polynomials on the interval [–2,2].

SOLUTION: We proceed by defining `hermitetable` to be the table consisting of the first five Hermite polynomials.

```
hermitetable=Table[HermiteH[n,x],{n,1,5}]
```

$$\{2 x, -2 + 4 x^2, -12 x + 8 x^3, 12 - 48 x^2 + 16 x^4,$$
$$120 x - 160 x^3 + 32 x^5 \}$$

We then use `->` to evaluate each member of `hermitetable` when x is replaced by 1.

```
hermitetable /. x->1
```

```
{2, 2, -4, -20, -8}
```

For (b), we use `Table` and `N` to evaluate the ordered pair `{i,hermitetable /
. x->i}` for i=1, 6/5, 7/5, ... , 2. Note that the elements of the resulting list are also lists.

```
Table[N[{i,hermitetable /. x->i}],{i,1,2,1/5}]
```

```
{{1., {2., 2., -4., -20., -8.}},
  {1.2, {2.4, 3.76, -0.576, -23.9424, -52.8538}},
  {1.4, {2.8, 5.84, 5.152, -20.6144, -98.9363}},
  {1.6, {3.2, 8.24, 13.568, -6.0224, -127.816}},
  {1.8, {3.6, 10.96, 25.056, 24.4416, -112.458}},
  {2., {4., 14., 40., 76., -16.}}}
```

In the same manner as when a built-in function is applied to a list of numbers, a built-in function applied to a list of functions results in each member of the list being evaluated by the given function. Therefore, we use `D` to compute the derivative of each term of `hermitetable`. Note that `int` could be used in the same manner to integrate each term of a table or list. .

```
D[hermitetable,x]
```

```
                    2              3
{2, 8 x, -12 + 24 x , -96 x + 64 x ,

          2        4
120 - 480 x  + 160 x }
```

To graph the list `hermitetable`, we use `Plot` to plot each function in the set `hermitetable` on the interval [–2,2]. Be sure to include `hermitetable` within the `Evaluate` command as indicated below. In this case, we specify that the displayed y-values consist of the interval [–50,50].

```
Plot[Evaluate[hermitetable],{x,-2,2},PlotRange->{-50,50}]
```

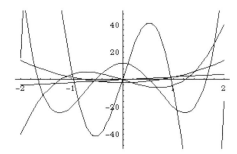

■

In the above example, applying D to the list `hermitetable` produces the list obtained from `hermitetable` by computing the derivative of each element of `hermitetable` with respect to x. If f is a function and `f[list]` returns

```
{f[list[[1]]],f[list[[2]]],...,f[list[[n]]]},
```

where `list={list[[1]],list[[2]],...,list[[n]]}`, then f is **listable**. Many built-in Mathematica functions, like D, are listable. To see if a built-in function `function` is listable, enter the command `Attributes[function]`; if `Listable` appears in the resulting list, the function `function` is listable.

A Word of Caution

As indicated above, when graphing a lists of functions `list`, the list must be included in the command using `Evaluate[list]` or errors result as indicated below.

```
funs={x,x^2,x^3};
Plot[funs,{x,-1,1}]
```

```
Plot::plnr: CompiledFunction[{x}, funs, -CompiledCode-][x]
    is not a machine-size real number at x = -1..
Plot::plnr: CompiledFunction[{x}, funs, -CompiledCode-][x]
    is not a machine-size real number at x = -0.916667.
Plot::plnr: CompiledFunction[{x}, funs, -CompiledCode-][x]
    is not a machine-size real number at x = -0.833333.
General::stop:
    Further output of Plot::plnr
    will be suppressed during this calculation.
```

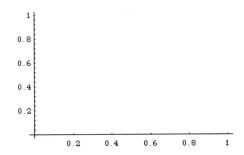

Entering the command `Plot[Evaluate[funs],{x,-1,1}]` graphs the functions x, x^2, and x^3 on the interval $[-1,1]$.

4.2 Operations on Lists

Extracting Elements of Lists

Individual elements of lists are obtained using double-square brackets [[...]] or Part. For example if table is a list, then entering table[[2]] or Part[table,2] returns the second element of the list table. The jth element (or part) of table is extracted with table[[j]] or Part[table,j]. Several elements can be extracted with Take. The first and last elements of table are extracted with First[table] and Last[table], respectively. The number of elements in a list table is obtained by entering the command Length[table].

EXAMPLE: A table corresponding to approximations of the first eight zeros of the Bessel function of the first kind of order zero, $J_0(x)$, is listed below. Use Mathematica to define this list to be zeros. Then, (a) determine the number of elements in zeros; (b) extract the third and fifth elements of zeros; (c) extract the fourth and sixth elements of zeros; (d) extract lists consisting of the first three elements of zeros, the fourth through sixth elements of zeros, and the last two elements of zeros; and (e) determine the location of the element 18.071.

| 2.4048 | 5.5201 | 8.6537 | 11.792 | 14.931 | 18.071 | 21.212 | 24.352 |

SOLUTION: We first define zeros to be the table of numbers listed above.

```
zeros={2.4048,5.5201,8.6537,11.792,14.931,18.071,21.212,24.352}

    {2.4048, 5.5201, 8.6537, 11.792, 14.931, 18.071, 21.212, 24.352}
```

The number of elements in the list zeros is obtained below with Length.

```
Length[zeros]

    8
```

The first and last elements of zeros are extracted with First and Last, respectively.

```
First[zeros]
Last[zeros]

    2.4048

    24.352
```

The third and seventh elements of zeros are extracted from zeros using double square brackets [[...]] and Part, respectively.

```
zeros[[3]]
```

>   8.6537

```
Part[zeros,7]
```

>   21.212

Below, we use `Part` to extract the fourth and sixth elements of `zeros` simultaneously.

```
Part[zeros,{4,6}]
```

>   {11.792, 18.071}

We use `Take` to extract the first three elements of zeros, the fourth through sixth elements of zeros, and the last two elements of zeros below.

```
Take[zeros,3]
Take[zeros,{4,6}]
Take[zeros,-2]
```

>   {2.4048, 5.5201, 8.6537}
>   {11.792, 14.931, 18.071}
>   {21.212, 24.352}

Last, we use `Position` to determine that the element 18.071 occurs in the sixth position of `zeros`.

```
Position[zeros,18.071]
```

>   {{6}}

■

Often, Mathematica's output is given to us as a list which we desire to use in subsequent calculations.

EXAMPLE: Let $f(x) = 3x^4 - 8x^3 - 30x^2 + 72x$. Locate and classify the critical points of f.

SOLUTION: We begin by clearing all prior definitions of f and then defining f. Since f is a polynomial, the critical numbers are found by solving the equation $f'(x) = 0$. The resulting list is named `critnums`.

```
Clear[f]
f[x_]=3x^4-8x^3-30x^2+72x;
critnums=Solve[f'[x]==0]
```

>   {{x -> -2}, {x -> 1}, {x -> 3}}

Note that `critnums` is actually a list of lists. For example, the number –2 is the second part of the first part of the second part of `critnums` as illustrated below.

```
critnums[[1]]
```

```
{x -> -2}
```

```
critnums[[1,1]]
```

```
x -> -2
```

```
critnums[[1,1,2]]
```

```
-2
```

Similarly, the numbers 1 and 3 are extracted with `critnums[[2,1,2]]` and `critnums[[3,1,2]]`, respectively.

```
critnums[[2,1,2]]
critnums[[3,1,2]]
```

```
1
3
```

We locate and classify the points by evaluating f and f″ for each of the numbers in `critnums`.

```
{x,f[x],f''[x]} /. critnums
```

```
{{-2, -152, 180}, {1, 37, -72}, {3, -27, 120}}
```

By the Second Derivative Test, we conclude that the points $(-2,-152)$ and $(3,-27)$ are relative minima while $(1,37)$ is a relative maximum. In fact, since $\lim_{x \to \pm\infty} f(x) = +\infty$, –152 is the absolute minimum of f. These results are confirmed by the graph of f shown below.

```
Plot[f[x],{x,-4,4}]
```

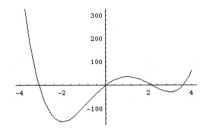

■

> **EXAMPLE:** Compute a 101-digit approximation of π. How many times does each digit occur in the approximation? What is the 66th digit to the right of the decimal place?

SOLUTION: The command `RealDigits[x]` yields a list of the decimal digits of x along with the number of digits to the left of the decimal; the command `IntegerDigits[n]` yields a list of the digits of the integer n. Below, we use `RealDigits` and `N` to compute a 101-digit approximation of π and then convert the approximation to a list of the decimal digits in the approximation. The resulting list is named `digits`.

```
digits=RealDigits[N[Pi,101]]
```

```
{{3, 1, 4, 1, 5, 9, 2, 6, 5, 3, 5, 8, 9, 7, 9, 3, 2,
  3, 8, 4, 6, 2, 6, 4, 3, 3, 8, 3, 2, 7, 9, 5, 0,
  2, 8, 8, 4, 1, 9, 7, 1, 6, 9, 3, 9, 9, 3, 7, 5,
  1, 0, 5, 8, 2, 0, 9, 7, 4, 9, 4, 4, 5, 9, 2, 3,
  0, 7, 8, 1, 6, 4, 0, 6, 2, 8, 6, 2, 0, 8, 9, 9,
  8, 6, 2, 8, 0, 3, 4, 8, 2, 5, 3, 4, 2, 1, 1, 7,
  0, 6, 8, 0}, 1}
```

Below we use `Length` to see that `digits` has two elements. The first element, extracted with `digits[[1]]`, consists of the list of the 101 digits in the approximation of π and the second element, extracted with `digits[[2]]`, is 1 which means there is only one digit (namely 3) to the left of the decimal.

```
Length[digits]
```

```
2
```

```
digits[[1]]
```

```
{3, 1, 4, 1, 5, 9, 2, 6, 5, 3, 5, 8, 9, 7, 9, 3, 2,
 3, 8, 4, 6, 2, 6, 4, 3, 3, 8, 3, 2, 7, 9, 5, 0, 2,
 8, 8, 4, 1, 9, 7, 1, 6, 9, 3, 9, 9, 3, 7, 5, 1, 0,
 5, 8, 2, 0, 9, 7, 4, 9, 4, 4, 5, 9, 2, 3, 0, 7, 8,
 1, 6, 4, 0, 6, 2, 8, 6, 2, 0, 8, 9, 9, 8, 6, 2, 8,
 0, 3, 4, 8, 2, 5, 3, 4, 2, 1, 1, 7, 0, 6, 8, 0}
```

The command Count[list,pattern] returns the number of elements in list which match the form defined by pattern. Thus, Count[digits[[1]],i] yields the number of elements in digits[[1]], corresponding to the digits in the 101-digit approximation of π, of form i. Below we use Table together with Count to count the number of occurrences of 0, 1, 2, 3, ... , 9 in digits[[1]]. The result is expressed in TableForm.

```
Table[{i,Count[digits[[1]],i]},{i,0,9}]//TableForm
```

```
0    9
1    8
2    12
3    12
4    10
5    8
6    9
7    7
8    13
9    13
```

Thus, we see that there are nine 0's, eight 1's, and so on, in the 101-digit approximation of π. The 66th digit to the right of the decimal in the approximation of π is the 67th element of digits[[1]] extracted below with digits[[1,67]]. Both the commands Part[digits,1,67] and Part[digits[[1]],67] would return the same result.

```
digits[[1,67]]
```

```
7
```

Thus, the 66th digit to the right of the decimal in the approximation of π is 7. ■

Graphing Lists of Points and Lists of Functions

If list={list[[1]],list[[2]],...,list[[n]]} is a list of numbers,

```
ListPlot[list]
```

plots the points (1,list[[1]]), (2,list[[2]]), ... , (n,list[[n]]). In general, the command ListPlot has the same options as the command Plot which can be viewed by entering the command Options[ListPlot].

Often it is desirable to suppress the output of lists, particularly when long lists are used. In general, a semi-colon ";" placed at the end of a command suppresses the resulting output. When dealing with a long Mathematica object expression, another useful Mathematica command is Short[expression]. This command produces an abbreviated, one-line output of expression. If list is a table, the command Short[list] produces a one-line output of list. If n is a positive integer greater than one, Short[list,n] produces an abbreviated n-line output of list. This abbreviated list includes an element of the form << n >>, which indicates the number of elements of the list that are omitted in the abbreviated output.

EXAMPLE: Graph the set of points $(x, \sin x)$ for x=1, 2, 3, ... ,1000.

SOLUTION: We first use `Table` and `N` to create a table of approximations of $\sin x$ for x=1, 2, 3, ... ,1000 and name the resulting table `sinvals`. Note that `sinvals` is not displayed since a semi-colon is placed at the end of the command. However, we do view portions of the list `sinvals` with `Short`.

```
sinvals=Table[N[Sin[x]],{x,1,1000}];
Short[sinvals]
```

> {0.841471, 0.909297, 0.14112, <<996>>, 0.82688}

```
Short[sinvals,3]
```

> {0.841471, 0.909297, 0.14112, −0.756802, −0.958924,
>
> −0.279415, 0.656987, <<989>>, <<8>>7, −0.855473,
>
> −0.0264608, 0.82688}

Then, we use `ListPlot[sinvals]` to graph the set of points $(x, \sin x)$ for $x = 1, 2, \ldots, 1000$.

```
ListPlot[sinvals]
```

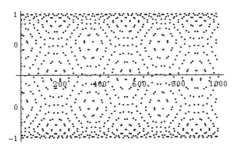

∎

Both tables of numbers, points, and functions can be graphed. In the following example, we illustrate another method to graph a set of points.

EXAMPLE: In the following, the percentage of the United States labor force which belonged to unions during certain years is displayed. Graph the data represented in the table.

Year	Union Membership as a Percentage of the Labor Force
1930	11.6
1935	13.2
1940	26.9
1945	35.5
1950	31.5
1955	33.2
1960	31.4
1965	28.4
1970	27.3
1975	25.5
1980	21.9
1985	18.0
1990	16.1

Source: *The World Almanac and Book of Facts,* 1993.

SOLUTION: We begin by entering the data represented in the table as `dataunion`: the x-coordinate of each point corresponds to the year, where x is the number of years past 1900, and the y-coordinate of each point corresponds to the percentage of the United States labor force which belonged to unions in the given year and then using `ListPlot` to graph the set of points represented in `dataunion`.

```
dataunion={{30,11.6},{35,13.2},{40,26.9},{45,35.5},{50,31.5},{55,33.2},
        {60,31.4},{65,28.4},{70,27.3},{75,25.5},{80,21.9},{85,18.0},
        {90,16.1}};
ListPlot[dataunion]
```

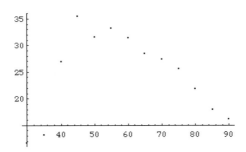

An alternative to using ListPlot is to use Show, Graphics, and Point to view the data represented in dataunion. The point (x_0, y_0) is represented with Point[{x0,y0}]. This object is then declared to be a graphics object with Graphics[Point[{x0,y0}]] and displayed with Show[Graphics[Point[{x0,y0}]]]. In the following command we use Map to apply the function Point to each pair of data in dataunion. The result is not a graphics object and cannot be displayed with Show.

```
Map[Point,dataunion]
```

```
{Point[{30, 11.6}], Point[{35, 13.2}], Point[{40, 26.9}],
   Point[{45, 35.5}], Point[{50, 31.5}], Point[{55, 33.2}],

  Point[{60, 31.4}], Point[{65, 28.4}], Point[{70, 27.3}],
  Point[{75, 25.5}], Point[{80, 21.9}], Point[{85, 18.}],

  Point[{90, 16.1}]}
```

Next, we use Show and Graphics to declare the set of points Map[Point,dataunion] as graphics objects and display the resulting graphics object. Note that the collection of all commands contained within the Graphics command are contained in braces {}. The command PointSize[.03] specifies that all Points be displayed as circles of radius 0.03 of the final displayed graphics object. The option Axes->Automatic instructs Mathematica to display the resulting graphics object with an axes.

```
datapts=Show[Graphics[{PointSize[.03],Map[Point,dataunion]}],
      Axes->Automatic]
```

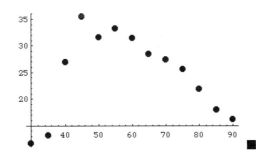

Tables of functions are graphed with Plot.

EXAMPLE: The **Laguerre polynomials**, $L_n^a(x)$, satisfy the ordinary differential equation $xy'' + (a+1-x)y' + ny = 0$. The built-in function LaguerreL[n,a,x] represents the Laguerre polynomial $L_n^a(x)$. Graph the Laguerre polynomials (a) $L_n^0(x)$ for $n = 1, 2, \ldots, 5$; and (b) $L_4^n(x)$ for $n = 1, 2, \ldots, 5$.

SOLUTION: For (a), we use Table and LaguerreL to generate a table consisting of $L_n^0(x)$ for $n = 1, 2, \ldots, 5$ and name the resulting output lpolys1.

```
lpolys1=Table[LaguerreL[n,0,x],{n,1,5}]
```

```
                    2                    2      3
           2 - 4 x + x     6 - 18 x + 9 x  - x
   {1 - x, ------------, ---------------------,
                2                   6

                    2       3     4
       24 - 96 x + 72 x - 16 x  + x
       -----------------------------,
                   24

                    2       3      4      5
       120 - 600 x + 600 x - 200 x + 25 x  - x
       ---------------------------------------}
                       120
```

Next, Plot is used to graph the set of functions lpolys1 on the interval [0,15]. Notice that within the Plot command, lpolys1 is enclosed by the command Evaluate. Evaluate[lpolys1] allows the elements of lpolys1 to be evaluated for the values of x on [0,15] instead of recreating the table for each value of x.

```
Plot[Evaluate[lpolys1],{x,0,15}]
```

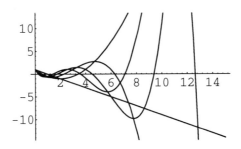

For (b), we use `Table` and `LaguerreL` to generate a table consisting of $L_4^n(x)$ for $n = 1, 2, \ldots, 5$ and name the resulting table `lpolys2`. We also use `Table` to generate a table of various `GrayLevels` which we will use to help distinguish our graphs in the final displayed graphics object.

```
lpolys2=Table[LaguerreL[4,n,x],{n,1,5}];
grays=Table[GrayLevel[i],{i,0,.4,.1}]
```

```
{GrayLevel[0], GrayLevel[0.1], GrayLevel[0.2], GrayLevel[0.3],

GrayLevel[0.4]}
```

Next, we use `Plot` to graph the functions in `lpolys2`. Each element of `lpolys2` is graphed on the interval [0,15] according to the `GrayLevel` specified in `grays`. Thus, the first function is graphed in `GrayLevel[0]`, corresponding to black, and the fifth function is graphed in `GrayLevel[0.4]`, corresponding to the lightest gray in the displayed graphics object.

```
Plot[Evaluate[lpolys2],{x,0,15},PlotStyle->grays]
```

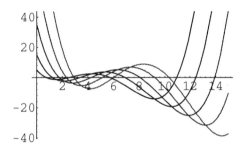

■

Evaluation of Lists by Functions

Another helpful command is `Map[f,list]` which creates a list consisting of elements obtained by evaluating `f` for each element of `list`, provided that each member of `list` is an element of the domain of `f`. Note that if `f` is listable, `f[list]` produces the same result as `Map[f,list]`.

To avoid errors, be sure to check that each element of `list` is in the domain of `f` prior to executing the command `Map[f,list]`.

> **EXAMPLE:** Create a table, named `oddints`, consisting of the first 25 odd integers. Square each number in `oddints`.

SOLUTION: We begin by using `Table` to create a table of the first 25 odd integers and name the resulting table `oddints`.

```
oddints=Table[2i-1,{i,1,25}]
```

> {1, 3, 5, 7, 9, 11, 13, 15, 17, 19, 21, 23, 25, 27, 29,
>
> 31, 33, 35, 37, 39, 41, 43, 45, 47, 49}

Next, we define $f(x) = x^2$ and use `Map` to compute f(x) for each x in `oddints`.

```
f[x_]=x^2;
Map[f,oddints]
```

> {1, 9, 25, 49, 81, 121, 169, 225, 289, 361, 441, 529,
>
> 625, 729, 841, 961, 1089, 1225, 1369, 1521, 1681,
>
> 1849, 2025, 2209, 2401}

Note that since f is `Listable`, `f[oddints]` produces the same results as `Map[f,oddints]`.

```
f[oddints]
```

> {1, 9, 25, 49, 81, 121, 169, 225, 289, 361, 441, 529,
>
> 625, 729, 841, 961, 1089, 1225, 1369, 1521, 1681,
>
> 1849, 2025, 2209, 2401}

∎

We can use `Map` on any list, including lists of functions.

EXAMPLE: The **Legendre polynomials**, $P_n(x)$, are solutions of the ordinary differential equation $(1-x^2)y'' - 2xy' + n(n+1)y = 0$. The built-in function `LegendreP[n,x]` represents the Legendre polynomial $P_n(x)$. Verify that $P_n(x)$ satisfies $(1-x^2)y'' - 2xy' + n(n+1)y = 0$ for n=1, 2, ... , 5.

SOLUTION: Below, we use `Table` to define `legendrepolys` to be the list consisting of the ordered pairs $(n, P_n(x))$ for n=1, 2, ... , 5.

```
legendrepolys=Table[{n,LegendreP[n,x]},{n,1,5}]
```

$$\left\{\{1, \text{x}\}, \left\{2, \frac{-1 + 3\, \text{x}^2}{2}\right\}, \left\{3, \frac{-3\, \text{x} + 5\, \text{x}^3}{2}\right\},\right.$$

$$\{4, \frac{3 - 30\ x^2 + 35\ x^4}{8}\}, \{5, \frac{15\ x^3 - 70\ x^3 + 63\ x^5}{8}\}\}$$

Next, we define the function f which given an ordered pair (n, y) computes and simplifies $(1 - x^2)y'' - 2xy' + n(n+1)y = 0$.

```
Clear[f]
f[{n_,y_}]:=Simplify[(1-x^2)D[y,{x,2}]-2x D[y,x]+n(n+1)y]
```

Last, we use Map to compute the value of f for each of the ordered pairs in legendrepolys. As expected, the resulting output is a list of five 0's.

```
Map[f,legendrepolys]
```

```
{0, 0, 0, 0, 0}
```  ∎

EXAMPLE: Compute a table of the values of the trigonometric functions $\sin x$, $\cos x$, and $\tan x$ for the principal angles.

SOLUTION: We first construct a table of the principal angles which is accomplished by defining t1 to be the table consisting of $\frac{n\pi}{4}$ for $n = 0, 1, ..., 8$ and t2 to be the table consisting of $\frac{n\pi}{6}$ for $n = 0, 1, ..., 12$. The principal angles are obtained by taking the union of t1 and t2. Note that Union[t1,t2] joins the lists t1 and t2, removes repeated elements, and sorts the results. If we did not wish to remove repeated elements and sort the result, the command Join[t1,t2] concatenates the lists t1 and t2.

```
t1=Table[n Pi/4,{n,0,8}];
t2=Table[n Pi/6,{n,0,12}];
prinangles=Union[t1,t2]
```

$$\{0, \frac{Pi}{6}, \frac{Pi}{4}, \frac{Pi}{3}, \frac{Pi}{2}, \frac{2\ Pi}{3}, \frac{3\ Pi}{4}, \frac{5\ Pi}{6}, Pi, \frac{7\ Pi}{6}, \frac{5\ Pi}{4},$$

$$\frac{4\ Pi}{3}, \frac{3\ Pi}{2}, \frac{5\ Pi}{3}, \frac{7\ Pi}{4}, \frac{11\ Pi}{6}, 2\ Pi\}$$

Next, we define f(x) to be the function which returns the ordered quadruple $(x, \sin x, \cos x, \tan x)$ and compute the value of f for each number in prinangles with Map naming the resulting table prinvalues. Note that prinvalues is not displayed since a semi-colon is included at the end of the command.

```
Clear[f]
f[x_]={x,Sin[x],Cos[x],Tan[x]}

    {x, Sin[x], Cos[x], Tan[x]}

prinvalues=Map[f,prinangles];
```

Finally, we use `TableForm` and `TableHeadings` to display `prinvalues` in row-and-column form; the columns are labeled x, sin$x$, cos$x$, and tan$x$.

```
TableForm[prinvalues,
        TableHeadings->{None,{"x","sin(x)","cos(x)","tan(x)"}}]
```

```
        x           sin(x)          cos(x)          tan(x)
        0           0               1               0
        Pi          1               Sqrt[3]         1
        --          -               -------         -------
        6           2                  2            Sqrt[3]
        Pi              1               1
        --          -------         -------
        4           Sqrt[2]         Sqrt[2]         1
        Pi          Sqrt[3]         1
        --          -------            -
        3              2               2            Sqrt[3]
        Pi
        --
        2           1               0               ComplexInfinity
        2 Pi        Sqrt[3]            1
        ----        -------         -(-)
         3             2               2            -Sqrt[3]
        3 Pi            1               1
        ----        -------         -(-------)
         4           Sqrt[2]          Sqrt[2]        -1
        5 Pi        1               -Sqrt[3]           1
        ----        -               --------        -(-------)
         6             2               2             Sqrt[3]
        Pi          0               -1              0
        7 Pi           1            -Sqrt[3]           1
        ----        -(-)            --------        -------
         6             2               2            Sqrt[3]
        5 Pi            1               1
        ----        -(-------)      -(-------)
         4            Sqrt[2]          Sqrt[2]       1
        4 Pi        -Sqrt[3]         1
        ----        --------        -(-)
         3              2               2            Sqrt[3]
        3 Pi
        ----
         2          -1              0               ComplexInfinity
        5 Pi        -Sqrt[3]        1
        ----        --------            -
         3             2               2            -Sqrt[3]
        7 Pi            1               1
        ----        -(-------)      -------
         4            Sqrt[2]        Sqrt[2]         -1
```

```
11 Pi      1        Sqrt[3]        1
-----    -(-)       -------    -(-------)
 6         2           2         Sqrt[3]
2 Pi       0           1            0        ■
```

Evaluation of Parts of Lists by Functions

Parts of lists may be evaluated by functions with the command MapAt:
MapAt[f,list,j] applies f to the jth part of list and returns the list

$$\{list[[1]],...,list[[j1]],f[list[[j]]],list[[j+1]],...,list[[n]]\};$$

similarly MapAt[f,list,{j1,j2,...,jk}] applies f to list[[j1,j2,...,jk]].

EXAMPLE: Generate a table of 10 random numbers between –5 and 5 and name the resulting table nums. (a) Reduce the third number in nums modulo 1. (b) Reduce all the numbers in nums modulo 1.

SOLUTION: We use Table and Random to generate a table of ten random numbers between -5 and 5 and name the result nums. Note that because the command Random is used, when you enter the following calculations, your results will most certainly be different from those here.

```
nums=Table[Random[Real,{-5,5}],{10}]

    {4.78995, 0.619918, -1.83003, 0.409594, -1.11787,

     1.92788, 3.09407, 1.31449, 3.4408, 2.4368}
```

The command Mod[a,b] represents the remainder generated by a/b which is known as a modulo b or a mod b. We define g(x) to reduce x modulo 1 and use MapAt to reduce the third number in nums modulo 1.

```
g[x_]:=Mod[x,1]
MapAt[g,nums,3]

    {4.78995, 0.619918, 0.169971, 0.409594, -1.11787,

     1.92788, 3.09407, 1.31449, 3.4408, 2.4368}
```

To reduce all the numbers in nums modulo 1, we use Map.

```
Map[g,nums]

    {0.789948, 0.619918, 0.169971, 0.409594, 0.882131,

     0.927875, 0.094066, 0.314495, 0.440797, 0.436799}  ■
```

Other List Operations

A specific operation can be applied to the elements of a list through the command Apply[operation, list]. Of course, in order to use this command, the given operation must be defined for the elements of list.

For example, if numbers is a list of real numbers, then the command Apply[Plus,numbers] adds together all the elements of numbers while Apply[Times,numbers] multiplies together all the elements of numbers.

EXAMPLE: Define list to be a list of the first 100 positive integers. Compute the sum and product of the elements of list.

SOLUTION: We use Range to define list to be a list of the first 100 positive integers. Then, Apply, Plus, and Times are used to compute the sum and product of the members of list.

```
list=Range[100];
Apply[Plus,list]

    5050

Apply[Times,list]

    93326215443944152681699238856266700490715968264381162\

    1468592963895217599993229915608941463976156518862\

    53697920827223758251185210916864000000000000000000\

    000000
```

In this example, Sum and Product can also be used to compute the sum and product, respectively.

```
Sum[i,{i,1,100}]

    5050

Product[i,{i,1,100}]

    93326215443944152681699238856266700490715968264381\

    21468592963895217599993229915608941463976156518\

    625369792082722375825118521091686400000000000000000\

    000000000
```

Some other Mathematica commands used with lists are:

Append[list,element], which appends element to list;
AppendTo[list,element], which appends element to list and names the result list;
Drop[list,n], which returns the list obtained by dropping the first n elements from list;
Drop[list,-n], which returns the list obtained by dropping the last n elements of list;
Drop[list,{n,m}], which returns the list obtained by dropping the nth through mth elements of list;
Drop[list,{n}], which returns the list obtained by dropping the nth element of list;
Prepend[list,element], which prepends element to list; and
PrependTo[list,element], which prepends element to list and names the result list.

Alternative Way to Evaluate Lists by Functions

Abbreviations of several of the commands discussed in this section are summarized below and illustrated in the following example.

| @@ | Apply | // | (function application) | {...} | List |
| /@ | Map | [[...]] | Part | | |

> **EXAMPLE:** Define polys to be the set of polynomials consisting of $15x^2 - 6x - 9$, $4x^2 - 39x + 56$, $14x^2 + 24x - 8$, and $8x^2 - 17x - 21$. (a) Factor each polynomial in polys. (b) Find the sum of the polynomials in polys.

SOLUTION: After defining polys, we use Map, //, and /@ to factor the list of polynomials polys.

```
Clear[polys,x]
polys={15x^2-6x-9,4x^2-39x+56,14x^2+24x-8,8x^2-17x-21};
Map[Factor,polys]
```

```
{3 (-1 + x) (3 + 5 x), (-8 + x) (-7 + 4 x),

  2 (2 + x) (-2 + 7 x), (-3 + x) (7 + 8 x)}
```

```
polys//Factor
```

```
{3 (-1 + x) (3 + 5 x), (-8 + x) (-7 + 4 x),

  2 (2 + x) (-2 + 7 x), (-3 + x) (7 + 8 x)}
```

```
Factor/@polys
```

> {3 (-1 + x) (3 + 5 x), (-8 + x) (-7 + 4 x),
>
>   2 (2 + x) (-2 + 7 x), (-3 + x) (7 + 8 x)}

For (b), we find the sum using @@ instead of `Apply`.

```
Plus @@; polys
```

>   2
>   18 - 38 x + 41 x   ■

4.3 *Mathematics of Finance*

The use of lists and tables are quite useful in economic applications which deal with interest rates, annuities, and amortization. Mathematica is, therefore, of great use in these types of problems through its ability to show the results of problems in tabular form. Also, if a change is made in the problem, Mathematica can easily recompute the results.

Application: Compound Interest

A common problem in economics is the determination of the amount of interest earned from an investment. If P dollars are invested for t years at an annual interest rate of r% compounded m times per year, the **compound amount**, A(t), at time t is given by

$$A(t) = P\left(1 + \frac{r}{m}\right)^{mt}.$$

If P dollars are invested for t years at an annual interest rate of r% compounded continuously, the **compound amount**, A(t), at time t is given by $A(t) = Pe^{mt}$.

A specific example is shown below where the amount of money accrued at time t represents the sum of the original investment and the amount of interest earned on that investment at time t.

> **EXAMPLE:** Suppose $12,500 is invested at an annual rate of 7% compounded daily. How much money has accumulated and how much interest has been earned at the end of each five year period for t = 0, 5, 10, 15, 20, 25, 30? How much money has accumulated if interest is compounded continuously instead of daily?

SOLUTION: Below, we define `ac[t]` to give the total value of the investment at the end of t years and `interest[t]` to yield the total amount of interest earned at the end of t years. Then `Table` and `TableForm` are used to produce the table of ordered triples corresponding to the year, total value of the investment, and total interest earned.

```
Clear[ac,interest]
ac[t_]=12500 (1+0.07/365)^(365 t);
interest[t_]=ac[t]-12500;
Table[{t,ac[t],interest[t]},{t,0,30,5}]//TableForm
```

```
0     12500      0
5     17737.7    5237.75
10    25170.2    12670.2
15    35717.     23217.
20    50683.2    38183.2
25    71920.5    59420.5
30    102057.    89556.6
```

The value of the investment if interest is compounded continuously is shown below.

```
Clear[ac]
ac[t_]=12500 Exp[.07 t];
Table[{t,ac[t]},{t,0,30,5}]//TableForm
```

```
0     12500
5     17738.3
10    25171.9
15    35720.6
20    50690.
25    71932.5
30    102077.
```

◼

The problem can be redefined for arbitrary values of t, P, r, and n as follows :

```
Clear[ac,interest,results]
ac[t_,P_,r_,n_]=P (1+r/n)^(n t);
interest[t_,P_,r_,n_]=ac[t,P,r,n]-P;
results[{t0_,t1_,m_},P_,r_,n_]:=
      Table[{t,ac[t,P,r,n],interest[t,P,r,n]},{t,t0,t1,m}]//TableForm
```

Hence, any problem of this type can be worked using the functions defined above.

EXAMPLE: Suppose $10,000 is invested at an interest rate of 12% compounded daily. Create a table consisting of the total value of the investment and the interest earned at the end of 0, 5, 10, 15, 20, and 25 years. What is the total value and interest earned on an investment of $15,000 invested at an interest rate of 15% compounded daily at the end of 0, 10, 20, and 30 years?

SOLUTION: In this case, we use the function `results` defined above. Here, t0=0, t1=25, m=5, P=10000, r=.12, and n=365:

```
results[{0,25,5},10000,0.12,365]
```

```
 0     10000      0
 5     18219.4    8219.39
10     33194.6    23194.6
15     60478.6    50478.6
20     110188.    100188.
25     200756.    190756.
```

Notice that if the conditions are changed to t0=0, t1=30, m=10, P=15000, r=.15, and n=365, the desired table can be quickly calculated:

```
results[{0,30,10},15000,0.15,365]
```

```
 0     15000         0
10     67204.6       52204.6
20     301097.       286097.
                 6                 6
30     1.34901 10    1.33401 10        ∎
```

Application: Future Value

If R dollars are deposited at the **end** of each period for n periods in an annuity that earns interest at a rate of j% per period, the **future value** of the annuity is given by:

$$S_{future} = R\frac{(1+j)^n - 1}{j}.$$

> **EXAMPLE:** Define a function future which calculates the future value of an annuity. Compute the future value of an annuity where $250 is deposited at the end of each month for 60 months at a rate of 7% per year. Make a table of the future values of the annuity where $150 is deposited at the end of each month for 12t months at a rate of 8% per year for t=1, 5, 9, 13, ... , 21, 25.

SOLUTION: After defining future, we use future to calculate that the future value of an annuity where $250 is deposited at the end of each month for 60 months at a rate of 7% per year is $17898.22.

```
Clear[r,n]
future[r_,j_,n_]=r ((1+j)^n-1)/j
```

```
                  n
(-1 + (1 + j) ) r
-----------------
        j
```

```
future[250,0.07/12,5 12]
```

```
17898.2
```

For the second problem, we use `Table` and `future` to compute the future values of the annuity where $150 is deposited at the end of each month for 12t months at a rate of 8% per year for t=1, 5, 9, 13, ... , 21, 25. Hence, the first column in the table below corresponds to the time (in years) and the second column corresponds to the future value of the annuity.

```
Table[{t,future[150,0.08/12,12 t]},{t,1,25,4}]//TableForm
```

```
1      1867.49
5      11021.5
9      23614.4
13     40938.1
17     64769.6
21     97553.8
25     142654.
```

■

Application: Annuity Due

Another type of annuity is as follows. If R dollars are deposited at the **beginning** of each period for n periods with an interest rate of j% per period, the **annuity due** is given by:

$$S_{due} = R\left(\frac{(1+j)^{n+1} - 1}{j} - 1\right).$$

> **EXAMPLE:** Define a function due that computes the annuity due. Use due to (a) compute the annuity due of $500 deposited at the beginning of each month at an annual rate of 12% compounded monthly for three years; and (b) calculate the annuity due of $100k deposited at the beginning of each month at an annual rate of 9% compounded monthly for 10 years for k=1, 2, 3, ... ,10.

SOLUTION: In the same manner as the previous example, we first define due and then use due to compute the annuity due of $500 deposited at the beginning of each month at an annual rate of 12% compounded monthly for three years.

```
due[r_,j_,n_]=r(((1+j)^(n+1)-1)/j)-r
```

```
                          1 + n
          (-1 + (1 + j)       ) r
 -r + ----------------------
                 j
```

```
due[500,0.12/12,3 12]
```

```
21753.8
```

We then use Table and due to calculate the annuity due of $100k deposited at the beginning of each month at an annual rate of 9% compounded monthly for 10 years for k=1, 2, 3, ... ,10. Notice that the first column corresponds to the amount deposited each month at an annual rate of 9% compounded monthly and the second column corresponds to the value of the annuity.

```
Table[{100 k,due[100 k,0.09/12,10 12]},{k,1,10}]//TableForm
```

```
100    19496.6
200    38993.1
300    58489.7
400    77986.3
500    97482.8
600    116979.
700    136476.
800    155973.
900    175469.
1000   194966.
```

■

We solve a similar problem below.

EXAMPLE: Compare the annuity due on $100k monthly investment at an annual rate of 8% compounded monthly for t=5, 10, 15, 20 and k=1, 2, 3, 4, 5.

SOLUTION: We use Table and due to calculate due[100 k,0.08/12,t 12], corresponding to the annuity due of $100k deposited monthly at an annual rate of 8% compounded monthly for t years, for k=1, 2, 3, 4, and t=5, 10, 15, and 20. Notice that the rows correspond to the annuity due on $100, $200, $300, $400, and $500 monthly investment for 5, 10, 15, and 20 years, respectively. For example, the annuity due on $300 deposited monthly at an annual rate of 8% compounded monthly for 15 years is $104,504.

```
Table[due[100 k,0.08/12,t 12],{k,1,5},{t,5,20,5}]//TableForm
```

```
7396.67  18416.6   34834.5   59294.7
14793.3  36833.1   69669.    118589.
22190.   55249.7   104504.   177884.
29586.7  73666.3   139338.   237179.
36983.4  92082.8   174173.   296474.
```

■

Application: Present Value

Yet another type of problem deals with determining the amount of money which must be invested in order to insure a particular return on the investment over a certain period of time. This is given with the following. The **present value**, P, of an annuity of n payments of R dollars each at the end of consecutive interest periods with interest compounded at a rate of interest j% per period is given by:

$$P = R\frac{1-(1+j)^{-n}}{j}.$$

EXAMPLE: Define a function `present` to compute the present value of an annuity. (a) Find the amount of money that would have to be invested at 7 1/2% compounded annually to provide an ordinary annuity income of $45,000 per year for 40 years; and (b) find the amount of money that would have to be invested at 8% compounded annually to provide an ordinary annuity income of $20000+$5000k per year for 35 years for k=0, 1, 2, 3, 4, and 5 years.

SOLUTION: In the same manner as in the previous examples, we first define the function `present` which calculates the present value of an annuity. We then use `present` to calculate the amount of money that would have to be invested at 7 1/2% compounded annually to provide an ordinary annuity income of $45,000 per year for 40 years.

```
present[r_,j_,n_]=r ((1-(1+j)^(-n))/j)

              -n
    (1 - (1 + j)  ) r
    -----------------
            j

present[45000,0.075,40]

     566748.
```

Also, we use `Table` to find the amount of money that would have to be invested at 8% compounded annually to provide an ordinary annuity income of $20000+$5000k per year for 35 years for k=0, 1, 2, 3, 4, and 5. Notice that the first column corresponds to the annuity income and the second column corresponds to the present value of the annuity.

```
Table[{20000+5000k,present[20000+5000 k, 0.08,35]},{k,0,5}]//TableForm
```

```
20000    233091.
25000    291364.
30000    349637.
35000    407910.
40000    466183.
45000    524456.  ■
```

Application: Deferred Annuities

Deferred annuities can also be considered. The present value of a **deferred annuity** of R dollars per period for n periods deferred for k periods with interest rate j per period is given by:

$$P_{def} = R\left[\frac{1-\left(1+j\right)^{-(n+k)}}{j} - \frac{1-\left(1+j\right)^{-k}}{j}\right].$$

EXAMPLE: Define a function def[r,n,k,j], which computes the value of a deferred annuity where r equals the amount of the deferred annuity, n equals the number of years in which the annuity is received, k equals the number of years in which the lump sum investment is made, and j equals the rate of interest. Use def to compute the lump sum that would have to be invested for 30 years at a rate of 15% compounded annually to provide an ordinary annuity income of $35,000 per year for 35 years. How much money would have to be invested at the ages of 25, 35, 45, 55, and 65 at a rate of 8 1/2% compounded annually to provide an ordinary annuity income of $30,000 per year for 40 years beginning at age 65?

SOLUTION: As in the previous examples, we first define def and then use def to compute the lump sum that would have to be invested for 30 years at a rate of 15% compounded annually to provide an ordinary annuity income of $35,000 per year for 35 years. The function which computes the present value of a deferred annuity is given below where

  r = the amount of the deferred annuity,
  n= the number of years in which in annuity is received,
  k = the number of years in which the lump sum investment is made, and
  j = the interest rate.

```
def[r_,n_,k_,j_]=r ((1-(1+j)^(-(n+k)))/j-(1-(1+j)^(-k))/j)

                    -k                   -k - n
      1 - (1 + j)            1 - (1 + j)
   (-(-------------) + ------------------) r
           j                   j
```

```
def[35000,35,30,0.15]

   3497.58
```

To answer the second question, we note that the number of years the annuity is deferred is equal to 65 (the age at retirement) minus the age at which the money is initially invested, and then use `Table` and `def` to compute the amount of money would have to be invested at the ages of 25, 35, 45, 55, and 65 at a rate of 8 1/2% compounded annually to provide an ordinary annuity income of $30,000 per year for 40 years beginning at age 65. Note that the first column corresponds to the current age of the individual, the second column corresponds to the number of years from retirement, and the third column corresponds to the present value of the annuity.

```
Table[{k,65-k,def[30000,40,65-k,0.085]},{k,25,65,10}]//TableForm

   25    40    12988.8
   35    30    29367.4
   45    20    66399.2
   55    10    150127.
   65    0     339436.
```

■

Application: Amortization

A loan is **amortized** if both the principal and interest are paid by a sequence of equal periodic payments. A loan of P dollars at interest rate j per period may be amortized in n equal periodic payments of R dollars made at the end of each period, where

$$R = \frac{pj}{1-(1+j)^{-n}} .$$

The function, `amort[p,j,n]`, defined below determines the monthly payment needed to amortize a loan of p dollars with an interest rate of j% compounded monthly over n months. A second function, `totintpaid[p,j,n]`, calculates the total amount of interest paid to amortize a loan of p dollars with an interest rate of j% compounded monthly over n months.

```
amort[p_,j_,n_]=(p j)/(1-(1+j)^(-n))

         j p
      -------------
                -n
      1 - (1 + j)

totintpaid[p_,j_,n_]= n amort[p,j,n]-p
```

$$-p + \frac{j\ n\ p}{1 - (1 + j)^{-n}}$$

EXAMPLE: What is the monthly payment necessary to amortize a loan of $75,000 with interest 9.5% compounded monthly over 20 years?

SOLUTION: The first calculation below uses `amort` to determine the necessary monthly payment to amortize the loan. The second calculation determines the total amount paid on a loan of $75,000 at a rate of 9.5% compounded monthly over twenty years, while the third shows how much of this amount was paid towards the interest.

```
amort[75000,0.095/12,20 12]
```
    699.098
```
240 amort[75000,0.095/12,240]
```
    167784.
```
totintpaid[75000,0.095/12,240]
```
    92783.6 ■

EXAMPLE: What is the monthly payment necessary to amortize a loan of $80,000 at an annual rate of j% in twenty years for j=8,8.5, 9, 9.5, 10, and 10.5?

SOLUTION: Below, we use `amort` to calculate the necessary monthly payments. The first column corresponds to the annual interest rate and the second column corresponds to the monthly payment.

```
Table[{j,amort[80000,j/12,20 12]},{j,0.08,0.105,0.005}]//TableForm
```
    0.08   669.152
    0.085   694.259
    0.09   719.781
    0.095   745.705
    0.1   772.017
    0.105   798.704 ■

In many cases, the amount paid towards the principal of the loan and the total amount which remains to be paid after a certain payment need to be computed. This is easily accomplished with the functions `unpaidbalance` and `curprinpaid` defined below using the function `amort[p,j,n]` that was previously defined:

```
unpaidbalance[p_,j_,n_,m_]=present[amort[p,j,n],j,n-m]

             m - n
   (1 - (1 + j)    ) p
   --------------------
              -n
    1 - (1 + j)

curprinpaid[p_,j_,n_,m_]=p-unpaidbalance[p,j,n,m]

               m - n
     (1 - (1 + j)    ) p
   p - --------------------
                  -n
      1 - (1 + j)
```

Note that Mathematica does not retain definitions of functions from previous Mathematica sessions. This means that in order to use a function definition from a previous Mathematica session, the definition must be re-entered.

> **EXAMPLE:** What is the unpaid balance of the principal at the end of the fifth year of a loan of $60,000 with an annual interest rate of 8% scheduled to be amortized with monthly payments over a period of ten years? What is the total interest paid immediately after the 60th payment?

SOLUTION: We use the functions unpaidbalance and curprinpaid, defined above, to calculate that of the original $60,000 loan, $24,097.90 has been paid at the end of five years; $35,902.10 is still owed on the loan.

```
unpaidbalance[60000,0.08/12,120,60]

   35902.1

curprinpaid[60000,0.08/12,120,60]

   24097.9  ■
```

Mathematica can also be used to determine the total amount of interest paid on a loan using the following function

```
curintpaid[p_,j_,n_,m_]=m amort[p,j,n]-curprinpaid[p,j,n,m]

                m - n
      (1 - (1 + j)    ) p          j m p
   -p + -------------------- + -------------
                   -n                    -n
        1 - (1 + j)          1 - (1 + j)
```

where curintpaid[p,j,n,m] computes the interest paid on a loan of $p amortized at a rate of j per period over n periods immediately after the mth payment.

EXAMPLE: What is the total interest paid on a loan of $60,000 with an interest rate of 8% compounded monthly amortized over a period of ten years (120 months) immediately after the 60th payment?

SOLUTION: Using `curintpaid`, we see that the total interest paid is $19,580.10.

```
curintpaid[60000,0.08/12,120,60]
```

```
   19580.1  ■
```

Using the functions defined above, amortization tables can be created which show a breakdown of the payments made on a loan. An example is given below.

EXAMPLE: What is the monthly payment necessary to amortize a loan of $45,000 with interest rate of 7% compounded monthly over a period of 15 years (180 months)? What is the total principal and interest paid after 0, 3, 6, 9, 12, and 15 years?

SOLUTION: We first use `amort` to calculate the monthly payment necessary to amortize the loan.

```
amort[45000,0.07/12,15 12]
```

```
   404.473
```

Next, we use `Table`, `curprinpaid`, and `curintpaid` to determine the interest and principal paid at the end of 0, 3, 6, 9, 12, and 15 years.

```
Table[{t,curprinpaid[45000,0.07/12,15 12,12 t],
       curintpaid[45000,0.07/12,15 12,12 t]},{t,0,15,3}]//TableForm
```

```
   0    0.        0.
   3    5668.99   8892.03
   6    12658.4   16463.6
   9    21275.9   22407.2
   12   31900.6   26343.5
   15   45000     27805.1
```

Note that the first column represents the number of years, the second column represents the principal paid, and the third column represents the interest paid. Thus, at the end of twelve years, $31,900.60 of the principal has been paid and $26,343.50 has been paid in interest. ■

Since `curintpaid[p,j,n,y]` computes the interest paid on a loan of $p amortized at a rate of j per period over n periods immediately after the yth payment, and `curintpaid[p,j,n,y-12]` computes the interest paid on a loan of $p amortized at a rate of j per period over n periods immediately after the (y−12)th payment,

```
curintpaid[p,j,n,y]-curintpaid[p,j,n,y-12]
```

yields the amount of interest paid on a loan of $p amortized at a rate of j per period over n periods between the (y−12)th and yth payment. Consequently, the interest paid and the amount of principal paid over a year can also be computed.

> **EXAMPLE:** Suppose that a loan of $45,000 with interest rate of 7% compounded monthly is amortized over a period of 15 years (180 months)? What is the principal and interest paid during each of the first five years of the loan?

SOLUTION: We begin by defining the functions `annualintpaid` and `annualprinpaid` which calculate the interest and principal paid during the yth year on a loan of $p amortized at a rate of j per period over n periods.

```
annualintpaid[p_,j_,n_,y_]:=curintpaid[p,j,n,y]-curintpaid[p,j,n,y-12];
annualprinpaid[p_,j_,n_,y_]:=curprinpaid[p,j,n,y]-
        curprinpaid[p,j,n,y-12];
```

We then use these functions along with `Table` to calculate the principal and interest paid during the first five years of the loan. Note that the first column represents the number of years the loan has been held, the second column represents the interest paid on the loan during the year, and the third column represents the amount of the principal that has been paid.

```
Table[{t,annualintpaid[45000,0.07/12, 15 12,12 t],
        annualprinpaid[45000,0.07/12,15 12,12 t]},{t,1,5,1}]//TableForm
```

1	3094.26	1759.41
2	2967.08	1886.6
3	2830.69	2022.98
4	2684.45	2169.22
5	2527.64	2326.03

For example, we see that during the third year of the loan, $2830.69 was paid in interest and $2022.98 was paid on the principal. ∎

Application: Financial Planning

We can use many of the functions defined above to help make decisions about financial planning.

> **EXAMPLE:** Suppose a retiree has $1,200,000. If she can invest this sum at 7%, compounded annually, what level payment can she withdraw annually for a period of forty years?

SOLUTION: The answer to the question is the same as the monthly payment necessary to amortize a loan of $1,200,000 at a rate of 7% compounded annually over a period of forty years. Thus, we use `amort` to see that she can withdraw $90,011 annually for forty years.

```
amort[1200000,.07,40]

   90011.
```

■

EXAMPLE: Suppose an investor begins investing at a rate of d dollars per year at an annual rate of j%. Each year the investor increases the amount invested by i%. How much has the investor accumulated after m years?

SOLUTION: The following table illustrates the amount invested each year and the value of the annual investment after m years.

Year	Rate of Increase	Annual Interest	Amount Invested	Value after m Years
0		$j\%$	d	$(1+j\%)^m d$
1	$i\%$	$j\%$	$(1+i\%)d$	$(1+i\%)(1+j\%)^{m-1}d$
2	$i\%$	$j\%$	$(1+i\%)^2 d$	$(1+i\%)^2(1+j\%)^{m-2}d$
3	$i\%$	$j\%$	$(1+i\%)^3 d$	$(1+i\%)^3(1+j\%)^{m-3}d$
k	$i\%$	$j\%$	$(1+i\%)^k d$	$(1+i\%)^k(1+j\%)^{m-k}d$
m	$i\%$	$j\%$	$(1+i\%)^m d$	$(1+i\%)^m d$

It follows that the total value of the amount invested for the first k years after m years is given by:

Year	Total Investment
0	$\left(1+j\%\right)^m d$
1	$\left(1+j\%\right)^m d + \left(1+i\%\right)\left(1+j\%\right)^{m-1} d$
2	$\left(1+j\%\right)^m d + \left(1+i\%\right)\left(1+j\%\right)^{m-1} d + \left(1+i\%\right)^2\left(1+j\%\right)^{m-2} d$
3	$\displaystyle\sum_{n=0}^{3}\left(1+i\%\right)^n\left(1+j\%\right)^{m-n} d$
k	$\displaystyle\sum_{n=0}^{k}\left(1+i\%\right)^n\left(1+j\%\right)^{m-n} d$
m	$\displaystyle\sum_{n=0}^{m}\left(1+i\%\right)^n\left(1+j\%\right)^{m-n} d$

The package **SymbolicSum.m**, contained in the **Algebra** folder (or directory), contains the command `SymbolicSum` which can be used to find a closed form of the sums $\displaystyle\sum_{n=0}^{k}\left(1+i\%\right)^n\left(1+j\%\right)^{m-n} d$ and $\displaystyle\sum_{n=0}^{m}\left(1+i\%\right)^n\left(1+j\%\right)^{m-n} d$. Below, we first load the package **SymbolicSum** and then use `SymbolicSum` to find the sum $\displaystyle\sum_{n=0}^{k}\left(1+i\%\right)^n\left(1+j\%\right)^{m-n} d$ and name the result `closedone`. We then use `Factor` and `Together` to first write `closedone` as a single fraction and then factor the numerator.

```
<<Algebra`SymbolicSum`
closedone=SymbolicSum[(1+i)^n (1+j)^(m-n) d,{n,0,k}]//Simplify

          -k + m
  (d (1 + j)

           k           k
    ((1 + i)  + i (1 + i)   -

           k           k
    (1 + j)  - j (1 + j) ))\

  / (i - j)

Factor[Together[closedone]]
```

```
                          -k + m
(d (1 + j)


                     k           k
        (-(1 + i)   - i (1 + i)   +


                  k           k
        (1 + j)   + j (1 + j)  ))\


     / (-i + j)
```

In the exact same manner as above, `SymbolicSum` is used to find a closed form of $\sum_{n=0}^{m}\left(1+i\%\right)^{n}\left(1+j\%\right)^{m-n}d$, naming the result `closedtwo`. In this case, however, the final result is displayed in a print cell in input form with the command `Print[InputForm[%]]`. Remember that the symbol `%` refers to the previous output.

```
closedtwo=SymbolicSum[(1+i)^n (1+j)^(m-n) d,{n,0,m}]

                  m           m
    (d ((1 + i)   + i (1 + i)   -


             m           m
    (1 + j)   - j (1 + j)  ))\


     / (i - j)
```

```
Factor[Together[closedtwo]]

                  m           m
    (d (-(1 + i)   - i (1 + i)   +


             m           m
    (1 + j)   + j (1 + j)  ))\


     / (-i + j)
```

```
Print[InputForm[%]]

    (d*(-(1 + i)^m - i*(1 + i)^m + (1 + j)^m + j*(1 + j)^m))/(-i + j)
```

The above results are used to define the functions `investment[{d,i,j},{k,m}]` and `investmenttot[{d,i,j},m]` which return the value of the investment after k and m years, respectively. In the second case, notice that print cells can be edited like any other input or text cell. Consequently, we use notebook editing features to copy and paste the above result when we define the function `investmenttot`.

```
investment[{d_,i_,j_},{k_,m_}]=(d*(1+j)^(-k+m)*((1+i)^k+i*
    (1+i)^k-(1+j)^k-j*(1+j)^k))/(i-j)
```

$$(d \ (1 + j)^{-k + m}$$

$$((1 + i)^{k} + i \ (1 + i)^{k} -$$

$$(1 + j)^{k} - j \ (1 + j)^{k}))\backslash$$

$$/ \ (i - j)$$

```
investmenttot[{d_,i_,j_},m_]=(d*(-(1+i)^m-i*(1+i)^m+(1+j)^m+
    j*(1+j)^m))/(-i+j)
```

$$(d \ (-(1 + i)^{m} - i \ (1 + i)^{m} +$$

$$(1 + j)^{m} + j \ (1 + j)^{m}))\backslash$$

$$/ \ (-i + j)$$

Finally, `investment` and `investmenttot` are used to illustrate various financial scenarios. In the first example, `investment` is used to compute the value after twenty-five years of investing $6500 the first year and then increasing the amount invested 5% per year for 5, 10, 15, 20, and 25 years assuming a 15% rate of interest on the amount invested. The built-in function `AccountingForm` is used to convert numbers expressed in exponential notation to ordinary notation. In the second example, `investmenttot` is used to compute the value after twenty-five years of investing $6500 the first year and then increasing the amount invested 5% per year for 25 years assuming various rates of interest. The results are displayed in `AccountingForm`.

```
results=Table[{t,investment[{6500,0.05,0.15},{t,25}]},
    {t,5,25,5}]//TableForm
```

5	$1.03506 \ 10^{6}$
10	$1.55608 \ 10^{6}$
15	$1.88668 \ 10^{6}$
20	$2.09646 \ 10^{6}$
25	$2.22957 \ 10^{6}$

```
TableForm[AccountingForm[results]]
```

5	1035065.
10	1556078.
15	1886680.
20	2096460.
25	2229573.

```
scenes=Table[{i,investmenttot[{6500,0.05,i},25]},{i,0.08,0.20,0.02}];
AccountingForm[TableForm[scenes]]
```

0.08	832147.
0.1	1087126.
0.12	1437837.
0.14	1921899.
0.16	2591636.
0.18	3519665.
0.2	4806524.

■

   Another interesting investment problem is discussed in the following example. In this case, Mathematica is useful in solving a recurrence equation which occurs in the problem. The command used to solve equations of this type is RSolve. In general,

```
RSolve[{equations},a[n],n]
```

attempts to solve the recurrence equations equations for the variable a[n] with no dependence on n. Note that the command RSolve is contained in the package **RSolve** located in the **DiscreteMath** folder (or directory) so it must first be loaded before using. We illustrate the use of this command in the following example.

EXAMPLE: I am fifty years old and I have $500,000 which I can invest at a rate of 7% annually. Furthermore, I wish to receive a payment of $50,000 the first year. Future annual payments should include cost-of-living adjustments at a rate of 3% annually. Is $500,000 enough to guarantee this amount of annual income if I live to be eighty- years old?

SOLUTION: Instead of directly solving the above problem, let's solve a more general problem. Let a denote the amount invested and p the first-year payment. Let a_n denote the balance of the principal at the end of year n. Then, the amount of the nth payment, the interest earned on the principal, the decrease in principal, and the principal balance at the end of year n is shown in the table for various values of n. Observe that if $(1+j)^{n-1} p > (1+j)a_{n-1}$, then the procedure terminates and the amount received in year n is $(1+j)a_{n-1}$.

Year	Amount	Interest	From Principal	Principal Balance
1	p	ia	$p - ia$	$a_1 = (1+i)a - p$
2	$(1+j)p$	ia_1	$(1+j)p - ia_1$	$a_2 = (1+i)a_1 - (1+j)p$
3	$(1+j)^2 p$	ia_2	$(1+j)^2 p - ia_2$	$a_3 = (1+i)a_2 - (1+j)^2 p$
4	$(1+j)^3 p$	ia_3	$(1+j)^3 p - ia_3$	$a_4 = (1+i)a_3 - (1+j)^3 p$
n	$(1+j)^{n-1} p$	ia_{n-1}	$(1+j)^{n-1} p - ia_{n-1}$	$a_n = (1+i)a_{n-1} - (1+j)^{n-1} p$

The recurrence equation $a_n = (1+i)a_{n-1} - (1+j)^{n-1}p$ is solved for a_n with no dependence on a_{n-1} with Mathematica below. After clearing several definitions of variable names, we use RSolve to solve the recurrence equation given above where the initial balance is represented by amount. Hence, a_n is given by the expression found in bigstep.

```
<<DiscreteMath`RSolve`
eq1=a[1]==(1+i)amount-p;
eq2=a[n]==(1+i)a[n-1]-(1+j)^(n-1)p;
bigstep=RSolve[{eq1,eq2},a[n],n]
```

```
                                    -1 + n
                    (-1 - j) (1 + j)       p
    {{a[n] -> -(-----------------------) +
                         i - j

                            -1 + n
        ((-1 - i) (1 + i)

            (-(amount i) + amount j + p)) / (i - j)}}
```

We then define am[n,amount,i,p,j] to be the explicit solution found in bigstep, extracted from bigstep with bigstep[[1,1,2]]. Last we compute am[n,a,i,p,j] which corresponds to the balance of the principal of a dollars invested under the above conditions at the end of the nth year.

```
am[n_,amount_,i_,p_,j_]=bigstep[[1,1,2]]//Together;
am[n,a,i,p,j]

                    n               n             n
    (-(a i (1 + i) ) + a (1 + i)   j + (1 + i)   p -

            n
    (1 + j)  p) / (-i + j)
```

To answer the question, we first define `annuitytable` in the following. For given a, i, p, j, and m, `annuitytable[a,i,p,j,m]` returns an ordered triple corresponding to the year, amount of income received in that year, and principal balance at the end of the year for m years.

```
annuitytable[a_,i_,p_,j_,m_]:=Table[{k,(1+j)^(k-1) p,
    am[k,a,i,p,j]},{k,1,m}]//TableForm
```

Then we compute `annuitytable[500000,.07,50000,.03,15]`. In this case, we see that the desired level of income is only guaranteed for thirteen years which corresponds to an age of 67 since the principal balance is negative after thirteen years.

```
annuitytable[500000,.07,50000,.03,15]
```

1	50000	485000.
2	51500.	467450.
3	53045.	447126.
4	54636.3	423789.
5	56275.4	397179.
6	57963.7	367018.
7	59702.6	333006.
8	61493.7	294823.
9	63338.5	252122.
10	65238.7	204532.
11	67195.8	151653.
12	69211.7	93057.4
13	71288.	28283.4
14	73426.7	-43163.5
15	75629.5	-121814.

An alternative method of defining `annuitytable` is presented below. In this case, the procedure terminates when the principal is negative or after fifty years.

```
Clear[annuitytable]
annuitytable[a_,i_,p_,j_]:=Module[{},
    For[k=1,am[k,a,i,p,j]>=0 && k<=50,k++,
        Print[{k,(1+j)^(k-1) p,am[k,a,i,p,j]}]];
    Print[{k,am[k-1,a,i,p,j],0}]
    ]
```

We see that if the first year payment is $29,000, 3% increases can occur annually for thirty years:

```
annuitytable[500000,.07,29000,.03]
```

```
{1, 29000, 506000.}
{2, 29870., 511550.}
{3, 30766.1, 516592.}
{4, 31689.1, 521065.}
{5, 32639.8, 524900.}
{6, 33618.9, 528024.}
{7, 34627.5, 530358}
```

```
{8, 35666.3, 531816.}
{9, 36736.3, 532307.}
{10, 37838.4, 531730.}
{11, 38973.6, 529978.}
{12, 40142.8, 526934.}
{13, 41347.1, 522472.}
{14, 42587.5, 516457.}
{15, 43865.1, 508744.}
{16, 45181.8, 499175.}
{17, 46536.5, 487581.}
{18, 47932.6, 473779.}
{19, 49370.6, 457573.}
{20, 50851.7, 438752.}
{21, 52377.2, 417087.}
{22, 53948.5, 329335.}
{23, 55567., 364231.}
{24, 57234., 332493..}
{25, 58951., 296817.}
{26, 60719.6, 256874.}
{27, 62541.1, 212314.}
{28, 64417.4, 162759.}
{29, 66349.9, 107802.}
{30, 68340.4, 47007.9}
{31, 47007.9, 0}
```

We can also investigate certain other problems. For example, a thirty-year mortgage of $80,000 with an annual interest rate of 8.125% requires monthly payments of approximately $600 ($7,200 annually) to amortize the loan in 30 years. However, using `annuitytable`, we see that if the amount of the payments is increased by 3% each year, the thirty-year mortgage is amortized in 17 years. In the following result, the first column corresponds to the year of the loan, the second column the annual payment, and the third column the principal balance.

```
annuitytable[80000,.08125,7200,.03]
```

```
{1, 7200, 79300.}
{2, 7416., 78327.1}
{3, 7638.48, 77052.7}
{4, 7867.63, 75445.6}
{5, 8103.66, 73471.9}
{6, 8346.77, 71094.7}
{7, 8597.18, 68274.}
{8, 8855.09, 64966.2}
{9, 9120.74, 61123.9}
{10, 9394.37, 56695.9}
{11, 9676.2, 51626.2}
{12, 9966.48, 45854.4}
{13, 10265.5, 39314.6}
{14, 10573.4, 31935.4}
{15, 10890.6, 23639.5}
{16, 11217.4, 14342.9}
{17, 11553.9, 3954.36}
{18, 3954.36, 0}
```

4.4 Other Applications

We now discuss several other interesting applications that require the manipulation of lists.

Application: Secant Lines, Tangent Lines, and Animations

In differential calculus, we learn that $f'(x) = \lim_{h \to 0} \dfrac{f(x+h) - f(x)}{h}$, provided this limit exists. One way we may interpret $f'(a)$ is as the limit as $h \to 0$ of the slopes of the secant lines passing through $(a, f(a))$ and $(a+h, f(a+h))$. Given a differentiable function f and a number a, we can use Mathematica to graph f and the secant line passing through $(a, f(a))$ and $(a+h, f(a+h))$ for various values of h and animate the result or display the result as a graphics array.

> **EXAMPLE:** Let $f(x) = x^3 - \dfrac{9}{2}x^2 + \dfrac{23}{4}x - \dfrac{15}{8}$. Graph f and the secant line passing through $(1, f(1))$ and $(1+h, f(1+h))$ for various values of h.

SOLUTION: We begin by defining and graphing f. We use the option `Ticks` to place to place tick marks corresponding to 1, 2, and 3 on the x-axis and −1, 1, and 2 on the y-axis. The option `PlotRange->{-1.5,2}` specifies that the range displayed consists of the y-values between −1.5 and 2.

```
Clear[f]
f[x_]=x^3-9/2x^2+23/4x-15/8;
plotf=Plot[f[x],{x,0,3},PlotRange->{-1.5,2},Ticks->{Range[3],{-1,1,2}}]
```

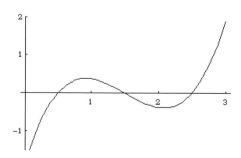

An equation of the line passing through the points $(a, f(a))$ and $(a+h, f(a+h))$ is given by $y = \dfrac{f(a+h) - f(a)}{h}(x-a) + f(a)$. Next, we define secant to be the function corresponding to the secant line passing through these points.

```
secant[a_,h_]:=(f[a+h]-f[a])/h(x-a)+f[a];
```

Since we will be graphing the secant line for $a = 1$ and various values of h, we define the function secgraph which, given h,

1. graphs the secant line passing through $(1, f(1))$ and $(1+h, f(1+h))$ and names the resulting graphics object s1;
2. generates the points $(1, f(1))$ and $(1+h, f(1+h))$, declares them to be graphics objects, and names them points; and
3. shows s1, points, and plotf.

Note that s1 and points are variables that are local to the function secgraph. The result of entering secgraph[h] for a particular value of h can be displayed by entering

```
Show[secgraph[h],DisplayFunction->$DisplayFunction].
```

```
Clear[secgraph,points]
secgraph[h_]:=Module[{s1,points},
      s1=Plot[secant[1,h],{x,0,3},
            DisplayFunction->Identity];
      points=Graphics[{
            PointSize[.02],
            Point[{1,f[1]}],Point[{1+h,f[1+h]}]}];
      Show[s1,plotf,points,PlotRange->{-1.5,2},
            Ticks->{Range[3],{-1,1,2}}]
            ]
```

To generate graphics that can be animated, we use a Do loop. The syntax of the Mathematica command Do is similar to the syntax of the command Table. The command Do[statement[i],{i,istart,istop,istep}] instructs Mathematica to execute statement[i] for values of i beginning with istart and continuing through istop in increments of istep.

The following two windows show the results of entering the command:

```
Do[Show[secgraph[h],DisplayFunction->$DisplayFunction],{h,2,.2,-.3}]
```

To animate graphics, select the cells of the graphics to be animated as shown below.

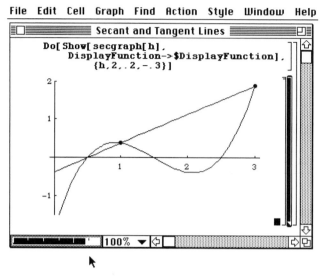

Then, go to **Graph** on the Mathematica menu and select **Animate Selected Graphics** or press ⌘y.

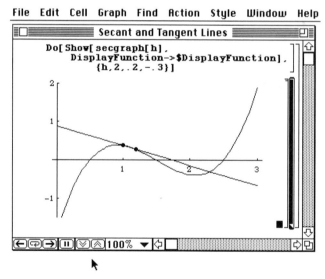

The six buttons in the lower left-hand corner of the window control the animation. From left to right, the buttons

    run the animation backward;
    run the animation cyclically;
    run the animation forward;
    pause the animation;
    slow the animation; and
    speed up the animation.

Animations may also be controlled by selecting **Animation...** under **Graph** on the Mathematica menu.

An alternative approach is to generate the desired graphs and display the result as a graphics array. In the following, we use `Table` to generate `secgraph[h]` for values of h from 1.7 to .2 in steps of −.3. The resulting list of six graphics objects is named `graphs`.

```
graphs=Table[secgraph[h],{h,1.7,.2,-.3}]
```

```
{-Graphics-,-Graphics-,-Graphics-,-Graphics-,-Graphics-, -Graphics-}
```

We then use `Partition` to partition the set of six graphs in graphs into two sets of three graphs named `toshow` and use `GraphicsArray` to display `toshow`.

```
toshow=Partition[graphs,3]
```

```
{{-Graphics-, -Graphics-, -Graphics-},

 {-Graphics-, -Graphics-, -Graphics-}}
```

```
Show[GraphicsArray[toshow]]
```

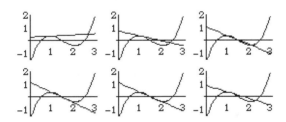

Similarly, we may also graph the line tangent to the graph of f at the point $(a, f(a))$ for many values of a and animate the result or display the results as a graphics array.

EXAMPLE: Let $f(x) = x^3 - \dfrac{9}{2}x^2 + \dfrac{23}{4}x - \dfrac{15}{8}$. Graph f and the tangent line passing through $(a, f(a))$ for various values of a.

SOLUTION: If f(x) is differentiable when $x = a$, the line tangent to the graph of f at the point $(a, f(a))$ is given by $y = f'(a)(x - a) + f(a)$. Below, we define `tangent[a]` to be a function corresponding to the line tangent to the graph of f at the point $(a, f(a))$ and define `tangraph` which, given a,

1. graphs the tangent line passing through $(a, f(a))$ and names the resulting graphics object `tl`;

2. generates the point $(a, f(a))$ declares it to be graphics objects, and names it point; and

3. shows tl, point, and plotf. Note that plotf was generated in the previous example.

Note that tl and point are variables that are local to the function tangraph. The result of entering tangraph[a] for a particular value of a can be displayed by entering

```
Show[tangraph[h],DisplayFunction->$DisplayFunction].
```

```
tangent[a_]:=f'[a](x-a)+f[a];
tangraph[a_]:=Module[{tl,point},
        tl=Plot[tangent[a],{x,0,3},
                DisplayFunction->Identity];
        point=Graphics[{
                PointSize[.02],Point[{a,f[a]}]}];
        Show[tl,plotf,point,PlotRange->{-1.5,2},
                Ticks->{Range[3],{-1,1,2}}]
                ]
```

As in the preceding example, we can use a Do loop to generate a set of graphics objects which can be animated. The results of entering the following command are shown below.

```
Do[Show[tangraph[a],DisplayFunction->$DisplayFunction],{a,.25,2.75,.25}]
```

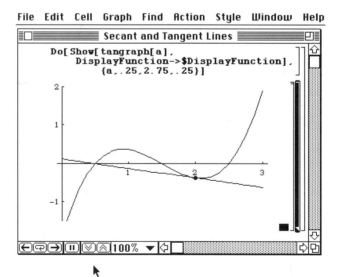

Alternatively, we can use `Table` and `Partition` to generate a table of graphics object, partition the result into an array of graphics objects, and use `GraphicsArray` to display the results.

```
graphs=Table[tangraph[a],{a,.25,2.75,.5}];
toshow=Partition[graphs,3];
Show[GraphicsArray[toshow]]
```

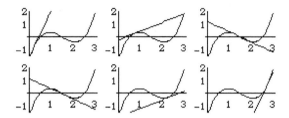

■

Application: Approximating Lists with Functions

Another interesting application of lists is that of curve fitting. The command

`Fit[data,functionset, variables]` fits the list of data points `data` using the functions in `functionset` by the method of least-squares. The functions in `functionset` are functions of the variables listed in `variables`; and `InterpolatingPolynomial[data,x]` fits the list of data points `data` with an $n-1$ degree polynomial in the variable `x`.

An example is shown below which gives a quadratic fit to the data points in `datalist`.

EXAMPLE: Define `datalist` to be the list of numbers consisting of 1.14479, 1.5767, 2.68572,2.5199, 3.58019, 3.84176, 4.09957, 5.09166, 5.98085,6.49449, and 6.12113. (a) Find a quadratic approximation of the points in `datalist`. (b) Find a fourth degree polynomial approximation of the points in `datalist`.

SOLUTION: The approximating function obtained above via the least-squares method can be plotted along with the data points. This is demonstrated below. Notice that many of the data points are not very close to the approximating function. Hence, a better approximation is obtained below using a polynomial of higher degree (4).

```
Clear[datalist]
datalist={1.14479, 1.5767, 2.68572,2.5199, 3.58019, 3.84176,
        4.09957, 5.09166, 5.98085,6.49449, 6.12113};
p1=ListPlot[datalist,DisplayFunction->Identity];
Clear[y]
y[x_]=Fit[datalist,{1,x,x^2},x]
```

$$0.508266 + 0.608688\ x - 0.00519281\ x^2$$

```
p2=Plot[y[x],{x,-1,11},DisplayFunction->Identity];
Show[p1,p2,DisplayFunction->$DisplayFunction]
```

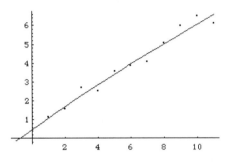

```
Clear[y]
y[x_]=Fit[datalist,{1,x,x^2,x^3,x^4},x]
```

$$-0.54133 + 2.02744\ x - 0.532282\ x^2 +$$

$$0.0709201\ x^3 - 0.00310985\ x^4$$

To check its accuracy, this second approximation is simultaneously with the data points.

```
p3=Plot[y[x],{x,-1,11},DisplayFunction->Identity];
Show[p1,p3,DisplayFunction->$DisplayFunction]
```

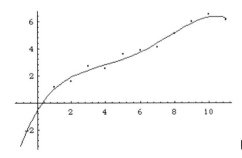

Next, consider a list of data points made up of ordered pairs.

EXAMPLE: The following table shows the average percentage of petroleum products imported to the United States for certain years. (a) Graph the points corresponding to the data in the table and connect the consecutive points with line segments. (b) Use `InterpolatingPolynomial` to find a function which approximates the data in the table. (c) Find a fourth degree polynomial approximation of the data in the table. (d) Find a trigonometric approximation of the data in the table.

Year	Percent
1973	34.8105
1974	35.381
1975	35.8167
1976	40.6048
1977	47.0132
1978	42.4577
1979	43.1319
1980	37.3182
1981	33.6343
1982	28.0988
1983	28.3107
1984	29.9822
1985	27.2542
1986	33.407
1987	35.4875
1988	38.1126
1989	41.57
1990	42.1533
1991	39.5108

Source: *The World Almanac and Book of Facts*, 1993.

SOLUTION: We begin by defining data to be the set of ordered pairs represented in the table: the x-coordinate of each point represents the number of years past 1900 and the y-coordinate represents the percentage of petroleum products imported to the United States.

```
data={{73., 34.8105}, {74., 35.381}, {75., 35.8167}, {76., 40.6048},
        {77., 47.0132}, {78., 42.4577}, {79., 43.1319}, {80., 37.3182},
        {81., 33.6343}, {82., 28.0988}, {83., 28.3107}, {84., 29.9822},
        {85., 27.2542}, {86., 33.407}, {87., 35.4875}, {88., 38.1126},
        {89., 41.57}, {90., 42.1533}, {91., 39.5108}};
```

Next, we use Graphics, Map, and Point to convert each of the ordered pairs in data to points and declare the result to be a graphics object named ps. Note that since PointSize[.03] is included within the Graphics command, the points will be larger than they would be if ListPlot had been used to graph the points. We also use ListPlot with the option PlotJoined->True to graph the set of points data and connect consecutive points with line segments. Then we use Show to display ps and lpdata simultaneously. Note that in the result, the points are easy to distinguish because of their larger size.

```
ps=Graphics[{PointSize[.03],Map[Point,data]}];
lpdata=ListPlot[data,PlotJoined->True,DisplayFunction->Identity];
Show[lpdata,ps,DisplayFunction->$DisplayFunction]
```

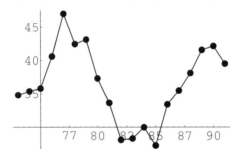

Next, we use InterpolatingPolynomial to find a polynomial approximation, p, of the data in the table. Note that the result is lengthy, so Short is used to display an abbreviated form of p. We then graph p and show the graph of p along with the data in the table for the years corresponding to 1971 to 1993. Although the interpolating polynomial agrees with the data exactly, the interpolating polynomial oscillates wildly.

```
p=InterpolatingPolynomial[data,x];
Short[p,3]
```

    34.8105 + (0.5705 + (-0.0674 +

            (0.747867 + <<1>>) (-75. + x)) (-74. + x))

        (-73. + x)

```
plotp=Plot[p,{x,71,93},DisplayFunction->Identity];
Show[plotp,ps,PlotRange->{0,50},DisplayFunction->$DisplayFunction]
```

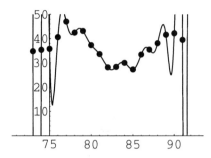

To find a polynomial which approximates the data but does not oscillate wildly, we use Fit. Again, we graph the fit and display the graph of the fit and the data simultaneously. In this case, the fit does not identically agree with the data and does not oscillate wildly.

```
Clear[p]
p=Fit[data,{1,x,x^2,x^3,x^4},x]
```

                                    2   3
    -198884. + 9597.83 x - 173.196 x + 1.38539 x -

                4
    0.00414481 x

```
plotp=Plot[p,{x,71,93},DisplayFunction->Identity];
Show[plotp,ps,PlotRange->{0,50},DisplayFunction->$DisplayFunction]
```

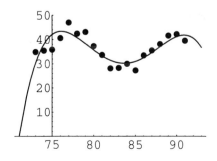

In addition to curve fitting with polynomials, Mathematica can also fit data with trigonometric functions. In this case, we use `Fit` to find an approximation of the data of the form $p = c_1 + c_2 \sin x + c_3 \sin\frac{x}{2} + c_4 \cos x + c_5 \cos\frac{x}{2}$. As in the previous two cases, we graph the fit and display the graph of the fit and the data simultaneously.

```
Clear[p]
p=Fit[data,{1,Sin[x],Sin[x/2],Cos[x],Cos[x/2]},x]
```

$$35.4237 + 4.25768 \; Cos[\tfrac{x}{2}] - 0.941862 \; Cos[x] +$$

$$6.06609 \; Sin[\tfrac{x}{2}] + 0.0272062 \; Sin[x]$$

```
plotp=Plot[p,{x,71,93},DisplayFunction->Identity];
Show[plotp,ps,PlotRange->{0,50},DisplayFunction->$DisplayFunction]
```

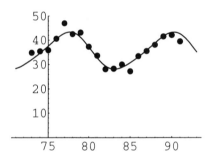

Mathematica supplies several packages which can be used to fit data using different techniques. We illustrate the command `NonlinearFit` in the following example.

EXAMPLE: The interest paid on the public debt of the United States of America as a percentage of Federal expenditures for selected years is shown in the following table. (a) Find a fifth degree polynomial approximation of the data in the table. (b) Find an approximation of the data of the form $h(x) = \dfrac{a_1 x^2 + a_2 x + a_3}{b_1 x^2 + b_2 x + b_3}$.

Year	Interest Paid as a Percentage of Federal Expenditures
1930	0
1940	10.5
1945	4.1
1950	13.4
1955	9.4
1960	10.0
1965	9.6
1970	9.9
1975	9.8
1980	12.7
1985	18.9
1990	21.1

Source: *The World Almanac and Book of Facts*, 1993

SOLUTION: Proceeding as in the previous example, we define `data` to be the set of ordered pairs represented in the table: the x-coordinate of each point represents the number of years past 1900 and the y-coordinate represents the interest paid on the public debt of the Untied States as a percentage of Federal expenditures. We also use `Graphics`, `Map`, and `Point` to convert each of the ordered pairs in `data` to points and declare the result to be a graphics object named `pts`. Note that since `PointSize[.03]` is included within the `Graphics` command, the points will be larger than they would be if `ListPlot` had been used to graph the points.

```
Clear[data]
data={{30,0},{40,10.5},{45,4.1},{50,13.4},{55,9.4},
      {60,10.0},{65,9.6},{70,9.9},{75,9.8},{80,12.7},
      {85,18.9},{90,21.1}};
pts=Graphics[{PointSize[.03],Map[Point,data]}];
```

Next, we use `Fit` to find a fifth degree polynomial approximation of the data in data. We graph the approximation and name the result p1 and then display both p1 and `pts` simultaneously, naming the result p2. Note that p2 is not displayed since p1 is not displayed.

```
Clear[f]
f[x_]=Fit[data,{1,x,x^2,x^3,x^4,x^5},x]
```

$$30.8223 - 6.35418\ x + 0.340698\ x^2 -$$

$$0.00726226\ x^3 + 0.0000681248\ x^4 - 2.32417\ 10^{-7}\ x^5$$

```
p1=Plot[f[x],{x,0,90},DisplayFunction->Identity];
p2=Show[p1,pts];
```

To find a nonlinear fit of the data, we use the command `NonlinearFit` which is contained in the package **NonlinearFit** located in the **Statistics** folder (or directory). Since `NonlinearFit` is not a built-in command, we first load the package **NonlinearFit** and then use `NonlinearFit` to find values of a_1, a_2, a_3, b_1, b_2, and b_3 so that $h(x) = \dfrac{a_1 x^2 + a_2 x + a_3}{b_1 x^2 + b_2 x + b_3}$ approximates the data in the table and name the resulting list `vals`.

```
<<Statistics`NonLinearFit`
Clear[h]
vals=NonlinearFit[data,
      (a1 x^2+a2 x+a3)/(b1 x^2+b2 x+b3),x,{a1,a2,a3,b1,b2,b3}]
```

```
NonlinearFit::lmpnocon:
    Warning: The values of the parameters given to
        NonlinearFit do not appear to have converged.
        The returned value may not be at the minimum.
{a1 -> -2.60692, a2 -> 476.384, a3 -> -11947.2,

 b1 -> -0.69463, b2 -> 93.2257, b3 -> -2312.4}
```

We then substitute the values obtained in `vals` into $h(x) = \dfrac{a_1 x^2 + a_2 x + a_3}{b_1 x^2 + b_2 x + b_3}$. As in the above, we graph the approximation and name the result p3 and then display both p3 and `pts` simultaneously, naming the result p4. Last, we use `GraphicsArray` to show both p2 and p4. In spite of the error messages obtained above, h appears to approximate the data in the table relatively well.

```
h[x_]=(a1 x^2+a2 x+a3)/(b1 x^2+b2 x+b3) /. vals;
p3=Plot[h[x],{x,0,90},DisplayFunction->Identity];
p4=Show[p3,pts];
Show[GraphicsArray[{{p2,p4}}]]
```

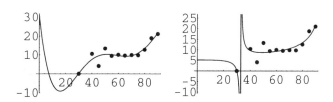

Application: Introduction to Fourier Series

Many problems in applied mathematics are solved through the use of Fourier series. Mathematica assists in the computation of these series in several ways. First, we restate the following standard definitions.

The Fourier series of a periodic function f(x) with period 2L is the trigonometric series

$$a_0 + \sum_{n=1}^{\infty}\left[a_n\cos\left(\frac{n\pi x}{L}\right) + b_n\sin\left(\frac{n\pi x}{L}\right)\right],$$

where $a_0 = \frac{1}{2L}\int_{-L}^{L}f(x)dx$, $a_n = \frac{1}{L}\int_{-L}^{L}f(x)\cos\left(\frac{n\pi x}{L}\right)dx$, and $b_n = \frac{1}{L}\int_{-L}^{L}f(x)\sin\left(\frac{n\pi x}{L}\right)dx$.

The **kth term of the Fourier series** $a_0 + \sum_{n=1}^{\infty}\left[a_n\cos\left(\frac{n\pi x}{L}\right) + b_n\sin\left(\frac{n\pi x}{L}\right)\right]$ is

$$a_k\cos\left(\frac{k\pi x}{L}\right) + b_k\sin\left(\frac{k\pi x}{L}\right).$$

The **kth partial sum of the Fourier series** $a_0 + \sum_{n=1}^{\infty}\left[a_n\cos\left(\frac{n\pi x}{L}\right) + b_n\sin\left(\frac{n\pi x}{L}\right)\right]$ is

$$a_0 + \sum_{n=1}^{k}\left[a_n\cos\left(\frac{n\pi x}{L}\right) + b_n\sin\left(\frac{n\pi x}{L}\right)\right].$$

It is a well-known theorem that if f(x) is a periodic function with period 2L and f'(x) is continuous on [–L,L] except at finitely many points, then at each point x the Fourier series corresponding to f converges and

$$a_0 + \sum_{n=1}^{\infty}\left[a_n\cos\left(\frac{n\pi x}{L}\right) + b_n\sin\left(\frac{n\pi x}{L}\right)\right] = \frac{\underset{y\to x+}{Lim}f(y) + \underset{y\to x-}{Lim}f(y)}{2}.$$

In fact, if the series $\sum_{n=1}^{\infty}\left(\left|a_n\right| + \left|b_n\right|\right)$ converges, then the Fourier series

$$a_0 + \sum_{n=1}^{\infty}\left[a_n\cos\left(\frac{n\pi x}{L}\right) + b_n\sin\left(\frac{n\pi x}{L}\right)\right]$$

converges uniformly on $\Re$.

EXAMPLE: Let $f(x) = \begin{cases} 1 \ if \ 0 \leq x \leq 1 \\ -x \ if \ -1 \leq x < 0 \\ f(x-2) \ if \ x > 1 \end{cases}$. Compute and graph the first few partial

sums of the Fourier series for f.

SOLUTION: We begin by clearing all prior definitions of f. We then define the piecewise function f and graph f on the interval [–1,5].

```
Clear[f]
f[x_]:=1 /; 0<=x<=1
f[x_]:=-x /; -1<=x<0
f[x_]:=f[x-2] /; x>1
graphf=Plot[f[x],{x,-1,5}]
```

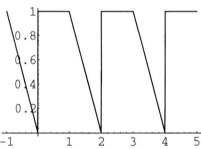

The Fourier series coefficients are computed with the integral formulas given earlier. Executing the commands

```
L=1;
a[0]=1/(2L) NIntegrate[f[x],{x,-L,L}]
```

defines L to be 1 and a[0] to be an approximation of the integral $\frac{1}{2L}\int_{-L}^{L} f(x)dx$.

Executing the commands

```
a[n_]:=1/L NIntegrate[f[x] Cos[n Pi x/L],{x,-L,L}]
b[n_]:=1/L NIntegrate[f[x] Sin[n Pi x/L],{x,-L,L}]
```

defines a[n] to be an approximation of the integral $\frac{1}{L}\int_{-L}^{L} f(x)\cos\left(\frac{n\pi x}{L}\right)dx$ and b[n]

to be an approximation of the integral $\frac{1}{L}\int_{-L}^{L} f(x)\sin\left(\frac{n\pi x}{L}\right)dx$.

```
Clear[a,b,fs,L]
L=1;
a[0]=1/(2L) NIntegrate[f[x],{x,-L,L}]
```

```
     0.75
```

```
a[n_]:=1/L NIntegrate[f[x] Cos[n*Pi x/L],{x,-L,L}]
b[n_]:=1/L NIntegrate[f[x] Sin[n*Pi x/L],{x,-L,L}]
```

A table containing the coefficients `a[i]` and `b[i]` for i = 1, 2, 3,..., 10 is created and named `coeffs`. Several error messages are generated because of the discontinuities but the resulting approximations are satisfactory for our purposes. The elements in the first column of the table represent the a_i's and the second column represents the b_i's . Notice how the elements of the table are extracted using double brackets with `coeffs`.

```
coeffs=Table[{a[i],b[i]},{i,1,10}];
```

```
NIntegrate::ncvb:
    NIntegrate failed to converge to
      prescribed accuracy after 7
        recursive bisections in x near x = -1..
NIntegrate::ncvb:
    NIntegrate failed to converge to
      prescribed accuracy after 7
        recursive bisections in x near x = -1..
```

```
TableForm[coeffs]
```

-0.202642	0.31831
$1.01644 \cdot 10^{-20}$	0.159155
-0.0225158	0.106103
$2.95932 \cdot 10^{-20}$	0.0795775
-0.00810569	0.063662
$-3.17637 \cdot 10^{-20}$	0.0530516
-0.00413556	0.0454873
$5.84453 \cdot 10^{-20}$	0.0397887
-0.203173	0.0357218
$7.48565 \cdot 10^{-20}$	0.031831

The first element of the list is extracted with `coeffs[[1]]`:

```
coeffs[[1]]
```

```
{-0.202642, 0.31831}
```

The first element of the second element of `coeffs` and the second element of the third element of `coeffs` are extracted with `coeffs[[2,1]]` and `coeffs[[3,2]]`, respectively.

```
coeffs[[2,1]]
```

$$1.01644 \cdot 10^{-20}$$

```
coeffs[[3,2]]
```

```
0.106103
```

Once the coefficients are calculated, the nth partial sum of the Fourier series is obtained with Sum. The kth term of the Fourier series, $a_k \cos(k\pi x) + b_k \sin(k\pi x)$, is defined in fs below. Hence, the nth partial sum of the series is given by

$$a_0 + \sum_{k=1}^{n} a_k \cos(k\pi x) + b_k \sin(k\pi x) = a[0] + \sum_{k=1}^{n} fs[k,x]$$

which is defined in fourier using Sum. We illustrate the use of fourier by finding fourier[2,x] and fourier[3,x].

```
fs[k_,x_]:=coeffs[[k,1]] Cos[k Pi x]+coeffs[[k,2]] Sin[k Pi x]
fourier[n_,x_]:=a[0]+Sum[fs[k,x],{k,1,n}]
fourier[2,x]
```

```
    0.75 - 0.202642 Cos[Pi x] +

                -20
      1.01644 10     Cos[2 Pi x] +

      0.31831 Sin[Pi x] +

      0.159155 Sin[2 Pi x]
```

```
fourier[3,x]
```

```
    0.75 - 0.202642 Cos[Pi x] +

                -20
      1.01644 10     Cos[2 Pi x] -

      0.0225158 Cos[3 Pi x] +

      0.31831 Sin[Pi x] +

      0.159155 Sin[2 Pi x] +

      0.106103 Sin[3 Pi x]
```

To see how the Fourier series approximates the periodic function, we plot the function simultaneously with the Fourier approximation for n=2 and n=5. The results are displayed together using GraphicsArray.

```
graphtwo=Plot[fourier[2,x],{x,-1,5},PlotStyle->GrayLevel[0.2],
        DisplayFunction->Identity];
bothtwo=Show[graphtwo,graphf];
graphfive=Plot[fourier[5,x],{x,-1,5},PlotStyle->GrayLevel[0.2],
        DisplayFunction->Identity];
bothfive=Show[graphfive,graphf];
Show[GraphicsArray[{bothtwo,bothfive}]]
```

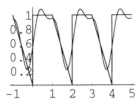 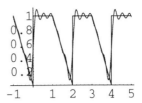

The package **FourierTransform** in the **Calculus** folder (or directory) contains several commands, such as `FourierTrigSeries`, `FourierSinSeriesCoefficient`, `FourierCosSeriesCoefficient,` and `NFourierTrigSeries`, which can be used to compute exact or approximate Fourier series of some functions.

Application: The One-Dimensional Heat Equation

A typical problem in applied mathematics which involves the use of Fourier series is that of the one-dimensional heat equation. This initial value problem which describes the temperature in a uniform rod with insulated surface is given by:

   i. $k\dfrac{\partial^2 u}{\partial x^2} = \dfrac{\partial u}{\partial t}, 0 < x < a, t > 0;$

   ii. $u(0,t) = T_0$, t>0;

   iii. $u(a,t) = T_a$, t>0; and

   iv. $u(x,0) = f(x)$, 0<x<a.

The solution to the problem is

$$u(x,t) = \underbrace{T_0 + \frac{1}{a}x(T_a - T_0)}_{v(x)} + \sum_{n=1}^{\infty} b_n \sin(\lambda_n x) e^{-\lambda_n^2 k t} \quad ,$$

where $\lambda_n = \dfrac{n\pi}{a}$ and $b_n = \dfrac{2}{a}\displaystyle\int_0^a (f(x) - v(x))\sin\left(\dfrac{n\pi x}{a}\right)dx$, and is obtained through separation of variables techniques. The coefficient b_n in the solution, $u(x,t)$, is the Fourier series coefficient b_n of the function $f(x) - v(x)$, where v(x) is the steady-state temperature.

EXAMPLE: Consider the heat equation with $k = 1$ and initial temperature distribution $f(x) = -(x-1)\cos(\pi x)$. The steady-state temperature for this problem is $v(x) = 1 - x$, and the eigenvalue, λ_n, is given by $\dfrac{n\pi}{4}$. Approximate the solution u(x,t) using these conditions.

SOLUTION: The function f is defined and plotted below. Also, the steady-state temperature, $v(x)$, and the eigenvalue are defined. Finally, `Integrate` is used to define a function which will be used to calculate the coefficients of the solution.

```
Clear[f]
f[x_]:=-(x-1) Cos[Pi x]
Plot[f[x],{x,0,4}]
```

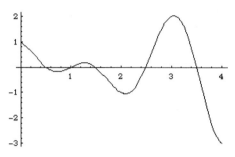

```
v[x_]:=1-x
lambda[n_]:=n Pi/4
b[n_]:=b[n]=Integrate[(f[x]-v[x])*Sin[n Pi x/4],{x,0,4}]
```

Notice that b[n] is defined using b[n_]:=b[n]=... so that Mathematica "remembers" the values of b[n] computed and thus avoids recomputing previously computed values. In the following table, we compute exact and approximate values of b[1], ..., b[10].

```
Table[{n,b[n],b[n]//N},{n,1,10}]//TableForm
```

	128	

1	15 Pi	2.71624
	-32	

2	3 Pi	-3.39531
	128	

3	21 Pi	1.94017
	-3	
	--	
4	Pi	-0.95493
	-128	

5	45 Pi	-0.905415
	32	

6	15 Pi	0.679061
	-128	

7	231 Pi	-0.17638
	2	

```
8    3 Pi      0.212207
     -128

     ------
9    585 Pi   -0.0696473
      32

     ------
10   105 Pi    0.0970087
```

Let $S_m = b_m \sin(\lambda_m x) e^{-\lambda_m^2 t}$. Then, the desired solution u(x,t) is given by

$$u(x,t) = v(x) + \sum_{m=1}^{\infty} S_m .$$

Let $u(x,t,n) = v(x) + \sum_{m=1}^{n} S_m$. Notice that $u(x,t,n) = u(x,t,n-1) + S_n$. Consequently, approximations of the solution to the heat equation are obtained recursively taking advantage of Mathematica's ability to compute recursively. The solution is first defined for n = 1 by u[x,t,1]. Subsequent partial sums, u[x,t,n], are obtained by adding the nth term of the series, $S_n = b_n \sin(\lambda_n x) e^{-\lambda_n^2 t}$, to u[x,t,n-1].

```
u[x_,t_,1]:=v[x]+b[1] Sin[lambda[1]*x]Exp[-lambda[1]^2 t]
u[x_,t_,n_]:=u[x,t,n-1]+b[n]*Sin[lambda[n] x] Exp[-lambda[n]^2 t]
```

By defining the solution in this manner a table can be created which includes the partial sums of the solution. In the following table, we compute the first, fourth, and seventh partial sums of the solution to the problem.

```
Table[u[x,t,n],{n,1,7,3}]//TableForm

                     Pi x
            128 Sin[----]
                      4
    1 - x + ------------------
                   2
                (Pi  t)/16
            15 E              Pi
                     Pi x                 Pi x
            128 Sin[----]        32 Sin[----]
                      4                    2
    1 - x + ------------------  - --------------- +
                   2                    2
                (Pi  t)/16            (Pi  t)/4
            15 E              Pi   3 E              Pi

                3 Pi x
        128 Sin[------]
                   4              3 Sin[Pi x]
    ------------------------ - -----------
               2                    2
```

```
      (9 Pi  t)/16          Pi  t
  21 E               Pi  E       Pi
                  Pi x                      Pi x
         128 Sin[----]         32 Sin[----]
                   4                         2
  1 - x + ----------------- - ---------------- +
                  2                     2
             (Pi  t)/16           (Pi  t)/4
       15 E             Pi  3 E             Pi

                3 Pi x
       128 Sin[------]
                  4                3 Sin[Pi x]
    ------------------- - ----------- -
               2                   2
       (9 Pi  t)/16          Pi  t
  21 E               Pi  E       Pi

              5 Pi x                   3 Pi x
     128 Sin[------]         32 Sin[------]
                4                        2
    ------------------- + ------------------- -
               2                     2
       (25 Pi  t)/16          (9 Pi  t)/4
  45 E               Pi  15 E             Pi

              7 Pi x
     128 Sin[------]
                4
    ---------------------
               2
       (49 Pi  t)/16
 231 E               Pi
```

To generate graphics which can be animated, we use a Do loop. The 10th partial sum of the solution is plotted below for t = 0 to t = 3 using a step-size in t of 3/20. Remember that u[x,t,n] is determined with a Table command. Therefore, Evaluate must be used in the Do command below so that Mathematica first computes the solution u and then evaluates u at the particular values of x. Otherwise, u is recalculated for each value of x. The plots of the solution obtained above can be animated as indicated in the following window.

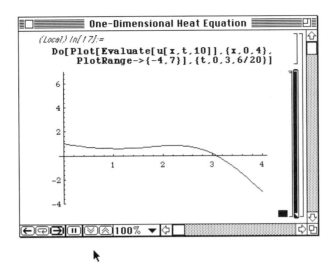

```
Do[Plot[Evaluate[u[x,t,10]],{x,0,4},PlotRange->{-4,7}],{t,0,3,6/20}]
```

Alternatively, we may generate several graphics and display the resulting set of graphics as a GraphicsArray. Below, we plot the 10th partial sum of the solution for t = 0 to t = 3 using a step-size in t of 3/8. The resulting nine graphs are named graphs which are then partitioned into three element subsets with Partition and named toshow. We then use Show and GraphicsArray to display toshow.

```
graphs=Table[Plot[Evaluate[u[x,t,10]],{x,0,4},Ticks->None,
        PlotRange->{-4,6.5},DisplayFunction->Identity],{t,0,3,3/8}];
toshow=Partition[graphs,3];
Show[GraphicsArray[toshow]]
```

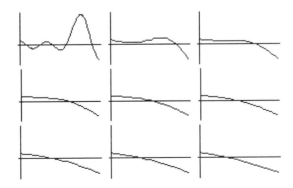

∎

Nested Lists: Matrices and Vectors

Chapter 5 discusses operations on matrices and vectors, including vector calculus and systems of equations. Several linear programming examples are discussed. Applications discussed in this chapter include linear programming, and vector calculus.

5.1 Nested Lists: Introduction to Matrices, Vectors, and Matrix Operations

Defining Nested Lists: Matrices and Vectors

Matrix algebra can be performed with Mathematica. Before introducing the operations involved in matrix algebra, the method by which a matrix is entered must first be discussed. In Mathematica, a **matrix** is simply a list of lists where each list represents a row of the matrix. Therefore, the $m \times n$ matrix

$$A = \left(a_{ij}\right) = \begin{pmatrix} a_{11} & a_{12} & a_{13} & \cdots & a_{1n} \\ a_{21} & a_{22} & a_{23} & \cdots & a_{2n} \\ a_{31} & a_{32} & a_{33} & \cdots & a_{3n} \\ \vdots & \vdots & \vdots & & \vdots \\ a_{m1} & a_{m2} & a_{m3} & \cdots & a_{mn} \end{pmatrix}$$

is entered in the following manner:

```
A={{a[1,1],a[1,2],...,a[1,n]},{a[2,1],a[2,2],...,a[2,n]},...,
    {a[m,1],a[m,2],...,a[m,n]}}.
```

For example, to use Mathematica to define m to be the matrix $\begin{pmatrix} a_{11} & a_{12} \\ a_{21} & a_{22} \end{pmatrix}$ enter the command

```
m={{a[1,1],a[1,2]},{a[2,1],a[2,2]}},
```

where $a[1,1]=a_{11}$, $a[1,2]=a_{12}$, $a[2,1]=a_{21}$, and $a[2,2]=a_{22}$.

Another way to create a matrix is to use the command `Array`. The command `m=Array[a,{2,2}]` produces the same result as above. Once a matrix has been entered, it can be placed in the usual form (with rows and columns) using the command `MatrixForm[A]`.

The following examples illustrate the definition of a 3×3 matrix and of a 2×4 matrix.

EXAMPLE: Use Mathematica to define the matrices $\begin{pmatrix} a_{11} & a_{12} & a_{13} \\ a_{21} & a_{22} & a_{23} \\ a_{31} & a_{32} & a_{33} \end{pmatrix}$ and $\begin{pmatrix} b_{11} & b_{12} & b_{13} & b_{14} \\ b_{21} & b_{22} & b_{23} & b_{24} \end{pmatrix}$.

SOLUTION: In this case, both `Table[a[i,j],{i,1,3},{j,1,3}]` and `Array[a,{3,3}]` produce the same result. Below, we use each to define `matrixa` to be the matrix

$$\begin{pmatrix} a_{11} & a_{12} & a_{13} \\ a_{21} & a_{22} & a_{23} \\ a_{31} & a_{32} & a_{33} \end{pmatrix}$$

The commands `MatrixForm` or `TableForm` are used to display the results in traditional matrix form.

```
Clear[a,b,matrixa,matrixb]
matrixa=Table[a[i,j],{i,1,3},{j,1,3}]

    {{a[1, 1], a[1, 2], a[1, 3]},

     {a[2, 1], a[2, 2], a[2, 3]},

     {a[3, 1], a[3, 2], a[3, 3]}}

MatrixForm[matrixa]

    a[1, 1]   a[1, 2]   a[1, 3]
    a[2, 1]   a[2, 2]   a[2, 3]
    a[3, 1]   a[3, 2]   a[3, 3]

matrixa=Array[a,{3,3}]

    {{a[1, 1], a[1, 2], a[1, 3]},

     {a[2, 1], a[2, 2], a[2, 3]},

     {a[3, 1], a[3, 2], a[3, 3]}}

MatrixForm[matrixa]

    a[1, 1]   a[1, 2]   a[1, 3]
    a[2, 1]   a[2, 2]   a[2, 3]
    a[3, 1]   a[3, 2]   a[3, 3]
```

We may also use Mathematica to define non-square matrices as indicated below. The same results would have been obtained by entering `Table[b[i,j],{i,1,2},{j,1,4}]`.

```
matrixb=Array[b,{2,4}]

    {{b[1, 1], b[1, 2], b[1, 3], b[1, 4]},

     {b[2, 1], b[2, 2], b[2, 3], b[2, 4]}}

MatrixForm[matrixb]

    b[1, 1]   b[1, 2]   b[1, 3]   b[1, 4]
    b[2, 1]   b[2, 2]   b[2, 3]   b[2, 4]   ■
```

More generally the commands `Table[f[i,j],{i,imax},{j,jmax}]` and `Array[f,{imax,jmax}]` yield nested lists corresponding to the $\mathrm{imax} \times \mathrm{jmax}$ matrix

$$\begin{pmatrix} f(1,1) & f(1,2) & \cdots & f(1,\mathrm{jmax}) \\ f(2,1) & f(2,2) & \cdots & f(2,\mathrm{jmax}) \\ \vdots & \vdots & & \vdots \\ f(\mathrm{imax},1) & f(\mathrm{imax},2) & \cdots & f(\mathrm{imax},\mathrm{jmax}) \end{pmatrix}$$

`Table [f[i,j],{i,imin,imax,istep},{j,jmin,jmax,jstep}]` calculates the list of lists

```
{{f[imin,jmin],f[imin,jmin+jstep],...,
    f[imin,jmax]},{f[imin+istep,jmin],...,f[imin+istep,jmax]}
        ,...,{f[imax,jmin],...,f[imax,jmax]}},
```

and the command

```
Table[f[i,j,k,...],{i,imin,imax,istep},{j,jmin,jmax,jstep},
    {k,kmin,kmax,kstep},...]
```

calculates a nested list; the list associated with `i` is outermost. If `istep` is omitted, the `stepsize` is one.

EXAMPLE: Define C to be the 3×4 matrix $\left(c_{ij}\right)$, where c$_{ij}$, the entry in the ith row and jth column of C, is the numerical value of $\cos(j^2 - i^2)\sin(i^2 - j^2)$.

SOLUTION: After clearing all prior definitions of c, if any, we define $c(i,j)$ to be the numerical value of $c(i,j) = \cos(j^2 - i^2)\sin(i^2 - j^2)$ and then use `Array` to compute the 3×4 matrix `matrixc`.

```
Clear[c,matrixc]
c[i_,j_]=N[Cos[j^2-i^2]*Sin[i^2-j^2]]

         2       2
    Cos[i  - 1. j ]

           2     2
      Sin[i  - 1. j ]

matrixc=Array[c,{3,4}]

    {{0., 0.139708, 0.143952, 0.494016},

      {-0.139708, 0., 0.272011, 0.452789},

      {-0.143952, -0.272011, 0., -0.495304}}
```

```
MatrixForm[matrixc]
```

```
0.          0.139708      0.143952      0.494016
-0.139708   0.            0.272011      0.452789
-0.143952   -0.272011     0.            -0.495304
```

■

EXAMPLE: Define the matrix $\begin{pmatrix} 1 & 0 & 0 \\ 0 & 1 & 0 \\ 0 & 0 & 1 \end{pmatrix}$.

SOLUTION: The matrix

$$\begin{pmatrix} 1 & 0 & 0 \\ 0 & 1 & 0 \\ 0 & 0 & 1 \end{pmatrix}$$

is the 3×3 identity matrix. The command `IdentityMatrix[n]` returns the $n \times n$ identity matrix.

```
IdentityMatrix[3]
```

```
{{1, 0, 0}, {0, 1, 0}, {0, 0, 1}}
```

■

EXAMPLE: Generate a 2×3 where the entries are randomly chosen integers between –4 and 4.

SOLUTION: Below, we use `Table`, `Random`, and `Integer` to generate the matrix. If you enter the following command, your results will almost certainly be different than the results shown here.

```
b=Table[Random[Integer,{-4,4}],{2},{3}];
MatrixForm[b]
```

```
-4   -2   -2
 2   -1   -1
```

■

In Mathematica, a **vector** is a list of numbers and, thus, is entered in the same manner as lists. For example, to use Mathematica to define the row vector `vectorv` to be $\begin{pmatrix} v_1 & v_2 & v_3 \end{pmatrix}$ enter `vectorv={v[1],v[2],v[3]}`. Similarly, to define the column vector `vectorv` to be

$$\begin{pmatrix} v_1 \\ v_2 \\ v_3 \end{pmatrix}$$

enter `vectorv={v[1],v[2],v[3]}`. Mathematica does not distinguish between row and column vectors. Nevertheless, Mathematica performs computations with vectors and matrices correctly as long as the computations are well-defined.

EXAMPLE: Define w to be the vector $\begin{pmatrix} -4 \\ -5 \\ 2 \end{pmatrix}$, `vectorv` to be the vector $\begin{pmatrix} v_1 & v_2 & v_3 & v_4 \end{pmatrix}$, and `zerovec` to be the vector $\begin{pmatrix} 0 & 0 & 0 & 0 & 0 \end{pmatrix}$.

SOLUTION: To define w, we enter:

```
w={-4,-5,2}
```

```
{-4, -5, 2}
```

Similarly, to define `vectorv`, we enter:

```
vectorv=Array[v,4]
```

```
{v[1], v[2], v[3], v[4]}
```

The same results as above would have been obtained by entering `Table[v[i],{i,1,4}]`. Last, to define `zerovec`, we enter:

```
zerovec=Table[0,{5}]
```

```
{0, 0, 0, 0, 0}
```

■

Extracting Elements of Matrices

For the 2×2 matrix `m={{a[1,1],a[1,2]},{a[2,1],a[2,2]}}` defined earlier, `m[[1]]` yields the first element of matrix m which is the list `{a[1,1],a[1,2]}`; `m[[2,1]]` yields the first element of the second element of matrix m which is `a[2,1]`. In general, if m is an m × n matrix, `m[[i,j]]` yields the unique element in the ith row and jth column. More specifically, `m[[i,j]]` yields the jth part of the ith part of m. Generally, `list[[i]]` or `Part[list,i]` yields the ith part of `list`; `list[[i,j]]` or `Part[list,i,j]` yields the jth part of the ith part of `list`, and so on.

EXAMPLE: Define mb to be the matrix $\begin{pmatrix} 10 & -6 & -9 \\ 6 & -5 & -7 \\ -10 & 9 & 12 \end{pmatrix}$. (a) Extract the third row of mb. (b) Extract the element in the first row and third column of mb. (c) Display mb in traditional matrix form.

SOLUTION: We begin by defining mb. mb[[i,j]] yields the (unique) number in the ith row and jth column of mb. Observe how various components of mb (rows and elements) can be extracted and how mb is placed in MatrixForm.

```
mb={{10,-6,-9},{6,-5,-7},{-10,9,12}}
```

```
{{10, -6, -9}, {6, -5, -7}, {-10, 9, 12}}
```

```
MatrixForm[mb]
```

```
10    -6    -9
 6    -5    -7
-10    9    12
```

```
mb[[3]]
```

```
{-10, 9, 12}
```

```
mb[[1,3]]
```

```
-9
```

In the previous example, we saw that the third row of mb is extracted with mb[[3]]. More generally, if m is a matrix, the ith row of m is extracted with m[[i]]. The command Transpose[m] yields the transpose of the matrix m, obtained by interchanging the rows and columns of m. We can use Transpose to extract a column from a matrix m by extracting rows from the transpose. Namely, if m is a matrix, Transpose[m][[i]] extracts the ith row from the transpose of m which is the same as the ith column of m.

EXAMPLE: Extract the second and third columns from A if $A = \begin{pmatrix} 0 & -2 & 2 \\ -1 & 1 & 3 \\ 2 & -4 & 1 \end{pmatrix}$.

SOLUTION: We first define matrixa and then use Transpose to compute the transpose of matrixa, naming the result ta, and then displaying ta in MatrixForm.

```
matrixa={{0,-2,2},{-1,1,-3},{2,-4,1}};

ta=Transpose[matrixa];
MatrixForm[ta]
```

$$\begin{array}{ccc} 0 & -1 & 2 \\ -2 & 1 & -4 \\ 2 & -3 & 1 \end{array}$$

Next, we extract the second column of `matrixa` using `Transpose`. Since we have already defined `ta` to be the transpose of `matrixa`, entering `ta[[2]]` would produce the same result.

```
Transpose[matrixa][[2]]
```

```
{-2, 1, -4}
```

To extract the third column, we take advantage of the fact that we have already defined `ta` to be the transpose of `matrixa`. Entering `Transpose[matrixa][[3]]` would produce the same result.

```
ta[[3]]
```

```
{2, -3, 1}
```

■

Once a matrix or array has been defined, we may use it in subsequent calculations.

EXAMPLE: The following table contains approximations of the first eight zeros for the Bessel functions of the first kind, $J_n(x)$, of order n=0, 1, 2, ... , 6. (a) List approximations of the first eight zeros of the Bessel function of the first kind of order 1. (b) What is an approximation of the fourth zero of the Bessel function of the first kind of order 2 and an approximation of the third zero of the Bessel function of the first kind of order 2? (c) Define a function `alpha` which, given n and m, returns an approximation of the mth zero of the Bessel function of the first kind of order n. (d) Use `alpha` to obtain an approximation of the third zero of the Bessel function of the first kind of order 0 and the third zero of the Bessel function of the first kind of order 5.

	1	2	3	4	5	6	7	8
$J_0(x)$	2.4048	5.5201	8.6537	11.792	14.931	18.071	21.212	24.352
$J_1(x)$	3.8317	7.0156	10.173	13.324	16.471	19.616	22.760	25.904
$J_2(x)$	5.1356	8.4172	11.620	14.796	17.960	21.117	24.270	27.421
$J_3(x)$	6.3802	9.7610	13.015	16.223	19.409	22.583	25.748	28.908
$J_4(x)$	7.5883	11.065	14.373	17.616	20.827	24.019	27.199	30.371
$J_5(x)$	8.7715	12.339	15.700	18.980	22.218	25.430	28.627	31.812
$J_6(x)$	9.9361	13.589	17.004	20.321	23.586	26.820	30.034	33.233

SOLUTION: We begin by defining zeros to be the array of numbers in the table above.

```
zeros={{2.4048,5.5201,8.6537,11.792,14.931,18.071,21.212,24.352},
{3.8317,7.0156,10.173,13.324,16.471,19.616,22.760,25.904},
{5.1356,8.4172,11.620,14.796,17.960,21.117,24.270,27.421},
{6.3802,9.7610,13.015,16.223,19.409,22.583,25.748,28.908},
{7.5883,11.065,14.373,17.616,20.827,24.019,27.199,30.371},
{8.7715,12.339,15.700,18.980,22.218,25.430,28.627,31.812},
{9.9361,13.589,17.004,20.321,23.586,26.820,30.034,33.233}};
```

The second element of `zeros`, corresponding to approximations of the first eight zeros of the Bessel function of the first kind, $J_1(x)$, is extracted with `zeros[[2]]`.

```
zeros[[2]]
```

```
{3.8317, 7.0156, 10.173, 13.324, 16.471, 19.616, 22.76, 25.904}
```

An approximation of the fourth zero of the Bessel function of the first kind of order 2 is the fourth element of the third element of `zeros`.

```
zeros[[3,4]]
```

```
14.796
```

On the other hand, the third zero of the Bessel function of the first kind of order 3 is the third element of the fourth element of `zeros`, extracted below with `Part`. The same result would be obtained by entering `zeros[[4,3]]`.

```
Part[zeros,4,3]
```

```
13.015
```

Below we define the function `alpha`. Given n and m, `alpha[n,m]` returns an approximation of the mth zero of the Bessel function of the first kind of order n. We use `alpha` to obtain an approximation of the third zero of the Bessel function of the first kind of order 0 and the third zero of the Bessel function of the first kind of order 5.

```
alpha[n_,m_]:=zeros[[n+1,m]]
alpha[0,3]

    8.6537

alpha[5,3]

    15.7
```

■

Basic Computations with Matrices and Vectors

Mathematica performs all of the usual operations on matrices. Matrix addition (A+B), scalar multiplication (kA), matrix multiplication, when defined, (A.B), and combinations of these operations are all possible. The **transpose** of A is obtained by interchanging the rows and columns of A and is found with the built-in command `Transpose[A]`. If A is a square matrix, the **determinant** of A is obtained with `Det[A]`.

If A and B are n × n matrices satisfying AB = BA = I, then B is called the **inverse** of A and is denoted by A^{-1}. The inverse of a matrix A, provided it exists, is found with the command `Inverse[A]`.

EXAMPLE: Define ma to be the matrix $\begin{pmatrix} 3 & -4 & 5 \\ 8 & 0 & -3 \\ 5 & 2 & 1 \end{pmatrix}$ and mb to be the matrix

$\begin{pmatrix} 10 & -6 & -9 \\ 6 & -5 & -7 \\ -10 & 9 & 12 \end{pmatrix}$. Compute (a) ma+mb; (b) mb−4ma; (c) the inverse of ma•mb; (d) the

transpose of (ma − 2mb)•mb; and (e) $\det \begin{pmatrix} 3 & -4 & 5 \\ 8 & 0 & -3 \\ 5 & 2 & 1 \end{pmatrix} = \begin{vmatrix} 3 & -4 & 5 \\ 8 & 0 & -3 \\ 5 & 2 & 1 \end{vmatrix}$.

SOLUTION: As described above, we enter ma and mb as nested lists where each element corresponds to a row of the matrix:

```
ma={{3,-4,5},{8,0,-3},{5,2,1}};
mb={{10,-6,-9},{6,-5,-7},{-10,9,12}}
```

Entering

```
ma+mb//TableForm
```

```
13   -10   -4
14   -5    -10
-5   11    13
```

adds matrix ma to mb and expresses the result in traditional matrix form. Entering

```
mb-4 ma//TableForm
```

```
-2    10    -29
-26   -5    5
-30   1     8
```

subtracts four times matrix ma from mb and expresses the result in traditional matrix form. Entering

```
Inverse[ma.mb]//TableForm
```

```
 59          53         167
---         ---       -(---)
380         190         380
   223         92      979
-(---)     -(--)       ---
   570         95      570
 49          18         187
---          --       -(---)
114          19         114
```

computes the inverse of ma•mb. Similarly, entering

```
Transpose[(ma-2 mb).mb]//TableForm
```

```
-352   -90   384
269    73    -277
373    98    -389
```

computes the transpose of $(ma - 2mb) \bullet mb$ and entering

```
Det[ma]
```

```
190
```

computes the determinant of ma. ■

As indicated in the previous example, matrix products, when defined, are computed with ... Note that . is also used to compute the dot product of two vectors, when defined.

EXAMPLE: Compute $A \bullet B$ and $B \bullet A$ if $A = \begin{pmatrix} -1 & -5 & -5 & -4 \\ -3 & 5 & 3 & -2 \\ -4 & 4 & 2 & -3 \end{pmatrix}$ and $B = \begin{pmatrix} 1 & -2 \\ -4 & 3 \\ 4 & -4 \\ -5 & -3 \end{pmatrix}$.

SOLUTION: Since A is a 3×4 matrix and B is a 4×2 `matrix`, $A \bullet B$ is defined and is a 3×2 matrix. Below we first define `matrixa` and `matrixb`, then compute the product, naming the result `ab`, and display `ab` in `MatrixForm`.

```
matrixa={{-1, -5, -5, -4}, {-3, 5, 3, -2}, {-4, 4, 2, -3}};
matrixb={{1, -2}, {-4, 3}, {4, -4}, {-5, -3}};
ab=matrixa.matrixb;
MatrixForm[ab]
```

```
      19    19
      -1    15
       3    21
```

However, the matrix product $B \bullet A$ is not defined and Mathematica produces error messages when we attempt to compute $B \bullet A$.

```
matrixb.matrixa
```

```
    Dot::dotsh: Tensors {{1, -2}, {-4, 3}, {4, -4}, {-5, -3}} and
        {{-1, -5, -5, -4}, {-3, 5, 3, -2}, {-4, 4, 2, -3}}
          have incompatible shapes.
    {{1, -2}, {-4, 3}, {4, -4}, {-5, -3}} .

      {{-1, -5, -5, -4}, {-3, 5, 3, -2}, {-4, 4, 2, -3}}
```

∎

Computations with vectors are performed in the same way.

EXAMPLE: Let $v = \begin{pmatrix} 0 \\ 5 \\ 1 \\ 2 \end{pmatrix}$ and $w = \begin{pmatrix} 3 \\ 0 \\ 4 \\ -2 \end{pmatrix}$. (a) Calculate $v - 2w$ and $v \bullet w$ (b) Find a unit vector with same direction as v and a unit vector with the same direction as w.

SOLUTION: We begin by defining v and w and then compute $v - 2w$ and $v \bullet w$.

```
v={0,5,1,2};
w={3,0,4,-2};
v-2w
```

```
    {-6, 5, -7, 6}
```

```
v.w
```

```
    0
```

The **norm** of a vector

$$v = \begin{pmatrix} v_1 \\ v_2 \\ \vdots \\ v_n \end{pmatrix} \quad \text{is} \quad \|v\| = \sqrt{v_1^2 + v_2^2 + \ldots + v_n^2} = \sqrt{v \bullet v}$$

If k is a scalar, the direction of kv is the same as the direction of v. Thus, if z is a nonzero vector, the vector $\dfrac{v}{\|v\|}$ has the same direction as v, and since

$\left\| \dfrac{v}{\|v\|} \right\| = \dfrac{1}{\|v\|}\|v\| = 1$, $\dfrac{v}{\|v\|}$ is a unit vector. Below, we define the function `norm` which,

given v, computes $\|v\|$. We then compute $\dfrac{v}{\|v\|}$ and $\dfrac{w}{\|w\|}$. The results correspond to

unit vectors with the same direction as v and w, respectively.

```
norm[v_]:=Sqrt[v.v]
uv=v/norm[v]
```

```
              5            1           2
    {0, Sqrt[-], --------, Sqrt[--]}
              6      Sqrt[30]      15
```

```
norm[uv]
```

```
    1
```

```
w/norm[w]
```

```
         3                  4           -2
    {--------, 0, --------, --------}
     Sqrt[29]       Sqrt[29]  Sqrt[29]    ■
```

Special attention must be given to the notation which must be used in taking the product of a matrix with itself. The following example illustrates how Mathematica interprets the expression `(matrixb)^3`. The command `(matrixb)^3` cubes each element of the matrix `matrixb`. The built-in command `MatrixPower` may be used to compute powers of matrices.

EXAMPLE: Let $B = \begin{pmatrix} -2 & 3 & 4 & 0 \\ -2 & 0 & 1 & 3 \\ -1 & 4 & -6 & 5 \\ 4 & 8 & 11 & -4 \end{pmatrix}$. (a) Compute B^2 and B^3. (b) Cube each entry of B.

SOLUTION: After defining B, we compute B^2. The same results would have been obtained by entering `MatrixPower[B,2]`.

```
matrixb={{-2,3,4,0},{-2,0,1,3},{-1,4,-6,5},{4,8,11,-4}};
matrixb.matrixb//MatrixForm
```

-6	10	-29	29
15	22	19	-7
20	13	91	-38
-51	24	-86	95

Next, we use `MatrixPower` to compute B^3. The same results would be obtained by entering `matrixb.matrixb.matrixb`.

```
MatrixPower[matrixb,3]//MatrixForm
```

137	98	479	-231
-121	65	-109	189
-309	120	-871	646
520	263	1381	-738

Last, we cube each entry of B with ^.

```
matrixb^3//MatrixForm
```

-8	27	64	0
-8	0	1	27
-1	64	-216	125
64	512	1331	-64

■

5.2 Linear Systems of Equations

Calculating Solutions of Linear Systems of Equations

To solve the system of linear equations $Ax=b$, where A is the coefficient matrix, b is the known vector, and x is the unknown vector, we proceed in the usual manner: if A^{-1} exists, then $A^{-1}Ax = A^{-1}b$ so $x = A^{-1}b$.

EXAMPLE: Solve the matrix equation $\begin{pmatrix} 3 & 0 & 2 \\ -3 & 2 & 2 \\ 2 & -3 & 3 \end{pmatrix}\begin{pmatrix} x \\ y \\ z \end{pmatrix} = \begin{pmatrix} 3 \\ -1 \\ 4 \end{pmatrix}$.

SOLUTION: The solution is given by

$$\begin{pmatrix} x \\ y \\ z \end{pmatrix} = \begin{pmatrix} 3 & 0 & 2 \\ -3 & 2 & 2 \\ 2 & -3 & 3 \end{pmatrix}^{-1} \begin{pmatrix} 3 \\ -1 \\ 4 \end{pmatrix}.$$

We proceed by defining `matrixa` and `b` and then using `Inverse` to calculate `Inverse[matrixa].b`, naming the resulting output `{x,y,z}`.

```
matrixa={{3,0,2},{-3,2,2},{2,-3,3}};
b={3,-1,4};
```

```
{x,y,z}=Inverse[matrixa].b
```

```
     13      7     15
    {--, -(--), --}
     23     23     23
```

We verify that the results are the desired solution by calculating `matrixa.{x,y,z}`. Because the result is

$$\begin{pmatrix} 3 \\ -1 \\ 4 \end{pmatrix},$$

we conclude that the solution to the system is

$$\begin{pmatrix} x \\ y \\ z \end{pmatrix} = \begin{pmatrix} 13/23 \\ -7/23 \\ 15/23 \end{pmatrix}.$$

```
matrixa.{x,y,z}
```

```
    {3, -1, 4}
```

■

Mathematica offers several commands for solving systems of linear equations, however, which do not depend on the computation of the inverse of A. These commands are discussed in the following examples.

The command

```
Solve[{eqn1,eqn2,...,eqnn},{var1,var2,...,varn}]
```

solves an n × n system of linear equations (n equations and n unknown variables). Note that both the equations as well as the variables are entered as lists. If one wishes to solve for all variables that appear in a system, the command `Solve[{eqn1,eqn2,...eqnn}]` attempts to solve `eqn1, eqn2, ..., eqnn` for all variables that appear in them. (Remember that a double equals sign (==) must be used in each equation.)

EXAMPLE: Solve the system of three equations $\begin{cases} x - 2y + z = -4 \\ 3x + 2y - z = 8 \\ -x + 3y + 5z = 0 \end{cases}$ for x, y, and z.

SOLUTION: In this case, entering either

```
Solve[{x-2y+z==-4,3x+2y==8,-x+3y+5z==0}]
```

or

```
Solve[{x-2y+z,3x+2y,-x+3y+5z}=={-4,8,0}]
```

yield the same result.

```
Solve[{x-2y+z==-4,3x+2y-z==8,-x+3y+5z==0},{x,y,z}]
```

```
{{x -> 1, y -> 2, z -> -1}}
```

Remark: Be sure to include the double equals signs between the left- and right-hand sides of each equation.

Another way to solve systems of equations is based on the matrix form of the system of equations, Ax=b. This system of equations is equivalent to the matrix equation

$$\begin{pmatrix} 1 & -2 & 1 \\ 3 & 2 & -1 \\ -1 & 3 & 5 \end{pmatrix} \begin{pmatrix} x \\ y \\ z \end{pmatrix} = \begin{pmatrix} -4 \\ 8 \\ 0 \end{pmatrix}.$$

The matrix of coefficients in the previous example is entered as `matrixa` along with the vector of right-hand side values `vectorb` . After defining the vector of variables, `vectorx`, the system Ax=b is solved explicitly with the command `Solve`.

```
matrixa={{1,-2,1},{3,2,-1},{-1,3,5}};
vectorb={-4,8,0};
vectorx={x1,y1,z1}
```

```
{x1, y1, z1}
```

```
Solve[matrixa.vectorx==vectorb,vectorx]
```

```
{{x1 -> 1, y1 -> 2, z1 -> -1}}
```

∎

In addition to using `Solve` to solve a system of linear equations, the command

```
LinearSolve[A,b]
```

calculates the solution x of the system Ax=b. `LinearSolve` generally solves a system more quickly than does `Solve`.

EXAMPLE: Solve the system $\begin{cases} 2x - 4y + z = -1 \\ 3x + y - 2z = 3 \\ -5x + y - 2z = 4 \end{cases}$. Verify that the results returned satisfy the system.

SOLUTION: To solve the system using `Solve`, we define `eqs` to be the set of three equations to be solved and `vars` to be the variables x, y, and z and then use `Solve` to solve the set of equations `eqs` for the variables in `vars`. The resulting output is named `sols`.

```
eqs={2x-4y+z==-1,3x+y-2z==3,-5x+y-2z==4};
vars={x,y,z};
sols=Solve[eqs,vars]
```

```
              1            15           51
    {{x -> -(-),  y -> -(--),  z -> -(--)}}
              8            56           28
```

To verify that the results given in `sols` are the desired solutions, we replace each occurrence of x, y, and z in `eqs` by the values found in `sols`. Since the results indicate each of the three equations is satisfied, we conclude that the values given in `sols` are the desired solutions.

```
eqs /. sols
```

```
    {{True, True, True}}
```

To solve the system using `LinearSolve`, we note that the system is equivalent to the matrix equation

$$\begin{pmatrix} 2 & -4 & 1 \\ 3 & 1 & -2 \\ -5 & 1 & -2 \end{pmatrix} \begin{pmatrix} x \\ y \\ z \end{pmatrix} = \begin{pmatrix} -1 \\ 3 \\ 4 \end{pmatrix},$$

define `matrixa` and `vectorb`, and use `LinearSolve` to solve this matrix equation.

```
matrixa={{2,-4,1},{3,1,-2},{-5,1,-2}};
vectorb={-1,3,4};
solvector=LinearSolve[matrixa,vectorb]
```

$$\{-(\tfrac{1}{8}),\ -(\tfrac{15}{56}),\ -(\tfrac{51}{28})\}$$

To verify that the results are correct, we compute `matrixa.solvector`. Since the result is

$$\begin{pmatrix} -1 \\ 3 \\ 4 \end{pmatrix},$$

we conclude that the solution to the system is

$$\begin{pmatrix} x \\ y \\ z \end{pmatrix} = \begin{pmatrix} -1/8 \\ -15/36 \\ -51/28 \end{pmatrix}.$$

```
matrixa.solvector
```

```
{-1, 3, 4}   ■
```

EXAMPLE: Solve the system of equations $\begin{cases} 4x_1 + 5x_2 - 5x_3 - 8x_4 - 2x_5 = 5 \\ 7x_1 + 2x_2 - 10x_3 - x_4 - 6x_5 = -4 \\ 6x_1 + 2x_2 + 10x_3 - 10x_4 + 7x_5 = -7 \\ -8x_1 - x_2 - 4x_3 + 3x_5 = 5 \\ 8x_1 - 7x_2 - 3x_3 + 10x_4 + 5x_5 = 7 \end{cases}$.

SOLUTION: We solve the system in two ways. First, we use `Solve` to solve the system. Note that in this case, we enter the equations in the form

```
set of left-hand sides==set of right-hand sides.
```

```
Solve[{4x[1]+5x[2]-5x[3]-8x[4]-2x[5],7x[1]+2x[2]-10x[3]-x[4]-6x[5],
       6x[1]+2x[2]+10x[3]-10x[4]+7x[5],-8x[1]-x[2]-4x[3]+3x[5],
       8x[1]-7x[2]-3x[3]+10x[4]+5x[5]}=={5,-4,-7,5,7}]
```

```
                38523            1245
{{x[4] -> -----, x[1] -> ----,
                6626            6626

          113174           7457
x[2] -> ------, x[3] -> -(----),
           9939            9939

          49327
x[5] -> -----}}
           9939
```

We also use `LinearSolve` after defining `matrixa` and `t2`. As expected, in each case, the results are the same.

```
Clear[matrixa]
matrixa={{4,5,-5,-8,-2},{7,2,-10,-1,-6},{6,2,10,-10,7},
        {-8,-1,-4,0,3},{8,-7,-3,10,5}};
t2={5,-4,-7,5,7};
LinearSolve[matrixa,t2]
```

$$\left\{\frac{1245}{6626}, \frac{113174}{9939}, -\left(\frac{7457}{9939}\right), \frac{38523}{6626}, \frac{49327}{9939}\right\}$$

∎

Gauss-Jordan Elimination

Given the matrix equation Ax=b, where

$$A = \begin{pmatrix} a_{11} & a_{12} & \cdots & a_{1n} \\ a_{21} & a_{22} & \cdots & a_{2n} \\ \vdots & \vdots & \ddots & \vdots \\ a_{m1} & a_{m2} & \cdots & a_{mn} \end{pmatrix}, \quad x = \begin{pmatrix} x_1 \\ x_2 \\ \vdots \\ x_n \end{pmatrix}, \quad \text{and} \quad b = \begin{pmatrix} b_1 \\ b_2 \\ \vdots \\ b_m \end{pmatrix},$$

the m × n matrix A is called the **coefficient matrix** for the matrix equation Ax=b and the $m \times (n+1)$ matrix

$$(A \mid b) = \begin{pmatrix} a_{11} & a_{12} & \cdots & a_{1n} & b_1 \\ a_{21} & a_{22} & \cdots & a_{2n} & b_2 \\ \vdots & \vdots & \ddots & \vdots & \vdots \\ a_{m1} & a_{m2} & \cdots & a_{mn} & b_m \end{pmatrix}$$

is called the **augmented matrix** for the matrix equation.

We may enter the augmented matrix associated with a linear system of equations directly or we can use the package **MatrixManipulation** contained in the **LinearAlgebra** folder (or directory) to help us construct the augmented matrix.

EXAMPLE: Solve the system $\begin{cases} -2x + y - 2z = 4 \\ 2x - 4y - 2z = -4 \\ x - 4y - 2z = 3 \end{cases}$ using Gauss-Jordan elimination.

SOLUTION: The system is equivalent to the matrix equation

$$\begin{pmatrix} -2 & 1 & -2 \\ 2 & -4 & -2 \\ 1 & -4 & -2 \end{pmatrix} \begin{pmatrix} x \\ y \\ z \end{pmatrix} = \begin{pmatrix} 4 \\ -4 \\ 3 \end{pmatrix}.$$

The augmented matrix associated with this system is

$$\begin{pmatrix} -2 & 1 & -2 & 4 \\ 2 & -4 & -2 & -4 \\ 1 & -4 & -2 & 3 \end{pmatrix}$$

which we construct using the command `AppendRows` contained in the **MatrixManipulation** package. We proceed by loading the **MatrixManipulation** package, defining `matrixa` and `b`, and then using `AppendRows` to construct the augmented matrix which we name `augm` and display in `MatrixForm`.

```
<<LinearAlgebra`MatrixManipulation`

matrixa={{-2,1,-2},{2,-4,-2},{1,-4,-2}};
b={{4},{-4},{3}};

augm=AppendRows[matrixa,b];
MatrixForm[augm]
```

```
-2    1    -2    4

 2   -4    -2   -4

 1   -4    -2    3
```

We calculate the solution by row-reducing `augm` using the built-in command `RowReduce`.

```
RowReduce[augm]//MatrixForm
```

```
1    0    0    -7

0    1    0    -4

0    0    1     3
```

From the result above, we see that the solution is

$$\begin{pmatrix} x \\ y \\ z \end{pmatrix} = \begin{pmatrix} -7 \\ -4 \\ 3 \end{pmatrix}.$$

We verify this below by replacing each occurrence of x, y, and z on the left-hand side of equation by –7, –4, and 3, respectively, and noting that the results are equal to the right-hand side of each equation.

```
Clear[x,y,z]
{-2x+y-2z,2x-4y-2z,x-4y-2z} /. {x->-7,y->-4,z->3}
```

```
{4, -4, 3}
```

■

EXAMPLE: Solve the system $\begin{pmatrix} 1 & -3 & -4 \\ 4 & 0 & -1 \\ 2 & -3 & -3 \end{pmatrix}\begin{pmatrix} x \\ y \\ z \end{pmatrix} = \begin{pmatrix} -3 \\ 3 \\ 4 \end{pmatrix}$ using Gauss-Jordan elimination.

SOLUTION: The augmented matrix associated with this system is

$$\left(\begin{array}{ccc|c} 1 & -3 & -4 & -3 \\ 4 & 0 & -1 & 3 \\ 2 & -3 & -3 & 4 \end{array}\right),$$

defined below as aug. We then proceed as in the previous example by using RowReduce to row-reduce the augmented matrix.

```
aug={{1,-3,-4,-3},{4,0,-1,3},{2,-3,-3,4}};
RowReduce[aug]
```

```
{{1, 0, 0, 2}, {0, 1, 0, -5}, {0, 0, 1, 5}}
```

From the results, we see that the desired solution is

$$\begin{pmatrix} x \\ y \\ z \end{pmatrix} = \begin{pmatrix} 2 \\ -5 \\ 5 \end{pmatrix},$$

which is verified below.

```
Clear[x,y,z]
eq1=x-3y-4z+3==0;
eq2=4x-z-3==0;
eq3=2x-3y-3z-4==0;

x=2;y=-5;z=5;

{eq1,eq2,eq3}
```

```
{True,True,True}
```
■

5.3 Selected Topics from Linear Algebra

Fundamental Subspaces Associated with Matrices

Let A denote the n × m matrix

$$A = \begin{pmatrix} a_{11} & a_{12} & \cdots & a_{1m} \\ a_{21} & a_{22} & \cdots & a_{2m} \\ \vdots & \vdots & \ddots & \vdots \\ a_{n1} & a_{n2} & \cdots & a_{nm} \end{pmatrix}.$$

The **row space of A**, row(A), is the spanning set of the rows of A; the **column space of A**, col(A), is the spanning set of the columns of A. If A is any matrix, then the dimension of the column space of A is equal to the dimension of the row space of A. The dimension of the row space (column space) of a matrix A is called the **rank** of A. The **nullspace** of A is the set of solutions to the system of equations Ax=0. The nullspace of A is a subspace and its dimension is called the **nullity** of A. In the same manner as the rank of A is equal to the number of non-zero rows in the row-echelon form of A, the nullity of A is equal to the number of zero rows in the row-echelon form of A. Thus, if A is a square matrix, the sum of the rank of A and the nullity of A is equal to the number of rows (columns) of A.

The built-in commands

> `NullSpace[m]` returns a list of vectors which form a basis for the nullspace (or kernel) of the matrix m; and
> `RowReduce[m]` yields the reduced row echelon form of the matrix m.

Below, we show how Mathematica can be used to determine the column space, rank, null space, and nullity of matrices.

EXAMPLE: Place the matrix $A = \begin{pmatrix} -1 & -1 & 2 & 0 & -1 \\ -2 & 2 & 0 & 0 & -2 \\ 2 & -1 & -1 & 0 & 1 \\ -1 & -1 & 1 & 2 & 2 \\ 1 & -2 & 2 & -2 & 0 \end{pmatrix}$ in reduced row echelon form. What is the rank of A? Find a basis for the nullspace of A.

SOLUTION: We begin by defining the matrix `matrixa`. Then, `RowReduce` is used to place `matrixa` in reduced row echelon form.

```
matrixa={{-1,-1,2,0,-1},{-2,2,0,0,-2},{2,-1,-1,0,1},{-1,-1,1,2,2},
       {1,-2,2,-2,0}};
```

```
RowReduce[matrixa]//MatrixForm
```

$$\begin{matrix} 1 & 0 & 0 & -2 & 0 \\ 0 & 1 & 0 & -2 & 0 \\ 0 & 0 & 1 & -2 & 0 \\ 0 & 0 & 0 & 0 & 1 \\ 0 & 0 & 0 & 0 & 0 \end{matrix}$$

Since the row-reduced form of `matrixa` contains four nonzero rows, the rank of A is 4 and thus the nullity is 1. We obtain a basis for the nullspace with `NullSpace`.

```
NullSpace[matrixa]
```

```
{{2, 2, 2, 1, 0}}
```

∎

EXAMPLE: Find a basis for the column space of $B = \begin{pmatrix} 1 & -2 & 2 & 1 & -2 \\ 1 & 1 & 2 & -2 & -2 \\ 1 & 0 & 0 & 2 & -1 \\ 0 & 0 & 0 & -2 & 0 \\ -2 & 1 & 0 & 1 & 2 \end{pmatrix}$.

SOLUTION: A basis for the column space of B is the same as a basis for the row space of the transpose of B. We begin by defining `matrixb` and then using `Transpose` to compute the transpose of `matrixb`, naming the resulting output `tb`.

```
matrixb={{1,-2,2,1,-2},{1,1,2,-2,-2},{1,0,0,2,-1},{0,0,0,-2,0},
       {-2,1,0,1,2}};
```

```
tb=Transpose[matrixb]
```

```
{{1, 1, 1, 0, -2}, {-2, 1, 0, 0, 1}, {2, 2, 0, 0, 0},
 {1, -2, 2, -2, 1}, {-2, -2, -1, 0, 2}}
```

Next, we use `RowReduce` to row reduce `tb` and name the result `rrtb`. A basis for the column space consists of the first four elements of `rrtb`. We also use `Transpose` to show that the first four elements of `rrtb` are the same as the first four columns of the transpose of `rrtb`. Thus, the jth column of a matrix m can be extracted from m with `Transpose[m][[j]]`.

```
rrtb=RowReduce[tb];
Transpose[rrtb]//MatrixForm
```

$$
\begin{matrix}
1 & 0 & 0 & 0 & 0 \\
0 & 1 & 0 & 0 & 0 \\
0 & 0 & 1 & 0 & 0 \\
0 & 0 & 0 & 1 & 0 \\
-\left(\dfrac{1}{3}\right) & \dfrac{1}{3} & -2 & -3 & 0
\end{matrix}
$$

We extract the first four elements of `rrtb` with `Take`. The results correspond to a basis for the column space of B.

```
Take[rrtb,4]
```

$$
\{\{1,\ 0,\ 0,\ 0,\ -\left(\tfrac{1}{3}\right)\},\ \{0,\ 1,\ 0,\ 0,\ \tfrac{1}{3}\},\ \{0,\ 0,\ 1,\ 0,\ -2\},
$$

$$
\{0,\ 0,\ 0,\ 1,\ -3\}\}\ \blacksquare
$$

EXAMPLE: Find a basis for the nullspace of $C = \begin{pmatrix} 0 & 2 & -2 & 1 & 1 \\ -1 & 3 & -3 & 3 & -1 \\ 0 & -1 & 1 & 1 & 2 \end{pmatrix}$.

SOLUTION: After defining `matrixc`, we use `NullSpace` to calculate a basis for the nullspace of C.

```
matrixc={{0,2,-2,1,1},{-1,3,-3,3,-1},{0,-1,1,1,2}};
NullSpace[matrixc]
```

$$
\{\{-15,\ 1,\ 0,\ -5,\ 3\},\ \{0,\ 1,\ 1,\ 0,\ 0\}\}
$$

$\blacksquare$

The Gram–Schmidt Process

A set of vectors $\{v_1, v_2, ..., v_n\}$ is **orthonormal** means that $\|v_i\| = 1$ for all values of i and $v_i \bullet v_j = 0$ for $i \neq j$. Given a set of linearly independent vectors $\{v_1, v_2, ..., v_n\}$, the set of all linear combinations of the elements of $\{v_1, v_2, ..., v_n\}$, $V = span\{v_1, v_2, ..., v_n\}$ is a vector space. Note that if $\{u_1, u_2, ..., u_n\}$ is an orthonormal set and $v \in span\{u_1, u_2, ..., u_n\}$, then $v = (v \bullet u_1)u_1 + (v \bullet u_2)u_2 + ... + (v \bullet u_n)u_n$. Thus, we may easily express v as a linear combination of the vectors in $\{u_1, u_2, \ldots, u_n\}$. Consequently, if we are given any vector space, V, it is frequently convenient to be able to find an orthonormal basis of V. We may use the Gram-Schmidt process to find an orthonormal basis of the vector space $V = span\{v_1, v_2, \ldots, v_n\}$. We summarize the algorithm of the Gram-Schmidt Process below.

1. Let $u_1 = \dfrac{v_1}{\|v_1\|}$;

2. Compute $proj_{\{u_1\}} v_2 = (u_1 \bullet v_2) u_1$, $v_2 - proj_{\{u_1\}} v_2$, and let $u_2 = \dfrac{v_2 - proj_{\{u_1\}} v_2}{\left\| v_2 - proj_{\{u_1\}} v_2 \right\|}$. Then,

   $span\{u_1, u_2\} = span\{v_1, v_2\}$ and $span\{u_1, u_2, v_3, \ldots, v_n\} = span\{v_1, v_2, v_3, \ldots, v_n\}$;

3. Generally, for $3 \le i \le n$, compute

   $proj_{\{u_1, u_2, \ldots, u_{i-1}\}} v_i = (u_1 \bullet v_i) u_1 + (u_2 \bullet v_i) u_2 + \ldots + (u_{i-1} \bullet v_i) u_{i-1}$,

   $v_i - proj_{\{u_1, u_2, \ldots, u_{i-1}\}} v_i$, and let $u_i = \dfrac{v_i - proj_{\{u_1, u_2, \ldots, u_{i-1}\}} v_i}{\left\| v_i - proj_{\{u_1, u_2, \ldots, u_{i-1}\}} v_i \right\|}$. Then,

   $span\{u_1, u_2, \ldots, u_i\} = span\{v_1, v_2, \ldots, v_i\}$ and
   $span\{u_1, u_2, \ldots, u_i, v_{i+1}, \ldots, v_n\} = span\{v_1, v_2, v_3, \ldots, v_n\}$; and

4. Since $span\{u_1, u_2, \ldots, u_n\} = span\{v_1, v_2, \ldots, v_n\}$ and $\{u_1, u_2, \ldots, u_n\}$ is an orthonormal set, $\{u_1, u_2, \ldots, u_n\}$ is an orthonormal basis of $span\{v_1, v_2, \ldots, v_n\}$.

The Gram-Schmidt procedure is well-suited to computer arithmetic. The following code performs each step of the Gram-Schmidt Process on a set of n linearly independent vectors $\{v_1, v_2, \ldots, v_n\}$. At the completion of each step of the procedure, `gramschmidt[vecs]` prints the list of vectors corresponding to $\{\mathbf{u}_1, \mathbf{u}_2, \ldots, \mathbf{u}_i, \mathbf{v}_{i+1}, \ldots, \mathbf{v}_n\}$ and returns the list of vectors $\{\mathbf{u}_1, \mathbf{u}_2, \ldots, \mathbf{u}_n\}$. Note how comments are inserted into the code using (*...*).

```
gramschmidt[vecs_]:=
      Module[{n,proj,u,capw},
      (*n represents the number of vectors in the
            list vecs*)
      n=Length[vecs];

      (*proj[v,capw] computes the projection of v
            onto capw*)
      proj[v_,capw_]:=
            Sum[(capw[[i]].v)capw[[i]],{i,1,Length[capw]}];

      u[1]=vecs[[1]]/Sqrt[vecs[[1]].vecs[[1]]];

      capw={};
```

```
u[i_]:=u[i]=
        Module[{stepone},
        stepone=vecs[[i]]-proj[vecs[[i]],capw];
        stepone/Sqrt[stepone.stepone]//Together
                ];
Do[
        u[i];
        AppendTo[capw,u[i]];
        Print[Join[capw,Drop[vecs,i]]]
        ,{i,1,n-1}];
u[n];
AppendTo[capw,u[n]]
]
```

EXAMPLE: Use the Gram-Schmidt process to transform the basis $\left\{ \begin{pmatrix} -2 \\ -1 \\ -2 \end{pmatrix}, \begin{pmatrix} 0 \\ -1 \\ 2 \end{pmatrix}, \begin{pmatrix} 1 \\ 3 \\ -2 \end{pmatrix} \right\}$ of $\Re^3$ into an orthonormal basis.

SOLUTION: We proceed by defining v1, v2, and v3 to be the vectors in the basis

$$\left\{ \begin{pmatrix} -2 \\ -1 \\ -2 \end{pmatrix}, \begin{pmatrix} 0 \\ -1 \\ 2 \end{pmatrix}, \begin{pmatrix} 1 \\ 3 \\ -2 \end{pmatrix} \right\}$$

and using gramschmidt[{v1,v2,v3}] to find an orthonormal basis.

```
v1={-2,-1,-2};
v2={0,-1,2};
v3={1,3,-2};
gramschmidt[{v1,v2,v3}]
```

```
        2    1    2
  {{-(-),  -(-),  -(-)},  {0, -1, 2},  {1, 3, -2}}
        3    3    3
        2    1    2     1    2   2
  {{-(-),  -(-),  -(-)},  {-(-),  -(-),  -},  {1, 3, -2}}
        3    3    3     3    3   3
        2    1    2     1    2   2     2   2   1
  {{-(-),  -(-),  -(-)},  {-(-),  -(-),  -},  {-(-),  -,  -}}
        3    3    3     3    3   3     3   3   3
```

■

EXAMPLE: Compute an orthonormal basis for the subspace of $\mathfrak{R}^4$ spanned by the

vectors $\begin{pmatrix} 2 \\ 4 \\ 4 \\ 1 \end{pmatrix}$, $\begin{pmatrix} -4 \\ 1 \\ -3 \\ 2 \end{pmatrix}$, and $\begin{pmatrix} 1 \\ 4 \\ 4 \\ -1 \end{pmatrix}$. Also, verify that the basis vectors are orthogonal and

have norm 1.

SOLUTION: With `gramschmidt` below, we compute the orthonormal basis vectors. The orthogonality of these vectors is then verified. Notice that `Together` must be used to simplify the result in the case of `oset[[2]].oset[[3]]`. The norm of each vector is then found to be 1.

```
oset=gramschmidt[{{2,4,4,1},{-4,1,-3,2},{1,4,4,-1}}]

            2           4           4           1
   {{--------, --------, --------, --------}, {-4, 1, -3, 2},
     Sqrt[37]  Sqrt[37]  Sqrt[37]  Sqrt[37]


     {1, 4, 4, -1}}
            2           4           4           1
   {{--------, --------, --------, --------},
     Sqrt[37]  Sqrt[37]  Sqrt[37]  Sqrt[37]


               32            93           -55
    {-15 Sqrt[-----], -----------, -----------,
              16909     Sqrt[33818] Sqrt[33818]


              32
    11 Sqrt[-----]}, {1, 4, 4, -1}}
            16909
            2           4           4           1
   {{--------, --------, --------, --------},
     Sqrt[37]  Sqrt[37]  Sqrt[37]  Sqrt[37]


               32            93           -55
    {-15 Sqrt[-----], -----------, -----------,
              16909     Sqrt[33818] Sqrt[33818]


              32            -449          268
    11 Sqrt[-----]}, {------------, ------------,
            16909       Sqrt[934565]  Sqrt[934565]


         156           -798
    ------------, ------------}}
    Sqrt[934565]  Sqrt[934565]
```

The three vectors are extracted with `oset` with `oset[[1]]`, `oset[[2]]`, and `oset[[3]]`.

```
oset[[1]].oset[[2]]
oset[[1]].oset[[3]]
    0
    0
oset[[2]].oset[[3]]//Together
    0
Sqrt[oset[[1]].oset[[1]]]
Sqrt[oset[[2]].oset[[2]]]
Sqrt[oset[[3]].oset[[3]]]
    1
    1
    1   ■
```

The package **Orthogonalization** in the **LinearAlgebra** folder (or directory) contains several useful commands which include

> `GramSchmidt[{v1,v2,...}]` returns an orthonormal set of vectors given the set of vectors $\{v_1, v_2, ...\}$. Note that this command does not illustrate each step of the Gram-Schmidt procedure as the `gramschmidt` function defined above;
>
> `Normalize[v1]` returns $\dfrac{v_1}{\|v_1\|}$ given the nonzero vector v_1; and
>
> `Projection[v1,v2]` returns the projection of v_1 onto v_2: $proj_{v_2} v_1 = \dfrac{v_1 \bullet v_2}{\|v_2\|^2} v_2$.

Linear Transformations

A function T:$\Re^n \to \Re^m$ is a **linear transformation** means that T satisfies the properties T(u+v)=T(u)+T(v) and T(cu)=cT(u) for all vectors u and v in $\Re^n$ and all real numbers c. Let T:$\Re^n \to \Re^m$ be a linear transformation and suppose T(e_1)=v_1, T(e_2)=v_2, ... T(e_n)=v_n where $\{e_1, e_2, ... , e_n\}$ represents the standard basis of $\Re^n$ and $v_1, v_2, ... , v_n$ are (column) vectors in $\Re^m$. The **associated matrix** of T is the m × n matrix $A = \begin{pmatrix} v_1 & v_2 & \cdots & v_n \end{pmatrix}$:

$$\text{if } x = \begin{pmatrix} x_1 \\ x_2 \\ \vdots \\ x_n \end{pmatrix}, \quad T(x) = T\left(\begin{pmatrix} x_1 \\ x_2 \\ \vdots \\ x_n \end{pmatrix} \right) = Ax = \begin{pmatrix} v_1 & v_2 & \cdots & v_n \end{pmatrix} \begin{pmatrix} x_1 \\ x_2 \\ \vdots \\ x_n \end{pmatrix}.$$

Moreover, if A is any $m \times n$ matrix, then A is the associated matrix of the linear transformation defined by T(x)=Ax. In fact, a linear transformation T is completely determined by its action on any basis.

The **kernel** of the linear transformation T, ker(T), is the set of all vectors **x** in $\Re^n$ such that T(**x**)=**0**: ker(T)={x∈ $\Re^n$: T(**x**)=**0**}. The kernel of T is a subspace of $\Re^n$. Since T(**x**)=A**x** for all x in $\Re^n$, ker(T)={x∈ $\Re^n$: T(**x**)=**0**}={x∈ $\Re^n$: A**x**=**0**} so the kernel of T is the same as the nullspace of A.

EXAMPLE: Let $T : \Re^5 \to \Re^3$ be the linear transformation defined by $T(x) = \begin{pmatrix} 0 & -3 & -1 & -3 & -1 \\ -3 & 3 & -3 & -3 & -1 \\ 2 & 2 & -1 & 1 & 2 \end{pmatrix} x$. (a) Calculate a basis for the kernel of the linear transformation. (b) Determine which of the vectors $\begin{pmatrix} 4 \\ 2 \\ 0 \\ 0 \\ -6 \end{pmatrix}$ and $\begin{pmatrix} 1 \\ 2 \\ -1 \\ -2 \\ 3 \end{pmatrix}$ is in the kernel of T.

SOLUTION: We begin by defining `matrixa` to be the matrix

$$\begin{pmatrix} 0 & -3 & -1 & -3 & -1 \\ -3 & 3 & -3 & -3 & -1 \\ 2 & 2 & -1 & 1 & 2 \end{pmatrix}$$

and then defining `t`. A basis for the kernel of T is the same as a basis for the nullspace of

$$\begin{pmatrix} 0 & -3 & -1 & -3 & -1 \\ -3 & 3 & -3 & -3 & -1 \\ 2 & 2 & -1 & 1 & 2 \end{pmatrix}$$

found with `NullSpace`.

```
Clear[t,matrixa]
matrixa={{0,-3,-1,-3,-1},{-3,3,-3,-3,-1},{2,2,-1,1,2}};
t[x_]=matrixa.x;
NullSpace[matrixa]

      {{-2, -1, 0, 0, 3}, {-6, -8, -15, 13, 0}}
```

Since

$$\begin{pmatrix} 4 \\ 2 \\ 0 \\ 0 \\ -6 \end{pmatrix}$$

is a linear combination of the vectors which form a basis for the kernel,

$$\begin{pmatrix} 4 \\ 2 \\ 0 \\ 0 \\ -6 \end{pmatrix}$$

is in the kernel while

$$\begin{pmatrix} 1 \\ 2 \\ -1 \\ -2 \\ 3 \end{pmatrix}$$

is not. These results are verified below by evaluating t for each vector.

```
t[{4,2,0,0,-6}]
```

    {0, 0, 0}

```
t[{1,2,-1,-2,3}]
```

    {-2, 9, 11} ∎

Application: Rotations

Let $x = \begin{pmatrix} x_1 \\ x_2 \end{pmatrix}$ be a vector in $\Re^2$ and θ an angle. Then, there are numbers r and ϕ given by

$r = \sqrt{x_1^2 + x_2^2}$ and $\phi = \tan^{-1}\dfrac{x_2}{x_1}$ so that $x_1 = r\cos\phi$ and $x_2 = r\sin\phi$. When we rotate

$$x = \begin{pmatrix} x_1 \\ x_2 \end{pmatrix} = \begin{pmatrix} r\cos\phi \\ r\sin\phi \end{pmatrix}$$

through the angle θ, we obtain the vector

$$x @ \begin{pmatrix} r\cos(\theta+\phi) \\ r\sin(\theta+\phi) \end{pmatrix},$$

as illustrated in the following diagram.

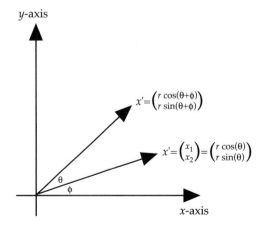

Using the trigonometric identities

$$\sin(\theta \pm \phi) = \sin\theta\cos\phi \pm \sin\phi\cos\theta \ \text{ and } \ \cos(\theta \pm \phi) = \cos\theta\cos\phi \mp \sin\theta\sin\phi$$

we rewrite

$$x \mapsto \begin{pmatrix} r\cos(\theta+\phi) \\ r\sin(\theta+\phi) \end{pmatrix} = \begin{pmatrix} r\cos\theta\cos\phi - r\sin\theta\sin\phi \\ r\sin\theta\cos\phi + r\sin\phi\cos\theta \end{pmatrix}$$

$$= \begin{pmatrix} \cos\theta & -\sin\theta \\ \sin\theta & \cos\theta \end{pmatrix} \begin{pmatrix} r\cos\phi \\ r\sin\phi \end{pmatrix} = \begin{pmatrix} \cos\theta & -\sin\theta \\ \sin\theta & \cos\theta \end{pmatrix} \begin{pmatrix} x_1 \\ x_2 \end{pmatrix}.$$

Thus, the vector x' is obtained from x by computing

$$\begin{pmatrix} \cos\theta & -\sin\theta \\ \sin\theta & \cos\theta \end{pmatrix} x .$$

Generally, if θ represents an angle, the linear transformation $T : \Re^2 \to \Re^2$ defined by

$$T(x) = \begin{pmatrix} \cos\theta & -\sin\theta \\ \sin\theta & \cos\theta \end{pmatrix} x$$

is called the **rotation of $\Re^2$ through the angle** θ.

Below, we write code to rotate a polygon through an angle θ. The procedure `rotate` uses a list of n points and the rotation matrix defined in `r` to produce a new list of points which are joined using the `Line` graphics directive. Entering

```
Line[{{x1,y1},{x2,y2},...,{xn,yn}}]
```

represents the graphics primitive for a line in two dimensions which connects the points listed in `{{x1,y1},{x2,y2},...,{xn,yn}}`. Entering

```
Show[Graphics[Line[{{x1,y1},{x2,y2},...,{xn,yn}}]]]
```

displays the line. This rotation can be determined for one value of t (which represents the angle θ). However, a more interesting result is obtained by creating a list of rotations for a sequence of angles and then displaying the graphics objects. This is done below for θ=0 to $\theta = \dfrac{\pi}{2}$ using increments of $\dfrac{\pi}{16}$. Hence, a list of nine graphs is given for the square with vertices (-1,1), (1,1), (1, -1), and (-1,-1).

```
r[theta_]={{Cos[theta],-Sin[theta]},{Sin[theta],Cos[theta]}}
rotate[pts_,angle_]:=
     Module[{newpts},
     newpts=Table[r[angle].pts[[i]],{i,1,Length[pts]}];
     newpts=AppendTo[newpts,newpts[[1]]];
     figure=Line[newpts];
     Show[Graphics[figure],AspectRatio->1,
          PlotRange->{{-1.5,1.5},{-1.5,1.5}},
          DisplayFunction->Identity]
     ]
```

```
graphs=Table[rotate[{{-1,1},{1,1},{1,-1},{-1,-1}},t],{t,0,Pi/2,Pi/16}];
array=Partition[graphs,3];
Show[GraphicsArray[array]]
```

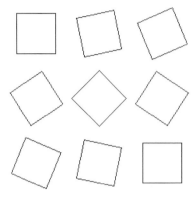

Eigenvalues and Eigenvectors

Let A be an n × n matrix with real components. Then the number λ is called an **eigenvalue** of A if there is a nonzero vector **v** which satisfies A**v**=λ**v.** This nonzero vector is called the **eigenvector** of A which corresponds to λ. The **characteristic matrix** of A is the matrix A− λI, where I represents the identity matrix. The eigenvalues are roots of the **characteristic equation** $|A - \lambda I| = 0$ which may have at most n real distinct roots; it may also have repeated roots and roots which are complex conjugates. The equation $p(\lambda)=|A - \lambda I|$ is called the characteristic polynomial. After obtaining the eigenvalues, the corresponding eigenvectors are found by substituting the eigenvalues into the homogeneous system of equations $(A - \lambda I)\mathbf{v} = \mathbf{0}$ and solving for **v.** Mathematica contains several commands that can be used to determine the characteristic matrix, characteristic polynomial, eigenvalues, and eigenvectors of an n × n matrix. We begin by discussing commands for determining the characteristic matrix and characteristic polynomial below.

The command

> `CharacteristicPolynomial[m,x]` gives the characteristic polynomial of m as a polynomial in x.
> `Eigenvalues[m]` gives a list of the eigenvalues of the square matrix m;
> `Eigenvectors[m]` gives a list of the eigenvectors of the square matrix m; and
> `Eigensystem[m]` gives a list of the eigenvalues and corresponding eigenvectors of the square matrix m.

Several examples are shown below.

EXAMPLE: If $A = \begin{pmatrix} 4 & -3 & 4 \\ 1 & -3 & 1 \\ -1 & -1 & 5 \end{pmatrix}$, find the characteristic polynomial of A (with respect to the variable x).

SOLUTI°ON: We begin by defining `matrixa`. We then compute the characteristic polynomial by computing the determinant of $A - xI$, where I represents the 3 ×3 identity matrix, with `Det` and then directly computing the characteristic polynomial with `CharacteristicPolynomial`. Note that `IdentityMatrix[n]` returns the n × n identity matrix.

```
Clear[matrixa]
matrixa={{4,-3,4},{1,-3,1},{-1,-1,5}};
Det[matrixa -x IdentityMatrix[3]]

                 2     3
    -54 - x + 6 x  - x

p=CharacteristicPolynomial[matrixa,x]

                 2     3
    -54 - x + 6 x  - x   ■
```

EXAMPLE: (a) If $A = \begin{pmatrix} 5 & 2/3 & 1 & -4/3 & -4 & -4/3 \\ 0 & -1/6 & -2 & -1/6 & 7 & 23/6 \\ -1/2 & -1/4 & 5/2 & -1/4 & 1 & 3/4 \\ 4 & 1/2 & 0 & 1/2 & -3 & -1/2 \\ 0 & -1 & 0 & 0 & 4 & 1 \\ -1 & 1/6 & -1 & 1/6 & 2 & 19/6 \end{pmatrix}$, find the eigenvalues

and eigenvectors of A. (b) If $B = \begin{pmatrix} 1 & 5 & 1 \\ -3 & 6 & -6 \\ -4 & 1 & 7 \end{pmatrix}$, find both exact and approximate values for the eigenvalues of B.

SOLUTION: In each case, we may calculate the eigenvalues by finding the characteristic polynomial of each matrix and then finding the zeros of each characteristic polynomial. For (a), we first define `matrixa` and then use `Eigenvalues` and `Eigenvectors` to find the eigenvalues and eigenvectors.

```
matrixa={{5,2/3,1,-4/3,-4,-4/3},{0,-1/6,-2,-1/6,7,23/6},
        {-1/2,-1/4,5/2,-1/4,1,3/4},{4,1/2,0,1/2,-3,-1/2},
        {0,-1,0,0,4,1},{-1,1/6,-1,1/6,2,19/6}};
Eigenvalues[matrixa]

    {2, 2, 2, 3, 3, 3}
```

```
Eigenvectors[matrixa]

        1         1
{{-(-), -1, -(-), 0, -1, 1}, {0, 0, 0, 0, 0, 0},
        2         2

   {0, 0, 0, 0, 0, 0}, {0, 1, 2, -1, 1, 0}, {0, 0, 0, 0, 0, 0},

   {0, 0, 0, 0, 0, 0}}
```

For (b), we first define `matrixb` and then use `Eigenvalues` to find the exact eigenvalues of the matrix.

```
matrixb={{1,5,1},{-3,6,-6},{-4,1,7}};
Eigenvalues[matrixb]

                              1/3
    14                    44 2
{-- - --------------------------- +
    3                             1/3
        3 (3346 + 6 Sqrt[320457])

                              1/3
    (3346 + 6 Sqrt[320457])
    ------------------------,
                1/3
            3 2

            1/3
    14      22 2     (1 + I Sqrt[3])
    -- + -------------------------- -
    3                             1/3
        3 (3346 + 6 Sqrt[320457])

                                                 1/3
    (1 - I Sqrt[3]) (3346 + 6 Sqrt[320457])
    ----------------------------------------,
                        1/3
                    6 2

            1/3
    14      22 2     (1 - I Sqrt[3])
    -- + -------------------------- -
    3                             1/3
        3 (3346 + 6 Sqrt[320457])

                                                 1/3
    (1 + I Sqrt[3]) (3346 + 6 Sqrt[320457])
    ----------------------------------------}
                        1/3
                    6 2
```

From the lengthy results obtained above, we see that approximate values may be more meaningful. To obtain numerical approximations, we use N as shown below.

```
Eigenvalues[N[matrixb]]
```

```
{8.68668, 2.65666 + 5.17562 I, 2.65666 - 5.17562 I}
```

∎

The next example illustrates how Eigensystem can be used to find both the eigenvalues and corresponding eigenvectors simultaneously.

EXAMPLE: Find the eigenvalues and corresponding eigenvectors of $B = \begin{pmatrix} 0 & 4 \\ 2 & -2 \end{pmatrix}$.

SOLUTION: Below, we define matrixb and then use Eigensystem to compute the eigenvalues and corresponding eigenvectors and name the resulting output eigsb.

```
matrixb={{0,4},{2,-2}};
eigsb=Eigensystem[matrixb]
```

```
{{-4, 2}, {{-1, 1}, {2, 1}}}
```

The eigenvalues correspond to the first element of eigsb while the corresponding eigenvectors are given in the second part of eigsb, extracted below with eigsb[[1]] and eigsb[[2]], respectively.

```
eigsb[[1]]
eigsb[[2]]
```

```
{-4, 2}
{{-1, 1}, {2, 1}}
```

Finally, we verify that the numbers and vectors given in eigsb are eigenvalues and corresponding eigenvectors. Below, we first verify that $B\begin{pmatrix} -1 \\ 1 \end{pmatrix} = -4\begin{pmatrix} -1 \\ 1 \end{pmatrix}$ and then verify that $B\begin{pmatrix} 2 \\ 1 \end{pmatrix} = 2\begin{pmatrix} 2 \\ 1 \end{pmatrix}$.

```
matrixb.eigsb[[2,1]]==eigsb[[1,1]] eigsb[[2,1]]
```

```
True
```

```
matrixb.eigsb[[2,2]]==eigsb[[1,2]] eigsb[[2,2]]
```

```
True
```

∎

Sometimes the matrix in which each element is numerically approximated is more useful than the matrix in its original form. This is obtained below for the matrix `matrixa` with `N[matrixa]`.

EXAMPLE: If $A = \begin{pmatrix} 3 & -5 & -4 \\ -5 & 6 & 3 \\ -3 & 2 & -2 \end{pmatrix}$, approximate the eigenvalues and corresponding eigenvectors of A.

SOLUTION: We first define `matrixa` and then use `Eigensystem` and `N` to approximate the eigenvalues and corresponding eigenvectors of the matrix, naming the resulting output `eigs`.

```
matrixa={{3,-5,-4},{-5,6,3},{-3,2,-2}};
eigs=Eigensystem[N[matrixa]]
```

```
{{10.9879, -3.77071, -0.217222},

  {{-0.601654, 0.756787, 0.255509},

   {0.505049, -0.00654559, 0.863066},

   {0.651499, 0.68315, -0.329933}}}
```

As in the previous example, the first part of `eigs` corresponds to the eigenvalues of the matrix while the second part corresponds to the eigenvectors. These are extracted from `eigs` with `eigs[[1]]` and `eigs[[2]]`.

```
eigs[[1]]
```

```
{10.9879, -3.77071, -0.217222}
```

```
eigs[[2]]
```

```
{{-0.601654, 0.756787, 0.255509},

  {0.505049, -0.00654559, 0.863066},

  {0.651499, 0.68315, -0.329933}}
```

Below we verify that these results are indeed approximations of the eigenvalues and corresponding eigenvectors of the matrix.

```
matrixa.eigs[[2,1]]
```

```
{-6.61094, 8.31552, 2.80752}
```

```
eigs[[1,1]] eigs[[2,1]]
```

```
{-6.61094, 8.31552, 2.80752}
```

The results obtained above appear to be the same. However, when we verify that the second element of each list is an eigenvalue and corresponding eigenvector, our subtraction does not result in zero. In fact, entering

```
matrixa.eigs[[2,2]]==eigs[[1,2]] eigs[[2,2]]
```

yields False.

```
verify2=matrixa.eigs[[2,2]]-eigs[[1,2]] eigs[[2,2]]
```

$$\{-4.33681\ 10^{-19}, \ 9.72394\ 10^{-19}, \ 4.33681\ 10^{-19}\}$$

However, these numbers are very "small" and can assume that they are 0. We use the command Chop to replace these "small" numbers by 0.

```
Chop[verify2]
```

```
{0, 0, 0}
```

Finally, we verify that the third element of each list is an eigenvalue and corresponding eigenvector.

```
verify3=Chop[matrixa.eigs[[2,3]]-eigs[[1,3]] eigs[[2,3]]]
```

```
{0, 0, 0}
```

∎

Jordan Canonical Form

Let $N_k = \left(n_{ij} \right) = \begin{cases} 1, j = i+1 \\ 0, \text{otherwise} \end{cases}$ represent a $k \times k$ matrix with indicated elements. The $k \times k$ **Jordan block matrix** is given by $B(\lambda) = \lambda I + N_k$ where λ is a constant. Hence, these matrices are defined by the following matrices.

$$N_k = \begin{pmatrix} 0 & 1 & 0 & \cdots & 0 \\ 0 & 0 & 1 & \cdots & 0 \\ \vdots & \vdots & \vdots & & \vdots \\ 0 & 0 & 0 & \cdots & 1 \\ 0 & 0 & 0 & \cdots & 0 \end{pmatrix} \quad \text{and} \quad B(\lambda) = \lambda I + N_k \begin{pmatrix} \lambda & 1 & 0 & \cdots & 0 & 0 \\ 0 & \lambda & 0 & \cdots & 0 & 0 \\ \vdots & \vdots & \vdots & & \vdots & \vdots \\ 0 & 0 & 0 & \cdots & \lambda & 1 \\ 0 & 0 & 0 & \cdots & 0 & \lambda \end{pmatrix}.$$

Hence, $B(\lambda)$ can be defined as

$$B(\lambda) = \left(b_{ij} \right) = \begin{cases} \lambda, i = j \\ 1, j = i+1 \\ 0, \text{otherwise} \end{cases}.$$

A **Jordan matrix** has the form

$$J = \begin{pmatrix} B_1(\lambda) & 0 & \cdots & 0 \\ 0 & B_2(\lambda) & \cdots & 0 \\ \vdots & \vdots & & \vdots \\ 0 & 0 & \cdots & B_n(\lambda) \end{pmatrix}$$

where the entries $B_j(\lambda)$, $j = 1, 2, \ldots, n$ represent Jordan block matrices. Suppose that A is an $n \times n$ matrix. Then there is an invertible $n \times n$ matrix C such that $C^{-1}AC = J$ where J is a Jordan matrix with the eigenvalues of A as diagonal elements. The matrix J is called the **Jordan canonical form** of A.

The command

`JordanDecomposition[m]` yields a list of matrices `{s,j}` such that `m=s.j.inverse[s]` and j is the Jordan canonical form of the matrix m.

For a given matrix A, the unique monic polynomial p of least degree satisfying p(A)=0 is called the **minimal polynomial of A**. Let q denote the characteristic polynomial of A. Since q(A)=0, it follows that p divides q. We can use the Jordan canonical form of a matrix to determine its minimal polynomial. We illustrate the procedures necessary to accomplish this in the example below.

EXAMPLE: Find the Jordan canonical form, J_A, of $A = \begin{pmatrix} 2 & 9 & -9 \\ 0 & 8 & -6 \\ 0 & 9 & -7 \end{pmatrix}$.

SOLUTION: After defining `matrixa`, we use `JordanDecomposition` to find the Jordan canonical form of A and name the resulting output `ja`.

```
matrixa={{2,9,-9},{0,8,-6},{0,9,-7}};
ja=JordanDecomposition[matrixa]

    {{{3, 0, 1}, {2, 1, 0}, {3, 1, 0}},

    {{-1, 0, 0}, {0, 2, 0}, {0, 0, 2}}}
```

The Jordan matrix corresponds to the second element of `ja` extracted below with `ja[[2]]` and displayed in `MatrixForm`.

```
ja[[2]]//MatrixForm

    -1   0   0
     0   2   0
     0   0   2
```

We also verify that the matrices `ja[[1]]` and `ja[[2]]` satisfy `matrixa=ja[[1]].ja[[2]].Inverse[ja[[1]]]`.

```
ja[[1]].ja[[2]].Inverse[ja[[1]]]
```

```
{{2, 9, -9}, {0, 8, -6}, {0, 9, -7}}
```

Next, we use `CharacteristicPolynomial` to find the characteristic polynomial of `matrixa` and then verify that `matrixa` satisfies its characteristic polynomial.

```
p=CharacteristicPolynomial[matrixa,x]
```

$$-4 + 3 x^2 - x^3$$

```
-4 IdentityMatrix[3]+3 MatrixPower[matrixa,2]-MatrixPower[matrixa,3]
```

```
{{0, 0, 0}, {0, 0, 0}, {0, 0, 0}}
```

From the Jordan form, we see that the minimal polynomial of A is $(x+1)(x-2)$. Below, we define the minimal polynomial to be q and then verify that `matrixa` satisfies its minimal polynomial.

```
q=Expand[(x+1)(x-2)]
```

$$-2 - x + x^2$$

```
-2 IdentityMatrix[3]-matrixa+MatrixPower[matrixa,2]
```

```
{{0, 0, 0}, {0, 0, 0}, {0, 0, 0}}
```

As expected, q divides p as verified below.

```
Cancel[p/q]
```

```
2 - x  ∎
```

EXAMPLE: Let $A = \begin{pmatrix} 3 & 8 & 6 & -1 \\ -3 & 2 & 0 & 3 \\ 3 & -3 & -1 & -3 \\ 4 & 8 & 6 & -2 \end{pmatrix}$. Find the characteristic and minimal polynomials of A.

SOLUTION: As in the previous example, we first define `matrixa` and then use `JordanDecomposition` to find the Jordan canonical form of A.

```
matrixa={{3,8,6,-1},{-3,2,0,3},{3,-3,-1,-3},{4,8,6,-2}};
ja=JordanDecomposition[matrixa]
```

$$\{\{\{3, -1, 1, 0\}, \{-1, -1, 0, -\tfrac{1}{2}\}, \{0, 2, 0, -(\tfrac{1}{2})\}, \{4, 0, 1, 0\}\},$$

$$\{\{-1, 0, 0, 0\}, \{0, -1, 0, 0\}, \{0, 0, 2, 1\}, \{0, 0, 0, 2\}\}\}$$

The Jordan canonical form of A is the second element of ja, extracted below and displayed in MatrixForm.

```
ja[[2]]//MatrixForm
```

$$\begin{matrix} -1 & 0 & 0 & 0 \\ 0 & -1 & 0 & 0 \\ 0 & 0 & 2 & 1 \\ 0 & 0 & 0 & 2 \end{matrix}$$

From the result above, we see that the minimal polynomial of A is $(x+1)(x-2)^2$. Below, we define q to be the minimal polynomial of A and then verify that matrixa satisfies q.

```
q=Expand[(x-2)^2(x+1)]
```

$$4 - 3 x^2 + x^3$$

```
4 IdentityMatrix[4]-3MatrixPower[matrixa,2]+MatrixPower[matrixa,3]
```

$$\{\{0, 0, 0, 0\}, \{0, 0, 0, 0\}, \{0, 0, 0, 0\}, \{0, 0, 0, 0\}\}$$

The characteristic polynomial is obtained below and named p. As expected, q divides p, verified below with Cancel.

```
p=CharacteristicPolynomial[matrixa,x]
```

$$4 + 4 x - 3 x^2 - 2 x^3 + x^4$$

```
Cancel[p/q]
```

$$1 + x$$

■

The QR Method

The **conjugate transpose** (or **Hermitian adjoint matrix**) of the m × n complex matrix A which is denoted by A^* is the transpose of the complex conjugate of A. Symbolically, we have $A^* = (\overline{A})^T$. An n × n complex matrix A is **unitary** if $A^* = A^{-1}$. Given a matrix A, there is a unitary matrix Q and an upper triangular matrix R such that A=QR. The matrices Q and R form the QR factorization of A.

The command `QRDecomposition[N[m]]` determines the QR decomposition of the matrix m by returning the list `{q,r}`, where q is an orthogonal matrix, r is an upper triangular matrix and `m=Transpose[q].r`.

EXAMPLE: Find the QR factorization of the matrix $A = \begin{pmatrix} 4 & -1 & 1 \\ -1 & 4 & 1 \\ 1 & 1 & 4 \end{pmatrix}$.

SOLUTION: We define `matrixa` and then use `QRDecomposition` to find the QR decomposition of `matrixa`, naming the resulting output `qrm`.

```
matrixa={{4,-1,1},{-1,4,1},{1,1,4}};
qrm=QRDecomposition[N[matrixa]]

    {{{-0.942809, 0.235702, -0.235702},

      {-0.142134, -0.92387, -0.355335},

      {0.301511, 0.301511, -0.904534}},

      {{-4.24264, 1.64992, -1.64992}, {0, -3.90868, -2.48734},

      {0, 0, -3.01511}}}
```

The first matrix in `qrm` is extracted with `qrm[[1]]` and the second with `qrm[[2]]`.

```
qrm[[1]]//MatrixForm

    -0.942809    0.235702    -0.235702
    -0.142134    -0.92387    -0.355335
    0.301511     0.301511    -0.904534
```

```
qrm[[2]]//MatrixForm

    -4.24264    1.64992     -1.64992
    0           -3.90868    -2.48734
    0           0           -3.01511
```

Below, we verify that the results returned are the QR Decomposition of A.

```
Transpose[qrm[[1]]].qrm[[2]]//MatrixForm

    4.     -1.    1.
    -1.    4.     1.
    1.     1.     4.
```

■

One of the most efficient and most widely used methods for numerically calculating the eigenvalues of a matrix is the QR Method. Given a matrix A, then there is a Hermitian matrix Q and an upper triangular matrix R such that $A = QR$. If we define a sequence of matrices

$$A_1 = A, A_m = Q_m R_m, A_{m+1} = R_m Q_m, m = 1, 2, \ldots,$$

then the sequence $\{A_m\}$ converges to a triangular matrix with the eigenvalues of A along the diagonal or to a nearly triangular matrix from which the eigenvalues of A can be calculated rather easily.

EXAMPLE: Consider the 3×3 matrix $A = \begin{pmatrix} 4 & -1 & 1 \\ -1 & 4 & 1 \\ 1 & 1 & 4 \end{pmatrix}$. Approximate the

eigenvalues of A with the QR Method.

SOLUTION: We define the sequence a and qr recursively. Note that we define a using the form a[n_]:=a[n]=... and qr using the form qr[n_]:=qr[n]=... so that Mathematica "remembers" the values of a and qr computed, and thus Mathematica avoids recomputing values previously computed. This is of particular advantage when computing a[n] and qr[n] for large values of n.

```
matrixa={{4,-1,1},{-1,4,1},{1,1,4}};
a[1]=N[matrixa];
qr[1]=QRDecomposition[a[1]];

a[n_]:=a[n]=qr[n-1][[2]].Transpose[qr[n-1][[1]]];
qr[n_]:=qr[n]=QRDecomposition[a[n]];
```

Below, we illustrate a[n] and qr[n] by computing qr[9] and a[10]. Note that computing a[10] requires the computation of qr[9]. From the results, we suspect that the eigenvalues of A are 5 and 2.

```
qr[9]
```

```
                        -7
{{{-1., 2.23173 10   , -0.000278046},

                -8
   {-8.92692 10   , -1., -0.000481589},

   {0.000278046, 0.000481589, -1.}},

                     -6
   {{-5., 1.56221 10   , -0.00194632}, {0, -5., -0.00337112},

   {0, 0, -2.}}}
```

```
a[10]//MatrixForm
```

$$
\begin{pmatrix}
5. & -1.78538\ 10^{-7} & 0.000556091 \\
-1.78538\ 10^{-7} & 5. & 0.000963178 \\
0.000556091 & 0.000963178 & 2.
\end{pmatrix}
$$

Next, we compute a[n] for n=5, 10, and 15, displaying the result in TableForm. We obtain further evidence that the eigenvalues of A are 5 and 2.

```
Table[a[n]//MatrixForm,{n,5,15,5}]//TableForm
```

$$
\begin{pmatrix}
4.99902 & -0.001701 & 0.0542614 \\
-0.001701 & 4.99706 & 0.0939219 \\
0.0542614 & 0.0939219 & 2.00393
\end{pmatrix}
$$

$$
\begin{pmatrix}
5. & -1.78538\ 10^{-7} & 0.000556091 \\
-1.78538\ 10^{-7} & 5. & 0.000963178 \\
0.000556091 & 0.000963178 & 2.
\end{pmatrix}
$$

$$
\begin{pmatrix}
5. & -1.87211\ 10^{-11} & 5.69438\ 10^{-6} \\
-1.87211\ 10^{-11} & 5. & 9.86295\ 10^{-6} \\
5.69438\ 10^{-6} & 9.86295\ 10^{-6} & 2.
\end{pmatrix}
$$

We verify that the eigenvalues of A are indeed 5 and 2 with Eigenvalues.

```
Eigenvalues[matrixa]
```

```
{2, 5, 5}
```

■

5.4 Maxima and Minima Using Linear Programming

The Standard Form of a Linear Programming Problem

We call the linear programming problem of the form: Minimize $Z = \underbrace{c_1 x_1 + c_2 x_2 + \ldots + c_n x_n}_{\text{function}}$,

subject to the restrictions

$$\begin{cases} a_{11}x_1 + a_{12}x_2 + \ldots + a_{1n}x_n \geq b_1 \\ a_{21}x_1 + a_{22}x_2 + \ldots + a_{2n}x_n \geq b_2 \\ \vdots \\ a_{m1}x_1 + a_{m2}x_2 + \ldots + a_{mn}x_n \geq b_m \end{cases}, \text{ and } x_1 \geq 0, \ x_2 \geq 0, \ldots, \ x_n \geq 0$$

the **standard form** of the linear programming problem. The command

```
ConstrainedMin[function,{inequalities},{variables}]
```

solves the standard form of the linear programming problem.

Similarly, the command

```
ConstrainedMax[function,{inequalities},{variables}]
```

solves the linear programming problem: Maximize $Z = \underbrace{c_1x_1 + c_2x_2 + \ldots + c_nx_n}_{function}$ subject to the

restrictions

$$\begin{cases} a_{11}x_1 + a_{12}x_2 + \ldots + a_{1n}x_n \geq b_1 \\ a_{21}x_1 + a_{22}x_2 + \ldots + a_{2n}x_n \geq b_2 \\ \vdots \\ a_{m1}x_1 + a_{m2}x_2 + \ldots + a_{mn}x_n \geq b_m \end{cases}, \text{ and } x_1 \geq 0, \ x_2 \geq 0, \ldots, \ x_n \geq 0.$$

EXAMPLE: Maximize $Z(x_1, x_2, x_3) = 4x_1 - 3x_2 + 2x_3$ subject to the constraints $3x_1 - 5x_2 + 2x_3 \leq 60$, $x_1 - x_2 + 2x_3 \leq 10$, $x_1 + x_2 - x_3 \leq 20$, and x1, x2, x3 all non-negative.

SOLUTION: In order to solve a linear programming problem with Mathematica, the variables {x1,x2,x3} and objective function z[x1,x2,x3] are first defined. In an effort to limit the amount of typing required to complete the problem, the set of inequalities is assigned the name ineqs while the set of variables is called vars. Notice that the symbol "<=", obtained by typing the "<" key and then the "=" key, represents "less than or equal to" and is used in ineqs. Hence, the maximization problem is solved with the command ConstrainedMax[z[x1,x2,x3],ineqs,vars].

```
Clear[x1,x2,x3,z,ineqs,vars]
vars={x1,x2,x3};
z[x1_,x2_,x3_]=4x1-3x2+2x3

    4 x1 - 3 x2 + 2 x3

ineqs={3x1-5x2+x3 <=60,x1-x2+2x3 <=10,x1+x2-x3 <=20};
ConstrainedMax[z[x1,x2,x3],ineqs,vars]

    {45, {x1 -> 15, x2 -> 5, x3 -> 0}}
```

The solution gives the maximum value of z subject to the given constraints, as well as the values of x1, x2, and, x3 which maximize z. Thus, we see that the maximum value of z is 45 when $x_1 = 15$, $x_2 = 5$, and $x_3 = 0$. ∎

We demonstrate the use of `ConstrainedMin` in the example below.

> **EXAMPLE:** Minimize $Z(x,y,z) = 4x - 3y + 2z$ subject to the constraints $3x - 5y + 2z \le 60$, $x - y + 2z \le 10$, $x + y - z \le 20$, and x, y, and z, all non-negative.

SOLUTION: After clearing all previously used names of functions and variable values, the variables, objective function, and set of constraints for this problem are defined and entered as they were in the first example. By using

$$\text{ConstrainedMin[z[x1,x2,x3],ineqs,vars]}$$

the minimum value of the objective function is obtained as well as the variable values which give this minimum.

```
Clear[x1,x2,x3,z,ineqs,vars]
vars={x1,x2,x3};
z[x1_,x2_,x3_]=4x1-3x2+2x3;

ineqs={3x1-5x2+x3 <= 60,x1-x2+2x3 <=10,x1+x2-x3 <=20};

ConstrainedMin[z[x1,x2,x3],ineqs,vars]

    {-90, {x1 -> 0, x2 -> 50, x3 -> 30}}
```

We conclude that the minimum value is -90 and occurs when $x_1 = 0$, $x_2 = 50$, and $x_3 = 30$. ∎

The Dual Problem

Given the standard form of the linear programming problem: Minimize $Z = \sum_{j=1}^{n} c_j x_j$ subject to the constraints $\sum_{j=1}^{n} a_{ij} x_j \ge b_i$ for i=1, 2, ... , m and $x_j \ge 0$ for j=1, 2, ... , n, the **dual problem** is: Maximize $Y = \sum_{i=1}^{m} b_i y_i$ subject to the constraints $\sum_{i=1}^{m} a_{ij} y_i \le c_j$ for j=1, 2, ... , n and $y_i \ge 0$ for i=1, 2, ... , m. Similarly, for the problem: Maximize $Z = \sum_{j=1}^{n} c_j x_j$ subject to the constraints

$$\sum_{j=1}^{n} a_{ij}x_j \leq b_i \text{ for } i=1, 2, \dots, m \text{ and } x_j \geq 0 \text{ for } j=1, 2, \dots, n, \text{ the dual problem is: Minimize}$$

$$Y = \sum_{i=1}^{m} b_i y_i \text{ subject to the constraints } \sum_{i=1}^{m} a_{ij}y_i \geq c_j \text{ for } j=1, 2, \dots, n \text{ and } y_i \geq 0 \text{ for } i=1, 2, \dots, m.$$

EXAMPLE: Maximize $Z = 6x + 8y$ subject to the constraints $5x + 2y \leq 20$, $x + 2y \leq 10$, $x \geq 0$, and $y \geq 0$. State the dual problem and find its solution.

SOLUTION: First, the original (primal) problem is solved. The objective function for this problem is represented by `zx`. Finally, the set of inequalities for the primal is defined to be `ineqsx`. Using the command

```
ConstrainedMax[zx,ineqsx,{x[1],x[2]}],
```

the maximum value of `zx` is found to be 45.

```
Clear[zx,zy,x,y,valsx,valsy,ineqsx,ineqsy]

zx=6x[1]+8x[2];
ineqsx={5x[1]+2x[2]<=20,x[1]+2x[2]<=10}

    {5 x[1] + 2 x[2] <= 20,

      x[1] + 2 x[2] <= 10}

ConstrainedMax[zx,ineqsx,{x[1],x[2]}]

            5          15
    {45, {x[1] -> -, x[2] -> --}}
            2           4
```

Because in this problem we have $c_1 = 6$, $c_2 = 8$, $b_1 = 20$, and $b_2 = 10$, the dual problem is: Minimize $Z = 20y_1 + 10y_2$ subject to the constraints $5y_1 + y_2 \geq 6$, $2y_1 + 2y_2 \geq 8$, $y_1 \geq 0$, and $y_2 \geq 0$. The dual is solved in a similar fashion by defining the objective function `zy` and the collection of inequalities `ineqsy`. The minimum value obtained by `zy` subject to the constraints `ineqsy` is 45 which agrees with the result of the primal and is found with

```
ConstrainedMin[zy,ineqsy,{y[1] , y[2]}].
```

```
zy=20y[1]+10y[2];
ineqsy={5y[1]+y[2]>=6,2y[1]+2y[2]>=8}

    {5 y[1] + y[2] >= 6,

      2 y[1] + 2 y[2] >= 8}
```

```
ConstrainedMin[zy,ineqsy,{y[1],y[2]}]
```

$$\{45, \{y[1] \rightarrow \frac{1}{2}, \ y[2] \rightarrow \frac{7}{2}\}\}$$

■

Of course, linear programming models can involve numerous variables. Consider the following: Given the standard form linear programming problem: Minimize $Z = \underbrace{c_1 x_1 + c_2 x_2 + \ldots + c_n x_n}_{function}$, subject to the restrictions

$$\begin{cases} a_{11}x_1 + a_{12}x_2 + \ldots + a_{1n}x_n \geq b_1 \\ a_{21}x_1 + a_{22}x_2 + \ldots + a_{2n}x_n \geq b_2 \\ \quad\vdots \\ a_{m1}x_1 + a_{m2}x_2 + \ldots + a_{mn}x_n \geq b_m \end{cases}, \text{ and } x_1 \geq 0, \ x_2 \geq 0, \ldots, \ x_n \geq 0.$$

Let

$$x = \begin{pmatrix} x_1 \\ x_2 \\ \vdots \\ x_n \end{pmatrix}, \quad b = \begin{pmatrix} b_1 \\ b_2 \\ \vdots \\ b_m \end{pmatrix}, \quad c = \begin{pmatrix} c_1 & c_2 & \cdots & c_n \end{pmatrix},$$

and A denote the m × n matrix

$$\begin{pmatrix} a_{11} & a_{12} & \cdots & a_{1n} \\ a_{21} & a_{22} & \cdots & a_{2n} \\ \vdots & \vdots & \ddots & \vdots \\ a_{m1} & a_{m2} & \cdots & a_{mn} \end{pmatrix}.$$

Then the standard form of the linear programming problem is equivalent to finding the vector x that maximizes $Z = c \bullet x$ subject to the restrictions $A \bullet x \geq b$ and $x \geq 0$. The dual problem of: Maximize the number $Z = c \bullet x$ subject to the restrictions $A \bullet x \geq b$ and $x \geq 0$ is: Minimize the number $Y = y \bullet b$ subject to the restrictions $y \bullet A \leq c$ and $y \geq 0$.

The command `LinearProgramming[c,A,b]` finds the vector x which minimizes the quantity `Z=c.x` subject to the restrictions `A.x > b` and `x > 0`. This command does not yield the minimum value of `Z` as did `ConstrainedMin` and `ConstrainedMax` and the value must be determined from the resulting vector.

EXAMPLE: Maximize $Z = 5x_1 - 7x_2 + 7x_3 + 5x_4 + 6x_5$ subject to the constraints $2x_1 + 3x_2 + 3x_3 + 2x_4 + 2x_5 \geq 10$, $6x_1 + 5x_2 + 4x_3 + x_4 + 4x_5 \geq 30$, $-3x_1 - 2x_2 - 3x_3 - 4x_4 \geq -5$, $-x_1 - x_2 - x_4 \geq -10$, and $x_i \geq 0$ for i=1, 2, 3, 4, and 5. State the dual problem. What is its solution?

SOLUTION: For this problem,

$$x = \begin{pmatrix} x_1 \\ x_2 \\ x_3 \\ x_4 \\ x_5 \end{pmatrix}, \quad b = \begin{pmatrix} 10 \\ 30 \\ -5 \\ -10 \end{pmatrix}, \quad c = \begin{pmatrix} 5 & -7 & 7 & 5 & 6 \end{pmatrix},$$

and

$$A = \begin{pmatrix} 2 & 3 & 3 & 2 & 2 \\ 6 & 5 & 4 & 1 & 4 \\ -3 & -2 & -3 & -4 & 0 \\ -1 & -1 & 0 & -1 & 0 \end{pmatrix}.$$

First, the vectors c and b are entered and then matrix A is entered and named matrixa.

```
Clear[matrixa,x,y,c,b]
c={5,-7,7,5,6};
b={10,30,-5,-10};
matrixa={{2,3,3,2,2},{6,5,4,1,4},{-3,-2,-3,-4,0},{-1,-1,0,-1,0}};
```

Next, we use Array[x,5] to create the list of 5 elements {x[1],x[2],...,x[5]} named xvec. The command Table[x[i],{i,1,5}] returns the same list. These variables must be defined before attempting to solve this linear programming problem.

```
xvec=Array[x,5]

    {x[1], x[2], x[3], x[4], x[5]}
```

After entering the objective function coefficients with the vector c , the matrix of coefficients from the inequalities with matrixa , and the right-hand side values found in b, the problem is solved with

LinearProgramming[c,matrixa,b].

The solution is called xvec . Hence, the maximum value of the objective function is obtained by evaluating the objective function at the variable values which yield a maximum. Since these values are found in xvec , the maximum is determined with the product of the vector c and the vector xvec . (Recall that this product is entered as c.xvec.) This value is found to be $35/4$.

```
xvec=LinearProgramming[c,matrixa,b]

         5        35
    {0, -, 0, 0, --}
         2         8

c.xvec

    35
    --
    4
```

Because the dual of the problem is Minimize the number Y=y.b subject to the restrictions y.A<c and y > 0, we use Mathematica to calculate y.b and y.A:

Remark: Notice that Mathematica does NOT make a distinction between row and column vectors; it interprets the vector correctly and consequently performs the calculation properly.

A list of the dual variables {y[1],y[2],y[3],y[4]} is created with Array[y,4]. This list includes 4 elements because there are four constraints in the original problem. The objective function of the dual problem is, therefore, found with yvec.b, and the left-hand sides of the set of inequalities are given with yvec.matrixa.

```
yvec=Array[y,4]

    {y[1], y[2], y[3], y[4]}

yvec.b

    10 y[1] + 30 y[2] - 5 y[3] - 10 y[4]

yvec.matrixa

    {2 y[1] + 6 y[2] - 3 y[3] - y[4],

     3 y[1] + 5 y[2] - 2 y[3] - y[4],

     3 y[1] + 4 y[2] - 3 y[3],

     2 y[1] + y[2] - 4 y[3] - y[4], 2 y[1] + 4 y[2]}
```

Hence, we may state the dual problem as follows:

$$\text{Minimize } Y = 10y_1 + 30y_2 - 5y_3 - 10y_4 \text{ subject to the constraints}$$
$$2y_1 + 6y_2 - 3y_3 - y_4 \leq 5,$$
$$3y_1 + 5y_2 - 2y_3 - y_4 \leq -7,$$
$$3y_1 + 4y_2 - 3y_3 \leq 7,$$
$$2y_1 + y_2 - 4y_3 - y_4 \leq 5,$$
$$2y_1 + 4y_2 \leq 6, \text{ and } y_i \geq 0 \text{ for } i = 1, 2, 3, \text{ and } 4. \blacksquare$$

Application: A Transportation Problem

A certain company has two factories, F1 and F2, each producing two products, P1 and P2, that are to be shipped to three distribution centers, D1, D2, and D3. The following table illustrates the cost associated with shipping each product from the factory to the distribution center, the minimum number of each product each distribution center needs, and the maximum output of each factory. How much of each product should be shipped from each plant to each distribution center to minimize the total shipping costs?

	F1/P1	F1/P2	F2/P1	F2/P2	Minimum
D1/P1	$0.75		$0.80		500
D1/P2		$0.50		$0.40	400
D2/P1	$1.00		$0.90		300
D2/P2		$0.75		$1.20	500
D3/P1	$0.90		$0.85		700
D3/P2		$0.80		$0.95	300
Maximum Output	1000	400	800	900	

SOLUTION: Let x_1 denote the number of units of P1 shipped from F1 to D1; x_2 the number of units of P2 shipped from F1 to D1; x_3 the number of units of P1 shipped from F1 to D2; x_4 the number of units of P2 shipped from F1 to D2; x_5 the number of units of P1 shipped from F1 to D3; x_6 the number of units of P2 shipped from F1 to D3; x_7 the number of units of P1 shipped from F2 to D1; x_8 the number of units of P2 shipped from F2 to D1; x_9 the number of units of P1 shipped from F2 to D2; x_{10} the number of units of P2 shipped from F2 to D2; x_{11} the number of units of P1 shipped from F2 to D3; and x_{12} the number of units of P2 shipped from F2 to D3.

Then, it is necessary to minimize the number

$$Z = .75x_1 + .5x_2 + x_3 + .75x_4 + .9x_5 + .8x_6 + .8x_7 + .4x_8 + .9x_9 + 1.2x_{10} + .85x_{11} + .95x_{12}$$

subject to the constraints $x_1 + x_3 + x_5 \le 1000$, $x_2 + x_4 + x_6 \le 400$, $x_7 + x_9 + x_{11} \le 800$, $x_8 + x_{10} + x_{12} \le 900$, $x_1 + x_7 \ge 500$, $x_3 + x_9 \ge 300$, $x_5 + x_{11} \ge 700$, $x_2 + x_8 \ge 400$, $x_4 + x_{10} \ge 500$, $x_6 + x_{12} \ge 300$, and x_i non-negative for i=1, 2, ... , 12.

In order to solve this linear programming problem, the objective function which computes the total cost, the 12 variables, and set of inequalities must be entered. The coefficients of the objective function are given in the vector c. Using the command `Array[x,12]` illustrated in the previous example to define the list of 12 variables `{x[1],x[2],...,x[12]}`, the objective function is given by the product z=xvec.c, where xvec is the name assigned to the list of variables.

```
Clear[xvec,z,constraints,vars,c]
c={0.75, 0.5, 1, 0.75, 0.9, 0.8, 0.8, 0.4, 0.9, 1.2, 0.85, 0.95};

xvec=Array[x,12]

    {x[1], x[2], x[3], x[4], x[5], x[6], x[7], x[8],
       x[9], x[10], x[11], x[12]}
```

```
z=xvec.c
```

$$0.75 \; x[1] \; + \; 0.5 \; x[2] \; + \; x[3] \; + \; 0.75 \; x[4] \; +$$

$$0.9 \; x[5] \; + \; 0.8 \; x[6] \; + \; 0.8 \; x[7] \; + \; 0.4 \; x[8] \; +$$

$$0.9 \; x[9] \; + \; 1.2 \; x[10] \; + \; 0.85 \; x[11] \; + \; 0.95 \; x[12]$$

The set of constraints is then entered and named `constraints` for easier use. Therefore, the minimum cost and the value of each variable which yields this minimum cost are found with the command

```
ConstrainedMin[z,constraints,xvec].
```

```
constraints={x[1]+x[3]+x[5]<=1000,x[2]+x[4]+x[6]<=400,
x[7]+x[9]+x[11]<=800,x[8]+x[10]+x[12] <=900,
x[1]+x[7]>=500, x[3]+x[9]>=300,x[5]+x[11]>=700, x[2]+x[8]>=400,
x[4]+x[10]>500, x[6]+x[12]>300};
```

```
values=ConstrainedMin[z,constraints,xvec]
```

```
{2115, {x[1] -> 500, x[2] -> 0, x[3] -> 0,

    x[4] -> 400, x[5] -> 200, x[6] -> 0, x[7] -> 0,

    x[8] -> 400, x[9] -> 300, x[10] -> 100,

    x[11] -> 500, x[12] -> 300}}
```

Notice that values is a list made up of two elements, the minimum value of the cost function, 2115, and the list of the variable values `{x[1]->500,x[2]->0,` `...}`. Hence, the minimum cost is obtained with the command `values[[1]]` and the list of variable values which yield the minimum cost is extracted with `values[[2]]`.

```
values[[1]]
```

```
    2115
```

```
values[[2]]
```

```
{x[1] -> 500, x[2] -> 0, x[3] -> 0, x[4] -> 400,

    x[5] -> 200, x[6] -> 0, x[7] -> 0, x[8] -> 400,

    x[9] -> 300, x[10] -> 100, x[11] -> 500,

    x[12] -> 300}
```

Using these extraction techniques, the number of units produced by each factory can be computed. Since x_1 denotes the number of units of P1 shipped from F1 to D1, x_3 the number of units of P1 shipped from F1 to D2, and x_5 the number of units of P1 shipped from F1 to D3, the total number of units of Product 1 produced by Factory 1 is given by the command `x[1]+x[3]+x[5] /. values[[2]]`, which evaluates this sum at the values of `x[1]`, `x[3]`, and `x[5]` given in the list `values[[2]]`.

```
x[1]+x[3]+x[5] /. values[[2]]
```

```
700
```

Also, the number of units of Products 1 and 2 received by each distribution center can be computed. The command `x[3]+x[9] /. values[[2]]` gives the total amount of Product 1 received at Dist 1 because

`x[3]` = amount of Product 1 received by Dist 2 from F1 and

`x[9]` = amount of Product 1 received by Dist 2 from F2.

Notice that this amount is the minimum number of units (300) of Product 1 requested by Dist 1.

```
x[3]+x[9] /. values[[2]]
```

```
300
```

The number of units of each product that each factory produces can be calculated, and the amount of Products 1 and 2 received at each distribution center are calculated in a similar manner and illustrated below.

```
{x[1]+x[3]+x[5],x[2]+x[4]+x[6],x[7]+x[9]+x[11],
    x[8]+x[10]+x[12],x[1]+x[7], x[3]+x[9],x[5]+x[11], x[2]+x[8],
    x[4]+x[10], x[6]+x[12]} /. values[[2]]//TableForm
```

```
700
400
800
800
500
300
700
400
500
300
```

From the results above, we see that factory 1 produces 700 units of Product 1, factory 1 produces 400 units of Product 2, factory 2 produces 800 units of Product 1, factory 2 produces 800 units of product 2, and each distribution center receives exactly the minimum number of each product it requests.

∎

5.5 Vector Calculus

Definitions and Notation

The terminology and notation used in *Mathematica By Example* is standard. Nevertheless, we review basic definitions briefly.

A **scalar field** is a function with domain a set of ordered triples and range a subset of the real numbers:

$$f:U \to V \text{ is a scalar field means } U \subseteq \Re^3 \text{ and } V \subseteq \Re.$$

The **gradient of the scalar field f** is defined to be the vector

$$grad\, f = \frac{\partial f}{\partial x}i + \frac{\partial f}{\partial y}j + \frac{\partial f}{\partial z}k = \left\langle \frac{\partial f}{\partial x}, \frac{\partial f}{\partial y}, \frac{\partial f}{\partial z} \right\rangle = \left\langle f_x, f_y, f_z \right\rangle,$$

where $i = \langle 1,0,0 \rangle$, $j = \langle 0,1,0 \rangle$, and $k = \langle 0,0,1 \rangle$.

A **vector field f** is a vector-valued function:

$f:V \to U$, $U \subseteq \Re^3$ and $V \subseteq \Re^3$ is a vector field means that f can be written in the form

$$f(x,y,z) = f_1(x,y,z)i + f_2(x,y,z)j + f_3(x,y,z)k = \left\langle f_1(x,y,z), f_2(x,y,z), f_3(x,y,z) \right\rangle$$

for each (x,y,z) in the domain of f.

A **conservative vector field f** is a vector field that is the gradient of a scalar field: f is a conservative vector field means that there is a scalar field g satisfying $f = \nabla^2 g$. In this case, g is usually called a **potential function** for f.

The **divergence of the vector field f** is defined to be the scalar

$$div\, f = div\, f(x,y,z) = div\left\langle f_1(x,y,z), f_2(x,y,z), f_3(x,y,z) \right\rangle$$
$$= \frac{\partial f_1}{\partial x} + \frac{\partial f_2}{\partial y} + \frac{\partial f_3}{\partial z} = \nabla \bullet f.$$

The **laplacian of the scalar field f** is defined to be div(grad f)):

$$laplacian(f) = \nabla^2 f = \Delta f = \frac{\partial^2 f}{\partial x^2} + \frac{\partial^2 f}{\partial y^2} + \frac{\partial^2 f}{\partial z^2} = f_{xx} + f_{yy} + f_{zz}$$

For three-dimensional vector analysis, the package **VectorAnalysis** contains the commands Grad, Div, Curl, and Laplacian, which we use to compute the gradient and divergence of vector fields and curl and laplacian of scalar fields.

Be sure to load the package **VectorAnalysis**, contained in the **Calculus** folder (or directory) by entering <<Calculus'VectorAnalysis' prior to using these functions.

Because Mathematica recognizes Cartesian [x,y,z], Cylindrical[r,phi,z], and Spherical[r,theta,phi] coordinates, and because the operations discussed in this section differ in the various coordinate systems, the desired coordinate system must be indicated. This is accomplished with

SetCoordinates[System],

where System is usually either Cartesian, Cylindrical, or Spherical.

However, the available coordinate systems are: Cartesian, Cylindrical, Spherical, Parabolic, ParabolicCylinder, ProlateEllipsoidal, EllipticCylinder, OblateEllipsoidal, Toroidal, Elliptic, and Bipolar.

In addition to the above commands, others included in the **VectorAnalysis** package include CoordinatesToCartesian[point,system] which gives the Cartesian coordinates of point when point is given in the coordinate system system, CoordinatesFromCartesian[point,system] which gives coordinates in the coordinate system system when point is given in Cartesian coordinates, DotProduct[u,v,system] which computes the dot product of u and v in the coordinate system system, CrossProduct[u,v] which computes the cross product of u and v in the coordinate system system, and ScalarTripleProduct[u,v,w,system] which computes the scalar triple product of u, v, and w in the coordinate system system. Other interesting commands include ArcLengthFactor, JacobianMatrix, and JacobianDeterminant. For a comprehensive discussion of the commands contained in the package **VectorAnalysis** see the *Technical Report: Guide to Standard Mathematica Packages* published by Wolfram Research, Inc.

> **EXAMPLE:** Let $f(x,y,z) = \cos(xyz)$. Compute ∇f, $\nabla^2 f$, and $div(\nabla f)$.

SOLUTION: After loading the package **VectorAnalysis**, we enter SetCoordinates[Cartesian] to specify that our calculations will be using Cartesian coordinates. We then use Grad, Laplacian, and Div to compute ∇f, $\nabla^2 f$, and $div(\nabla f)$.

```
<<Calculus'VectorAnalysis'
SetCoordinates[Cartesian];

Clear[f]
f[x_,y_,z_]=Cos[x y z];

gradientf[x_,y_,z_]=Grad[f[x,y,z]]

    {-(y z Sin[x y z]), -(x z Sin[x y z]), -(x y Sin[x y z])}
```

```
Laplacian[f[x,y,z]]

      2  2                    2  2                   2  2
   -(x  y  Cos[x y z]) - x   z  Cos[x y z] - y   z  Cos[x y z]

Div[gradientf[x,y,z]]

      2  2                    2  2                   2  2
   -(x  y  Cos[x y z]) - x   z  Cos[x y z] - y   z  Cos[x y z]
```

■

If S is the graph of f(x,y) and $g(x,y,z)=z-f(x,y)$, then the gradient $\nabla g(x,y,z)$ is a normal vector to the graph of g(x,y,z)=0. At the point (x,y,z), a **unit normal vector**, n, can be obtained via:

$$n = \frac{\nabla g(x,y,z)}{\|\nabla g(x,y,z)\|} = \frac{-f_x(x,y)i - f_y(x,y)j + k}{\sqrt{\left(f_x(x,y)\right)^2 + \left(f_y(x,y)\right)^2 + 1}} = \frac{\left\langle -f_x(x,y), -f_y(x,y), 1 \right\rangle}{\sqrt{\left(f_x(x,y)\right)^2 + \left(f_y(x,y)\right)^2 + 1}}.$$

The **curl of the vector field f** is defined to be the vector field:

$$curl\, f = curl\, f(x,y,z) = curl \left\langle f_1(x,y,z), f_2(x,y,z), f_3(x,y,z) \right\rangle$$

$$= \left(\frac{\partial f_3}{\partial y} - \frac{\partial f_2}{\partial z} \right) i + \left(\frac{\partial f_1}{\partial z} - \frac{\partial f_3}{\partial x} \right) j + \left(\frac{\partial f_2}{\partial x} - \frac{\partial f_1}{\partial y} \right) k$$

$$= \det \begin{pmatrix} i & j & k \\ \frac{\partial}{\partial x} & \frac{\partial}{\partial y} & \frac{\partial}{\partial z} \\ f_1 & f_2 & f_3 \end{pmatrix}.$$

EXAMPLE: Let $f(x,y,z)= xy\,i + x\,yz^2\,j - e^{2z}k = \left\langle xy, xyz^2, -e^{2z} \right\rangle$. Compute $curl\, f$, $div\, f$, $laplacian(div\, f)$, and $grad(laplacian(div\, f)) = grad\left(\nabla^2(div\, f) \right)$.

SOLUTION: The first step towards solving this problem is to enter the unit vectors in cartesian coordinates i={1,0,0}, j={0,1,0}, and k={0,0,1}. The vector-valued function f[x,y,z] can then be defined using these three unit vectors as follows:

```
f[x_,y_,z_]=x y i+x z^2 y j-Exp[2z] k
```

(remembering to place appropriate spaces between variables for multiplication). Alternatively, we could define f by entering

```
f[x_,y_,z_]={x y,x z^2 y,-Exp[2z]}.
```

Be sure to load the package **VectorAnalysis**, as done below, if you have not already loaded it during your current Mathematica session.

Notice that the coordinate system has not been set in this problem. However, the correct system can be indicated in each command. For example, the curl of f in Cartesian coordinates is determined with

```
Curl[f[x,y,z],Cartesian].
```

The curl could similarly be obtained in the other systems by replacing `Cartesian` with `Cylindrical`, `Spherical`, or one of the other available coordinate systems, in the command above.

```
<<Calculus'VectorAnalysis'

Clear[i,j,k]
i={1,0,0};
j={0,1,0};
k={0,0,1};

Clear[f]
f[x_,y_,z_]=x y i+x z^2 y j-Exp[2z] k;
```

Next we use `Curl` to compute the curl of the vector-valued function f.

```
curlf[x_,y_,z_]=Curl[f[x,y,z],Cartesian]

                      2
    {-2 x y z, 0, -x + y z }
```

As was the case with computing the curl of f, the divergence of f can be calculated in Cartesian coordinates with

```
Div[f[x,y,z],Cartesian]].
```

Again, since the divergence is a function of (x,y,z), it is named `divf[x,y,z]` for later use. The Laplacian of the divergence of f is computed with

```
Laplacian[divf[x,y,z],Cartesian]].
```

This function is called `ladivf[x,y,z]` so that $grad\,(laplacian\,(div\,f)) = grad\left(\nabla^2(div\,f)\right)$ can be found with

```
Grad[ladivf[x,y,z],Cartesian]].
```

```
divf[x_,y_,z_]=Div[f[x,y,z],Cartesian]

         2 z         2
    -2 E    + y + x z
```

```
ladivf[x_,y_,z_]=Laplacian[divf[x,y,z],Cartesian]
```

$$-8 \; E^{2 \; z} \; + \; 2 \; x$$

```
Grad[ladivf[x,y,z],Cartesian]
```

$$\{2, \; 0, \; -16 \; E^{2 \; z} \}$$

■

We demonstrate the computation of a unit normal vector in the example below.

EXAMPLE: Let $w(x,y) = \cos(4x^2 + 9y^2)$. Let n(x,y) denote a unit vector normal to the graph of w at the point $(x,y,w(x,y))$. Find a formula for n.

SOLUTION: In order to visualize the unit normal vector at points $(x,y,w(x,y))$ to the surface $w(x,y)$, this function is plotted below using several of the options available with Plot3D. The option Boxed->False specifies that the Graphics3D object be displayed without a bounding box, while the option PlotPoints->35 specifies that the number of sample points used consist of 35 along the x-axis and 35 along the y-axis, for a total of $35 \times 35 = 1225$ sample points used in the generation of the graph. The options Axes->Automatic and Shading->False indicate that Mathematica is to automatically place axes in the final displayed graph and the results will not be shaded.

```
Clear[w]
w[x_,y_]=Cos[4x^2+9y^2];

plotw=Plot3D[w[x,y],{x,-1,1},{y,-1,1},Boxed->False, Axes->Automatic,
    PlotPoints->35, Shading->False]
```

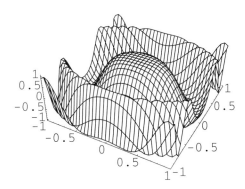

The equation $z = w(x,y)$ is written as $z - w(x,y) = 0$. The left-hand side of this equation is a function of x, y, and z and is defined as `wz[x_,y_,z_]=z-w[x,y]`. Since the partial derivative of `wz` with respect to z is -1, the gradient of `wz` is a function of x and y only. Hence, the gradient of `wz` is named `gw[x_,y_]` and is computed with `Grad[wz[x,y,z],Cartesian]`. The length of the gradient of `wz` which is necessary in determining the unit normal vector is the square root of the dot product of the gradient of `wz` with itself. This product is computed with `gw[x,y].gw[x,y]`.

```
wz[x_,y_,z_]=z-w[x,y]
```

$$z - \text{Cos}[4\ x^2 + 9\ y^2]$$

```
gw[x_,y_]=Grad[wz[x,y,z],Cartesian]
```

$$\{8\ x\ \text{Sin}[4\ x^2 + 9\ y^2],\ 18\ y\ \text{Sin}[4\ x^2 + 9\ y^2],\ 1\}$$

```
gw[x,y].gw[x,y]
```

$$1 + 64\ x^2\ \text{Sin}[4\ x^2 + 9\ y^2]^2 + 324\ y^2\ \text{Sin}[4\ x^2 + 9\ y^2]^2$$

Therefore, the unit normal vector is the gradient of g, `gw[x,y]`, divided by the square root of `gw[x,y].gw[x,y]`, $\dfrac{\nabla g(x,y,z)}{\|\nabla g(x,y,z)\|}$, as shown below. This is also a function of the variables x and y since the unit normal vector differs from point to point on the surface. Hence, this vector is assigned the name `normalw[x,y]` so that the unit vector at any point $(x,y,w(x,y))$ can be easily determined by evaluating `normalw[x,y]` at any point (x,y).

```
normalw[x_,y_]=gw[x,y]/Sqrt[gw[x,y].gw[x,y]]
```

$$\{(8\ x\ \text{Sin}[4\ x^2 + 9\ y^2])\ /$$

$$\text{Sqrt}[1 + 64\ x^2\ \text{Sin}[4\ x^2 + 9\ y^2]^2 +$$

$$324\ y^2\ \text{Sin}[4\ x^2 + 9\ y^2]^2\ ],$$

$$(18\ y\ \text{Sin}[4\ x^2 + 9\ y^2])\ /$$

$$\text{Sqrt}[1 + 64\ x^2\ \text{Sin}[4\ x^2 + 9\ y^2]^2 +$$

$$324\ y^2\ \text{Sin}[4\ x^2 + 9\ y^2]^2\ ],$$

```
              2          2       2 2
 1 / Sqrt[1 + 64 x  Sin[4 x  + 9 y ] +

        2          2      2 2
   324 y  Sin[4 x  + 9 y ] ]}
```

We can graph various normal vectors with the command `PlotVectorField3D` which is contained in the package **PlotField3D** located in the **Graphics** folder (or directory). After loading the **PlotField3D** package, we graph `normalw[x,y]` in the cube given by $[-1,1]\times[-1,1]\times[-1,1]$ and name the resulting graph `plotn`. We then use `Show` to display `plotw` and `plotn` together.

```
<<Graphics'PlotField3D'
plotn=PlotVectorField3D[normalw[x,y],{x,-1,1},{y,-1,1},{z,-1,1}]
```

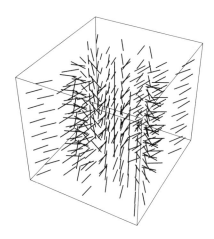

```
Show[plotw,plotn]
```

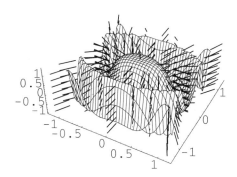

Similarly, we may graph the gradient vector field of the scalar function `wz` with the command `PlotGradientField3D`, also contained in the **PlotField3D** package. In the following command, we include the option `VectorHeads->True` so we can see the direction of the resulting arrows.

```
PlotGradientField3D[wz[x,y,z],{x,-1,1},{y,-1,1},{z,-1,1},
       VectorHeads->True]
```

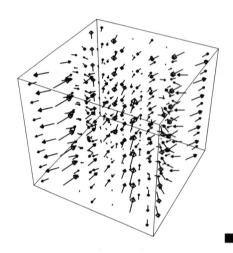

Application: Green's Theorem

Green's Theorem: Let C be a piecewise smooth simple closed curve and let R be the region consisting of C and its interior. If f and g are functions that are continuous and have continuous first partial derivatives throughout an open region D containing R, then

$$\oint_C \left(m(x,y)dx + n(x,y)dy \right) = \iint_R \left(\frac{\partial n}{\partial x} - \frac{\partial m}{\partial y} \right) dA \ .$$

EXAMPLE: Use Green's Theorem to evaluate $\oint_C \left(x + e^{\sqrt{y}} \right) dx + (2y + \cos(x)) dy$, where C is the boundary of the region enclosed by the parabolas $y = x^2$ and $x = y^2$.

SOLUTION: To calculate the limits of integration, we use Mathematica to graph the functions x^2 and $\sqrt{x}$. Note that the two functions intersect at the points (0,0) and (1,1).

```
Plot[{x^2,Sqrt[x]},{x,0,1.2}]
```

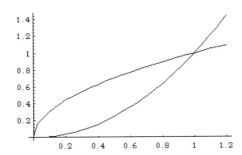

In this example, $m(x,y) = x + e^{\sqrt{y}}$ and $n(x,y) = 2y + \cos(x)$. Therefore, applying Green's theorem,

$$\oint_C \left(x + e^{\sqrt{y}}\right)dx + \left(2y + \cos(x)\right)dy = \oint_C m(x,y)dx + n(x,y)dy$$

$$= \iint_R \left(\frac{\partial n}{\partial x} - \frac{\partial m}{\partial y}\right)dA = \int_0^1 \int_{x^2}^{\sqrt{x}} \left(\frac{\partial n}{\partial x} - \frac{\partial m}{\partial y}\right)dy\,dx.$$

Next, we will use Mathematica to define m(x,y), n(x,y), and to compute $\frac{\partial n}{\partial x}$, $\frac{\partial m}{\partial y}$,

and $\int_0^1 \int_{x^2}^{\sqrt{x}} \left(\frac{\partial n}{\partial x} - \frac{\partial m}{\partial y}\right)dy\,dx$. First, the functions m(x,y), and n(x,y) are defined. Recall that in computing the partial derivatives, the variable of differentiation must be specified. These partial derivatives are calculated in nx and my, respectively. Integrate cannot be used to find an exact value of this integral (as shown in our final calculation) so we approximate it with NIntegrate.

```
Clear[m,n]
m[x_,y_]=x+Exp[Sqrt[y]];
n[x_,y_]=2y+Cos[x];

nx=D[n[x,y],x]

     -Sin[x]

my=D[m[x,y],y]

      Sqrt[y]
     E
     ---------
     2 Sqrt[y]

NIntegrate[nx-my,{x,0,1},{y,x^2,Sqrt[x]}]

     -0.676441
```

```
Integrate[nx-my,{x,0,1},{y,x^2,Sqrt[x]}]
```

```
General::intinit:
    Loading integration packages -- please wait.
                                    Pi          2
    -26 + 8 E + 2 Cos[1] - Sqrt[--] FresnelC[Sqrt[--]] +
                                    2                    Pi

                    2
            Sqrt[x ]
    Integrate[E        , {x, 0, 1}] + 2 Sin[1]
```

∎

Application: The Divergence Theorem

The Divergence Theorem: Let Q be any domain with the property that each straight line through any interior point of the domain cuts the boundary in exactly two points, and such that the boundary S is a piecewise smooth closed, oriented surface with unit outer normal n. If f is a vector field that has continuous partial derivatives on Q, then

$$\iint_S f \bullet n\, dS = \iiint_Q div\, f\, dV = \iiint_Q \nabla \bullet f\, dV \;.$$

$\iint_S f \bullet n\, dS$ is called the **outward flux** of the vector field f across the surface S. If S is a portion of the level curve g(x,y)=c for some g, then a unit normal vector n may be taken to be either $n = \dfrac{\nabla g}{\|\nabla g\|}$ or $n = \dfrac{-\nabla g}{\|\nabla g\|}$.

Recall the following formulas for the evaluations of surface integrals: Let S be the graph of z=f(x,y) (y=h(x,z) or x=k(y,z)) and let R_{xy} (R_{xz} or R_{yz}) be the projection of S on the xy- (xz- or yz-) plane. Then,

$$\iint_S g(x,y,z)dS = \begin{cases} \iint_{R_{xy}} g(x,y,f(x,y))\sqrt{(f_x(x,y))^2 + (f_y(x,y))^2 + 1}\, dA \\ \iint_{R_{xz}} g(x,h(x,z),z)\sqrt{(h_x(x,z))^2 + (h_z(x,z))^2 + 1}\, dA. \\ \iint_{R_{yz}} g(k(y,z),y,z)\sqrt{(k_y(y,z))^2 + (k_z(y,z))^2 + 1}\, dA \end{cases}$$

EXAMPLE: Use the Divergence Theorem to compute the outward flux of the field

$$vf(x,y,z) = \langle xy + x^2yz, yz + xy^2z, xz + xyz^2 \rangle$$

through the surface of the cube cut from the first octant by the planes x=2, y=2, and z=2.

SOLUTION: By the Divergence Theorem, $\underset{Cube\ Surface}{\iint} vf \bullet n\, dA = \underset{Cube\ Interior}{\iiint} \nabla \bullet vf\, dV$. Notice that

without the Divergence theorem, calculating $\underset{Cube\ Surface}{\iint} vf \bullet n\, dA$ would require six

separate integrals. However, with the Divergence Theorem, calculating the flux can be accomplished by integrating the divergence. Because we need the command Div, we load the **VectorAnalysis** package. The vector field is defined in vf as a list of three elements, the x, y, and z components, so that the divergence can be determined in divvf. The divergence is then integrated over the cube [0,2] × [0,2] × [0,2] to yield a value of 72.

```
<<Calculus'VectorAnalysis'
vf[x_,y_,z_]={x y+x^2 z y,y z+x y^2 z, x z+x y z^2}

        2               2
   {x y + x  y z, y z + x y  z,

               2
     x z + x y z }

divvf[x_,y_,z_]=Div[vf[x,y,z],Cartesian]

   x + y + z + 6 x y z

Integrate[divvf[x,y,z],{x,0,2},{y,0,2},{z,0,2}]

   72
```

In the same manner as in the previous example, we can use the command PlotVectorField3D contained in the **PlotField3D** package to graph the vector field vf. After loading the **PlotField3D** package, we graph vf in the cube $[0,2] \times [0,2] \times [0,2]$.

```
<<Graphics'PlotField3D'
PlotVectorField3D[vf[x,y,z],{x,0,2},{y,0,2},{z,0,2},VectorHeads->True]
```

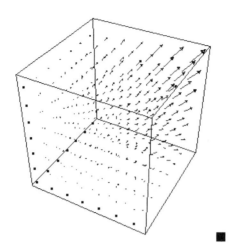

Application: Stoke's Theorem

Stoke's Theorem: Let S be an oriented surface with finite surface area, unit normal n, and boundary C. Let F be a continuous vector field defined on S such that the component functions of F have continuous partial derivatives at each non-boundary point of S. Then, $\oint_C F \bullet dr = \iint_S (curl f) \bullet n \, dS$. In other words, the surface integral of the normal component of the curl of F taken over S equals the line integral of the tangential component of the field taken over C: $\oint_C F \bullet T \, ds = \iint_S (curl f) \bullet n \, dS$. In particular, if $F = \langle M, N, P \rangle = M i + N j + P k$, then

$$\int_C M(x,y,z)dx + N(x,y,z)dy + P(x,y,z)dz = \iint_S (curl f \, f) \bullet n \, dS .$$

EXAMPLE: Verify Stoke's Theorem for the vector field $vf(x,y,z) = \langle y^2 - z, z^2 + x, x^2 - y \rangle$ and S the paraboloid $z = f(x,y) = 4 - (x^2 + y^2)$, z non-negative.

SOLUTION: Since we must show $\oint_C vf \bullet dr = \iint_S (curl \, vf) \bullet n \, dS$, we must compute curl **vf**, n, $\iint_S (curl \, vf) \bullet n \, dS$, r, dr, and $\oint_C vf \bullet dr$. We begin by loading the **VectorAnalysis** package and defining the vector field **vf** and the function **f**. The curl of **vf** is then computed in **curlvf**. The function $h(x,y,z) = z - f(x,y)$, which will be used in the computation of the unit normal vector, is also defined. Hence, the normal vector to the surface is given by ∇h , which is found below in **normal**.

```
<<Calculus'VectorAnalysis'

Clear[vf,f,h,normal,un,g,curlvf,n]
vf[x_,y_,z_]={y^2-z,z^2+x,x^2-y};
f[x_,y_]=4-(x^2+y^2);

curlvf[x_,y_,z_]=Curl[vf[x,y,z],Cartesian]

    {-1 - 2 z, -1 - 2 x, 1 - 2 y}

h[x_,y_,z_]=z-f[x,y]

        2   2
    -4 + x + y + z

normal[x_,y_,z_]=Grad[h[x,y,z],Cartesian]

    {2 x, 2 y, 1}
```

Since normal is a normal vector to the surface, $\frac{\nabla h}{\|\nabla h\|} = \frac{normal[x,y,z]}{\|normal[x,y,z]\|}$ represents a unit normal vector. This vector is found below in un. Recall that

$$\|normal[x,y,z]\| = \sqrt{normal[x,y,z]\bullet normal[x,y,z]}.$$

Note that normal[x,y,z] is a list (of three elements) and normal[x,y,z][[i]] yields the ith element of the list normal[x,y,z]. Therefore,

||normal[x,y,z]|| is given by the command

```
    Sqrt[Sum[(normal[x,y,z][[i]])^2,{i,1,3}]].
```

Thus, an alternative approach is to define un by entering:

```
un[x_,y_,z_]=normal[x,y,z]/Sqrt[
        Sum[(normal[x,y,z][[i]])^2,{i,1,3}]]
```

In order to easily use the surface integral evaluation formula, define g[x,y,z] to be the dot product of curlvf[x,y,z] and un[x,y,z].

```
un[x_,y_,z_]=normal[x,y,z]/Sqrt[normal[x,y,z].normal[x,y,z]]

            2 x
    {--------------------,
            2     2
     Sqrt[1 + 4 x + 4 y ]

            2 y
     --------------------,
            2     2
     Sqrt[1 + 4 x + 4 y ]
```

```
             1
   ------------------}
        2      2
   Sqrt[1 + 4 x  + 4 y ]
```

```
g[x_,y_,z_]=Together[curlvf[x,y,z].un[x,y,z]]
```

```
   1 - 2 x - 4 y - 4 x y - 4 x z
   ----------------------------
              2      2
       Sqrt[1 + 4 x  + 4 y ]
```

By the surface integral evaluation formula,

$$\iint_S (curl\,vf)\bullet n\,dS = \iint_S g(x,y,z)dS = \iint_R g(x,y,f(x,y))\sqrt{(f_x(x,y))^2 + (f_y(x,y))^2 + 1}\,dA\,,$$

where R is the projection of f(x,y) on the xy-plane. Hence, in this example, R is the region bounded by the graph of the circle $x^2 + y^2 = 4$. Thus,

$$\iint_R g(x,y,f(x,y))\sqrt{(f_x(x,y))^2 + (f_y(x,y))^2 + 1}\,dA =$$

$$\int_{-2}^{2}\int_{-\sqrt{4-x^2}}^{\sqrt{4-x^2}} g(x,y,f(x,y))\sqrt{(f_x(x,y))^2 + (f_y(x,y))^2 + 1}\,dA.$$

This surface integral is computed below to yield a value of 4π.

```
function=g[x,y,f[x,y]] Sqrt[(D[f[x,y],x])^2+(D[f[x,y],y])^2+1]
```

```
   1 - 2 x - 4 y - 4 x y -

          2    2
    4 x (4 - x  - y )
```

```
Integrate[function,{x,-2,2},{y,-Sqrt[4-x^2],Sqrt[4-x^2]}]
```

```
   4 Pi
```

Notice that the integral

$$\int_{-2}^{2}\int_{-\sqrt{4-x^2}}^{\sqrt{4-x^2}} g(x,y,f(x,y))\sqrt{(f_x(x,y))^2 + (f_y(x,y))^2 + 1}\,dA$$

can be easily evaluated using polar coordinates. To do so, replace each occurrence of x and y in $g(x,y,f(x,y))\sqrt{(f_x(x,y))^2 + (f_y(x,y))^2 + 1}$ by $r\cos t$ and $r\sin t$, respectively.

```
function=g[x,y,f[x,y]] Sqrt[(D[f[x,y],x])^2+(D[f[x,y],y])^2+1] /.
    {x->r Cos[t],y->r Sin[t]}

  1 - 2 r Cos[t] - 4 r Sin[t] -

        2
    4 r  Cos[t] Sin[t] -

                  2        2
    4 r Cos[t] (4 - r  Cos[t]  -

        2       2
      r  Sin[t] )
```

We then simplify function with `Expand` using the option `Trig->True` which applies basic trigonometric identities to attempt to simplify `function`. The expression in `polarfunction` is then integrated over the circular region R: $0 \leq r \leq 2, 0 \leq t \leq 2\pi$ to yield the value of 4π which was obtained in the integral in Cartesian coordinates above.

```
polarfunction=Expand[function,Trig->True]

                    3
  1 - 18 r Cos[t] + 4 r  Cos[t] -

              2
  4 r Sin[t] - 2 r  Sin[2 t]
```

```
Integrate[polarfunction r,{r,0,2},{t,0,2Pi}]

  4 Pi
```

Now, to verify Stoke's Theorem, we must compute the associated line integral. We begin by noticing that the boundary of $z=f(x,y)=4-\left(x^2+y^2\right), z \geq 0$ is the circle $x^2+y^2=4$ which has parameterization x=2*Cos[s], y=2*Sin[s], and z=0 for $0 \leq s \leq 2\pi$. This parameterization is substituted into `vf` and named `pvf` below. In order to evaluate the line integral along the circle, we must define the parameterization of the circle, `r[s]`, and calculate `r'[s]`. The dot product of `pvf` and `r'[s]` represents the integrand of the line integral.

```
pvf=vf[x,y,z] /. {x->2 Cos[s],y->2 Sin[s],z->0}

          2
  {4 Sin[s] , 2 Cos[s],

              2
    4 Cos[s]  - 2 Sin[s]}
```

```
r[s_]={2 Cos[s],2 Sin[s],0}

  {2 Cos[s], 2 Sin[s], 0}
```

```
r'[s]
```

```
    {-2 Sin[s], 2 Cos[s], 0}
```

```
pvf.r'[s]
```

$$4\ Cos[s]^2\ -\ 8\ Sin[s]^3$$

The resulting expression is then integrated along the circle to yield a value of 4π, which verifies Stoke's Theorem.

```
Integrate[pvf.r'[s],{s,0,2Pi}]
```

```
    4 Pi
```

∎

Applications Related to Ordinary and Partial Differential Equations

Mathematica can perform calculations necessary when computing solutions of various differential equations and, in some cases, can be used to find the exact solution of certain differential equations using the built-in command DSolve. In addition, Mathematica contains the command NDSolve which can be used to obtain numerical solutions of other differential equations. The purpose of Chapter 6 is to illustrate various computations Mathematica can perform when solving differential equations. Applications discussed in this chapter include the Falling Bodies Problem, Spring Problems, Classification of Equilibrium Points, and the Wave Equation.

6.1 First-Order Ordinary Differential Equations

Separable Differential Equations

A differential equation that can be written in the form $g(y)y' = f(x)$ is called a **separable differential equation**. Rewriting $g(y)y' = f(x)$ in the form $g(y)\dfrac{dy}{dx} = f(x)$ yields $g(y)dy = f(x)dx$ so that $\int g(y)dy = \int f(x)dx + C$, where C represents an arbitrary constant. An equation of this type is solved with Mathematica in the following example.

EXAMPLE: Solve the initial value problems $y\cos(x)dx - (1 + y^2)dy = 0, y(0) = 1$.

SOLUTION: We first try to solve the equation with DSolve by defining the equation and then entering the command DSolve[eq,y[x],x] which attempts to solve the equation eq for y[x].

```
eq=y'[x]==y[x] Cos[x]/(1+y[x]^2);
DSolve[eq,y[x],x]
```

>   Solve::tdep: The equations appear to involve transcendental functions of
>   the variables in an essentially non-algebraic way.
>   Solve::tdep: The equations appear to involve transcendental functions of
>   the variables in an essentially non-algebraic way.
>   2
>   y[x]
>   Solve[Log[y[x]] - Sin[x] + ----- == C[1], y[x]]
>   2

However, in this case, DSolve is unable to solve this nonlinear equation so we rewrite the equation in the form $\cos(x)dx = \dfrac{1+y^2}{y}dy$. To solve the equation, we must integrate both the left- and right-hand sides, which we do below with Integrate, naming the resulting output lhs and rhs, respectively.

```
lhs=Integrate[Cos[x],x]
rhs=Integrate[(1+y^2)/y,y]
```

>   Sin[x]
>   2
>   y
>   -- + Log[y]
>   2
```
```

Therefore, a general solution to the equation is $\sin x + C_1 = \ln|y| + \frac{1}{2}y^2$. Below, we use

`ContourPlot` to graph $\sin x + C_1 = \ln|y| + \frac{1}{2}y^2$ for various values of C_1 by observing

that the level curves of $\sin x - \ln|y| + \frac{1}{2}y^2$ correspond to the graph of

$\sin x + C_1 = \ln|y| + \frac{1}{2}y^2$ for various values of C_1.

```
ContourPlot[lhs-rhs,{x,0,10},{y,0,10},ContourShading->False,
       Frame->False,Axes->Automatic,AxesOrigin->{0,0}]
```

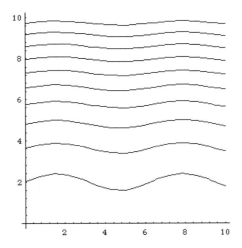

By substituting y(0)=1 into this equation, we find that $C_1 = \frac{1}{2}$, so the implicit

solution is given by $\sin x + \frac{1}{2} = \ln|y| + \frac{1}{2}y^2$.

```
gensol=lhs==rhs+c

                 2
                y
    Sin[x] == c + -- + Log[y]
                 2

initeq=gensol /. {x->0,y->1}

          1
    0 == - + c
          2

Solve[initeq]

          1
    {{c -> -(-)}}
          2
```

■

Homogeneous Differential Equations

A differential equation that can be written in the form M(x,y)dx+N(x,y)dy=0 where $M(tx,ty)=t^nM(x,y)$ and $N(tx,ty)=t^nN(x,y)$ is called a **homogeneous differential equation** (of degree n). This type of equation can be solved with the help of Mathematica as illustrated in the following example.

EXAMPLE: Solve the equation $(x^2-y^2)dx+xy\,dy=0$.

SOLUTION: Proceeding as in the previous example, we first define eq to be the equation $(x^2-y^2)dx+xy\,dy=0$, and then we attempt to use DSolve to solve the equation.

```
Clear[eq]
eq=x y y'[x]==(y[x]^2-x^2);
DSolve[eq,y[x],x]
```

$$DSolve[x\ y\ y'[x]\ ==\ -x^2\ +\ y[x]^2\ ,\ y[x],\ x]$$

Since DSolve is unsuccessful, let $M(x,y)=x^2-y^2$ and $N(x,y)=xy$. Then, $M(tx,ty)=t^2M(x,y)$ and $N(tx,ty)=t^2N(x,y)$, which means that $(x^2-y^2)dx+xy\,dy=0$ is a homogeneous equation of degree 2.

```
Clear[m,n,x,y]
m[x_,y_]=x^2-y^2;
n[x_,y_]=x y;
m[t x,t y]//Factor
n[t x,t y]//Factor
```

$$t^2\ (x\ -\ y)\ (x\ +\ y)$$
$$t^2\ x\ y$$

Assume x=vy. Then, $dx=v\,dy+y\,dv$, and directly substituting into the equation and simplifying yields $y^2v^3\,dy+y^3(v^2-1)dv=0$.

```
leqone=m[x,y] Dt[x]+n[x,y] Dt[y]
```

$$(x^2\ -\ y^2)\ Dt[x]\ +\ x\ y\ Dt[y]$$

```
x=v y;
leqtwo=leqone//ExpandAll
```

$$-(y^3\ Dt[v]) + v^2\ y^3\ Dt[v] + v^3\ y^2\ Dt[y]$$

```
leqthree=Collect[leqtwo,{Dt[v],Dt[y]}]
```

$$(-y^3 + v^2\ y^3)\ Dt[v] + v^3\ y^2\ Dt[y]$$

Dividing this equation by y^3v^3 yields the separable differential equation

$$\frac{dy}{y} + \frac{(v^2-1)dv}{v^3} = 0.$$

```
leqfour=Cancel[Apart[leqthree/(y^3 v^3)]]
```

$$\frac{(-1 + v^2)\ Dt[v]}{v^3} + \frac{Dt[y]}{y}$$

We solve this equation by rewriting it in the form

$$\frac{dy}{y} = \frac{(1-v^2)dv}{v^3} = \left(\frac{1}{v^3} - \frac{1}{v}\right)dv$$

and integrating each side with Integrate. Note how [[...]] and Take are used to extract the terms to be integrated.

```
leqfour[[1,1]]
```

$$v^{-3}$$

```
leqfour[[1,2]]
```

$$-1 + v^2$$

```
Take[leqfour[[1]],2]
```

$$\frac{-1 + v^2}{v^3}$$

```
leqfour[[2,1]]
```

$$\frac{1}{y}$$

```
first=Integrate[Take[leqfour[[1]],2],v]
```

```
    1
 ---- + Log[v]
    2
 2 v
```

```
second=Integrate[leqfour[[2,1]],y]
```

```
Log[y]
```

This yields

$$\ln y = \frac{-2}{v^2} - \ln v + C_1$$

which can be simplified as $\ln(vy) = \frac{-2}{v^2} + C_1$, so

$$vy = Ce^{-2/v^2}, \text{ where } C = e^{C_1}.$$

Since x=vy, $v = \frac{x}{y}$, resubstituting into the above equation yields

$$x = Ce^{-2y^2/x^2}$$

as a general solution of the equation $(x^2 - y^2)dx + xy\,dy = 0$. Of course, the same results are obtained by substituting $v = \frac{x}{y}$ into **first**.

```
Clear[x,v,y]
first /. v->x/y
```

```
     2
    y            x
  ---- + Log[-]
     2         y
  2 x
```

To graph $x = Ce^{-2y^2/x^2}$ for various values of C, we note that the graph of $x = Ce^{-2y^2/x^2}$ for various values of C is the same as the level curves of xe^{2y^2/x^2} which we graph with `ContourPlot`. We graph the level curves of xe^{2y^2/x^2} corresponding to the C-values defined in `vals`, which is specified in the `ContourPlot` command with `Contours->vals`. Including the option `PlotPoints->60` increases the number of points sampled and, thus, helps assure that the resulting graphs are smooth.

```
vals=Table[i,{i,.5,5.5,.5}]
```

```
{0.5, 1., 1.5, 2., 2.5, 3., 3.5, 4., 4.5, 5., 5.5}
```

```
ContourPlot[x Exp[2y^2/x^2],{x,.01,6},{y,-3,3},
        ContourShading->False,Frame->False,Contours->vals,
        PlotPoints->60,Axes->Automatic,AxesOrigin->{0,0}]
```

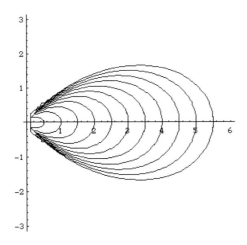

Exact Equations

A differential equation that can be written in the form $M(x,y)dx + N(x,y)dy = 0$ where $\frac{\partial N}{\partial x} = \frac{\partial M}{\partial y}$ is called an **exact differential equation**. If $M(x,y)dx + N(x,y)dy = 0$ is exact, there is a function F such that the total differential of F, dF, satisfies the equation $df = M(x,y)dx + N(x,y)dy = 0$. The solution of the exact differential equation is F(x,y)=c where c is a constant. The method by which F(x,y) is determined with Mathematica is illustrated in the following example.

EXAMPLE: Find a general solution of the equation

$$(-1 + e^{xy}y + y\cos(xy))dx + (1 + e^{xy}x + x\cos(xy))dy = 0.$$

SOLUTION: We begin by defining $m(x,y) = -1 + e^{xy}y + y\cos(xy)$, $n(x,y) = 1 + e^{xy}x + x\cos(xy)$,and then trying to use DSolve to solve the equation.

```
Clear[m,n]
m[x_,y_]=-1+Exp[x y]y +y Cos[x y];
n[x_,y_]=1+Exp[x y]x +x Cos[x y];
equation=DSolve[m[x,y[x]]+n[x,y[x]]*y'[x]==0,y[x],x]
```

```
    Solve::tdep:
       The equations appear to
          involve transcendental
          functions of the
          variables in an
          essentially non-algebraic
          way.
              x y[x]
    Solve[E          - x +

           Sin[x y[x]] + y[x] == C[1]

           , y[x]]
```

Since `DSolve` is unsuccessful, we verify that $\dfrac{\partial m}{\partial y} = \dfrac{\partial n}{\partial x}$ and consequently the equation must be exact.

```
D[m[x,y],y]==D[n[x,y],x]
```

```
    True
```

We then use `Integrate` to compute $\int m(x,y)dx$ and name the resulting output stepone.

```
stepone=Integrate[m[x,y],x]
```

```
    x y
    E    - x + Sin[x y]
```

The result means that the desired solution is of the form $e^{xy} - x + \sin(xy) + g(y)$. Therefore, we define steptwo to be the partial derivative of stepone+g[y] with respect to y.

```
steptwo=D[stepone+g[y],y]
```

```
    x y
    E    x + x Cos[x y] + g'[y]
```

Since $\dfrac{\partial}{\partial y}$(stepone+g[y])$= n(x,y)$, we use the `Solve` command to find the value of $g'(y)$.

```
stepthree=Solve[steptwo==n[x,y],g'[y]]
```

```
    {{g'[y] -> 1}}
```

Therefore, $g(y) = y + c$ and a general solution of the equation is $e^{xy} - x + y + \sin(xy) = c$.

```
stepfour=Integrate[g'[y] /. stepthree[[1]],y]
```

```
   y
```

```
solution=stepone+stepfour
```

```
    x y
   E    - x + y + Sin[x y]
```

In this case, we can graph various solutions with the command `ContourPlot` by observing that level curves of the function $e^{xy} - x + y + \sin(xy)$ correspond to the graphs of $e^{xy} - x + y + \sin(xy) = c$ for various values of c. As in the previous example, including the option `PlotPoints->30` increases the number of points sampled and, consequently, helps to assure that the resulting graphs are smooth. The option `Contours->20` instructs Mathematica to graph 20 contours, while the option `PlotRange->{-10,10}` specifies that the level curves correspond to c-values between −10 and 10.

```
ContourPlot[solution,{x,-Pi,Pi},{y,-Pi,Pi},Contours->20,PlotPoints->30,
    PlotRange->{-10,10},ContourShading->False]
```

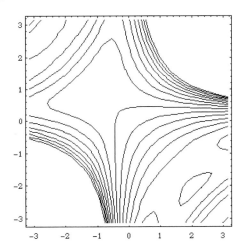

Linear Equations

A differential equation that can be written in the form $\dfrac{dy}{dx} = p(x)y = q(x)$ is called a **first-order linear differential equation**. If $\dfrac{dy}{dx} = p(x)y = q(x)$, then multiplying by $e^{\int p(x)dx}$ results in

$e^{\int p(x)dx}\dfrac{dy}{dx}+e^{\int p(x)dx}p(x)y=e^{\int p(x)dx}q(x)$. The term $e^{\int p(x)dx}$ is called the **integrating factor**. Applying the product rule and Fundamental Theorem of Calculus yields

$$\frac{d}{dx}\left(e^{\int p(x)dx}\,y\right)=e^{\int p(x)dx}\frac{dy}{dx}+e^{\int p(x)dx}p(x)y$$

so the equation

$$e^{\int p(x)dx}\frac{dy}{dx}+e^{\int p(x)dx}p(x)y=e^{\int p(x)dx}q(x)$$

is equivalent to the equation

$$\frac{d}{dx}\left(e^{\int p(x)dx}\,y\right)=e^{\int p(x)dx}q(x).$$

Integrating, we obtain $e^{\int p(x)dx}y=\displaystyle\int e^{\int p(x)dx}q(x)dx$. Dividing by $e^{\int p(x)dx}$ results in the solution

$$y=e^{-\int p(x)dx}\int e^{\int p(x)dx}q(x)dx$$

Mathematica's DSolve command can solve most first-order linear differential equations without having to calculate the integrating factor and following the procedure described above. We show this in the following example.

EXAMPLE: Find the general solution of $x\dfrac{dy}{dx}+3y=x\sin(x)$. Graph the solution for the values of c=−6, −4, −2, 0, 2, 4, and 6.

SOLUTION: In this case, we are able to use DSolve to directly solve the equation. Note that the resulting output is named sol.

```
sol=DSolve[x y'[x]+3y[x]==x Sin[x],y[x],x]


                                3                                 2
            C[1]    6 x Cos[x] - x  Cos[x] - 6 Sin[x] + 3 x  Sin[x]
  {{y[x] -> ---- + -----------------------------------------------}}
             3                            3
            x                            x
```

We extract the explicit solution from sol with sol[[1,1,2]] below.

```
sol[[1,1,2]]
```

$$C[1] \quad 6 \; x \; Cos[x] \; - \; x^3 \; Cos[x] \; - \; 6 \; Sin[x] \; + \; 3 \; x^2 \; Sin[x]$$

$$\frac{C[1]}{x^3} \; + \; \frac{6 \, x \, Cos[x] - x^3 \, Cos[x] - 6 \, Sin[x] + 3 \, x^2 \, Sin[x]}{x^3}$$

To graph the solution for the indicated values of c, we use `Evaluate` and `Table`. The command

```
Table[sol[[1,1,2]] /. C[1]->i,{i,-6,6,2}]
```

generates a table of the functions to be graphed. Be sure to include the `Table` command in the `Evaluate` command so that Mathematica first computes the table and then graphs each function in the table.

```
Plot[Evaluate[Table[sol[[1,1,2]] /. C[1]->i,{i,-6,6,2}]],
     {x,.01,3/2Pi},PlotRange->{-5,5}]
```

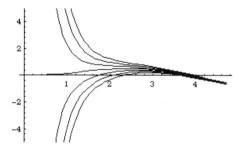

The effects of various forcing functions f(x) in the equation $\frac{dy}{dx} + a(x)y = f(x)$ are demonstrated in the example below.

EXAMPLE: Compare the solutions of $\frac{dy}{dx} + y = f(x)$ subject to y(0)=0 where f(x)=x, $\sin x$, $\cos x$, e^x, e^{-x}, $e^{-x}\sin x$, $x\cos x$, and xe^{-x}.

SOLUTION: To compute each solution, the table `funs` is first defined and then the `Table` and `DSolve` commands are used to find the solution of each of the eight equations. The command

```
DSolve[{y'[x]+y[x]==funs[[i]],y[0]==0},y[x],x]
```

solves the differential equation $y' + y = $`funs[[i]]`, where `funs[[i]]` is the ith element of `funs`, subject to the initial condition y(0)=0. The result of the `Table` command is named `sols` which we display in a two-line abbreviated form with `Short`.

```
funs={x,Sin[x],Cos[x],Exp[x],Exp[-x],Sin[x]Exp[-x],x Cos[x],x Exp[-x]};
sols=Table[DSolve[{y'[x]+y[x]==funs[[i]],y[0]==0},y[x],x],{i,1,8}];
Short[sols,2]
```

```
                    -x                        1     -Cos[x] + Sin[x]
    {{{y[x] -> -1 + E    + x}}, {{y[x] -> ---- + ----------------}},
                                           x            2
                                        2 E


                                                           2
                 -1                                       x
    {{y[x] -> ---- + <<1>>}}, <<4>>, {{y[x] -> ----}}}
               x                                    x
            2 E                                  2 E
```

Observe that the first element of `sols` is the list $\{y[x] \rightarrow -1+E^{-x}+x\}$ which can be obtained with the command `sols[[1]]`. To evaluate the expression $-1+E^{-x}+x$ for explicit values of x, we must either reenter the expression or extract it from `sols`. One way of extracting the expression $-1+E^{-x}+x$ from the list `sols` is to enter

$$y[x] \ /. \ sols[[1]],$$

which replaces `y[x]` by the expression $-1+E^{-x}+x$, or to enter `sols[[1,1,2]]`.

To graph each of the explicit solutions in `sols`, we must extract the explicit solutions. One way of extracting the solutions is to create a table of values of `y[x]` where `y[x]` is replaced by the rule in the ith element of `sols` as done in the following command. The resulting list of functions is named `toplot` for future use and displayed in an abbreviated two-line form with `Short`. Alternatively, the table can be created by entering the command `Table[sols[[i,1,2]],{i,1,8}]`.

```
toplot=Table[y[x] /. sols[[i,1]],{i,1,8}];
Short[toplot,2]
```

```
           -x         1     -Cos[x] + Sin[x]    -1    Cos[x] + Sin[x]
    {-1 + E    + x, ---- + ----------------, ---- + ----------------,
                     x            2            x            2
                  2 E                      2 E
```

$$x \, Cos[x] + <<1>> + x \, Sin[x] \qquad x^2$$
$$<<3>>, \; \text{----------------------------}, \; \text{----}\}$$
$$2 \qquad\qquad\qquad\qquad x$$
$$2 \, E$$

To graph each of the functions in toplot, we define g[i] which graphs the ith element of toplot on the interval $[-\pi, 2\pi]$. Note that the results of g are not displayed since the option DisplayFunction->Identity is included. We then use g to graph each function in toplot on the interval $[-\pi, 2\pi]$ and partition the resulting set of eight graphics into two element subsets with Partition. The resulting eight graphics objects are displayed as a graphics array for easy comparison.

```
g[i_]:=Plot[toplot[[i]],{x,-Pi,2Pi},DisplayFunction->Identity];
graphs=Partition[Table[g[i],{i,1,8}],2];
Show[GraphicsArray[graphs]]
```

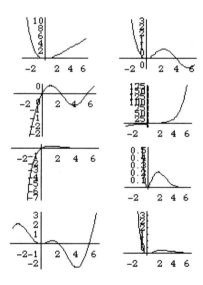

Numerical Solutions of First-Order Ordinary Differential Equations

Numerical approximations of solutions to differential equations can be obtained with NDSolve. This command is particularly useful when working with nonlinear equations for which DSolve is unable to find an explicit solution. This command is entered in the form

```
NDSolve[{deq,ics},fun,{var,varmin,varmax}],
```

where deq is solved for fun and the solution is valid over the interval [varmin,varmax]. In some cases, the interval on which the solution is valid is smaller than the interval requested. Note that the number of initial conditions in ics must equal the order of the differential equation indicated in deq. In order to illustrate the command NDSolve, we consider the nonlinear equations below.

EXAMPLE: Graph the solution of $\dfrac{dy}{dx} = \sin(2x - y)$ subject the initial condition $y(0) = 0.5$ on the interval $[0, 15]$.

SOLUTION: First, we define eq to be the equation $\dfrac{dy}{dx} = \sin(2x - y)$ and then use NDSolve to approximate the solution of eq subject to the initial condition $y(0) = 0.5$, naming the resulting output sol. The resulting output is an InterpolatingFunction which represents an approximate function obtained through interpolation. This solution is extracted from sol with sol[[1,1,2]]. The interval {0., 15.} is the range of values over which the approximation is valid.

```
Clear[x,y]
eq=y'[x]==Sin[2x-y[x]];
sol=NDSolve[{eq,y[0]==.5},y[x],{x,0,15}]
```

```
{{y[x] -> InterpolatingFunction[{0., 15.}, <>][x]}}
```

We then graph the solution by replacing y[x] by the result obtained in sol. The same result is obtained if y[x] /. sol is replaced by sol[[1,1,2]].

```
Plot[y[x] /. sol,{x,0,15}]
```

We can also use NDSolve to generate approximations of solutions to a differential equation under changing initial conditions.

> **EXAMPLE:** Graph the solution of $y' = \sin(xy)$ subject to the initial condition $y(0) = i$ on the interval $[0,7]$ for $i = 0.5, 1.0, 1.5, 2.0,$ and 2.5.

SOLUTION: We begin by defining `eq` to be the equation $y' = \sin xy$. We then define `sol[i]` to return the approximate function obtained from

```
NDSolve[{eq,y[0]==i},y[x],{x,0,7}].
```

```
Clear[x,y,sol]
eq=y'[x]==Sin[x y[x]];
sol[i_]:=Module[{sol},
      sol=NDSolve[{eq,y[0]==i},y[x],{x,0,7}];
      sol[[1,1,2]]]
```

Next, we define `toplot` to be a table consisting of `sol[i]` for $i = 0.5, 1.0, 1.5, 2.0,$ and 2.5. We display an abbreviated form of `toplot` with `Short` to show that the list `toplot` consists of `InterpolatingFunctions`. Finally, `Plot` is used to graph the functions in `toplot` on the interval $[0,7]$.

```
toplot=Table[sol[i],{i,.5,2.5,.5}];
Short[toplot]
```

```
{InterpolatingFunction[{0., 7.}, <>][x], <<4>>}
```

```
Plot[Evaluate[toplot],{x,0,7}]
```

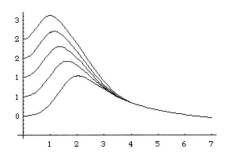

■

Application: Population Growth and the Logistic Equation

The **logistic equation** (or **Verhulst equation**), first introduced by the Belgian mathematician Pierre Verhulst to study population growth, is the equation

$$y'(t) = (r - a y(t))y(t),$$

where r and a are constants, subject to the condition $y(0) = y_0$. This equation can be written as $\frac{dy}{dt} = (r - ay)y = ry - ay^2$ where the term $(-y^2)$ represents an inhibitive factor or "death rate." Hence, the population under these assumptions is not allowed to grow out of control as it is in some other models like the Malthus model. Also, the population does not grow or decay constantly.

The logistic equation is separable, and, thus, can be solved by separation of variables. We proceed by using `DSolve` to find a general solution of the equation:

```
Clear[logistic,y]
logistic=y'[t]==(r-a y[t])y[t];
sol=DSolve[logistic,y[t],t]
```

```
                   r t
                  E    r
     {{y[t] -> ---------------}, {y[t] -> 0}}
                   r t
                a E    + r C[1]
```

We see that the function y=0 is a (trivial) solution to the equation. We are only interested in the first solution which we extract from sol with `sol[[1,1,2]]`.

```
sol[[1,1,2]]
```

```
          r t
         E    r
     ---------------
          r t
       a E    + r C[1]
```

Applying the initial condition $y(0) = y_0$ to solve for C[1], we find that

```
cval=Solve[Evaluate[sol[[1,1,2]] /. t->0]==y0,C[1]]
```

```
                 r - a y0
     {{C[1] -> --------}}
                 r y0
```

and evaluating `sol[[1,1,2]]` for the value obtained above yields the solution which we define as y. We define y as a function of t, y0, r, and a so that we can refer to this solution in other problems without solving the differential equation again.

```
y[t_,y0_,r_,a_]=sol[[1,1,2]] /. cval[[1]]//Together
```

```
            r t
           E    r y0
     --------------------
                    r t
      r - a y0 + a E    y0
```

The solution can also be written as

$$y = \frac{ry_0}{ay_0 + (r - ay_0)e^{-rt}}.$$

Notice that $\lim_{t \to \infty} y(t) = \frac{r}{a}$.

EXAMPLE: Use the logistic equation to approximate the population of the United States using $r = 0.03$, $a = 0.0001$, and $y_0 = 5.3$. Compare this result with the actual census values given in the table below. Use the model obtained to predict the population of the United States in the year 2000.

Year (t)	Population (in millions)	Year (t)	Population (in millions)
1800 (0)	5.30	1900 (100)	76.21
1810 (10)	7.24	1910 (110)	92.23
1820 (20)	9.64	1920 (120)	106.02
1830 (30)	12.68	1930 (130)	123.20
1840 (40)	17.06	1940 (140)	132.16
1850 (50)	23.19	1950 (150)	151.33
1860 (60)	31.44	1960 (160)	179.32
1870 (70)	38.56	1970 (170)	203.30
1880 (80)	50.19	1980 (180)	226.54
1890 (90)	62.98	1990 (190)	248.71

Source: The World Almanac and Book of Facts, 1993

SOLUTION: We substitute the indicated values of r, a, and y_0 into $y = \frac{ry_0}{ay_0 + (r - ay_0)e^{-rt}}$ to obtain the approximation of the population of the United States at time t, where t represents the number of years since 1800,

$$y(t) = \frac{0.03 \bullet 5.3}{0.0001 \bullet 5.3 + (0.03 - 0.0001 \bullet 5.3)e^{-.03t}} = \frac{0.159}{0.00053 + 0.02947e^{-0.3t}}.$$

We compare the approximation of the population of the United States given by the approximation y(t) with the actual population obtained from census figures. First, we enter the data represented in the table as **data** and then graph the points in

data using Graphics, Map, and Point, naming the resulting graphics object
dots. We then graph y[t,5.3,.03,.0001] for the years corresponding to 1800
to 2000 and name the resulting graph ploty. Finally, Show is used to display
dots and ploty together.

```
data={{0,5.30},{10,7.24},{20,9.64},{30,12.68},{40,17.06},
{50,23.19},{60,31.44},{70,38.56},{80,50.19},{90,62.98},
{100,76.21},{110,92.23},{120,106.02},{130,123.20},
{140,132.16},{150,151.33},{160,179.32},{170,203.30},
{180,226.54},{190,248.71}};
dots=Graphics[{PointSize[.015],Map[Point,data]}];
ploty=Plot[y[t,5.3,.03,.0001],{t,0,200},DisplayFunction->Identity];
Show[ploty,dots,DisplayFunction->$DisplayFunction]
```

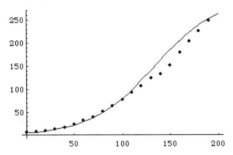

We can also compare the data by making a table of the year, actual population,
and population predicted by y[t,5.3,.03,.0001].

```
Table[{data[[i,1]]+1800,data[[i,2]],y[data[[i,1]],5.3,.03,.0001]},
       {i,1,20}]//TableForm
```

1800	5.3	5.3
1810	7.24	7.1103
1820	9.64	9.51898
1830	12.68	12.7082
1840	17.06	16.9038
1850	23.19	22.3766
1860	31.44	29.437
1870	38.56	38.417
1880	50.19	49.6339
1890	62.98	63.3328
1900	76.21	79.6105
1910	92.23	98.3335
1920	106.02	119.081
1930	123.2	141.141
1940	132.16	163.594
1950	151.33	185.448
1960	179.32	205.817
1970	203.3	224.047
1980	226.54	239.782
1990	248.71	252.941

To predict the population of the United States in the year 2000 with this model, we evaluate

```
y[200,5.3,.03,.0001]

    263.66
```

Thus, we predict that the population will be approximately 263.66 million in the year 2000. Note that projections of the population of the United States in the year 2000 made by the Bureau of the Census range from 259.57 million to 278.23 million. ■

Application: Newton's Law of Cooling

Newton's Law of Cooling states that the rate at which the temperature T(t) changes in a cooling body is proportional to the difference between the temperature of the body and the constant temperature T_s of the surrounding medium. This situation is represented as the first-order initial value problem $\frac{dT}{dt} = k(T - T_s)$ subject to $T(0) = T_0$, where T_0 is the initial temperature of the body and k is the constant of proportionality. We solve a problem involving Newton's law of cooling in the following example.

> **EXAMPLE:** A pie is removed from a 350° oven. In 15 minutes, the pie has a temperature of 150°. Determine the time required to cool the pie to a temperature of 80° so that it may be eaten.

SOLUTION: Newton's Law of Cooling states that an object of higher temperature than its environment cools at a rate that is proportional to the difference in temperature: $\frac{dT}{dt} = k(A - T)$, where k is a positive constant, A is the surrounding temperature, and T is the temperature of the object. The general solution, which depends on the parameters of the problem, is determined. Here, the resulting function is called `temp`, the surrounding temperature `tempS`, the initial temperature `temp0`, and the constant of proportionality k. The solution based on the data indicated in this example is then easily found.

```
del=DSolve[{tp'[t]==-k (tp[t]-tempS),tp[0]==temp0},tp[t],t]

    {{tp[t] ->

                  -tempS + temp0
          tempS + --------------}}
                       k t
                      E
```

```
temp[tempS_,temp0_,k_,t_]=del[[1,1,2]]
```

$$\text{tempS} + \frac{-\text{tempS} + \text{temp0}}{E^{k\ t}}$$

The solution using the parameter values needed for this problem is given below.

```
temp[75,350,k,15]
```

$$75 + \frac{275}{E^{15\ k}}$$

Since the constant k is unknown, it is determined below with `Solve` and called `k1` for convenience. (Note that `FindRoot` could have been used to determine the constant of proportionality above instead of `Solve`, in order to avoid the warning messages which result with `Solve`.) In this case, only a portion of the result from the `Solve` command is displayed.

```
k1=Solve[temp[75,350,k,15]==150,k]//N
```

```
Solve::ifun:
    Warning: Inverse functions
        are being used by Solve,
        so some solutions may not
        be found.
{{k -> 0.0866189},
```

This number is extracted in the usual manner so that it can be used to determine the time at which the pie reaches its desired temperature.

```
k1[[1,1,2]]
```

```
0.0866189
```

This is accomplished with `FindRoot` by, first, plotting the solution to obtain an estimate of the time at which the temperature is 80 degrees and then, using this initial approximation with `FindRoot`. Since the value of the function seems to equal 80 near t = 40, the initial guess of 40 is used to achieve the more accurate value of t = 46.264.

```
Plot[temp[75,350,k1[[1,1,2]],t],{t,0,50}]
```

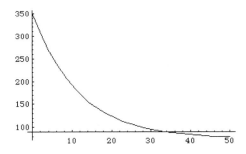

```
FindRoot[temp[75,350,k1[[1,1,2]],t]==80,{t,40}]
```

```
{t -> 46.264}
```

Application: Free-Falling Bodies

The motion of objects can be determined through the solution of a first-order equation. We begin by explaining some of the theory which is needed to set up the differential equation that models the situation.

> **Newton's Second Law of Motion**: The rate at which the momentum of a body changes with respect to time is equal to the resultant force acting on the body.

Because the body's momentum is defined as the product of its mass and velocity, this statement is modeled as

$$\frac{d}{dt}(mv) = F$$

where m and v represent the body's mass and velocity, respectively, and F is the sum of the forces acting on the body. Because m is constant, differentiation leads to the well-known equation

$$m\frac{dv}{dt} = F.$$

If the body is subjected to the force due to gravity, then its velocity is determined by solving the differential equation

$$m\frac{dv}{dt} = mg \text{ or } \frac{dv}{dt} = g$$

where $g \cong 32 \text{ ft/s}^2$ (English system) and 9.8 m/s^2 (metric system).

This differential equation is applicable only when the resistive force due to the medium (such as air resistance) is ignored. If this offsetting resistance is considered, we must discuss all of the forces acting on the object. Mathematically, we write the equation as

$$m\frac{dv}{dt} = \sum \left(\text{forces acting on the object}\right)$$

where the direction of motion is taken to be the positive direction.

We use a force diagram to set up the differential equation which models the situation. Because air resistance acts against the object as it falls and g acts in the same direction of the motion, we state the initial value problem in the form given below.

$$m\frac{dv}{dt} = mg + \left(-F_R\right) \text{ or } m\frac{dv}{dt} = mg - F_R$$

where F_R represents this resistive force. Note that down is assumed to be the positive direction. The resistive force is typically proportional to the body's velocity (v) or the square of its velocity (v^2). Hence, the differential equation is linear or nonlinear based on the resistance of the medium taken into account.

negative direction

object

g

positive direction

Force Diagram

EXAMPLE: An object of mass m = 1 is dropped from a height of 50 feet above the surface of a small pond. While the object is in the air, the force due to air resistance is v. However, when the object is in the pond, it is subjected to a buoyancy force equivalent to 6v. Determine how much time is required for the object to reach a depth of 25 feet in the pond.

SOLUTION: This problem must be broken into two parts: an initial value problem for the object above the pond, and an initial value problem for the object below the surface of the pond. Using techniques discussed in previous examples, the initial value problem above the pond's surface is found to be

$$\frac{dv}{dt} = 32 - v, \, v(0) = 0.$$

However, to define the initial value problem to find the velocity of the object beneath the pond's surface, the velocity of the object when it reaches the surface must be known. Hence, the velocity of the object above the surface must be determined by solving the initial value problem above. The equation $\dfrac{dv}{dt} = 32 - v$ is separable and solved with DSolve in d1.

```
Clear[v,y]
d1=DSolve[{v'[t]==32-v[t],v[0]==0},v[t],t]
```

$$\{\{v[t] \to 32 - \frac{32}{t}\}\}$$
$$E$$

In order to find the velocity when the object hits the pond's surface we must know the time at which the position of the object is 0. Thus, we must find the position function, which is done by integrating the velocity function, obtaining $y(t) = 32e^{-t} + 32t - 32$.

```
p1=DSolve[{y'[t]==d1[[1,1,2]],y[0]==0},y[t],t]
```

$$\{\{y[t] \to -32 + \frac{32}{t} + 32\ t\}\}$$
$$E$$

The position function is graphed below The value of t at which the object has traveled 50 feet is needed. This time appears to be approximately 2.5 seconds.

```
Plot[{p1[[1,1,2]],50},{t,0,5}]
```

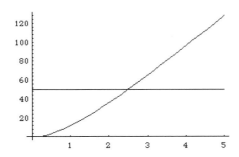

A more accurate value of the time at which the object hits the surface is found using FindRoot. In this case, we obtain $t \approx 2.47864$. The velocity at this time is then determined by substitution into the velocity function resulting in $v(2.47864) \approx 29.3166$. Note that this value is the initial velocity of the object when it hits the surface of the pond.

```
t1=FindRoot[p1[[1,1,2]]==50,{t,2.5}]
```

$$\{t \to 2.47864\}$$

```
v1=d1[[1,1,2]] /. t1
```

>   29.3166

Thus, the initial value problem which determines the velocity of the object beneath the surface of the pond is given by $\frac{dv}{dt} = 32 - 6v$, $v(0) = 29.3166$. The solution of this initial value problem is $v(t) = \frac{16}{3} + 23.9833\,e^{-t}$, and integrating to obtain the position function (the initial position is 0), we obtain $y(t) = 3.99722 - 3.99722\,e^{-6t} + \frac{16}{3}t$. These steps are carried out in d2 and p2 below.

```
d2=DSolve[{v'[t]==32-6v[t],v[0]==v1},v[t],t]
```

```
            16    23.9832
{{v[t] -> -- + -------}}
            3       6 t
                   E
```

```
p2=DSolve[{y'[t]==d2[[1,1,2]],y[0]==0},y[t],t]
```

```
                     3.99721    16 t
{{y[t] -> 3.99721 - ------- + ----}}
                       6 t      3
                      E
```

This position function is then plotted to determine when the object is 25 feet beneath the surface of the pond. This time appears to be near 4 seconds.

```
Plot[{p2[[1,1,2]],25},{t,0,5}]
```

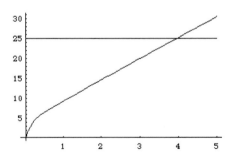

A more accurate approximation of the time at which the object is 25 feet beneath the pond's surface is obtained with FindRoot. In this case, we obtain $t \approx 3.93802$. Finally, the time required for the object to reach the pond's surface is added to the time needed for it to travel 25 feet beneath the surface, to see that approximately 6.41667 seconds are required for the object to travel from a height of 50 feet above the pond to a depth of 25 feet below the surface.

```
t2=FindRoot[p2[[1,1,2]]==25,{t,4}]

    {t -> 3.93802}

t1[[1,2]]+t2[[1,2]]

    6.41667
```

■

6.2 *Higher-Order Ordinary Differential Equations*

An ordinary differential equation of the form

$$\sum_{k=0}^{n} a_k(x)y^{(k)}(x) = a_n(x)y^{(n)}(x) + a_{n-1}(x)y^{(n-1)}(x) + \ldots + a_1(x)y'(x) + a_0(x)y(x) = f(x)$$

is called an **nth order ordinary linear differential equation**. If $f(x)$ is identically the zero function, the equation is said to be **homogeneous**; if $f(x)$ is not the zero function, the equation is said to be **nonhomogeneous**; and if the functions $a_i(x)$, $i=0, 1, 2, \ldots , n$ are constants, the equation is said to have **constant coefficients**.

Let $f_1(x)$, $f_2(x)$, $f_3(x)$, $\ldots$, $f_{n-1}(x)$, and $f_n(x)$ be a set of n functions at least $n-1$ times differentiable. S is **linearly dependent** on an interval I means that there are constants c_1, $c_2, \ldots , c_n$, not all zero, so that $\sum_{k=1}^{n} c_k f_k(x) = 0$ for every value of x in the interval I. S is **linearly independent** means that S is not linearly dependent. The **Wronskian** of S, denoted by $W(S) = W\big(f_1(x), f_2(x), f_3(x), \ldots , f_{n-1}(x), f_n(x)\big)$, is the determinant

$$W(S) = \begin{vmatrix} f_1(x) & f_2(x) & \cdots & f_n(x) \\ f_1'(x) & f_2'(x) & \cdots & f_n'(x) \\ \vdots & \vdots & \vdots & \vdots \\ f_1^{(n-1)}(x) & f_2^{(n-1)}(x) & \cdots & f_n^{(n-1)}(x) \end{vmatrix}.$$

The following theorem can help us determine if a set of functions is either linearly dependent or linearly independent.

> **Theorem:** Let $f_1(x)$, $f_2(x)$, $f_3(x)$, $\ldots$, $f_{n-1}(x)$, and $f_n(x)$ be a set of n functions at least $n-1$ times differentiable. If $W(S) \neq 0$ for at least one value of x in the interval I, S is linearly independent.

Application of this theorem with the help of Mathematica is illustrated in the example below.

EXAMPLE: Show that $S = \{e^x, x e^x, x^2 e^x\}$ is linearly independent.

SOLUTION: The Wronskian of S is

$$W(S) = \begin{vmatrix} e^x & x e^x & x^2 e^x \\ \dfrac{d}{dx}(e^x) & \dfrac{d}{dx}(x e^x) & \dfrac{d}{dx}(x^2 e^x) \\ \dfrac{d^2}{dx^2}(e^x) & \dfrac{d^2}{dx^2}(x e^x) & \dfrac{d^2}{dx^2}(x^2 e^x) \end{vmatrix} = \begin{vmatrix} e^x & x e^x & x^2 e^x \\ e^x & (x+1)e^x & (x^2+2x)e^x \\ e^x & (x+2)e^x & (x^2+4x+2)e^x \end{vmatrix}.$$

We compute this below with Mathematica by defining `caps` to be the list of functions consisting of e^x, $x e^x$; and $x^2 e^x$; and `matrix` to be the matrix

$$\begin{pmatrix} e^x & x e^x & x^2 e^x \\ \dfrac{d}{dx}(e^x) & \dfrac{d}{dx}(x e^x) & \dfrac{d}{dx}(x^2 e^x) \\ \dfrac{d^2}{dx^2}(e^x) & \dfrac{d^2}{dx^2}(x e^x) & \dfrac{d^2}{dx^2}(x^2 e^x) \end{pmatrix}.$$

We then use `Det` to compute the determinant of `matrix`.

```
caps={Exp[x],x Exp[x],x^2 Exp[x]};
matrix={caps,D[caps,x],D[caps,{x,2}]};
TableForm[matrix]
```

```
    x    x                 x  2
    E    E  x              E  x
    x    x     x           x        x  2
    E    E  + E  x         2 E  x + E  x
    x       x     x        x        x      x  2
    E    2 E  + E  x       2 E  + 4 E  x + E  x
```

```
Det[matrix]
```

```
      3 x
    2 E
```

Since the Wronskian is $2 e^{3x} \neq 0$, the set of functions is linearly independent. ∎

An alternative approach, which will allow us to quickly compute the Wronskian of other sets of functions, begins by defining the function `wronskian`. The command `wronskian` is defined to compute the Wronskian of a list of functions in the variable x. `wronksian[list]` computes the Wronskian of the list `list` by:

1. Defining the variables n, r, and `matrix` local to the procedure `wronskian`;
2. Defining n to be the number of elements of `list`;
3. Defining `r[1]` to be the $1 \times n$ matrix `list`. Note that `r[1]` corresponds to the vector $\begin{pmatrix} f_1(x) & f_2(x) & \cdots & f_n(x) \end{pmatrix}$, which corresponds to the top row of the matrix

$$\begin{pmatrix} f_1(x) & f_2(x) & \cdots & f_n(x) \\ f_1'(x) & f_2'(x) & \cdots & f_n'(x) \\ \vdots & \vdots & \vdots & \vdots \\ f_1^{(n-1)}(x) & f_2^{(n-1)}(x) & \cdots & f_n^{(n-1)}(x) \end{pmatrix};$$

4. Defining `r[k]` to be the derivative of `r[k-1]`. `r[k]` corresponds to the kth row of the matrix

$$\begin{pmatrix} f_1(x) & f_2(x) & \cdots & f_n(x) \\ f_1'(x) & f_2'(x) & \cdots & f_n'(x) \\ \vdots & \vdots & \vdots & \vdots \\ f_1^{(n-1)}(x) & f_2^{(n-1)}(x) & \cdots & f_n^{(n-1)}(x) \end{pmatrix};$$

5. Defining `matrix` to be the matrix

$$\begin{pmatrix} f_1(x) & f_2(x) & \cdots & f_n(x) \\ f_1'(x) & f_2'(x) & \cdots & f_n'(x) \\ \vdots & \vdots & \vdots & \vdots \\ f_1^{(n-1)}(x) & f_2^{(n-1)}(x) & \cdots & f_n^{(n-1)}(x) \end{pmatrix}; \text{ and}$$

6. Computing and returning the determinant of `matrix` corresponding to the Wronskian of `list`.

We define this function below.

```
wronskian[list_]:=Module[{n,r,matrix},
       n=Length[list];
       r[1]=list;
       r[k_]:=r[k]=D[r[k-1],x];
       matrix=Table[r[i],{i,1,n}];
       Det[matrix]];
```

EXAMPLE: Determine if the set of functions $\{\cos x, \cos 2x, \cos 3x, \cos 4x\}$ is linearly independent.

SOLUTION: We use `wronskian`, defined above, to compute the Wronskian of the set of functions.

```
trigex=wronskian[{Cos[x],Cos[2x],Cos[3x],Cos[4x]}]
```

$$-42 \, \text{Cos}[3 \, x] \, \text{Cos}[4 \, x] \, \text{Sin}[x] \, \text{Sin}[2 \, x] +$$

$$288 \, \text{Cos}[2 \, x] \, \text{Cos}[4 \, x] \, \text{Sin}[x] \, \text{Sin}[3 \, x] -$$

$$450 \, \text{Cos}[x] \, \text{Cos}[4 \, x] \, \text{Sin}[2 \, x] \, \text{Sin}[3 \, x] -$$

$$300 \, \text{Cos}[2 \, x] \, \text{Cos}[3 \, x] \, \text{Sin}[x] \, \text{Sin}[4 \, x] +$$

$$768 \, \text{Cos}[x] \, \text{Cos}[3 \, x] \, \text{Sin}[2 \, x] \, \text{Sin}[4 \, x] -$$

$$252 \, \text{Cos}[x] \, \text{Cos}[2 \, x] \, \text{Sin}[3 \, x] \, \text{Sin}[4 \, x]$$

To see that this is not the zero function, we use `Simplify` to simplify `trigex`.

```
Simplify[trigex]
```

$$96 \, (18 + 16 \, \text{Cos}[2 \, x] + \text{Cos}[4 \, x]) \, \text{Sin}[x]^6$$

The output above is not the zero function since it is not zero when $x = \dfrac{\pi}{2}$ as shown below.

```
trigex /. x->Pi/2
```

$$288$$

∎

A set $S = \left\{ f_1(x), f_2(x), f_3(x), \ldots, f_{n-1}(x), f_n(x) \right\}$ of n linearly independent non-trivial solutions of the nth order linear homogeneous equation

$$a_n(x)y^{(n)}(x)+a_{n-1}(x)y^{(n-1)}(x)+\ldots+a_1(x)y^{(1)}(x)+a_0(x)=0$$

is called a **fundamental set of solutions** of the equation. Observe that if $S = \left\{ f_i(x) \right\}_{i=1}^{n}$ is a fundamental set of solutions of

$$\sum_{i=0}^{n} a_i(x)y^{(i)}(x)=a_n(x)y^{(n)}(x)+a_{n-1}(x)y^{(n-1)}(x)+\ldots+a_1(x)y'(x)+a_0(x)y(x)=0$$

and $\left\{ c_i \right\}_{i=1}^{n}$ is a set of n numbers, then $f(x) = \displaystyle\sum_{i=1}^{n} c_i f_i(x)$ is also a solution of $\displaystyle\sum_{i=0}^{n} a_i(x)y^{(i)}(x)=0$. The following two theorems tell us that under reasonable conditions the nth-order homogeneous equation $a_n(x)y^{(n)}(x)+a_{n-1}(x)y^{(n-1)}(x)+\ldots+a_1(x)y^{(1)}(x)+a_0(x)=0$ has a fundamental set of n solutions.

Theorem: If $a_i(x)$ is continuous on an open interval I for i=0, 1, ... , n, then the nth-order linear homogeneous equation $\sum_{i=0}^{n} a_i(x)y^{(i)}(x) = 0$ has a fundamental set of solutions on I.

Theorem: Any set of n+1 solutions of the nth-order linear homogeneous equation $\sum_{i=0}^{n} a_i(x)y^{(i)}(x) = 0$ is linearly dependent.

If $S = \{f_i(x)\}_{i=1}^{n}$ is a fundamental set of solutions of the nth-order linear homogeneous equation $\sum_{i=0}^{n} a_i(x)y^{(i)}(x) = 0$, then a **general solution** of the equation is $f(x) = \sum_{i=1}^{n} c_i f_i(x)$, where $\{c_i\}_{i=1}^{n}$ is a set of n arbitrary constants.

The equation

$$a_n m^n + a_{n-1}m^{n-1} + ... + a_1 m + a_0 = \sum_{k=0}^{n} a_k m^k = 0$$

is called the **characteristic equation** of the nth-order homogeneous linear differential equation with constant coefficients $a_n y^{(n)}(x) + a_{n-1}y^{(n-1)}(x) + ... + a_1 y'(x) + a_0 y(x) = \sum_{k=0}^{n} a_k y^{(k)}(x) = 0$. The general solutions of the nth-order homogeneous linear differential equation with constant coefficients are determined by the solutions of its characteristic equation.

The Homogeneous Second-Order Equation with Constant Coefficients

Let $ay'' + by' + cy = 0$ be a homogeneous second-order equation with constant coefficients, and let m_1 and m_2 be the solutions of the characteristic equation $am^2 + bm + c = 0$.

(a) If $m_1 \neq m_2$ and both m_1 and m_2 are real, a general solution of $ay'' + by' + cy = 0$ is
$$y(t) = c_1 e^{m_1 t} + c_2 e^{m_2 t};$$

(b) If $m_1 = m_2$ and both m_1 and m_2 are real, a general solution of $ay'' + by' + cy = 0$ is
$$y(t) = c_1 e^{m_1 t} + c_2 t e^{m_1 t}; \text{ and}$$

(c) If $m_1 = \alpha + i\beta$, $\beta \neq 0$, and $m_1 = \overline{m_2}$, a general solution of $ay'' + by' + cy = 0$ is

$$y(t) = c_1 e^{\alpha t} \cos \beta t + c_2 e^{\alpha t} \sin \beta t.$$

In (c) above, $\overline{m_2}$ is the **complex conjugate** of m_2: $\overline{m_2} = \overline{\alpha - i\beta} = \alpha + i\beta$.

Mathematica is useful in solving these equations and plotting the corresponding solutions.

EXAMPLE: Find the solution of each problem:

(a) $3y'' + 2y' - 5y = 0$;

(b) $2y'' + 5y' + 5y = 0$ subject to the initial conditions y(0)=0 and $y'(0) = \dfrac{1}{2}$; and

(c) $y'' + 4y' + 4y = 0$ subject to the initial conditions y(0)=0 and $y'(0) = -\dfrac{1}{2}$.

SOLUTION: In each case, DSolve is used to find an exact solution. For (a), we have:

```
solution=DSolve[3y''[x]+2y'[x]-5y[x]==0,y[x],x]

                 C[1]       x
{{y[x] -> -------- + E   C[2]}}
             (5 x)/3
          E
```

When DSolve is used to solve (b), the resulting solution is expressed as a complex exponential. To see that the solution is real, we use ComplexExpand.

```
solution=DSolve[{2y''[x]+5y'[x]+5y[x]==0,y[0]==0,y'[0]==1/2},y[x],x]

{{y[x] ->

         ((-5 - I Sqrt[15]) x)/4
    I E
    -------------------------- -
              Sqrt[15]

         ((-5 + I Sqrt[15]) x)/4
    I E
    --------------------------}}
              Sqrt[15]
```

Notice that solution is a nested list. solution[[1,1,2]] yields the second element of the first element of the first element of solution. In other words, solution[[1,1,2]] yields the expression corresponding to the desired solution. ComplexExpand is used to expand solution[[1,1,2]] assuming that x is real. The result is clearly a real-valued function.

```
simp=solution[[1,1,2]]//ComplexExpand
```

```
        Sqrt[15] x
2 Sin[----------]
           4
-------------------
            (5 x)/4
 Sqrt[15] E
```

Finally, the solution is graphed on the interval $[-\pi/2, \pi]$.

```
Plot[simp,{x,-Pi/2,Pi}]
```

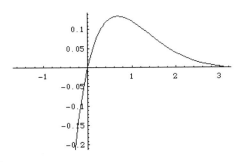

Similarly DSolve successfully solves (c).

```
solution=DSolve[{y''[x]+4y'[x]+4y[x]==0,y[0]==1,y'[0]==-1/2},y[x],x]
```

```
              -2 x     3 x
 {{y[x] -> E        + ------}}
                       2 x
                      2 E
```

The result is then graphed on the interval $[-1,1]$. Note that the command Plot[solution[[1,1,2]],{x,-1,1}] would produce the same result.

```
Plot[y[x]/.solution,{x,-1,1}]
```

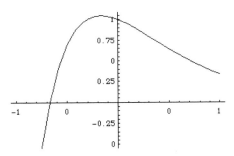

■

In the same manner as in the case for a second-order homogeneous equation with real constant coefficients, a general solution is also determined by the solutions of the characteristic equation. Instead of stating an exact rule for the numerous situations encountered, we illustrate how a general solution is found in the following examples.

The command DSolve can be used to solve nth-order linear homogeneous differential equations with constant coefficients as long as n is smaller than 5. In cases when the roots of the characteristic equation are symbolically complicated, approximations of the roots of the characteristic equation can be computed with the commands Solve or NRoots.

EXAMPLE: Find a general solution of $9y^{(4)} - 6y''' + 46y'' - 6y' + 37y = 0$.

SOLUTION: The characteristic equation of $9y^{(4)} - 6y''' + 46y'' - 6y' + 37y = 0$ is $9x^4 - 6x^3 + 46x^2 - 6x + 37 = 0$, solved below with Solve.

```
Solve[9x^4-6x^3+46x^2-6x+37==0]
```

$$\{\{x \to -I\}, \{x \to I\}, \{x \to \tfrac{1}{3} - 2\,I\}, \{x \to \tfrac{1}{3} + 2\,I\}\}$$

Since the solutions of the characteristic equation are $x = \pm i$ and $x = \frac{1}{3} \pm 2i$, a general solution of the equation is given by $y = c_1 \cos x + c_2 \sin x + e^{x/3}(c_3 \cos 2x + c_4 \sin 2x)$. Since the order of the equation is 4, which is smaller than 5, DSolve can also be used to find a general solution. Below, we first define eq to be the equation $9y^{(4)} - 6y''' + 46y'' - 6y' + 37y = 0$, and then use DSolve to find a general solution of eq, naming the resulting output sol.

```
Clear[eq,sol]
eq=9D[y[x],{x,4}]-6D[y[x],{x,3}]+46y''[x]-6y'[x]+37y[x]==0;
sol=DSolve[eq,y[x],x]
```

$$\{\{y[x] \to C[2]\,\text{Cos}[x] + E^{x/3}\,C[4]\,\text{Cos}[2\,x] - C[1]\,\text{Sin}[x] - E^{x/3}\,C[3]\,\text{Sin}[2\,x]\}\}$$

Note that the explicit form of the solution is extracted from sol with sol[[1,1,2]]. To graph the solution for various values of the constants, we define tograph to be the table of functions obtained by replacing each occurrence of C[1], C[2], C[3], and C[4] in sol[[1,1,2]] by i, j, k, and m, respectively, for i=0 and 1, j=−1 and 0, k=0 and 1, and m=−1 and 0. The result of the Table command is a 2×2×2×2-dimensional array so Flatten is used to remove parentheses from the result of the Table command. Thus, tograph is a 1-dimensional array consisting of 16 functions.

```
tograph=Table[sol[[1,1,2]] /. {C[1]->i,C[2]->j,C[3]->k,C[4]->m},
       {i,0,1},{j,-1,0},{k,0,1},{m,-1,0}]//Flatten;
Length[tograph]
```

         16

To avoid having messy graphs, we graph the first eight functions in `tograph` by defining `first` to be the first eight functions in `tograph`. Similarly, we graph the second eight by defining `second` to be the last eight functions in `tograph`. Both `first` and `second` are displayed in an abbreviated one-line form with `Short`.

```
first=Take[tograph,8];
Short[first]
second=Take[tograph,-8];
Short[second]
```

$$\{-\text{Cos}[x] - E^{x/3}\text{Cos}[2\ x],\ -\langle\langle1\rangle\rangle,\ \langle\langle5\rangle\rangle,\ -(E^{x/3}\ \text{Sin}[2\ x])\}$$

$$\{-\text{Cos}[x] - E^{x/3}\ \text{Cos}[2\ x] - \text{Sin}[x],\ \langle\langle6\rangle\rangle,\ -\langle\langle1\rangle\rangle + \langle\langle1\rangle\rangle\}$$

```
p1=Plot[Evaluate[first],{x,0,2Pi}]
```

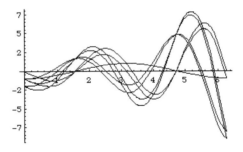

```
p2=Plot[Evaluate[second],{x,0,2Pi}]
```

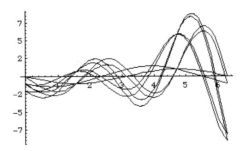

∎

Nonhomogeneous Equations with Constant Coefficients: Variation of Parameters

Let p(x), q(x), and f(x) be continuous on an interval I. The associated homogeneous equation of $y''(x)+p(x)y'(x)+q(x)y(x)=f(x)$ is $y''(x)+p(x)y'(x)+q(x)y(x)=0$. Let $y_1(x)$ and $y_2(x)$ form a fundamental set of solutions for the associated homogeneous equation of $y''(x)+p(x)y'(x)+q(x)y(x)=f(x)$.   Let $u_1(x)=\int \dfrac{-y_2(x)f(x)}{y_1(x)y_2'(x)-y_1'(x)y_2(x)}dx$ and

$u_2(x)=\int \dfrac{y_1(x)f(x)}{y_1(x)y_2'(x)-y_1'(x)y_2(x)}dx$. Then, $y_p(x)=y_1(x)u_1(x)+y_2(x)u_2(x)$ is a particular solution of $y''(x)+p(x)y'(x)+q(x)y(x)=f(x)$, and a general solution is $y(x)=c_1y_1(x)+c_2y_2(x)+y_p(x)$.

We show how Mathematica can be used to assist in the Method of Variation of Parameters in the example below.

EXAMPLE: Solve $y''+4y'+13y=x\cos^2 3x$.

SOLUTION: The associated homogenous equation of the equation $y''+4y'+13y=x\cos^2 3x$ is $y''+4y'+13y=0$, which has characteristic equation $m^2+4m+13=0$. Since the symbols `y1`, `y2`, `yc`, `yp`, `u1`, and `u2` will be used in constructing the solution, all prior definitions are first cleared and then the characteristic equation is solved for m:

```
Clear[y1,y2,yc,yp,y,u1,u2,f]
Solve[m^2+4m+13==0]
```

    {{m -> -2 - 3 I}, {m -> -2 + 3 I}}

Since the solutions of the characteristic equation are $-2-3i$ and $-2+3i$, a fundamental set of solutions of $y''+4y'+13y=0$ is $\{e^{-2x}\cos 3x, e^{-2x}\sin 3x\}$. Therefore, we define $f(x)=x\cos^2 3x$, $y_1(x)=e^{-2x}\cos 3x$, and $y_2(x)=e^{-2x}\sin 3x$:

```
f[x_]=x Cos[3x]^2;
y1[x_]=Exp[-2x]Cos[3x];
y2[x_]=Exp[-2x]Sin[3x];
```

and wronskian $=\begin{vmatrix} y_1(x) & y_2(x) \\ y_1'(x) & y_2'(x) \end{vmatrix} = 3e^{-4x}$.

```
wronskian=Det[{{y1[x],y2[x]},D[{y1[x],y2[x]},x]}]//Simplify
```

        3
       ----
        4 x
       E

To find a particular solution of $y'' + 4y' + 13y = x\cos^2 3x$, we first define $\text{u1prime} = \dfrac{-y_2(x)f(x)}{\text{wronskian}}$

```
u1prime=-y2[x] f[x]/wronskian
```

$$
\dfrac{-(E^{2\ x}\ x\ Cos[3\ x]^2\ Sin[3\ x])}{3}
$$

and then compute $u_1(x) = \displaystyle\int \text{u1prime}\,dx = \int \dfrac{-y_2(x)f(x)}{\text{wronskian}}\,dx$.

```
u1[x_]=Integrate[u1prime,x]
```

$$
\begin{aligned}
(&-86700\ E^{2\ x}\ Cos[3\ x] + 281775\ E^{2\ x}\ x\ Cos[3\ x]\ -\\
&6084\ E^{2\ x}\ Cos[9\ x] + 129285\ E^{2\ x}\ x\ Cos[9\ x]\ -\\
&36125\ E^{2\ x}\ Sin[3\ x] - 187850\ E^{2\ x}\ x\ Sin[3\ x]\ -\\
&13013\ E^{2\ x}\ Sin[9\ x] - 28730\ E^{2\ x}\ x\ Sin[9\ x]) \ /\ 14652300
\end{aligned}
$$

Similarly, we define $\text{u2prime} = \dfrac{y_1(x)f(x)}{\text{wronskian}}$:

```
u2prime=y1[x] f[x]/wronskian
```

$$
\dfrac{E^{2\ x}\ x\ Cos[3\ x]^3}{3}
$$

and then compute $u_2(x) = \displaystyle\int \text{u2prime}\,dx = \int \dfrac{y_1(x)f(x)}{\text{wronskian}}\,dx$.

```
u2[x_]=Integrate[u2prime,x]
```

$$
\begin{aligned}
(&108375\ E^{2\ x}\ Cos[3\ x] + 563550\ E^{2\ x}\ x\ Cos[3\ x]\ +\\
&13013\ E^{2\ x}\ Cos[9\ x] + 28730\ E^{2\ x}\ x\ Cos[9\ x]\ -\\
&260100\ E^{2\ x}\ Sin[3\ x] + 845325\ E^{2\ x}\ x\ Sin[3\ x]\ -\\
&6084\ E^{2\ x}\ Sin[9\ x] + 129285\ E^{2\ x}\ x\ Sin[9\ x]) \ /\ 14652300
\end{aligned}
$$

Then a particular solution of $y'' + 4y' + 13y = x\cos^2 3x$ is given by $y_p(x) = y_1(x)u_1(x) + y_2(x)u_2(x)$:

```
yp[x_]=y1[x]u1[x]+y2[x]u2[x]
```

$$
\begin{aligned}
&(\text{Cos}[3\ x]\ (-86700\ E^{2x}\ \text{Cos}[3\ x] + 281775\ E^{2x}\ x\ \text{Cos}[3\ x] - \\
&\quad 6084\ E^{2x}\ \text{Cos}[9\ x] + 129285\ E^{2x}\ x\ \text{Cos}[9\ x] - \\
&\quad 36125\ E^{2x}\ \text{Sin}[3\ x] - 187850\ E^{2x}\ x\ \text{Sin}[3\ x] - \\
&\quad 13013\ E^{2x}\ \text{Sin}[9\ x] - 28730\ E^{2x}\ x\ \text{Sin}[9\ x])) / \\
&(14652300\ E^{2x}) + (\text{Sin}[3\ x] \\
&\quad (108375\ E^{2x}\ \text{Cos}[3\ x] + 563550\ E^{2x}\ x\ \text{Cos}[3\ x] + \\
&\quad 13013\ E^{2x}\ \text{Cos}[9\ x] + 28730\ E^{2x}\ x\ \text{Cos}[9\ x] - \\
&\quad 260100\ E^{2x}\ \text{Sin}[3\ x] + 845325\ E^{2x}\ x\ \text{Sin}[3\ x] - \\
&\quad 6084\ E^{2x}\ \text{Sin}[9\ x] + 129285\ E^{2x}\ x\ \text{Sin}[9\ x])) / \\
&(14652300\ E^{2x})
\end{aligned}
$$

and a complimentary solution of $y'' + 4y' + 13y = 0$ is given by $y_c(x) = c_1 y_1(x) + c_2 y_2(x)$:

```
yc[x_]=c1 y1[x]+c2 y2[x]
```

$$
\frac{c1\ \text{Cos}[3\ x]}{E^{2x}} + \frac{c2\ \text{Sin}[3\ x]}{E^{2x}}
$$

so a general solution of $y'' + 4y' + 13y = x\cos^2 3x$ is given by $y(x) = y_c(x) + y_p(x)$.

```
y[x_]=yc[x]+yp[x]
```

$$
\frac{c1\ \text{Cos}[3\ x]}{E^{2x}} + \frac{c2\ \text{Sin}[3\ x]}{E^{2x}} +
$$

```
                       2 x                      2 x
(Cos[3 x] (-86700 E    Cos[3 x] + 281775 E    x Cos[3 x] -

             2 x                2 x
    6084 E    Cos[9 x] + 129285 E    x Cos[9 x] -

             2 x                 2 x
    36125 E    Sin[3 x] - 187850 E    x Sin[3 x] -

             2 x                2 x
    13013 E    Sin[9 x] - 28730 E    x Sin[9 x])) /

              2 x
(14652300 E    ) + (Sin[3 x]

              2 x                    2 x
   (108375 E    Cos[3 x] + 563550 E    x Cos[3 x] +

             2 x                2 x
    13013 E    Cos[9 x] + 28730 E    x Cos[9 x] -

              2 x                 2 x
    260100 E    Sin[3 x] + 845325 E    x Sin[3 x] -

            2 x                2 x
    6084 E    Sin[9 x] + 129285 E    x Sin[9 x])) /

              2 x
(14652300 E    )
```

In order to graph various solutions corresponding to different values of c_1 and c_2, we first create a table of functions tograph which we display in an abbreviated six-line form with Short:

```
tograph=Table[y[x], {c1,-5,5,5},{c2,-4,4,2}];
Short[tograph,6]
```

```
     -5 Cos[3 x]    4 Sin[3 x]
  {{----------- - ---------- + <<1>> +
        2 x            2 x
       E              E

                           2 x
   (Sin[3 x] (108375 E    Cos[3 x] +

             2 x                    2 x
    563550 E    x Cos[3 x] + 13013 E    Cos[9 x] +

             2 x                 2 x
    28730 E    x Cos[9 x] - 260100 E    Sin[3 x] +

              2 x                2 x
    845325 E    x Sin[3 x] - 6084 E    Sin[9 x] +
```

```
                  2 x                                      2 x
       129285 E    x Sin[9 x])) / (14652300 E   ), <<4>>}\

  , <<1>>, {<<5>>}}
```

and then graph the table `tograph` on the interval $[-1,1]$:

```
Plot[Evaluate[tograph],{x,-1,1},PlotRange->{-20,20},PlotPoints->100]
```

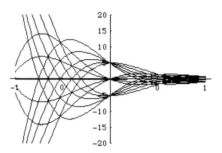

DSolve can frequently be used to find solutions of equations that can be solved using the method of Variation of Parameters.

EXAMPLE: Solve $y'' - 2y' + y = e^x \ln x, x > 0$.

SOLUTION: We use `DSolve` to find a general solution of the equation, naming the resulting output `sol`. The explicit form of the solution is extracted from `sol` with `sol[[1,1,2]]`.

```
sol=DSolve[y''[x]-2y'[x]+y[x]==Exp[x]Log[x],y[x],x]
```

```
                   x  2                          x  2
             -3 E  x      x          x      E  x  Log[x]
  {{y[x] ->  -------- + E   C[1] + E   x C[2] + ------------}}
                4                                    2
```

To graph the solution for various values of the constants, we define `tograph` to be the table obtained by replacing each occurrence of `C[1]` and `C[2]` in `sol[[1,1,2]]` by i and j, respectively, for i=-3, -2, and -1 and j=1 and 2.

```
tograph=Table[sol[[1,1,2]] /. {C[1]->i,C[2]->j},{i,-3,-1},{j,1,2}];
```

We then use `Plot` to graph the functions in `tograph`. Note that the solutions obtained are only valid for $x > 0$; thus we obtain several error messages, since we request that the solutions be graphed on the interval $[0,5]$. Nevertheless, the resulting graphs are displayed correctly.

```
Plot[Evaluate[tograph],{x,0,5}]
```

```
Infinity::indet:
                         0. 1. (-Infinity)
    Indeterminate expression ----------------- encountered.
                                2
```

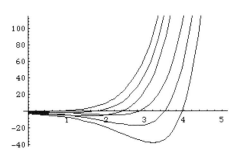

Cauchy-Euler Equations

A **Cauchy-Euler** differential equation is a differential equation of the form

$$a_n x^n y^{(n)}(x) + a_{n-1} x^{n-1} y^{(n-1)}(x) + \ldots + a_1 x y'(x) + a_0 y(x) = g(x),$$

where $\{a_i\}_{i=0}^{n}$ is a collection of constants.

Let $ax^2 y'' + bxy' + cy = 0$ be the general second-order homogeneous Cauchy-Euler equation. The equation $am(m-1) + bm + c = 0$ is called the **auxiliary equation** of the Cauchy-Euler equation of order two. The solutions of the auxiliary equation completely determine the general solution of the homogeneous Cauchy-Euler equation of order two. Let m_1 and m_2 denote the two solutions of the equation $am(m-1) + bm + c = 0$, which is obtained by assuming solutions of the form $y = x^m$, $x > 0$.

(a) If $m_1 \neq m_2$ are real, then a general solution of $ax^2 y'' + bxy' + cy = 0$ is

$$y = c_1 x^{m_1} + c_2 x^{m_2};$$

(b) If $m_1 = m_2$, then a general solution of $ax^2 y'' + bxy' + cy = 0$ is

$$y = c_1 x^{m_1} + c_2 x^{m_1} \ln(x); \text{ and}$$

(c) If $m_1 = \overline{m_2} = \alpha + i\beta$, $\beta \neq 0$, then a general solution of $ax^2 y'' + bxy' + cy = 0$ is

$$y = x^\alpha \left[c_1 \cos(\beta \ln(x)) + c_2 \sin(\beta \ln(x)) \right].$$

The auxiliary equation of higher-order Cauchy-Euler equations is defined in the same way, and solutions of higher-order homogeneous Cauchy-Euler equations are determined in the same manner as solutions of second-order homogeneous differential equations with constant coefficients. Note that in some cases the method of variation of parameters can be used to solve nonhomogeneous Cauchy-Euler equations. Below, we solve a third-order homogeneous Cauchy-Euler equation.

EXAMPLE: Solve $x^3 y''' + 16x^2 y'' + 79 x y' + 125 y = 0$.

SOLUTION: We proceed by defining eq to be the equation

$$x^3 y''' + 16x^2 y'' + 79 x y' + 125 y = 0$$

and then using DSolve to find a general solution of the equation, naming the resulting output sol.

```
Clear[x,y,eq]
eq=x^3 y'''[x]+16x^2 y''[x]+79x y'[x]+125y[x]==0;
sol=DSolve[eq,y[x],x]

              C[1]    C[3] Cos[3 Log[x]]    C[2] Sin[3 Log[x]]
  {{y[x] -> ---- + ------------------ - ------------------}}
              5              4                     4
              x              x                     x
```

To graph the solution for various values of the constants, we define tograph to be the set of functions obtained by replacing each occurrence of C[1], C[2], and C[3] in sol[[1,1,2]] by i, j, and k, respectively, for i=−1 and i, j=0 and 4, and k=−4 and 0. The resulting eight functions are graphed with Plot on the interval [0.25,1.5]. The option PlotRange->{{0,3/2},{-20,20}} specifies that the resulting graph be displayed with x-coordinates corresponding to the interval $\left[0, \dfrac{3}{2}\right]$ and y-coordinates corresponding to the interval [−20,20].

```
tograph=Table[sol[[1,1,2]] /. {C[1]->i,C[2]->j,C[3]->k},
       {i,-1,1,2},{j,0,4,4},{k,-4,0,4}];
Plot[Evaluate[tograph],{x,.25,1.5},PlotRange->{{0,3/2},{-20,20}}]
```

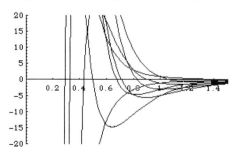

We may also solve this equation by traditional methods. If we assume that $y(x) = x^m$, then the value of eq becomes:

```
y[x_]=x^m;
eq
```

$$\begin{array}{l} m & m & m & m \\ 125\ x\ + 79\ m\ x\ + 16\ (-1 + m)\ m\ x\ + (-2 + m)\ (-1 + m)\ m\ x\ == 0 \end{array}$$

We can solve this equation directly or we can divide the left-hand side of the equation by x^m and factor the result. We interpret the resulting output to mean that the auxiliary equation of $x^3 y''' + 16 x^2 y'' + 79 x y' + 125 y = 0$ is $(m+5)(m^2 + 8m + 25) = 0$.

```
eq[[1]]/x^m//Cancel//Factor
```

$$\begin{array}{c} 2 \\ (5 + m)\ (25 + 8\ m + m\ ) \end{array}$$

We may use `Solve` to solve the auxiliary equation. Solving eq for m results in:

```
Solve[eq,m]
```

```
Solve::ifun: Warning: Inverse functions are being used by Solve, so
     some solutions may not be found.
{{m -> -5}, {m -> -4 - 3 I}, {m -> -4 + 3 I}, {m -> -Infinity}}
```

Since we are only interested in the real and complex solutions, we conclude that the solutions of the auxiliary equation are $m = -5$ and $m = -4 \pm 3i$. Thus, a general solution of the equation is given by $y = c_1 x^{-5} + x^{-4}(c_2 \cos(3\ln x) + c_3 \sin(3\ln x))$. ∎

Application: Harmonic Motion

Suppose that a mass is attached to an elastic spring which is suspended from a rigid support such as a ceiling. According to Hooke's law, the spring exerts a restoring force in the upward direction which is proportional to the displacement of the spring. Mathematically, this is stated as follows:

> **Hooke's law:** F=ks, where k>0 is the constant of proportionality or spring constant, and s is the displacement of the spring.

Using this law and assuming that x(t) represents the position of the mass, we obtain the initial value problem $m\dfrac{d^2 x}{dt^2} + kx = 0$ subject to $x(0) = \alpha$ and $x'(0) = \beta$. Note that the initial conditions give the initial position and velocity, respectively. The solution, x(t), to this problem represents the position of the mass at time t. This differential equation disregards all retarding forces acting on the motion of the mass, and a more realistic model which takes these forces into account is needed. Studies in mechanics reveal that resistive forces due to damping are proportional to a power of the velocity of the motion. Hence, $F_R = c\dfrac{dx}{dt}$ or $F_R = c\left(\dfrac{dx}{dt}\right)^2$, where c>0, are typically used to represent the damping force. Then, we have the following initial value problem, assuming that $F_R = c\dfrac{dx}{dt}$: $m\dfrac{d^2x}{dt^2} + c\dfrac{dx}{dt} + kx = 0$ subject to $x(0) = \alpha$ and $x'(0) = \beta$. Problems of this type are characterized by the value of $c^2 - 4mk$ as follows:

(a) $c^2 - 4mk > 0$. This situation is said to be **overdamped** since the damping coefficient c is large in comparison with the spring constant k.

(b) $c^2 - 4mk = 0$. This situation is described as **critically damped** since the resulting motion is oscillatory with a slight decrease in the damping coefficient c.

(c) $c^2 - 4mk < 0$. This situation is called **underdamped** because the damping coefficient c is small in comparison with the spring constant k.

Mathematica can be used to investigate the solutions of various problems involving harmonic motion as illustrated in the example below.

EXAMPLE: Classify the following differential equations as overdamped, underdamped, or critically damped. Also, solve the corresponding initial value problem using the given initial conditions, and investigate the behavior of the solutions.

(a) $\dfrac{d^2x}{dt^2} + 8\dfrac{dx}{dt} + 16x = 0$ subject to x(0)=0 and $x'(0) = 1$;

(b) $\dfrac{d^2x}{dt^2} + 5\dfrac{dx}{dt} + 4x = 0$ subject to x(0)=1 and $x'(0) = 1$; and

(c) $\dfrac{d^2x}{dt^2} + \dfrac{dx}{dt} + 16x = 0$ subject to x(0)=0 and $x'(0) = 1$.

SOLUTION: For (a), we identify m=1, c=8, and k=16 so that $c^2 - 4mk = 0$, which means that the differential equation $\dfrac{d^2x}{dt^2} + 8\dfrac{dx}{dt} + 16x = 0$ is critically damped. After defining de1, we solve the equation subject to the initial conditions and name the resulting output sol1. We then graph the solution, extracted from sol1 with sol1[[1,1,2]], on the interval [0,4]. Note that replacing sol1[[1,1,2]] with x[t] /. sol1 in the Plot command produces the same results.

```
Clear[de1,x,t]
de1=x''[t]+8x'[t]+16x[t]==0;
sol1=DSolve[{de1,x[0]==0,x'[0]==1},x[t],t]
```

```
                 t
    {{x[t] -> ----}}
             4 t
            E
```

```
Plot[sol1[[1,1,2]],{t,0,4}]
```

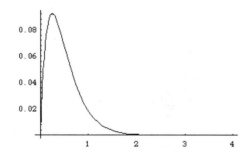

For (b), we proceed in the same manner. We identify m=1, c=5, and k=4 so that $c^2 - 4mk = 9$, and the equation $\dfrac{d^2x}{dt^2} + 5\dfrac{dx}{dt} + 4x = 0$ is overdamped. We then define de2 to be the equation and the solution of the equation obtained with DSolve, sol2, and then graph x(t) on the interval [0,4].

```
Clear[de2,x,t]
de2=x''[t]+5x'[t]+4x[t]==0;
sol2=DSolve[{de2,x[0]==1,x'[0]==1},x[t],t]
```

```
               -2        5
    {{x[t] -> ------ + ----}}
             4 t       t
            3 E       3 E
```

```
Plot[sol2[[1,1,2]],{t,0,4}]
```

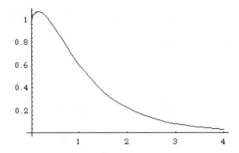

For (c), we proceed in the same manner as in (a) and (b) to show that the equation is underdamped because the value of $c^2 - 4mk$ is -63.

```
Clear[de3,x,t]
de3=x''[t]+x'[t]+16x[t]==0;
sol3=DSolve[{de3,x[0]==0,x'[0]==1},x[t],t]
```

```
            I  ((-1 - 3 I Sqrt[7]) t)/2   I  ((-1 + 3 I Sqrt[7]) t)/2
          - E                           - E
          3                             3
{{x[t] -> -------------------------- - --------------------------}}
                  Sqrt[7]                      Sqrt[7]
```

```
Plot[sol3[[1,1,2]],{t,0,4}]
```

```
    Plot::plnr: CompiledFunction[{t}, <<1>>, -CompiledCode-][t]
        is not a machine-size real number at t = 0..
```

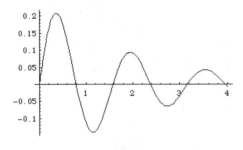

Numerical Solutions of Higher-Order Ordinary Differential Equations

As in the case with first-order ordinary differential equations, numerical approximations of solutions to higher-order differential equations can also be obtained with NDSolve. This command is particularly useful when working with nonlinear equations for which DSolve is unable to find an explicit solution. In order to illustrate the command NDSolve for higher-order ordinary differential equations, we consider the nonlinear pendulum equation below.

Application: The Simple Pendulum

Another situation which leads to a second-order ordinary differential equation is that of the simple pendulum. In this case, a mass m is attached to the end of a rod of length L which is suspended from a rigid support. Because the motion is best described in terms of the angular displacement θ, we let θ=0 correspond to the rod hanging vertically. The objective is to find the motion of the mass as a function of θ, an initial position, and an initial velocity. Assuming that the pendulum is allowed to rotate without friction, the only force acting on the pendulum is that of gravity. Newton's second law and the relationship s=Lθ are used to establish the following initial value problem which models this situation:

$L\dfrac{d^2\theta}{dt^2}+g\sin(\theta)=0$ subject to the initial conditions $\theta(0)=\theta_0 \text{ and } \theta'(0)=v_0$. Notice that this differential equation is nonlinear. However, this nonlinear equation can be approximated by making use of the power series expansion of $\sin(\theta)$ given by:

$\sin(\theta)=\displaystyle\sum_{n=0}^{\infty}\dfrac{(-1)^n\theta^{2n+1}}{(2n+1)!}=\theta-\dfrac{\theta^3}{3!}+\dfrac{\theta^5}{5!}+\cdots$. Hence, for small displacements, we have the

approximation $\sin(\theta)\approx\theta$. Therefore, the initial value problem becomes $L\dfrac{d^2\theta}{dt^2}+g\theta=0$ subject

to $\theta(0)=\theta_0 \text{ and } \theta'(0)=v_0$. Notice that this problem is linear and can easily be solved. Suppose that the pendulum undergoes a damping force which is proportional to the instantaneous

velocity. Then, the force due to damping is given as $F_D=-b\dfrac{d\theta}{dt}$. Incorporating this force

into the sum of the forces acting on the pendulum, we have $L\dfrac{d^2\theta}{dt^2}+b\dfrac{d\theta}{dt}+g\sin(\theta)=0$ subject

to $\theta(0)=\theta_0 \text{ and } \theta'(0)=v_0$. We now investigate the properties of this nonlinear differential equation.

EXAMPLE: Use NDSolve to investigate the solutions to the damped pendulum

problem $\dfrac{d^2\theta}{dt^2}+0.50\dfrac{d\theta}{dt}+\sin(\theta)=0$ subject to the initial conditions $\theta(0)=\theta_0 \text{ and } \theta'(0)=v_0$

using the following initial conditions:

(a) $\theta(0)=i \text{ and } \theta'(0)=0$ for i =−1, −0.5, 0.5, and 1;

(b) $\theta(0)=0 \text{ and } \theta'(0)=i$ for i=−2, −1, 1, and 2;

(c) $\theta(0)=1 \text{ and } \theta'(0)=1$, $\theta(0)=1 \text{ and } \theta'(0)=-1$, $\theta(0)=-1 \text{ and } \theta'(0)=1$, and
$\theta(0)=-1 \text{ and } \theta'(0)=-1$;

(d) $\theta(0)=1 \text{ and } \theta'(0)=2$, $\theta(0)=1 \text{ and } \theta'(0)=3$, $\theta(0)=-1 \text{ and } \theta'(0)=4$, and
$\theta(0)=-1 \text{ and } \theta'(0)=5$; and

(e) $\theta(0)=-1 \text{ and } \theta'(0)=2$, $\theta(0)=-1 \text{ and } \theta'(0)=3$, $\theta(0)=1 \text{ and } \theta'(0)=-4$, and
$\theta(0)=1 \text{ and } \theta'(0)=-5$.

SOLUTION: Notice that, in this case, the damping coefficient is relatively small compared to the other coefficients. The differential equation is defined below as eq. To make the calculations in solving the problem easier, we define the function s[i,j], which uses NDSolve to solve the initial value problem with initial position i and initial velocity j. The solution is extracted from s[i,j] with s[i,j][[1,1,2]].

```
Clear[eq,s]
eq=x''[t]+0.5 x'[t]+Sin[x[t]]==0
```

$$Sin[x[t]] + 0.5 x'[t] + x''[t] == 0$$

```
s[i_,j_]:=NDSolve[{eq,x[0]==i,x'[0]==j},x[t],{t,0,15}];
```

For (a), the function s is used with the values of initial positive given in table1 below and j=0 to generate a list of four interpolating functions.

```
table1={-1,-0.5,0.5,1};
sols1=Table[s[table1[[i]],0][[1,1,2]],{i,1,4}]
```

```
    {InterpolatingFunction[{0., 15.}, <>][t],

      InterpolatingFunction[{0., 15.}, <>][t],

      InterpolatingFunction[{0., 15.}, <>][t],

      InterpolatingFunction[{0., 15.}, <>][t]}
```

These four solutions are graphed below in one.

```
one=Plot[Evaluate[sols1],{t,0,15}]
```

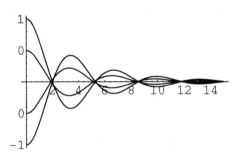

Next, a list of solutions is found with s using i=0 and values of initial velocity given in table2. These functions are then graphed in two.

```
table2={-2,-1,1,2};
sols2=Table[s[0,table2[[i]]][[1,1,2]],{i,1,4}];
two=Plot[Evaluate[sols2],{t,0,15}]
```

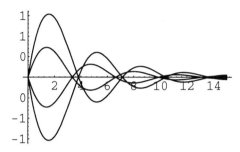

For (c), (d), and (e), we proceed in the same manner as in (a) and (b).

```
table3={{1,1},{1,-1},{-1,1},{-1,-1}};
sols3=Table[s[table3[[i,1]],table3[[i,2]]][[1,1,2]],{i,1,4}]
three=Plot[Evaluate[sols3],{t,0,15}]
```

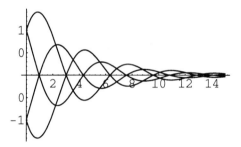

```
table4={{1,2},{1,3},{-1,4},{-1,5}};
sols4=Table[s[table4[[i,1]],table4[[i,2]]][[1,1,2]],{i,1,4}];
four=Plot[Evaluate[sols4],{t,0,15}]
```

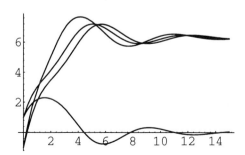

```
table5={{-1,2},{-1,3},{1,-4},{1,-5}};
sols5=Table[s[table5[[i,1]],table5[[i,2]]][[1,1,2]],{i,1,4}]
five=Plot[Evaluate[sols5],{t,0,15}]
```

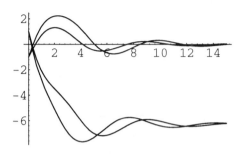

Finally, all five of the plots obtained above are displayed together.

```
six=Show[one,two,three,four,five]
```

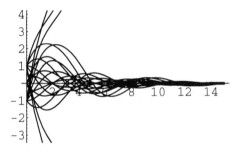

These solutions are also displayed in the form of a `GraphicsArray`.

```
Show[GraphicsArray[{{one,two},{three,four},{five,six}}]]
```

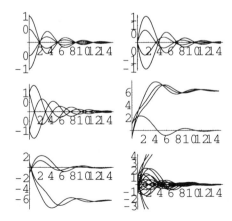

■

6.3 Power Series Solutions of Ordinary Differential Equations

Power Series Solutions about Ordinary Points

Mathematica can also be used to help construct power series solutions of ordinary differential equations. This topic was discussed briefly in section 3.5.

Let $a_2(x)y''(x)+a_1(x)y'(x)+a_0(x)y(x)=0$ and let $p(x)=\dfrac{a_1(x)}{a_2(x)}$ and $q(x)=\dfrac{a_0(x)}{a_2(x)}$. Then, $a_2(x)y''(x)+a_1(x)y'(x)+a_0(x)y(x)=0$ is equivalent to $y''(x)+p(x)y'(x)+q(x)y(x)=0$. A number x_0 is an **ordinary point** means that both p(x) and q(x) are analytic at x_0. If x_0 is not an ordinary point, then x_0 is called a **singular point.**

EXAMPLE: Solve the equation $y''-2xy'+2\bullet 4y=0$ subject to the initial conditions y(0)=12 and $y'(0)=0$.

SOLUTION: We begin by defining lhs to be the left-hand side of the equation $y''-2xy'+2\bullet 4y=0$ and then defining serleft to be the power series for lhs about x=0.

```
Clear[x,y,lhs,serleft,eqs,roots,sol]
lhs=y''[x]-2 x y'[x]+2 4y[x];
serleft=Series[lhs,{x,0,6}]
```

$$\left(8\,y[0] + y''[0]\right) + \left(6\,y'[0] + y^{(3)}[0]\right)\,x +$$

$$\left(2\,y''[0] + \frac{y^{(4)}[0]}{2}\right)\,x^2 + \left(\frac{y^{(3)}[0]}{3} + \frac{y^{(5)}[0]}{6}\right)\,x^3 +$$

$$\frac{y^{(6)}[0]\,x^4}{24} + \left(\frac{-y^{(5)}[0]}{60} + \frac{y^{(7)}[0]}{120}\right)\,x^5 +$$

$$\left(\frac{-y^{(6)}[0]}{180} + \frac{y^{(8)}[0]}{720}\right)\,x^6 + O[x]^7$$

Since the coefficient of x^i must be 0 for all values of i, we use LogicalExpand to equate the coefficients of serleft and 0, the right-hand side of the equation, and name the resulting system of equations eqs.

```
eqs=LogicalExpand[serleft==0]
```

$$8\ y[0] + y''[0] == 0\ \&\&\ 6\ y'[0] + y^{(3)}[0] == 0\ \&\&$$

$$2\ y''[0] + \frac{y^{(4)}[0]}{2} == 0\ \&\&$$

$$\frac{y^{(3)}[0]}{3} + \frac{y^{(5)}[0]}{6} == 0\ \&\&\ \frac{y^{(6)}[0]}{24} == 0\ \&\&$$

$$\frac{-y^{(5)}[0]}{60} + \frac{y^{(7)}[0]}{120} == 0\ \&\&\ \frac{-y^{(6)}[0]}{180} + \frac{y^{(8)}[0]}{720} == 0$$

The command `Table[D[y[x],{x,i}],{i,2,8}] /. x->0]` generates the list consisting of $y''(0)$, $y'''(0)$, ... , $y^{(8)}(0)$. We then solve `eqs` for $y''(0)$, $y'''(0)$, ... , $y^{(8)}(0)$. The result, named `roots`, is in terms of y(0) and $y'(0)$.

```
roots=Solve[eqs,Evaluate[Table[D[y[x],{x,i}],{i,2,8}] /. x->0]]
```

$$\{\{y^{(4)}[0] \rightarrow 32\ y[0],\ y^{(7)}[0] \rightarrow 24\ y'[0],$$

$$y^{(8)}[0] \rightarrow 0,\ y''[0] \rightarrow -8\ y[0],$$

$$y^{(3)}[0] \rightarrow -6\ y'[0],\ y^{(5)}[0] \rightarrow 12\ y'[0],$$

$$y^{(6)}[0] \rightarrow 0\}\}$$

The solution is obtained by computing the power series for y(x) about x=0 and then replacing each unknown by the values obtained in `roots`. The resulting series is named `sol`.

```
sol=Series[y[x],{x,0,5}] /. roots[[1]]
```

$$y[0] + y'[0]\ x - 4\ y[0]\ x^2 - y'[0]\ x^3 + \frac{4\ y[0]\ x^4}{3} +$$

$$\frac{y'[0]\ x^5}{10} + O[x]^6$$

We then compute the value of `sol` when y(0)=12 and $y'(0)=0$. The same result is obtained with `HermiteH[4,x]`.

```
y[0]=12;
y'[0]=0;
sol
```

$$12 - 48\ x^2 + 16\ x^4 + O[x]^6$$

```
HermiteH[4,x]
```

$$12 - 48\ x^2 + 16\ x^4$$

In fact, the **Hermite polynomials**, $H_n(x)$, are solutions of the ordinary differential equation $y'' - 2xy' + 2ny = 0$. The command `HermiteH[n,x]` yields the Hermite polynomial $H_n(x)$. The following commands compute a table of the first five Hermite polynomials, name the resulting table `ths`, display `ths` in `TableForm`, and then graph each function in `ths` on the interval $[-4,4]$.

```
ths=Table[HermiteH[n,x],{n,1,5}];
TableForm[ths]
```

$$2\ x$$
$$-2 + 4\ x^2$$
$$-12\ x + 8\ x^3$$
$$12 - 48\ x^2 + 16\ x^4$$
$$120\ x - 160\ x^3 + 32\ x^5$$

```
Plot[Evaluate[ths],{x,-4,4}]
```

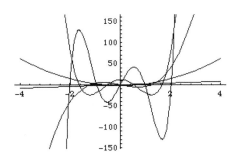

In the next example, we construct a power series solution of an equation which cannot be solved with `DSolve`.

EXAMPLE: Find a power series solution of $y'' + f(x)y' + y = \cos x$, where $f(x) = \begin{cases} \dfrac{\sin x}{x}, & \text{if } x \neq 0 \\ 1, & \text{if } x = 0 \end{cases}$, subject to the initial conditions y(0)=1 and $y'(0) = -1$. Graph the ninth Maclaurin polynomial of the power series solution to the problem.

SOLUTION: We begin by trying unsuccessfully to use `DSolve` to solve the equation. Because `DSolve` does not solve the equation, we then define `lhs` to be the left-hand side of the equation, and `rhs` to be the right-hand side.

```
DSolve[y''[x]+Sin[x]/x y'[x]+y[x]==Cos[x],y[x],x]
```

```
                   Sin[x] y'[x]
        DSolve[y[x] + ------------ + y''[x] == Cos[x], y[x], x]
                        x
```

```
lhs=y''[x]+Sin[x]/x y'[x]+y[x];
rhs=Cos[x];
```

We then use `Series` to compute the power series expansion of `lhs` about $x = 0$ and name the resulting output `ser`. Note that even though $\dfrac{\sin x}{x}$ is undefined when $x = 0$, Mathematica is able to compute the correct series expansion.

```
ser=Series[lhs,{x,0,7}]
```

```
   (y[0] + y'[0] + y''[0]) +


                          (3)
      (y'[0] + y''[0] + y   [0]) x +


                         (3)        (4)
       -y'[0]   y''[0]   y   [0]    y   [0]    2
      (------ + ------ + ------- + -------) x   +
         6        2         2         2


                   (3)        (4)        (5)
       -y''[0]   y   [0]    y   [0]    y   [0]    3
      (------- + ------- + ------- + -------) x   +
          6         6          6          6


               (3)        (4)        (5)        (6)
       y'[0]   y   [0]    y   [0]    y   [0]    y   [0]    4
      (----- - ------- + ------- + ------- + -------) x   +
        120       12         24         24         24


               (4)        (5)        (6)        (7)
       y''[0]   y   [0]    y   [0]    y   [0]    y   [0]    5
      (------ - ------- + ------- + ------- + -------) x   +
        120        36        120        120        120
```

$$
\left(\frac{-y'[0]}{5040} + \frac{y^{(3)}[0]}{240} - \frac{y^{(5)}[0]}{144} + \frac{y^{(6)}[0]}{720} + \frac{y^{(7)}[0]}{720} + \right.
$$

$$
\left. \frac{y^{(8)}[0]}{720} \right) x^6 + \left(\frac{-y''[0]}{5040} + \frac{y^{(4)}[0]}{720} - \frac{y^{(6)}[0]}{720} + \right.
$$

$$
\left. \frac{y^{(7)}[0]}{5040} + \frac{y^{(8)}[0]}{5040} + \frac{y^{(9)}[0]}{5040} \right) x^7 + O[x]^8
$$

We then apply the initial conditions y(0)=1 and $y'(0)=-1$ by replacing each occurrence of y[0] and y'[0] in ser by 1 and −1, respectively, naming the resulting output serone.

```
serone=ser /. {y[0]->1,y'[0]->-1}
```

$$
y''[0] + (-1 + y''[0] + y^{(3)}[0]) \, x +
$$

$$
\left(\frac{1}{6} + \frac{y''[0]}{2} + \frac{y^{(3)}[0]}{2} + \frac{y^{(4)}[0]}{2} \right) x^2 +
$$

$$
\left(\frac{-y''[0]}{6} + \frac{y^{(3)}[0]}{6} + \frac{y^{(4)}[0]}{6} + \frac{y^{(5)}[0]}{6} \right) x^3 +
$$

$$
\left(-\left(\frac{1}{120}\right) - \frac{y^{(3)}[0]}{12} + \frac{y^{(4)}[0]}{24} + \frac{y^{(5)}[0]}{24} + \frac{y^{(6)}[0]}{24} \right) x^4 +
$$

$$
\left(\frac{y''[0]}{120} - \frac{y^{(4)}[0]}{36} + \frac{y^{(5)}[0]}{120} + \frac{y^{(6)}[0]}{120} + \frac{y^{(7)}[0]}{120} \right) x^5 +
$$

$$
\left(\frac{1}{5040} + \frac{y^{(3)}[0]}{240} - \frac{y^{(5)}[0]}{144} + \frac{y^{(6)}[0]}{720} + \frac{y^{(7)}[0]}{720} + \right.
$$

$$
\left. \frac{y^{(8)}[0]}{720} \right) x^6 + \left(\frac{-y''[0]}{5040} + \frac{y^{(4)}[0]}{720} - \frac{y^{(6)}[0]}{720} + \right.
$$

$$\left(\frac{y^{(7)}[0]}{5040} + \frac{y^{(8)}[0]}{5040} + \frac{y^{(9)}[0]}{5040}\right) x^7 + O[x]^8$$

In the same manner as above, we define `sertwo` to be the power series of $\cos x$ about $x = 0$.

```
sertwo=Series[Cos[x],{x,0,7}]
```

$$1 - \frac{x^2}{2} + \frac{x^4}{24} - \frac{x^6}{720} + O[x]^8$$

Since two power series are equal if and only if their corresponding coefficients are equal, `LogicalExpand` is used to equate the coefficients of the series `serone` and `sertwo`. The resulting system of equations is named `equations`.

```
equations=LogicalExpand[serone==sertwo]
```

$$-1 + y''[0] == 0 \;\&\&\; -1 + y''[0] + y^{(3)}[0] == 0 \;\&\&$$

$$\frac{2}{3} + \frac{y''[0]}{2} + \frac{y^{(3)}[0]}{2} + \frac{y^{(4)}[0]}{2} == 0 \;\&\&$$

$$\frac{-y''[0]}{6} + \frac{y^{(3)}[0]}{6} + \frac{y^{(4)}[0]}{6} + \frac{y^{(5)}[0]}{6} == 0 \;\&\&$$

$$-\left(\frac{1}{20}\right) - \frac{y^{(3)}[0]}{12} + \frac{y^{(4)}[0]}{24} + \frac{y^{(5)}[0]}{24} + \frac{y^{(6)}[0]}{24} == 0 \;\&\&$$

$$\frac{y''[0]}{120} - \frac{y^{(4)}[0]}{36} + \frac{y^{(5)}[0]}{120} + \frac{y^{(6)}[0]}{120} + \frac{y^{(7)}[0]}{120} == 0 \;\&\&$$

$$\frac{1}{630} + \frac{y^{(3)}[0]}{240} - \frac{y^{(5)}[0]}{144} + \frac{y^{(6)}[0]}{720} + \frac{y^{(7)}[0]}{720} +$$

$$\frac{y^{(8)}[0]}{720} == 0 \;\&\&\; \frac{-y''[0]}{5040} + \frac{y^{(4)}[0]}{720} - \frac{y^{(6)}[0]}{720} +$$

```
      (7)         (8)          (9)
    y    [0]    y    [0]    y    [0]
    ------- +  ------- +  ------- == 0
     5040        5040       5040
```

Then, `equations` is solved for the unknowns and the resulting solution list is named `roots`.

```
roots=Solve[equations]
```

```
      (9)          358   (8)          1741   (7)              554
   {{y    [0] -> ---, y    [0] -> ----, y    [0] -> -(---),
                 105              63                    45
      (5)         10   (6)         1   (3)
    y    [0] -> --, y    [0] -> -, y    [0] -> 0,
                3                5


      (4)          7
    y    [0] -> -(-), y''[0] -> 1}}
                 3
```

To display the first few terms of the series, we first compute the power series for y(x) about $x = 0$ and name the resulting series `sery`, and then replace y(0) by 1 $y'(0)$ by −1, and the remaining unknowns by the values specified in `roots`. The resulting series is converted to a normal expression with `Normal`, and the resulting output is named `solapprox`.

```
sery=Series[y[x],{x,0,9}];
solapprox=Normal[sery] /. {y[0]->1,y'[0]->-1} /.roots[[1]]
```

```
           2       4      5     6        7          8
          x     7 x     x     x      277 x     1741 x
   1 - x + -- - ---- + -- + ---- - ------ + ------- +
           2     72    36   3600   113400   2540160


         9
    179 x
   --------
   19051200
```

Finally, we graph `solapprox` on the interval [0,3].

```
pone=Plot[solapprox,{x,0,3}]
```

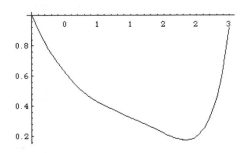

Power Series Solutions about Regular Singular Points

Let x_0 be a singular point of $y''(x)+p(x)y'(x)+q(x)y(x)=0$. x_0 is a **regular singular point** means that both $(x-x_0)p(x)$ and $(x-x_0)^2q(x)$ are analytic at $x=x_0$. If x_0 is not a regular singular point, x_0 is called an **irregular singular point**.

Let $x=0$ be a regular singular point of the equation $y''(x)+p(x)y'(x)+q(x)y(x)=0$. Then, $xp(x)$ is analytic at $x=0$, so $p(x)=\sum_{n=0}^{\infty}p_nx^{n-1}$ and $x^2q(x)$ is analytic at $x=0$, so $q(x)=\sum_{n=0}^{\infty}q_nx^{n-2}$. If we assume there is a constant r so that $y(x)=x^r\sum_{n=0}^{\infty}a_nx^n$ is a solution of $y''(x)+p(x)y'(x)+q(x)y(x)=0$, substituting this solution into the equation and equating coefficients results in the equation $r^2+(p_0-1)r+q_0=0$. This equation is called the **indicial equation** of the problem. The solutions of the problem are determined by the solutions of the indicial equation. Let $r_1=\frac{1}{2}\left(1-p_0+\sqrt{1-2p_0+p_0^2-4q_0}\right)$ and $r_2=\frac{1}{2}\left(1-p_0-\sqrt{1-2p_0+p_0^2-4q_0}\right)$ be the two solutions of the indicial equation. If r_1-r_2 is not an integer, then there are two linearly independent solutions of the problem of the form $y_1(x)=x^{r_1}\sum_{n=0}^{\infty}a_{1n}x^n$ and $y_2(x)=x^{r_2}\sum_{n=0}^{\infty}a_{2n}x^n$. If r_1-r_2 is a non-zero integer, then there are two linearly independent solutions of the form $y_1(x)=x^{r_1}\sum_{n=0}^{\infty}a_{1n}x^n$ and $y_2(x)=cy_1(x)\ln x+x^{r_2}\sum_{n=0}^{\infty}a_{2n}x^n$. If r_1-r_2 is zero, then there are two linearly independent solutions of the problem of the form $y_1(x)=x^{r_1}\sum_{n=0}^{\infty}a_{1n}x^n$ and $y_2(x)=y_1(x)\ln(x)+x^{r_1}\sum_{n=0}^{\infty}a_{1n}x^n$. In any case, if $y_1(x)$ is a solution of the problem, a second linearly independent solution is given by $y_2(x)=y_1(x)\int\frac{e^{-\int p(x)dx}}{[y_1(x)]^2}dx$.

EXAMPLE: Find a general solution of $y''-\left(\frac{2}{3x}-1\right)y'+\left(\frac{4}{9x^2}+x\right)y=0$.

SOLUTION: We identify $p(x) = \dfrac{-2}{3x} + 1$ and $q(x) = \dfrac{4}{9x^2} + x$ so that the indicial equation is $r^2 + \left(\dfrac{-2}{3} - 1\right)r + \dfrac{4}{9} = 0$. In this case, factoring yields the equation

$$r^2 - \frac{5}{3}r + \frac{4}{9} = \left(r - \frac{4}{3}\right)\left(r - \frac{1}{3}\right) = 0$$

so that the solutions of the indicial equation are $r_1 = \dfrac{4}{3}$ and $r_2 = \dfrac{1}{3}$ and $r_1 - r_2 = 1$. Since the roots of the indicial equation differ by an integer, we search for one solution of the form

$$y_1(x) = \sum_{n=0}^{\infty} a_n x^{n+4/3}$$

and another linearly independent solution of the form

$$y_2(x) = c\, y_1(x)\ln x + \sum_{n=0}^{\infty} b_n x^{n+1/3},$$

where c is a constant that may be zero. Let $y_1(x) = \sum_{n=0}^{\infty} a_n x^{n+4/3}$. Then,

$$y_1'(x) = \sum_{n=0}^{\infty} a_n \left(n + \frac{4}{3}\right) x^{n+1/3} \quad \text{and} \quad y_1''(x) = \sum_{n=0}^{\infty} a_n \left(n + \frac{4}{3}\right)\left(n + \frac{1}{3}\right) x^{n-2/3}.$$

Substituting $y_1(x)$ into the equation and simplifying yields

$$\sum_{n=0}^{\infty} a_n n(n+1) x^{n-2/3} + \sum_{n=0}^{\infty} a_n \left(n + \frac{4}{3}\right) x^{n+1/3} + \sum_{n=0}^{\infty} a_n x^{n+7/3} = 0.$$

Expanding and reindexing produces

$$\left(2a_1 + \frac{4}{3}a_0\right)x^{1/3} + \left(6a_2 + \frac{7}{3}a_1\right)x^{4/3} +$$

$$\sum_{n=0}^{\infty}\left[(n+4)(n+3)a_{n+3} + \left(n + \frac{10}{3}\right)a_{n+2} + a_n\right]x^{n+7/3} = 0.$$

Because the coefficient of $x^{i-2/3}$ must be 0 for all values of i,

$$\begin{cases} 2a_1 + \frac{4}{3}a_0 = 0 \\ 6a_2 + \frac{7}{3}a_1 = 0 \\ (n+4)(n+3)a_{n+3} + \left(n+\frac{10}{3}\right)a_{n+2} + a_n = 0 \ for \ n = 0, \dots \end{cases}$$

We then use Mathematica to find the values of a_n. With the following command, we solve for a_1 in terms of a_0 and name the resulting output a1.

```
Clear[a,b,a1,a2,as,b1,b2,bs,c]
a1=Solve[2a[1]+4/3a[0]==0,a[1]]
```

```
             -2 a[0]
{{a[1] ->  -------}}
               3
```

Similarly, we solve for a_2 in terms of a_1 and then replace a_1 by the value obtained in a1:

```
a2=Solve[6a[2]+7/3a[1]==0,a[2]]
```

```
             -7 a[1]
{{a[2] ->  -------}}
              18
```

```
a2 /. a1[[1]]
```

```
             7 a[0]
{{a[2] ->  ------}}
              27
```

Finally, we solve $(n+4)(n+3)a_{n+3} + \left(n+\frac{10}{3}\right)a_{n+2} + a_n = 0$ for a_{n+3}, naming the resulting output an3, and then replace each occurrence of n in an3 by $n-3$.

```
an3=Solve[(n+4)(n+3)a[n+3]+(n+10/3)a[n+2]+a[n]==0,a[n+3]]
```

```
              -(3 a[n] + 10 a[2 + n] + 3 n a[2 + n])
{{a[3 + n] -> -------------------------------------}}
                      3 (3 + n) (4 + n)
```

```
an3 /. n->n-3//ExpandAll
```

```
             -3 a[-3 + n]    a[-1 + n]     3 n a[-1 + n]
{{a[n] ->  ------------ - ---------- - -------------}}
                  2              2              2
             3 n + 3 n      3 n + 3 n     3 n + 3 n
```

The result means that for $n \geq 3$, $a_n = \dfrac{-3a_{n-3} - a_{n-1} - 3na_{n-1}}{3n^2 + 3n}$. Let

$$y_2(x) = c\,y_1(x)\ln x + \sum_{n=0}^{\infty} b_n x^{n+1/3} = c\ln x \sum_{n=0}^{\infty} a_n x^{n+4/3} + \sum_{n=0}^{\infty} b_n x^{n+1/3}$$

be a second linearly independent solution of the equation. Then,

$$y_2'(x) = \sum_{n=0}^{\infty} c a_n x^{n+1/3} + c y_1' \ln x + \sum_{n=0}^{\infty} b_n \left(n + \frac{1}{3} \right) x^{n-2/3}$$

and

$$y_2''(x) = \sum_{n=0}^{\infty} c a_n \left(n + \frac{1}{3} \right) x^{n-2/3} + c y_1'' \ln x + \sum_{n=0}^{\infty} b_n \left(n + \frac{1}{3} \right)\left(n - \frac{2}{3} \right) x^{n-5/3}\ .$$

Substituting into the equation and simplifying yields

$$\sum_{n=0}^{\infty} n(n-1) b_n x^{n-5/3} + \sum_{n=0}^{\infty} \left[\frac{c(3n-1)}{3} a_n + \frac{3n+1}{3} b_n \right] x^{n-2/3} +$$

$$\sum_{n=0}^{\infty} c a_n x^{n+1/3} + \sum_{n=0}^{\infty} b_n x^{n+4/3} = 0.$$

Expanding and reindexing results in

$$\left(\frac{-c}{3} a_0 + \frac{1}{3} b_0 \right) x^{-2/3} +$$

$$\left(2b_2 + \frac{2c}{3} a_1 + \frac{4}{3} b_1 + c a_0 \right) x^{1/3} +$$

$$\sum_{n=0}^{\infty} \left[(n+3)(n+2) b_{n+3} + \frac{3(3n+5)}{3} a_{n+2} + \frac{3n+7}{3} b_{n+2} + c a_{n+1} + b_n \right] x^{n+4/3} = 0.$$

Because the coefficient of $x^{i-2/3}$ is 0 for all values of i,

$$\begin{cases} \dfrac{-c}{3} a_0 + \dfrac{1}{3} b_0 = 0 \\[2mm] 2b_2 + \dfrac{2c}{3} a_1 + \dfrac{4}{3} b_1 + c a_0 = 0 \\[2mm] (n+3)(n+2) b_{n+3} + \dfrac{3(3n+5)}{3} a_{n+2} + \dfrac{3n+7}{3} b_{n+2} + c a_{n+1} + b_n = 0 \ \text{for } n = 0, \ldots \end{cases}$$

In the same manner as above, we solve for b_0 in terms of a_0 and name the resulting output b0.

```
Clear[a,b]
b0=Solve[-c/3a[0]+1/3b[0]==0,b[0]]
```

```
{{b[0] -> c a[0]}}
```

Similarly, we solve for b_2 in terms of a_1, a_0, and b_1. (b_1 is arbitrary.)

```
b2=Solve[2b[2]+2c/3a[1]+4/3b[1]+c a[0]==0,b[2]]
```

```
         -3 c a[0] - 2 c a[1] - 4 b[1]
{{b[2] -> ------------------------------}}
                      6
```

Finally, we solve

$$(n+3)(n+2)b_{n+3} + \frac{3(3n+5)}{3}a_{n+2} + \frac{3n+7}{3}b_{n+2} + ca_{n+1} + b_n = 0$$

for b_{n+3}, naming the resulting output bn3, and then replace each occurrence of n in bn3 by $n-3$.

```
bn3=Solve[(n+3)(n+2)b[n+3]+3(3n+5)/3a[n+2]+
        (3n+7)/3b[n+2]+c a[n+1]+b[n]==0,b[n+3]]
```

```
{{b[3 + n] ->

    -(3 c a[1 + n] + 15 a[2 + n] + 9 n a[2 + n] + 3 b[n] +

     7 b[2 + n] + 3 n b[2 + n]) / (3 (2 + n) (3 + n))}}
```

```
bn=bn3 /.n->n-3//ExpandAll
```

```
          -3 c a[-2 + n]   12 a[-1 + n]   9 n a[-1 + n]
{{b[n] -> -------------- + ------------ - ------------- -
               2                2               2
          -3 n + 3 n       -3 n + 3 n       -3 n + 3 n

    3 b[-3 + n]   2 b[-1 + n]   3 n b[-1 + n]
    ----------- + ----------- - -------------}}
         2             2              2
    -3 n + 3 n    -3 n + 3 n     -3 n + 3 n
```

The result means that for $n \geq 3$,

$$b_n = \frac{-3c\,a_{n-2} + 12a_{n-1} - 9na_{n-1} - 3b_{n-3} + 2b_{n-1} - 3nb_{n-1}}{3n^2 - 3n}.$$

Because we have computed recurrence relations that yield the value of a_n and b_n for all values of n, we may construct our solutions $y_1(x)$ and $y_2(x)$.

In the following commands, we define $a_0=1$, $a_1=-2/3$, $a_2=7/27$, and then a_n as above and then compute a table of values of a_n for n=0, 1, 2, ... , 10, name the resulting table as, and display as in TableForm. Note that a is defined using the form $a[n\_]:=a[n]=\ldots$ so that Mathematica "remembers" the values of $a[n]$ computed and thus avoids recomputing values previously computed. This is particularly advantageous and time-saving when computing $a[n]$ (and, subsequently, $b[n]$) for large values of n.

```
Clear[a,b]
a[0]=1;
a[1]=-2/3;
a[2]=7/27;
a[n_]:=a[n]=(-3a[n-3]-a[n-1]-3n a[n-1])/(3n+3n^2)
as=Table[{n,a[n]},{n,0,10}];
TableForm[as]
```

```
    0     1
                2
              -(-)
    1         3
              7
              --
    2        27
                151
              -(---)
    3          972
             3907
             -----
    4        58320
                3371
              -(------)
    5          164025
             561971
             --------
    6        82668600
                57955759
              -(----------)
    7          27776649600
             3161469847
             ------------
    8        5999756313600
                1075908049
              -(------------)
    9          8264970432000
             4169289225091
             -----------------
   10        133644571885440000
```

In this case, we let c=1, $b_0=1$, $b_1=1$, and b_2 and b_n, as above, then compute a table of values of b_n for n=0, 1, 2, ... , 10, name the resulting table bs, and display bs in TableForm.

```
b[0]=1;
b[1]=1;
b[2]=-(3a[0]+2a[1]+4b[1])/6;
b[n_]:=b[n]=(-3 a[n-2]+12a[n-1]-9n a[n-1]-
      3b[n-3]+2b[n-1]-3n b[n-1])/(3n^2-3n)
bs=Table[{n,b[n]},{n,0,10}];
TableForm[bs]
```

```
    0      1
    1      1
              17
            -(--)
    2        18
           31
           ---
    3      324
             163
           -(----)
    4       5832
           84679
           -------
    5      3499200
               3509
            -(--------)
    6        26244000
              109479869
            -(----------)
    7        69441624000
              4644389783
            --------------
    8      11666192832000
                2775418878709
             -(----------------)
    9          151119385910272000
              94843769731
            ----------------
    10     1388515032576000
```

We then compute the first eleven terms of the series for $y_1(x)$ and name the resulting function y1approx:

```
y1approx[x_]=Sum[a[n]x^(n+4/3),{n,0,10}]
```

$$x^{4/3} - \frac{2 x^{7/3}}{3} + \frac{7 x^{10/3}}{27} - \frac{151 x^{13/3}}{972} + \frac{3907 x^{16/3}}{58320} -$$

$$\frac{3371 x^{19/3}}{164025} + \frac{561971 x^{22/3}}{82668600} - \frac{57955759 x^{25/3}}{27776649600} +$$

$$\frac{3161469847\ x^{28/3}}{5999756313600} - \frac{1075908049\ x^{31/3}}{8264970432000} + \frac{4169289225091\ x^{34/3}}{133644571885440000}$$

and compute the first eleven terms of the series for $y_2(x)$ and name the result
y2approx.

```
y2approx[x_]=y1approx[x] Log[x]+Sum[b[n]x^(n+1/3),{n,0,10}]
```

$$x^{1/3} + x^{4/3} - \frac{17\ x^{7/3}}{18} + \frac{31\ x^{10/3}}{324} - \frac{163\ x^{13/3}}{5832} +$$

$$\frac{84679\ x^{16/3}}{3499200} - \frac{3509\ x^{19/3}}{26244000} - \frac{109479869\ x^{22/3}}{69441624000} +$$

$$\frac{4644389783\ x^{25/3}}{11666192832000} - \frac{2775418878709\ x^{28/3}}{15119385910272000} +$$

$$\frac{94843769731\ x^{31/3}}{1388515032576000} + (x^{4/3} - \frac{2\ x^{7/3}}{3} + \frac{7\ x^{10/3}}{27} -$$

$$\frac{151\ x^{13/3}}{972} + \frac{3907\ x^{16/3}}{58320} - \frac{3371\ x^{19/3}}{164025} + \frac{561971\ x^{22/3}}{82668600} -$$

$$\frac{57955759\ x^{25/3}}{27776649600} + \frac{3161469847\ x^{28/3}}{5999756313600} - \frac{1075908049\ x^{31/3}}{8264970432000} +$$

$$\frac{4169289225091\ x^{34/3}}{133644571885440000}) \text{ Log}[x]$$

We then graph both y1approx and y2approx on [0,1] and display the two
graphs as a graphics array. Note that several error messages are generated when
Mathematica graphs y2approx, due to the logarithm term, but the resulting
graphs are displayed correctly.

```
py1=Plot[y1approx[x],{x,0,1},DisplayFunction->Identity];
py2=Plot[y2approx[x],{x,0,1},DisplayFunction->Identity];
Show[GraphicsArray[{py1,py2}]]
```

```
Infinity::indet:
    Indeterminate expression 0. (-Infinity) encountered.
Infinity::indet:
    Indeterminate expression 0. (-Infinity) encountered.
Plot::plnr: CompiledFunction[{x}, <<1>>, -CompiledCode-]
        [<<1>>] is not a machine-size real number at x = 0..
```

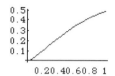 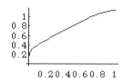

6.4 Using the Laplace Transform to Solve Ordinary Differential Equations

Definition of the Laplace Transform

Let f(t) be a function defined on the interval [0,+∞). The **Laplace transform** of f(t) is the function (of s)

$$L\{f\}(s) = \int_0^{+\infty} e^{-st} f(t)\,dt,$$

provided the integral exists.

f(t) is the **inverse Laplace transform** of F(s) means that L{f}(s)=F(s) and we write $L^{-1}\{F(s)\}(t) = f(t)$.

Commands which can be used to compute Laplace transforms and inverse Laplace transforms are located in the **LaplaceTransform** package contained in the **Calculus** folder (or directory). The command `InverseLaplaceTransform[f[s],s,t]` computes the inverse Laplace transform of f[s] and the result is a function of t, while `LaplaceTransform[g[t],t,s]` yields the Laplace transform of g[t] as a function of s. Several examples are given below.

EXAMPLE: Find the Laplace transform of (a) $f(t) = t^3$; (b) $f(t) = \sin at$; and (c) $f(t) = \cos at$.

SOLUTION: For (b) and (c) we will use the command `LaplaceTransform` contained in the `LaplaceTransform` package so we begin by loading the `LaplaceTransform` package. For (a), we use the definition of the Laplace transform and compute $\int_0^A t^3 e^{-st}dt$, naming the resulting output `stepone`.

```
<<Calculus'LaplaceTransform'
stepone=Integrate[t^3 Exp[-s t],{t,0,A}]
```

$$-\frac{6}{s^4} - \frac{6A}{s^3} - \frac{3A^2}{s^2} - \frac{A^3}{s} \over E^{As} + \frac{6}{s^4}$$

Then, the Laplace transform of $f(t) = t^3$ is

$$\lim_{A \to \infty} \int_0^A t^3 e^{-st}dt = \lim_{A \to \infty} \text{stepone}$$

$$= \lim_{A \to \infty} \left(\frac{-6s^{-4} - 6As^{-3} - 3A^2s^{-2} - A^3s^{-1}}{e^{As}} + \frac{6}{s^4} \right) = \frac{6}{s^4}.$$

For (b) and (c) we use the command `LaplaceTransform`.

```
LaplaceTransform[Sin[a t],t,s]
```

$$\frac{a}{a^2 + s^2}$$

```
LaplaceTransform[Cos[a t],t,s]
```

$$\frac{s}{a^2 + s^2}$$

In this case, we see that `LaplaceTransform` is successful and that the Laplace transform of $f(t) = \sin at$ is $\frac{a}{a^2 + s^2}$, while the Laplace transform of $f(t) = \cos at$ is $\frac{s}{a^2 + s^2}$. ■

Although `LaplaceTransform` can be used to compute the Laplace transform of many "standard" functions, in other cases it is best to proceed directly and use Mathematica to perform the calculations necessary in computing the Laplace transform of a function.

EXAMPLE: Find the Laplace transform of the function f defined by $f(t)=\begin{cases}1-t, if\ 0\le t\le 1\\ f(t-1),\ if\ t>1\end{cases}$. Hence, f represents the periodic extension of the function $1-t$ on $[0,1]$.

SOLUTION: In this case, we illustrate how to use Mathematica to define and graph a piecewise defined function. We begin by defining and graphing the function $f(t)=\begin{cases}1-t, if\ 0\le t\le 1\\ f(t-1),\ if\ t>1\end{cases}$.

```
Clear[f]
f[x_]:=1-x /; 0<=x<=1
f[x_]:=f[x-1] /; x>1
Plot[f[x],{x,0,5},PlotRange->{0,3/2},Ticks->{Automatic,{0,.5,1,1.5}}]
```

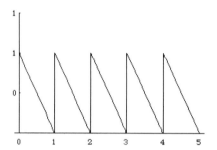

The Laplace transform of the periodic function f with period P is given by

$$L\{f\}(s)=\frac{1}{1-e^{-Ps}}\int_{0}^{P}e^{-st}f(t)dt\ .$$

Therefore, the Laplace transform of f is given by $\dfrac{1}{1-e^{-s}}\displaystyle\int_{0}^{1}e^{-st}f(t)dt$. With the following commands, we compute and simplify $\displaystyle\int_{0}^{1}(1-t)e^{-st}\,dt$.

```
stepone=Integrate[(1-t)Exp[-s t],{t,0,1}]
```

$$\frac{\dfrac{1-s}{s^2}+\dfrac{1}{s}}{s}-\frac{1-s}{s^2}$$

```
steptwo=Together[stepone]
```

```
      s     s
  1 - E   + E   s
  -------------
       s   2
       E   s
```

We then compute $\dfrac{1}{1-e^{-s}}$steptwo and name the result lf. Therefore, the Laplace

transform of f(t) is $\dfrac{1-e^s+se^s}{s^2(e^s-1)}$.

```
lf=1/(1-Exp[-s]) steptwo//Simplify
```

```
        s     s
    1 - E   + E   s
    -------------
          s   2
    (-1 + E ) s
```

■

The following example illustrates how to use the command
InverseLaplaceTransform to compute the inverse Laplace transform of some
functions.

EXAMPLE: Find the inverse Laplace transform of $\dfrac{4}{s^2+16}$.

SOLUTION: After loading the package LaplaceTransform, we use
InverseLaplaceTransform to see that the inverse Laplace transform of $\dfrac{4}{s^2+16}$
is $\sin 4t$.

```
<<Calculus'LaplaceTransform'
InverseLaplaceTransform[4/(s^2+16),s,t]
```

```
    Sin[4 t]
```

■

Solving Ordinary Differential Equations with the Laplace Transform

Laplace transforms can be used to solve a variety of differential equations. Typically, when we use Laplace transforms to solve a differential equation for a function y, we will compute the Laplace transform of each term of the equation, solve the resulting equation for the Laplace transform of y, L{y}, and finally determine y by computing the inverse Laplace transform of L{y}. This step-by-step procedure can be carried out with Mathematica as illustrated in the example below.

EXAMPLE: Let f(t) be defined recursively by $f(t) = \begin{cases} 1, if\ 0 \le t < 1 \\ -1, if\ 1 \le t \le 2 \end{cases}$ and f(t)=f(t–2) if $t \ge 2$. Solve $y'' + 4y' + 20y = f(x)$.

SOLUTION: We begin by defining and graphing f and u where $u(t) = \begin{cases} 1\ if\ t \ge 0 \\ 0\ if\ t < 0 \end{cases}$ and then displaying the resulting graphs as a graphics array.

```
Clear[f,g,u,y1,y2,sol]
f[t_]:=1 /; 0<=t<1
f[t_]:=-1 /; 1<=t<=2
f[t_]:=f[t-2] /; t>2
u[t_]:=1 /; t>=0
u[t_]:=0 /; t<0
plotf=Plot[f[t],{t,0,5},Ticks->{Automatic,{-2,-1,0,1,2}},
        PlotRange->{-2,2},DisplayFunction->Identity];
plotu=Plot[u[t],{t,-2,2},AxesOrigin->{0,0},
        Ticks->{Automatic,{-2,-1,0,1,2}},
        PlotRange->{-2,2},DisplayFunction->Identity];
Show[GraphicsArray[{plotf,plotu}]]
```

We then define lhs to be the left-hand side of the equation $y'' + 4y' + 20y = f(t)$.

```
Clear[y,x,lhs,stepone,steptwo]
lhs=y''[t]+4y'[t]+20y[t]

    20 y[t] + 4 y'[t] + y''[t]
```

Let `ly` denote the Laplace transform of y. Then, the Laplace transform of y' is $s\,\mathtt{ly}-y(0)$, and the Laplace transform of y'' is $s^2\,\mathtt{ly}-s\,y(0)-y'(0)$. These relationships are defined below in `laplacerule`. In the second command, `laplacerule` is applied to `lhs`, and the simplified result is named `stepone`.

```
laplacerule={y[t]->ly,y'[t]->s ly-y[0],y''[t]->s^2 ly-s y[0]-y'[0]};
```

```
stepone=lhs /. laplacerule//Simplify
```

```
                 2
  20 ly + 4 s ly + s  ly - 4 y[0] - s y[0] - y'[0]
```

Let `lr` denote the Laplace transform of the right-hand side of the equation, f(t). We then solve the equation $20\,\mathtt{ly}+4s\,\mathtt{ly}+s^2\,\mathtt{ly}-4y(0)-s\,y(0)-y'(0)=\mathtt{lr}$ for `ly` and name the resulting output `steptwo`.

```
steptwo=Solve[stepone==lr,ly]
```

```
          lr + 4 y[0] + s y[0] + y'[0]
  {{ly -> ----------------------------}}
                        2
                20 + 4 s + s
```

To compute y, we must compute the inverse Laplace transform of `ly` which is explicitly obtained from `steptwo` with `steptwo[[1,1,2]]`. We begin by collecting those terms which contain `lr` and name the resulting output `stepthree`.

```
stepthree=Collect[steptwo[[1,1,2]],lr]
```

```
       lr                4 y[0]            s y[0]             y'[0]
  -------------  +  -------------  +  -------------  +  -------------
             2                2                 2                 2
  20 + 4 s + s      20 + 4 s + s      20 + 4 s + s      20 + 4 s + s
```

Since the first term of `stepthree` is the only term containing `lr`, we drop the first term from `stepthree` and name the result `stepfour`.

```
stepfour=Drop[stepthree,1]
```

```
      4 y[0]            s y[0]             y'[0]
  -------------  +  -------------  +  -------------
             2                2                 2
  20 + 4 s + s      20 + 4 s + s      20 + 4 s + s
```

Completing the square yields $s^2+4s+20=(s+2)^2+16$. Because the inverse Laplace transform of $\dfrac{b}{(s-a)^2+b^2}$ is $e^{at}\sin bt$ and the inverse Laplace transform of $\dfrac{s-a}{(s-a)^2+b^2}$ is $e^{at}\cos bt$, the inverse Laplace transform of

$$\text{stepfour} = \frac{4y(0)+sy(0)+y'(0)}{s^2+4s+20} = y(0)\frac{s+2}{(s+2)^2+4^2}+\frac{y'(0)+2y(0)}{4}\frac{4}{(s+2)^2+4^2}$$

is $y(0)e^{-2t}\cos 4t+\dfrac{y'(0)+2y(0)}{4}e^{-2t}\sin 4t$ which is defined below as $y_1(t)$.

```
y1[t_]=(4 Cos[4t] y[0]+2 Sin[4t] y[0]+Sin[4t] y'[0])/(4 Exp[2t])

   4 Cos[4 t] y[0] + 2 Sin[4 t] y[0] + Sin[4 t] y'[0]
   ---------------------------------------------------
                         2 t
                      4 E
```

To compute the inverse Laplace transform of $\dfrac{1r}{s^2+4s+20}$, we begin by computing

$1r$. Let $u_a(t)=\begin{cases}1\ if\ t\ge a\\0\ if\ t<a\end{cases}$. Then, $u_a(t)=u(t-a)$. The periodic function

$f(t)=\begin{cases}1,\ if\ 0\le t<1\\-1,\ if\ 1\le t\le 2\end{cases}$ and f(t)=f(t–2) if $t\ge 2$ can be written in terms of step functions

as

$$f(x) = u_0(t)-2u_1t+2u_2(t)-2u_3(t)+2u_4(t)-\dots$$
$$= u(t)-2u(t-1)+2u(t-2)-2u(t-3)+2u(t-4)-\dots$$
$$= u(t)+2\sum_{n=1}^{\infty}(-1)^n u(t-n).$$

In general, the Laplace transform of $u_a(t)=u(t-a)$ is $\dfrac{e^{-as}}{s}$ and the Laplace transform

of $f(t-a)u_a(t)=f(t-a)u(t-a)$ is $e^{-as}F(s)$, where F(s) is the Laplace transform of f(t). Then,

$$1r = L\{f\}(s)=\frac{1}{s}-2\frac{e^{-s}}{s}+2\frac{e^{-2s}}{s}-2\frac{e^{-3s}}{s}+\dots$$
$$= \frac{1}{s}(1-2e^{-s}+2e^{-2s}-2e^{-3s}+\dots)$$

and

$$\frac{1r}{s^2+4s+20}=\frac{1}{s(s^2+4s+20)}(1-2e^{-s}+2e^{-2s}-2e^{-3s}+\dots)$$

$$= \frac{1}{s(s^2+4s+20)}+2\sum_{n=1}^{\infty}(-1)^n\frac{e^{-ns}}{s(s^2+4s+20)}.$$

In the following command we extract $\dfrac{1r}{s^2+4s+20}$ from `stepthree` and name the result `stepfive`.

```
stepfive=stepthree[[1]]
```

```
        1r
   -------------
              2
   20 + 4 s + s
```

We then use `Cancel` to obtain the expression $\dfrac{1}{s(s^2+4s+20)}$ and name it `stepsix`.

```
stepsix=Cancel[1/(s 1r) stepfive]
```

```
          1
   -----------------
                  2
   s (20 + 4 s + s )
```

Because the inverse Laplace transform of $\dfrac{1}{s^2+4s+20}=\dfrac{1}{4}\dfrac{4}{(s+2)^2+4^2}$

is $\dfrac{1}{4}e^{-2t}\sin 4t$, the inverse Laplace transform of $\dfrac{1}{s(s^2+4s+20)}$ is $\displaystyle\int_0^t \dfrac{1}{4}e^{-2\alpha}\sin 4\alpha\, d\alpha$, computed below and defined to be the function g(t).

```
g[t_]=Integrate[1/4Exp[-2a]Sin[4a],{a,0,t}]
```

```
        -2 Cos[4 t]    Sin[4 t]
        -----------  - --------
            2 t           2 t
    1       E             E
    -- + ----------------------
    20            40
```

Then, the inverse Laplace transform of $2(-1)^n\dfrac{e^{-ns}}{s(s^2+4s+20)}$

is $2(-1)^n g(t-n)u(t-n)$ and the inverse Laplace transform of

$\dfrac{1}{s(s^2+4s+20)}+2\displaystyle\sum_{n=1}^{\infty}(-1)^n\dfrac{e^{-ns}}{s(s^2+4s+20)}$ is $y_2(t)=g(t)+2\displaystyle\sum_{n=1}^{\infty}(-1)^n g(t-n)u(t-n)$. It then follows that

$$y(t) = y_1(t) + y_2(t)$$

$$= y(0)e^{-2t}\cos 4t + \frac{y'(0) + 2y(0)}{4}e^{-2t}\sin 4t + g(t) + 2\sum_{n=1}^{\infty}(-1)^n g(t-n)u(t-n),$$

where $g(t) = \dfrac{1}{20} - \dfrac{1}{20}e^{-2t}\cos 4t - \dfrac{1}{40}e^{-2t}\sin 4t$.

To graph the solution for various initial conditions on the interval [0,5], we define $y_2(t) = g(t) + 2\sum_{n=1}^{5}(-1)^n g(t-n)u(t-n)$, $\mathtt{sol}$, and $\mathtt{inits}$. Note that we can graph the solution for various initial conditions on the interval [0,m] by defining $y_2(t) = g(t) + 2\sum_{n=1}^{m}(-1)^n g(t-n)u(t-n)$.

```
y2[t_]:=g[t]+2 Sum[(-1)^n*g[t-n]u[t-n],{n,1,5}]
sol[t_]:=y1[t]+y2[t]
inits={-1/2,0,1/2};
```

We then create a table of graphs of $\mathtt{sol[t]}$ on the interval [0,5] corresponding to replacing y(0) and y'(0) by the values −1/2, 0, and 1/2 and then displaying the resulting graphics array.

```
graphs=Table[Plot[sol[t] /. {y[0]->inits[[i]],
               y'[0]->inits[[j]]},{t,0,5},DisplayFunction->Identity],
               {i,1,3},{j,1,3}]//Flatten;
array=Partition[graphs,3];
Show[GraphicsArray[array]]
```

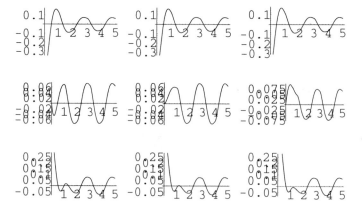

■

Application: The Convolution Theorem

In many cases, we are required to determine the inverse Laplace transform of a product of two functions. Just as in differential and integral calculus, when the derivative and integral of a product of two functions did not produce the product of the derivatives and integrals, respectively, neither did the inverse Laplace transform of the product yield the product of the inverse Laplace transforms. The Convolution Theorem tells us how to compute the inverse Laplace transform of a product of two functions.

> **The Convolution Theorem:** Suppose that f(t) and g(t) are piecewise continuous on $[0, +\infty)$ and both are of exponential order. Further, suppose that the Laplace transform of f(t) is F(s) and that of g(t) is G(s). Then,
>
> $$L^{-1}\{F(s)G(s)\} = L^{-1}\{L\{(f * g)(t)\}\} = (f * g)(t) = \int_0^t f(t - v)g(v)dv.$$

Note that $(f * g)(t) = \int_0^t f(t - v)g(v)dv$ is called the **convolution integral**.

We show how Mathematica can be used to apply the Convolution Theorem in the example below.

EXAMPLE: The differential equation used to determine the charge q(t) on the capacitor in an L-R-C circuit is $\bar{L}\dfrac{d^2q}{dt^2} + R\dfrac{dq}{dt} + \dfrac{1}{C}q = v(t), q(0) = 0, q'(0) = 0$, where $\bar{L}$ denotes inductance (The bar is used so that it will not be confused with the notation for Laplace transforms.), $\dfrac{dq}{dt} = i$, i(t) current, R resistance, C capacitance, and v(t) voltage supply. Since $\dfrac{dq}{dt} = i$, this differential equation can be represented

as $\bar{L}\dfrac{di}{dt} + Ri + \dfrac{1}{C}\displaystyle\int_0^t i(u)du = v(t)$. Note also that the initial condition q(0)=0 is satisfied

since $q(0) = \dfrac{1}{C}\displaystyle\int_0^0 i(u)du = 0$. The condition $q'(0) = 0$ is replaced by i(0)=0. (a) Solve this

integrodifferential equation, an equation which involves a derivative as well as an integral of the unknown function, by using the Convolution Theorem. (b) Consider this example with constant values $\bar{L} = C = R = 1$ and $v(t) = \begin{cases} \sin(t), & \text{if } 0 \le t \le \pi/2 \\ 0, & \text{if } t > \pi/2 \end{cases}$. Determine i(t) and graph the solution.

SOLUTION: We proceed as in the case of a differential equation by taking the Laplace transform of both sides of the equation. The Convolution Theorem is used in determining the Laplace transform of the integral as follows:

$$L\left\{\int_0^t i(u)\,du\right\} = L\{(1*i(t))(t)\} = L\{1\}L\{i(t)\} = \frac{I(s)}{s},$$

where I(s) denotes the Laplace transform of i(t). Therefore, application of the Laplace transform yields

$$\bar{L}sI(s) - si(0) + RI(s) + \frac{1}{C}\frac{I(s)}{s} = V(s),$$

where V(s) denotes the Laplace transform of v(t). Since i(0)=0, we have $\bar{L}sI(s) + RI(s) + \frac{1}{C}\frac{I(s)}{s} = V(s)$. Simplifying and solving for I(s) results in $I(s) = \dfrac{V(s)}{\bar{L}Cs^2 + RCs + 1}$ and, hence,

$$i(t) = L^{-1}\left\{\frac{V(s)}{\bar{L}Cs^2 + RCs + 1}\right\}.$$

For (b), we note that $v(t) = \begin{cases} \sin(t), & if\ 0 \le t \le \pi/2 \\ 0, & if\ t > \pi/2 \end{cases}$ can be written as $v(t) = \sin(t)u\left(\dfrac{\pi}{2} - t\right)$, where $u(t) = \begin{cases} 1\ if\ t \ge 0 \\ 0\ if\ t < 0 \end{cases}$. We first define the unit step function, u, and then define and plot the forcing function f on the interval [0,π].

```
Clear[u,f]
<<Calculus'LaplaceTransform'
u[t_,a_]:=0 /; t<a
u[t_,a_]:=1 /; t>=a
f[t_]:=Sin[t]*(u[t,0]-u[t,Pi/2])
p1=Plot[f[t],{t,0,Pi}]
```

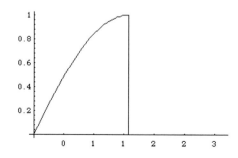

Next, we define 1pt and invlpt. lpt[g[t],a] computes $L\{g(t)u(t-a)\} = e^{-as}L\{g(t+a)\}$, the Laplace transform of functions involving unit step functions, while invlpt[G[s],a] computes $L^{-1}\{e^{-as}G(s)\} = g(t-a)u(t-a)$, the inverse Laplace transform of functions involving exponential functions.

```
lpt[g_,a_]:=Exp[-a s]*LaplaceTransform[g /.t->t+a,t,s]
invlpt[lpg_,a_]:=(InverseLaplaceTransform[lpg,s,t]/.t->t-a)*u[t,a]
```

We, therefore, compute the Laplace transform of v(t) using a combination of LaplaceTransform and lpt (since g[1,t]=1). We call this result capv.

```
capv=LaplaceTransform[Sin[t],t,s]-lpt[Sin[t],Pi/2]
```

```
    1                 s
  ------  -  -------------------
    2       (Pi s)/2      2
  1 + s     E          (1 + s )
```

Using the general formula obtained for the Laplace transform of i(t), we note that the denominator of this expression is given by $s^2 + s + 1$, which is entered as denom below. Hence, the Laplace transform of i, called capi, is given below by the ratio capv/denom.

```
denom=s^2+s+1;
capi=capv/denom;
sol1=Simplify[capi]
```

```
          (Pi s)/2
         E          - s
  ----------------------------------
  (Pi s)/2        2    3    4
  E         (1 + s + 2 s + s + s )
```

Simplifying the expression given above in sol1, we notice that one component involves $e^{-\pi s/2}$. Hence, we employ the user-defined function invlpt to determine the inverse Laplace transform of this part of sol1 and use InverseLaplaceTransform to determine that of the rest of it. The solution which results is defined as i.

```
i[t_]=InverseLaplaceTransform[1/(1+s+2s^2+s^3+s^4),s,t]-
      invlpt[s/(1+s+2s^2+s^3+s^4),Pi/2]
```

```
                    Sqrt[3] t          Sqrt[3] t
                Cos[---------]    Sin[---------]
                        2                2
  -Cos[t] +  --------------  + --------------  -
                  t/2                  t/2
                 E             Sqrt[3] E
```

```
                                          -Pi
                              Sqrt[3] (--- + t)
               (Pi/2 - t)/2              2
          2 E                   Sin[----------------]
                                          2
 (-Cos[t]  - -------------------------------------)
                        Sqrt[3]


              Pi
      u[t, --]
              2
```

This solution is plotted below in p2 and displayed with the forcing function in the plot which follows. Notice the effect that the forcing function has on the solution to the differential equation.

```
p2=Plot[i[t],{t,0,10},DisplayFunction->Identity];
Show[p1,p2,PlotRange->All,DisplayFunction->$DisplayFunction]
```

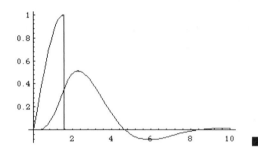

Application: The Dirac Delta Function

Let δ denote the function with the two properties (i) $\delta(t-t_0)=0$ if $t \neq t_0$; and (ii) $\int_{-\infty}^{+\infty}\delta(t-t_0)dt=1$. The function $\delta(t-t_0)$ is known as the **Dirac delta function** and is quite useful in the definition of impulse forcing functions which arise in some differential equations. The Laplace transform of $\delta(t-t_0)$ is $L\{\delta(t-t_0)\}=e^{-st_0}$. Mathematica contains a definition of the Dirac delta function, `DiracDelta`, which is contained in the package **DiracDelta** located in the **Calculus** folder (or directory). We illustrate how problems involving the Dirac delta function can be solved through the use of Mathematica and Laplace transforms in the following example.

EXAMPLE: Find the solution to the initial value problem $x''+x'+x=\delta(t)+u(t-2\pi)$, $x(0)=0$ and $x'(0)=0$, where $u(t)=\begin{cases}1 \text{ if } t \geq 0 \\ 0 \text{ if } t < 0\end{cases}$.

SOLUTION: After loading the packages LaplaceTransform and DiracDelta, we define eq to be the left-hand side of the equation $x'' + x' + x = \delta(t) + u(t-2\pi)$ and then use LaplaceTransform to compute the Laplace transform of eq, naming the resulting output leq. Note that the symbol LaplaceTransform[x[t],t,s] represents the Laplace transform of x. We then apply the initial conditions x(0)=0 and $x'(0) = 0$, to leq and name the resulting output ics.

```
<<Calculus'LaplaceTransform'
<<Calculus'DiracDelta'
Clear[x,eq]
eq=x''[t]+x'[t]+x[t];
leq=LaplaceTransform[eq,t,s]
```

```
   LaplaceTransform[x[t], t, s] + s LaplaceTransform[x[t], t, s] +

     2
    s  LaplaceTransform[x[t], t, s] - x[0] - s x[0] - x'[0]
```

```
ics=leq /. {x[0]->0,x'[0]->0}
```

```
   LaplaceTransform[x[t], t, s] + s LaplaceTransform[x[t], t, s] +

     2
    s  LaplaceTransform[x[t], t, s]
```

In addition to containing the command DiracDelta, the package **DiracDelta** also contains the command UnitStep, which represents the unit step function: $\text{UnitStep[t]} = \begin{cases} 1 \text{ if } t \geq 0 \\ 0 \text{ if } t < 0 \end{cases}$. In rhs, we use LaplaceTransform, DiracDelta, and UnitStep to compute the Laplace transform of the right-hand side of the equation $x'' + x' + x = \delta(t) + u(t-2\pi)$.

```
rhs=LaplaceTransform[DiracDelta[t]-UnitStep[t-2Pi],t,s]
```

```
          1
    1 - ---------
         2 Pi s
        E       s
```

Next, we use Solve to solve the equation ics=rhs for the Laplace transform of x. The expression for the Laplace transform is extracted from soln with soln[[1,1,2]].

```
soln=Solve[ics==rhs,LaplaceTransform[x[t],t,s]]
```

```
                                          2 Pi s
                                     1 - E      s
    {{LaplaceTransform[x[t], t, s] -> -(-------------------)}}
                                     2 Pi s          2
                                    E      s (1 + s + s )
```

To find x, we must compute the inverse Laplace transform of the Laplace transform of x obtained above. Below, we use `InverseLaplaceTransform` to compute the inverse Laplace transform of `soln[[1,1,2]]` and name the resulting function x.

```
x[t_]=InverseLaplaceTransform[soln[[1,1,2]],s,t]
```

```
          Sqrt[3] t
  2 Sin[---------]
              2
  ---------------- - UnitStep[-2 Pi + t] +
           t/2
    Sqrt[3] E

      Pi - t/2      Sqrt[3] (-2 Pi + t)
    2 E          Sin[-------------------] UnitStep[-2 Pi + t]
                            2
  ------------------------------------------------------- +
                      Sqrt[3]

     Pi - t/2      Sqrt[3] (-2 Pi + t)
    (E           Cos[-------------------] -
                            2

      Pi - t/2      Sqrt[3] (-2 Pi + t)
      E          Sin[-------------------]
                            2
  ---------------------------------) UnitStep[-2 Pi + t]
              Sqrt[3]
```

Finally, we use `Plot` to graph the solution on the interval $[0, 8\pi]$.

```
Plot[x[t],{t,0,8Pi}]
```

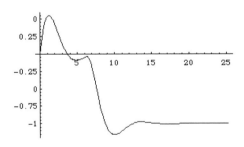

∎

6.5 Systems of Ordinary Differential Equations

Homogeneous Linear Systems with Constant Coefficients

Let

$$\mathbf{A} = \begin{pmatrix} a_{11} & a_{12} & \cdots & a_{1n} \\ a_{21} & a_{22} & \cdots & a_{2n} \\ \vdots & \vdots & \ddots & \vdots \\ a_{n1} & a_{n2} & \cdots & a_{nn} \end{pmatrix}$$

be an n × n real matrix and let $\{\lambda_k\}_{k=1}^n$ be the eigenvalues and $\{\mathbf{v}_k\}_{k=1}^n$ the corresponding eigenvectors of $\mathbf{A}$. The general solution of the system $\mathbf{X}'(t) = \mathbf{A}\mathbf{X}(t)$ is determined by the eigenvalues of A. If the eigenvalues $\{\lambda_k\}_{k=1}^n$ are distinct and real, then a general solution of $\mathbf{X}'(t) = \mathbf{A}\mathbf{X}(t)$ is

$$\mathbf{X}(t) = c_1\mathbf{v}_1 e^{\lambda_1 t} + c_2\mathbf{v}_2 e^{\lambda_2 t} + \ldots + c_n\mathbf{v}_n e^{\lambda_n t} = \sum_{i=1}^n c_i\mathbf{v}_i e^{\lambda_i t}.$$

If the eigenvalues $\{\lambda_k = \alpha_k + \beta_k i\}_{k=1}^m$, where $\beta_k \neq 0$, are complex and the corresponding eigenvectors $\{\mathbf{v}_k\}_{k=1}^n$ are distinct, then a general solution of $\mathbf{X}'(t) = \mathbf{A}\mathbf{X}(t)$ is

$$\mathbf{X}(t) = c_1\mathbf{w}_{11} e^{\lambda_1 t} + c_2\mathbf{w}_{12} e^{\lambda_1 t} + c_3\mathbf{w}_{21} e^{\lambda_2 t} + c_4\mathbf{w}_{22} e^{\lambda_2 t} + \ldots + c_{2m-1}\mathbf{w}_{m1} e^{\lambda_m t} +$$
$$c_{2m}\mathbf{w}_{m2} e^{\lambda_m t} + c_{2m+1}\mathbf{v}_{2m+1} e^{\lambda_{2m+1} t} + \ldots + c_n\mathbf{v}_n e^{\lambda_n t}, \text{ where}$$

$$\mathbf{w}_{i1} = \frac{1}{2}\left[\mathbf{v}_i + \overline{\mathbf{v}_i}\right]\cos(\beta_i t) + \frac{i}{2}\left[\mathbf{v}_i - \overline{\mathbf{v}_i}\right]\sin(\beta_i t) \text{ and}$$

$\mathbf{w}_{i2} = \frac{i}{2}\left[\mathbf{v}_i - \overline{\mathbf{v}_i}\right]\cos(\beta_i t) - \frac{1}{2}\left[\mathbf{v}_i + \overline{\mathbf{v}_i}\right]\sin(\beta_i t)$. Mathematica can solve many systems of differential equations.

In order to solve the 2 × 2 system with constant coefficients,

$$\begin{cases} \dfrac{dx}{dt} = ax + by \\ \dfrac{dy}{dt} = cx + dy \end{cases}$$

we enter the command

```
DSolve[{x'[t]==a x[t]+b y[t],y'[t]==c x[t]+d y[t]},{x[t],y[t]},t]
```

We illustrate how systems can be solved with Mathematica through the use of eigenvalues as well as DSolve in the examples below.

EXAMPLE: Solve the system of equations $\begin{cases} \dfrac{dx}{dt} = -y \\ \dfrac{dy}{dt} = -x \end{cases}$.

SOLUTION: We begin by finding the eigenvalues and associated eigenvectors of the matrix of coefficients $A = \begin{pmatrix} 0 & -1 \\ -1 & 0 \end{pmatrix}$ with Eigensystem. This gives us $\lambda_1 = -1$ and $\lambda_2 = 1$. An eigenvector corresponding to $\lambda_1 = -1$ is given by $v_1 = \begin{pmatrix} 1 \\ 1 \end{pmatrix}$, while that corresponding to $\lambda_2 = 1$ is $v_2 = \begin{pmatrix} 1 \\ -1 \end{pmatrix}$. Therefore, a general solution is $\begin{pmatrix} x \\ y \end{pmatrix} = c_1 \begin{pmatrix} 1 \\ 1 \end{pmatrix} e^{-t} + c_2 \begin{pmatrix} 1 \\ -1 \end{pmatrix} e^{t}$.

```
Eigensystem[{{0,-1},{-1,0}}]

        {{-1, 1}, {{1, 1}, {-1, 1}}}
```

We can graph the solutions for various values of the constants c_1 and c_2. Notice that x and y both depend on the variable t where x(t) represents the x-coordinate at a particular time t and y(t) represents the y-coordinate at a particular time t. Hence, we can plot these solutions parametrically in the xy-plane. (This type of graph is known as the **phase plane** of the system of equations.) First, the solutions are defined as x and y using the formula obtained above. Several members of the family of solutions are created in fncarray by substituting the values –6, –4, –2, 0, 2, 4, and 6 for the constants c1 and c2. Note that fncarray is a $7 \times 7 \times 2$. We then use Flatten to remove all but the innermost set of braces naming the result tograph. tograph consists of 49 sets of functions which are then plotted with ParametricPlot in graphone and displayed in an abbreviated form with Short.

```
x[t_]:=c1 Exp[-t]+c2 Exp[t]
y[t_]:=c1 Exp[-t]- c2 Exp[t]
fncarray=Table[{x[t],y[t]}/.{c1->i,c2->j},{i,-6,6,2},{j,-6,6,2}];
tograph=Flatten[fncarray,1];
Short[tograph]
```

```
graphone=ParametricPlot[Evaluate[tograph],{t,-2,2},
     PlotRange->{{-15,15},{-15,15}}]
```

```
      -6        t  -6          t                        6
 {{-- - 6 E ,  -- + 6 E }, <<47>>, {-- + <<1>>, <<1>>}}
       t            t                  t
     E            E                                    E
```

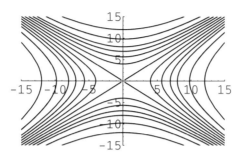

In order to determine the direction associated with these solutions, we consider the direction field (i.e., the collection of vectors which represent the tangent line at points on the solutions. Note that the slope of these tangent lines is given by

$$\frac{dy}{dx} = \frac{\dfrac{dy}{dt}}{\dfrac{dx}{dt}} = \frac{cx+dy}{ax+by}$$

at each point (x,y)). The direction fields are graphed with the command `PlotVectorField` located in the **PlotField** package contained in the **Graphics** folder (or directory). Finally, the direction field is displayed with the solutions to illustrate the associated motion. Notice that when the associated direction field is plotted, solutions near the line in the direction of the eigenvector corresponding the positive eigenvalue move away from the equilibrium point. On the other hand, solutions near the line in the direction of the eigenvector corresponding to the negative eigenvalue move towards the equilibrium point.

```
<<Graphics'PlotField'
graphtwo=PlotVectorField[{-y,-x},{x,-15,15},{y,-15,15},
     DisplayFunction->Identity];
Show[graphone,graphtwo]
```

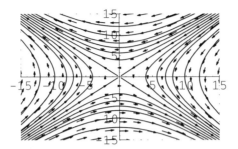

■

> **EXAMPLE:** Find a general solution of the system of equations $\begin{cases} \dfrac{dx}{dt} = y \\ \dfrac{dy}{dt} = -x \end{cases}$.

SOLUTION: The matrix of coefficients is defined in `mat` below, and the eigenvalues and eigenvectors determined with `Eigensystem`. The result means that the eigenvalues are $\lambda = \pm i$ and the eigenvectors are $\mathbf{v}_1 = \begin{pmatrix} i \\ 1 \end{pmatrix}$ and $\mathbf{v}_2 = \begin{pmatrix} -i \\ 1 \end{pmatrix}$. Hence, the solution in given in x and y (in terms of sines and cosines). Note that the exponential function is not included because the eigenvalues are imaginary with no real part. A collection of solutions is created in `fncarray` by substituting values of - 6, - 4, - 2, 0, 2, 4, and 6 for the arbitrary constants `c1` and `c2`. A shortened list of these solutions is then displayed with `Short`.

```
mat={{0,1},{-1,0}};
Eigensystem[mat]

    {{-I, I}, {{I, 1}, {-I, 1}}}

x[t_]:=-c1 Sin[t]+c2 Cos[t]
y[t_]:=c1 Cos[t]+c2 Sin[t]
fncarray=Table[{x[t],y[t]}/.{c1->i,c2->j},{i,-6,6,2},{j,-6,6,2}];
tograph=Flatten[fncarray,1];
Short[tograph]

    {{-6 Cos[t] + 6 Sin[t], -6 <<1>> + <<1>>}, <<48>>}
```

`ParametricPlot` is used to graph the phase plane in `graphthree`. In order to determine the direction associated with the motion of these curves as t increases, we plot the direction field in `graphdf`. This vector is then displayed with the family of solutions to show that the motion is clockwise. Because these solutions remain at a constant distance from the origin, we say that the point (0,0) is a **center**.

```
graphthree=ParametricPlot[Evaluate[tograph],{t,-1,1},
      PlotRange->{{-10,10},{-10,10}},AspectRatio->1,
      DisplayFunction->Identity];
<<Graphics`PlotField`
graphdf=PlotVectorField[{y,-x},{x,-10,10},{y,-10,10},
      DisplayFunction->Identity];
Show[graphthree,graphdf,DisplayFunction->$DisplayFunction]
```

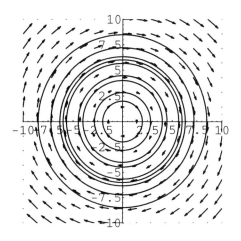

We now illustrate how DSolve can be used to solve systems of differential equations.

EXAMPLE: Find a general solution of $\begin{cases} x' = -5x + 3y \\ y' = -2x - 10 \end{cases}$.

SOLUTION: After clearing all prior definitions of x, y, and sol, we use DSolve to find a general solution of $\begin{cases} x' = -5x + 3y \\ y' = -2x - 10 \end{cases}$, naming the resulting output sol. The expressions for x(t) and y(t) are extracted from sol with sol[[1,1,2]] and sol[[1,2,2]], respectively.

```
Clear[x,y,sol]
sol=DSolve[{x'[t]==-5x[t]+3y[t],y'[t]==-2x[t]-10y[t]},{x[t],y[t]},t]

              -2      3          -3      3
   {{x[t] -> (---- + ----) C[1] + (---- + ----) C[2],
              8 t    7 t          8 t    7 t
              E      E            E      E


             2      2          3      2
   y[t] -> (---- - ----) C[1] + (---- - ----) C[2]}}
            8 t    7 t          8 t    7 t
            E      E            E      E
```

To graph the solution for various values of C[1] and C[2], we define funs to be the table of functions obtained by replacing each occurrence of C[1] and C[2] in {sol[[1,1,2]],sol[[1,2,2]]}, corresponding to the pair of functions $(x(t), y(t))$, by i and j for i=−6, −3, 0, 3, and 6 and j=−6, −3, 0, 3, and 6. Note that funs is a 5×5×2 array. In order to graph this list of functions, with ParametricPlot, we must convert funs to an array consisting of ordered pairs of functions, which we accomplish with Flatten, naming the resulting output toplot. The list toplot consists of 25 pairs of functions which are then graphed with ParametricPlot in pptwo. We also use the command PlotVectorField to graph the associated direction fields in graph4. Show is used to display both pptwo and graph4 together.

```
funs=Table[{sol[[1,1,2]],sol[[1,2,2]]} /.
      {C[1]->i,C[2]->j},{i,-6,6,3},{j,-6,6,3}];
toplot=Flatten[funs,1];
Length[toplot]
```

```
     25
```

```
<<Graphics`PlotField`
pptwo=ParametricPlot[Evaluate[toplot],{t,-2,1},
      Compiled->False,PlotRange->{{-10,10},{-10,10}},
      DisplayFunction->Identity];
graph4=PlotVectorField[{-5x+3y,-2x-10y},{x,-10,10},{y,-10,10},
      DisplayFunction->Identity];
Show[pptwo,graph4,DisplayFunction->$DisplayFunction]
```

Variation of Parameters

We now consider nonhomogeneous systems of equations of the form $X'=AX+F(t)$. Recall that the solution to the corresponding homogeneous system of equations $X'=AX$ can be represented in terms of the fundamental matrix $\Phi(t)$ and the n x 1 constant vector C with $X=\Phi(t)C$. Hence, by assuming a particular solution to the nonhomogeneous system of the form $X_p=\Phi(t)U(t)$, where $U(t)$ is a vector of the form

$$\mathbf{U}(t) = \begin{pmatrix} u_1(t) \\ u_2(t) \\ \vdots \\ u_n(t) \end{pmatrix},$$

we find that a particular solution is given by $\mathbf{X}_p = \Phi(t)\int \Phi^{-1}(t)\mathbf{F}(t)dt$. Hence a general solution is determined with

$$\mathbf{X} = \Phi(t)\mathbf{C} + \Phi(t)\int \Phi^{-1}(t)\mathbf{F}(t)dt.$$

In addition to determining the solution of differential equations, Mathematica can also be used to plot the solutions. In the following example, we illustrate how this is accomplished.

EXAMPLE: Solve $\begin{cases} x' - y = e^{-t} \\ y' + 5x + 2y = \sin(3t) \end{cases}$ subject to the initial conditions $x(0) = x_0$ and

$y(0) = y_0$. Graph the solution for various initial conditions.

SOLUTION: We use `DSolve` to solve the equation $\begin{cases} x' - y = e^{-t} \\ y' + 5x + 2y = \sin(3t) \end{cases}$ subject to

the initial conditions $x(0) = x_0$ and $y(0) = y_0$, naming the resulting output `sol`. The expressions for x(t) and y(t) are extracted from `sol` with `sol[[1,1,2]]` and `sol[[1,2,2]]`, respectively.

```
Clear[x,y,x0,y0,t,sol]
sol=DSolve[{x'[t]-y[t]==Exp[-t],y'[t]+5x[t]+2y[t]==Sin[3t],
      y[0]==y0,x[0]==x0},{x[t],y[t]},t]


              1         5      I    (-1 - 2 I) t
  {{x[t] -> ---- + (--- + ---) E
             t       104    104
           4 E

       (7 I + (11 + 3 I) x0 + (1 + 5 I) y0) +

          1      5 I    (-1 + 2 I) t
     (-(---)  - ---) E
        104     104

                                    3 Cos[3 t]    Sin[3 t]
     (7 + (3 + 11 I) x0 + (5 + I) y0) - ---------- - --------,
                                            26          13
```

```
              -5        3     11 I   (-1 - 2 I) t
    y[t] -> ----  + (-(---) - ----) E
              t         104    104
         4 E


    (7 I + (11 + 3 I) x0 + (1 + 5 I) y0) +


    11    3 I   (-1 + 2 I) t
   (--- + ---) E                    (7 + (3 + 11 I) x0 + (5 + I) y0) -
    104   104


    3 Cos[3 t]   9 Sin[3 t]
    ---------- + ----------}}
        13           26
```

To see that the expressions obtained above are real, we proceed by defining x and y.

```
Clear[x,y]
x[t_,x0_,y0_]=sol[[1,1,2]];
y[t_,x0_,y0_]=sol[[1,2,2]];
```

Note that when we evaluate x and y, as illustrated below, an imaginary component, although 0, is given in the resulting output.

```
{x[.4,.5,.5],y[.5,.5,.5]}

    {0.788798 + 0. I, -0.751764 + 0. I}
```

These 0-valued imaginary components are removed with Chop.

```
Chop[{x[.4,.5,.5],y[.5,.5,.5]}]

    {0.788798, -0.751764}
```

We will graph the solution for the initial conditions given in orderedpairs, below.

```
orderedpairs=Flatten[Table[{i,j},{i,-1,1,2/3},{j,-1,1,2/3}],1]

                     1             1             1           1       1
    {{-1, -1}, {-1, -(-)}, {-1, -}, {-1, 1}, {-(-), -1}, {-(-), -(-)},
                     3             3             3           3       3


       1   1       1        1        1        1       1  1       1
    {-(-), -}, {-(-), 1}, {-, -1}, {-, -(-)}, {-, -}, {-, 1},
       3   3       3        3        3        3       3  3       3


                     1             1
    {1, -1}, {1, -(-)}, {1, -}, {1, 1}}
                     3             3
```

Next, we define `solgraph`, which given a and b, graphs the parametric equations `Chop[{x[t,a,b],y[t,a,b]}]` for $0 \le t \le 7$. This corresponds to graphing the solution of the equation $\begin{cases} x' - y = e^{-t} \\ y' + 5x + 2y = \sin(3t) \end{cases}$ subject to the initial conditions $x(0) = a$ and $y(0) = b$. Note that the results of `solgraph` are not displayed. We then use `Map` to compute `solgraph` for each of the ordered pairs in `orderedpairs`. The resulting set of sixteen graphs is partitioned into four-graph subsets with `Partition`, naming the resulting array `toshow`. The array `toshow` is displayed with `Show` and `GraphicsArray`.

```
solgraph[{a_,b_}]:=
        ParametricPlot[Chop[{x[t,a,b],y[t,a,b]}],
        {t,0,7},Ticks->None,Compiled->False,DisplayFunction->Identity]
graphs=Map[solgraph,orderedpairs];
toshow=Partition[graphs,4];
Show[GraphicsArray[toshow]]
```

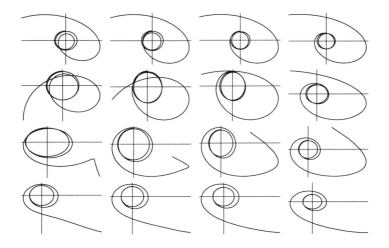

■

Nonlinear Systems, Linearization, and Classification of Equilibrium Points

An **equilibrium point** (x_0, y_0) of the system of differential equations

$$\begin{cases} \dfrac{dx}{dt} = f(x,y) \\ \dfrac{dy}{dt} = g(x,y) \end{cases}$$

is a point which satisfies $\begin{cases} f(x_0, y_0) = 0 \\ g(x_0, y_0) = 0 \end{cases}$. For the 2×2 system of linear differential equations

$x' = Ax$, in which the matrix of coefficients A has eigenvalues λ_1 and λ_2, the equilibrium point (0,0) is classified according to the following criteria.

Eigenvalues:	Classification:
Real: $\lambda_1 \leq \lambda_2 < 0$	Stable Node
Real: $\lambda_1 < 0 < \lambda_2$	Saddle
Real: $0 < \lambda_1 \leq \lambda_2$	Unstable Node
Complex: $\lambda_1 = \overline{\lambda_2} = \alpha + \beta i, \beta \neq 0, \alpha < 0$	Stable Spiral
Complex: $\lambda_1 = \overline{\lambda_2} = \alpha + \beta i, \beta \neq 0, \alpha > 0$	Unstable Spiral
Complex: $\lambda_1 = \overline{\lambda_2} = \alpha + \beta i, \beta \neq 0, \alpha = 0$	Center

The general form of the autonomous system (in which there is no dependence on t) is

$$\begin{cases} \dfrac{dx}{dt} = f(x, y) \\ \dfrac{dy}{dt} = g(x, y) \end{cases}.$$

Approximate solutions to problems of this type can be found by considering the linearized system about each equilibrium point (x_0, y_0), which in this case satisfy $\{f(x_0, y_0) = 0, g(x_0, y_0) = 0\}$. This linearized system is given by

$$\begin{cases} \dfrac{dx}{dt} = f_x(x_0, y_0)x + f_y(x_0, y_0)y + d_1 \\ \dfrac{dy}{dt} = g_x(x_0, y_0)x + g_y(x_0, y_0)y + d_2 \end{cases},$$

where $f_x(x_0, y_0) = \dfrac{\partial f}{\partial x}(x_0, y_0)$, $f_y(x_0, y_0) = \dfrac{\partial f}{\partial y}(x_0, y_0)$, $g_x(x_0, y_0) = \dfrac{\partial g}{\partial x}(x_0, y_0)$, $g_y(x_0, y_0) = \dfrac{\partial g}{\partial y}(x_0, y_0)$, and d_1, d_2 are constants.

Note that

$$J(x,y) = \begin{pmatrix} f_x(x,y) & f_y(x,y) \\ g_x(x,y) & g_y(x,y) \end{pmatrix}$$

is known as the **Jacobian matrix**. Hence, the linearized system can be written as

$$\begin{pmatrix} \dfrac{dx}{dt} \\ \dfrac{dy}{dt} \end{pmatrix} = \begin{pmatrix} f_x(x_0,y_0) & f_y(x_0,y_0) \\ g_x(x_0,y_0) & g_y(x_0,y_0) \end{pmatrix}\begin{pmatrix} x-x_0 \\ y-y_0 \end{pmatrix} = J(x_0,y_0)\begin{pmatrix} x-x_0 \\ y-y_0 \end{pmatrix}.$$

Numerical Solutions of Systems of Ordinary Differential Equations

Mathematica's `NDSolve` command can be used to approximate the solution of many nonlinear systems of differential equations. The correct number of initial conditions must be supplied within the `NDSolve` command.

This command is entered in the form

```
NDSolve[{desys,ics},funs,{var,varmin,varmax}],
```

where the equations `desys` subject to the initial conditions `ics` are solved for the functions `funs` and the solution is requested to be valid over the interval [`varmin`,`varmax`]. Each component of the result is given in the form

```
InterpolatingFunction[{varmin,varmax},<>].
```

In the following example, we illustrate the use of this command to solve a first-order system of nonlinear differential equations.

Application: Predator—Prey

EXAMPLE: The **Lotka-Volterra system** (Predator-Prey model) is the system

$$\begin{cases} x' = a_1 x - a_2 x y \\ y' = -b_1 y + b_2 x y' \end{cases}$$

where a_1, a_2, b_1, and b_2 are constants. Find and classify the equilibrium points of the Lotka-Volterra equations.

SOLUTION: We begin by defining `eqonerhs` and `eqtworhs` to be $a_1 x - a_2 x y$ and $-b_1 y + b_2 x y$, respectively, and then solving the system of equations $\begin{cases} a_1 x - a_2 x y = 0 \\ -b_1 y + b_2 x y = 0 \end{cases}$ for x and y to locate the equilibrium points.

```
Clear[a,b,x,y]
eqonerhs=a[1]x-a[2]x y;
eqtworhs=-b[1]y+b[2]x y;
cps=Solve[{eqonerhs==0,eqtworhs==0},{x,y}]
```

$$\left\{\{x \to 0,\ y \to 0\},\ \left\{x \to \frac{b[1]}{b[2]},\ y \to \frac{a[1]}{a[2]}\right\}\right\}$$

To classify the equilibrium points, we first define `linmatrix` to be the matrix

$$\begin{pmatrix} \dfrac{d}{dx}\left(a_1 x - a_2 x y\right) & \dfrac{d}{dy}\left(a_1 x - a_2 x y\right) \\[2ex] \dfrac{d}{dx}\left(-b_1 y + b_2 x y\right) & \dfrac{d}{dy}\left(-b_1 y + b_2 x y\right) \end{pmatrix}$$

and display `linmatrix` in `MatrixForm`.

```
linmatrix={{D[eqonerhs,x],D[eqonerhs,y]},{D[eqtworhs,x],D[eqtworhs,y]}};
MatrixForm[linmatrix]
```

```
a[1] - y a[2]    -(x a[2])
y b[2]           -b[1] + x b[2]
```

We then compute the value of `linmatrix` when $x = \dfrac{b_1}{b_2}$ and $y = \dfrac{a_1}{a_2}$:

```
linmatrix /. cps[[2]] // MatrixForm
```

$$\begin{pmatrix} 0 & -\left(\dfrac{a[2]\ b[1]}{b[2]}\right) \\[2ex] \dfrac{a[1]\ b[2]}{a[2]} & 0 \end{pmatrix}$$

and then compute the eigenvalues. Since the eigenvalues are complex conjugates with the real part equal to 0, we conclude that the equilibrium point $\left(\dfrac{b_1}{b_2}, \dfrac{a_1}{a_2}\right)$ is a center.

```
linmatrix /. cps[[2]] // Eigenvalues
```

```
{-I Sqrt[a[1]] Sqrt[b[1]], I Sqrt[a[1]] Sqrt[b[1]]}
```

Similarly we compute the value of linmatrix when x=0 and y=0:

```
linmatrix /. cps[[1]] // MatrixForm
```

```
a[1]      0
0        -b[1]
```

and then compute the eigenvalues. Since the eigenvalues are real and have opposite signs, we conclude that the equilibrium point (0,0) is a saddle.

```
linmatrix /. cps[[1]] // Eigenvalues
```

```
{a[1], -b[1]}
```

Unsuccessfully, we attempt to use DSolve to solve the system in the special case when $a_1=2$, $a_2=1$, $b_1=3$, and $b_2=1$:

```
Clear[x,y,eqone,eqtwo]
eqone=x'[t]==2 x[t]-x[t] y[t];
eqtwo=y'[t]==-3y[t]+x[t]y[t];
DSolve[{eqone,eqtwo},{x[t],y[t]},t]
```

```
DSolve[{x'[t] == 2 x[t] - x[t] y[t],

    y'[t] == -3 y[t] + x[t] y[t]}, {x[t], y[t]}, t]
```

However, we are able to use NDSolve to solve the system when x(0)=1 and y(0)=1 for $0 \le t \le 3$.

```
solone=NDSolve[{eqone,eqtwo,x[0]==1,y[0]==1},{x[t],y[t]},{t,0,3}]
```

```
{{x[t] -> InterpolatingFunction[{0., 3.}, <>][t],

    y[t] -> InterpolatingFunction[{0., 3.}, <>][t]}}
```

We then use ParametricPlot to graph the solution, solone, obtained above. Note that the resulting error message indicates that the functions to be graphed cannot be compiled, which normally results in faster computations. In this case, the functions are not compiled and still graphed.

```
ParametricPlot[{x[t],y[t]} /. solone,{t,0,3}]
```

```
ParametricPlot::ppcom:
    Function {x[t], y[t]} /. solone
        cannot be compiled; plotting will proceed with the
        uncompiled function.
```

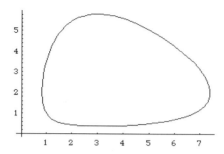

We define a function `sol` to graph various numerical solutions of the system above.

```
Clear[sol]
sol[s_]:=Module[{solt,y,x,t,eqone,eqtwo},
        eqone=x'[t]==2 x[t]-x[t] y[t];
        eqtwo=y'[t]==-3y[t]+x[t]y[t];
        solt=NDSolve[{eqone,eqtwo,x[0]==3s,y[0]==2s},
             {x[t],y[t]},{t,0,4}];
        ParametricPlot[{x[t],y[t]} /. solt,{t,0,4},Compiled->False,
             DisplayFunction->Identity]
                       ]
```

We plot the solution with `sol` for values of t from t = 1/8 to t = 7/8 using increments of 3/40

```
graphs=Table[sol[t],{t,1/8,7/8,3/40}];
```

and display these graphs below. Notice that all of the solutions oscillate about the center. These solutions reveal the relationship between the two populations: prey, x(t), and predator, y(t). As we follow one cycle counterclockwise beginning, for example, near the point (2,0), we notice that as x(t) increases, then y(t) increases until y(t) becomes overpopulated. Then, since the prey population is too small to supply the predator population, y(t) decreases which leads to an increase in the population of x(t). Since the number of predators becomes too small to control the number in the prey population, x(t) becomes overpopulated and the cycle repeats itself.

```
Show[graphs,PlotRange->All,DisplayFunction->$DisplayFunction]
```

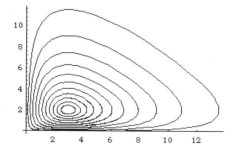

In fact, we can view these changes by graphing x(t) and y(t). Below, we use NDSolve to approximate the solution to the problem for $0 \leq t \leq 10$. We then graph x(t) and y(t) with Plot, naming the results plotx and ploty, respectively, and graph $(x(t), y(t))$ with ParametricPlot, naming the result param. Last, we use Show and GraphicsArray to display all three graphs.

```
sol=NDSolve[{eqone,eqtwo,x[0]==1,y[0]==1},{x[t],y[t]},{t,0,10}]

    {{x[t] -> InterpolatingFunction[{0., 10.}, <>][t],

      y[t] -> InterpolatingFunction[{0., 10.}, <>][t]}}

plotx=Plot[x[t] /. sol,{t,0,10},DisplayFunction->Identity];
ploty=Plot[y[t] /. sol,{t,0,10},DisplayFunction->Identity];
param=ParametricPlot[{x[t],y[t]} /. sol,{t,0,10},
       DisplayFunction->Identity];
Show[GraphicsArray[{plotx,ploty,param}]]
```

Next, we consider the solution of a second-order nonlinear equation by transforming the equation into the corresponding system of equations. We then use NDSolve to approximate the solutions to this system

> **EXAMPLE:** The **Van-der-Pol equation** $x'' + \mu(x^2 - 1)x' + x = 0$ is equivalent to the system $\begin{cases} x' = y \\ y' = \mu(1 - x^2)y - x \end{cases}$. Classify the equilibrium points, use NDSolve to approximate the solutions to this nonlinear system, and plot the phase plane.

SOLUTION: We find the equilibrium point of this well-known system below in roots. The associated linear system is then entered as linmatrix.

```
roots=Solve[{y==0,mu(1-x^2)y-x==0},{x,y}]

    {{y -> 0, x -> 0}}

linmatrix={{0,1},{-2mu x y-1,mu(1-x^2)}};
MatrixForm[linmatrix]

    0                    1
                                  2
    -1 - 2 mu x y    mu (1 - x )
```

The eigenvalues of the linearized system at the equilibrium point (0,0) are given below.

```
linmatrix /. roots[[1]] // Eigenvalues
```

```
            2                    2
   mu - Sqrt[-4 + mu ]   mu + Sqrt[-4 + mu ]
  {-------------------, -------------------}
           2                    2
```

Notice that these eigenvalues simplify to $\lambda = \dfrac{\mu \pm \sqrt{\mu^2 - 4}}{2}$, which are:

(a) both positive, real if $\mu > 2$ since $\mu^2 - 4 > 0$. Hence, (0,0) is an unstable node.

(b) complex conjugates with positive real part if $0 < \mu < 2$. Hence, (0,0) is an unstable spiral. (Note that μ is assumed positive since Van der Pol's equation came about from the study of nonlinear damping. Therefore, μ represents the damping coefficient in spring-mass systems. We disregard the case with $\mu = 2$ since it results in a repeated eigenvalue.)

We now employ NDSolve to determine and plot solutions which correspond to Van der Pol's equation with μ=1. This means that the equilibrium point (0,0) is an unstable focus according to our classification above. The two equations are defined in eqone and eqtwo and then used with NDSolve to determine the solution to the initial value problem x[0]=0 on the interval [0,10].

```
eqone=x'[t]==y[t];
eqtwo=y'[t]==(1-x[t]^2)y[t]-x[t];
solone=NDSolve[{eqone,eqtwo,x[0]==1,y[0]==1},{x[t],y[t]},{t,0,10}]

  {{x[t] -> InterpolatingFunction[{0., 10.}, <>][t],

     y[t] -> InterpolatingFunction[{0., 10.}, <>][t]}}
```

The approximate solution is then plotted with ParametricPlot below.

```
ParametricPlot[{x[t],y[t]} /. solone,{t,0,10}]

  ParametricPlot::ppcom:
     Function {x[t], y[t]} /. solone
       cannot be compiled; plotting will proceed with the
       uncompiled function.
```

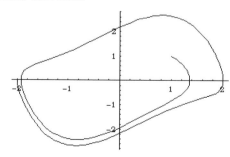

We now attempt to plot the phase plane associated with Van der Pol's equation. This is done in a manner similar to the previous example by defining a function `sol` which, given s, numerically approximates the solution using the initial conditions $x(0) = \frac{s}{24}\cos s$ and $y(0) = \frac{s}{24}\sin s$ and plots the solution parametrically over the interval $[0,10]$.

```
Clear[sol,eqone,eqtwo,x,y,t]
sol[s_]:=Module[{solt,x,y,t,eqone,eqtwo},
        eqone=x'[t]==y[t];
        eqtwo=y'[t]==(1-x[t]^2)y[t]-x[t];
        solt=NDSolve[{eqone,eqtwo,
                x[0]==s/24 Cos[s],y[0]==s/24 Sin[s]},
                {x[t],y[t]},{t,0,10}];
        ParametricPlot[{x[t],y[t]} /. solt,{t,0,10},
                Compiled->False,DisplayFunction->Identity]
                ]
```

A table of solutions is produced in `graphs` below for s = 1/4 to $s = 8\pi - \frac{1}{4}$ using increments of $(8\pi - 1/4)/15$.

```
graphs=Table[sol[t],{t,1/4,8Pi,(8Pi-1/4)/15}];
```

The solutions which were found are then shown simultaneously to reveal the phase plane. Notice that the solutions seem to approach a closed path as the variable t increases. (Recall that (0,0) is an unstable spiral, so the solutions are directed away from the origin.) This closed path is called a limit cycle because all solutions approach it as t increases.

```
Show[graphs,PlotRange->All,DisplayFunction->$DisplayFunction]
```

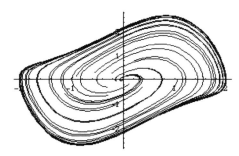

■

Application: The Double Pendulum

EXAMPLE: The motion of a double pendulum is modeled by the following system of equations using the approximation $\sin\theta \approx \theta$ for small displacements:

$$\begin{cases} (m_1 + m_2)\ell_1^2\theta_1'' + m_2\ell_1\ell_2\theta_2'' + (m_1 + m_2)\ell_1 g\theta_1 = 0 \\ m_2\ell_2^2\theta_2'' + m_2\ell_1\ell_2\theta_1'' + m_2\ell_2 g\theta_2 = 0 \end{cases},$$

where θ_1 represents the displacement of the upper pendulum, and θ_2 that of the lower pendulum. Also, m_1 and m_2 represent the mass attached to the upper and lower pendulums, respectively, while the length of each is given by ℓ_1 and ℓ_2. Suppose that $m_1 = 3$, $m_2 = 1$, and each pendulum has length 16. If $\theta_1(0) = 1$, $\theta_1'(0) = 0$, $\theta_2(0) = -1$, and $\theta_2'(0) = 0$, then solve the double pendulum problem using $g = 32$. Also, plot the solution.

SOLUTION: Application of the system of equations given above yields the following system of second order equations

$$4(16)^2\,\theta_1'' + (16)^2\,\theta_2'' + 4(16)(32)\,\theta_1 = 0,$$

$$(16)^2\,\theta_2'' + (16)^2\,\theta_1'' + (16)(32)\,\theta_2 = 0,$$

$$\theta_1(0) = 1,\ \theta_1'(0) = 0,\ \theta_2(0) = 1,\ \theta_2'(0) = 0.$$

For convenience, we refer to θ_1 as x and θ_2 as y in the commands below. We define the left-hand sides of the equations in eq1 and eq2 as well as the transformation rules in rule.

```
Clear[x,rule,eq1,eq2]
<<Calculus`LaplaceTransform`

eq1=4 16^2x''[t]+16^2 y''[t]+64 32x[t];
eq2=16^2 y''[t]+16^2 x''[t]+16 32 y[t];

rule={x[t]->lx,x'[t]->s lx-x[0],x''[t]->s^2 lx-s x[0]-x'[0],
       y[t]->ly,y'[t]->s ly-y[0],y''[t]->s^2 ly-s y[0]-y'[0]};
```

The Laplace transform is applied below in eqs.

```
eqs={eq1,eq2} /. rule

                     2
  {2048 lx + 1024 (lx s  - s x[0] - x'[0]) +

            2
    256 (ly s  - s y[0] - y'[0]),
```

```
             2
512 ly + 256 (lx s  - s x[0] - x'[0]) +

          2
256 (ly s  - s y[0] - y'[0])}
```

Since the system is homogeneous, each of the components of eqs is equated to zero and the Laplace transform of x and y, lx and ly, are found.

```
sols=Solve[eqs=={0,0},{lx,ly}]

            2   2
{{lx -> ((2 + s ) (s  (-4 s x[0] - s y[0] - 4 x'[0] -

                    2
          y'[0]) - 4 (2 + s )

          (-(s x[0]) - s y[0] - x'[0] - y'[0]))) /

      2          2     4
    (s  (-16 - 16 s  - 3 s )) -

    -(s x[0]) - s y[0] - x'[0] - y'[0]
    ----------------------------------,
                  2
                 s

          2
  ly -> -((s  (-4 s x[0] - s y[0] - 4 x'[0] - y'[0]) -

              2
    4 (2 + s ) (-(s x[0]) - s y[0] - x'[0] - y'[0])) /

          2     4
  (-16 - 16 s  - 3 s ))}}
```

Below, the initial conditions are applied.

```
conds=sols /. {x[0]->1,y[0]->-1,x'[0]->0,y'[0]->0}

                  2                        3
         -3 s (2 + s )                   3 s
{{lx -> -----------------, ly -> -----------------}}
              2     4                  2     4
        -16 - 16 s  - 3 s          -16 - 16 s  - 3 s
```

InverseLaplaceTransform is used to obtain the formulas for x and y. These are given below.

```
x[t_]=InverseLaplaceTransform[conds[[1,1,2]],s,t]

                      2 t
              Cos[-------]
3 Cos[2 t]        Sqrt[3]
---------- + ------------
    4              4
```

```
y[t_]=InverseLaplaceTransform[conds[[1,2,2]],s,t]
```

$$-3 \frac{\cos[2\ t]}{2} + \frac{\cos\left[\frac{2\ t}{\text{Sqrt}[3]}\right]}{2}$$

The position functions are then plotted with the dashed curve representing the
second spring and the darker curve the first spring.

```
Plot[{x[t],y[t]},{t,0,10},PlotStyle->{GrayLevel[0],Dashing[{.01}]}]
```

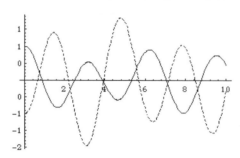

We can generate the graphics far more easily viewing the motion of the double
pendulum. We do this by defining the function pen2, which depends on the time
t as well as the length of the two pendulums, len1 and len2, below. Since the
angles are measured from the vertical axis, polar coordinates with the reference
angle at $3\pi/2$ are used. In this function, pt1 represents the position of the mass
attached to the end of the first pendulum and pt2 that of the mass at the end of
the second spring. pen2 uses Line to produce the graphics of the lines joining the
points representing the masses.

```
Clear[pen2]
pen2[t_,len1_,len2_]:=Module[{pt1,pt2},
        pt1={len1 Cos[3Pi/2+x[t]],
                len1 Sin[3Pi/2+x[t]]};
        pt2={len1 Cos[3Pi/2+x[t]]+len2 Cos[3Pi/2+y[t]],
                len1 Sin[3Pi/2+x[t]]+len2 Sin[3Pi/2+y[t]]};
        Show[Graphics[{
                    Line[{{0,0},pt1}],
                    PointSize[.05],Point[pt1],
                    Line[{pt1,pt2}],
                    PointSize[.05],Point[pt2]}
                        ],
                Axes->Automatic,Ticks->None,
                PlotRange->{{-32,32},{-32,0}},
                DisplayFunction->Identity]
                                                            ]
```

Below, we generate the graphics of the pendulum for t =0 to t =8 using increments of one. These graphics are partitioned into groups of three and displayed as a graphics array. In the same manner as in the previous examples, an alternative to producing an array of graphics cells is to use the command `Do[pen2[t,1,6,16],{t,0,8}]` and then animate the resulting graphics cells.

```
graphs=Table[pen2[t,16,16],{t,0,8}];
groups=Partition[graphs,3];
Show[GraphicsArray[groups]]
```

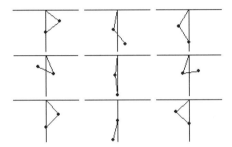

■

6.6 *Some Partial Differential Equations*

The One-Dimensional Wave Equation

Suppose that we pluck a string, like a guitar or violin string, of length a and constant mass density that is fixed at each end. What is the position of the string at a particular instance of time? The problem of determining the position of a string of length a and mass density c is modeled by the following initial-boundary value problem where f(x) and g(x) in (iii) represent the initial position and velocity functions, respectively. The boundary conditions in (ii) represent the fixed ends of the string at x=0 and x=a.

$$(i) \ c^2 \frac{\partial^2 u}{\partial x^2} = \frac{\partial^2 u}{\partial t^2}, \ 0 < x < a, \ t > 0;$$

$$(ii) \ u(0,t) = 0, \ u(a,t) = 0, \ t \geq 0; \ and$$

$$(iii) \ u(x,0) = f(x), \ \frac{\partial u}{\partial t}\bigg|_{t=0} = g(x), \ 0 \leq x \leq a.$$

This problem is typically solved through separation of variables by assuming a solution of the form u(x,t)=X(x)T(t). Substituting this solution into the partial differential equation (i), we obtain $c^2 X''T = XT''$. Dividing by XT yields $\dfrac{X''}{X} = \dfrac{T''}{c^2 T} = -\lambda^2$ where $-\lambda^2$ is the constant of separation. Hence, we have the two ordinary differential equations $X'' + \lambda^2 X = 0$ and $T'' + \lambda^2 c^2 T = 0$. The boundary conditions in (ii) correspond to X(0)=X(a)=0. The corresponding boundary value problem $\begin{cases} X'' + \lambda^2 X = 0 \\ X(0) = X(a) = 0 \end{cases}$ is an eigenvalue problem with eigenvalues $\lambda_n = \dfrac{n\pi x}{a}$ and corresponding eigenfunctions $X_n(x) = \sin(\lambda_n x) = \sin\left(\dfrac{n\pi x}{a}\right)$ for n=1, 2, ... Similarly, the solutions to $T'' + \lambda^2 c^2 T = 0$ are $T_n(t) = a_n \sin(\lambda_n ct) + b_n \cos(\lambda_n ct)$, so the solutions of this problem are

$$u_n(x,t) = X_n(x)T_n(t)$$
$$= \left(a_n \sin(\lambda_n ct) + b_n \cos(\lambda_n ct) \right) \sin(\lambda_n x)$$
$$= \left(a_n \sin\left(\frac{n\pi ct}{a}\right) + b_n \cos\left(\frac{n\pi ct}{a}\right) \right) \sin\left(\frac{n\pi x}{a}\right).$$

Therefore, the linear combination of these solutions is also a solution. This gives us

$$u(x,t) = \sum_{n=1}^{\infty} \left(a_n \sin\left(\frac{n\pi ct}{a}\right) + b_n \cos\left(\frac{n\pi ct}{a}\right) \right) \sin\left(\frac{n\pi x}{a}\right).$$

Application of the initial position function gives us $u(x,0) = \displaystyle\sum_{n=1}^{\infty} b_n \sin\left(\dfrac{n\pi x}{a}\right) = f(x)$. Use of the orthogonality conditions yields $b_n = \dfrac{2}{a}\displaystyle\int_0^a f(x)\sin\left(\dfrac{n\pi x}{a}\right)dx$. In order to apply the initial velocity, we first differentiate u(x,t) with respect to t:

$$u_t(x,t) = \sum_{n=1}^{\infty} \left(a_n \frac{a}{n\pi c}\cos\left(\frac{n\pi ct}{a}\right) - b_n \frac{a}{n\pi c}\sin\left(\frac{n\pi ct}{a}\right) \right) \sin\left(\frac{n\pi x}{a}\right).$$

Therefore, we have $u_t(x,0) = \displaystyle\sum_{n=1}^{\infty} a_n \frac{a}{n\pi c}\sin\left(\frac{n\pi x}{a}\right) = g(x)$, which through the use of the orthogonality condition yields $a_n = \dfrac{2n\pi c}{a}\displaystyle\int_0^a g(x)\sin\left(\frac{n\pi x}{a}\right)dx$.

We show how Mathematica is used to solve this problem in the following example.

EXAMPLE: Solve the wave equation with c=1 and a=1 subject to the indicated initial conditions:

$$(i)\ \frac{\partial^2 u}{\partial x^2} = \frac{\partial^2 u}{\partial t^2}, 0 < x < 1, t > 0;$$

$$(ii)\ u(0,t) = 0, u(a,t) = 0, t \geq 0;\ and$$

$$(iii)\ u(x,0) = \sin(\pi x), \left.\frac{\partial u}{\partial t}\right|_{t=0} = 3x+1, 0 \leq x \leq 1.$$

SOLUTION: The appropriate parameters and initial conditions are entered below.

```
Clear[alpha,beta]
a=1;
c=1;
f[x_]:=Sin[Pi x];
g[x_]=3x+1;
```

Next, the functions to determine the coefficients α_n and β_n in the series approximation of the solution u(x,t) are defined in alpha and beta. alpha and beta are defined using the form alpha[n_]:=alpha[n]=... and beta[n_]:=beta[n]=..., respectively, so that Mathematica "remembers" the values of alpha[n] and beta[n] computed and thus avoids recomputing previously computed values. The use of NIntegrate in these functions causes the calculations to be performed more quickly in most cases.

```
alpha[n_]:=alpha[n]=2/(n Pi c)*
        NIntegrate[g[x]Sin[n Pi x/a],{x,0,a}]//N//Chop;
beta[n_]:=b[n]=2/a*NIntegrate[f[x]Sin[n Pi x/a],{x,0,a}]//Chop;
```

A table of the first five α_n and β_n is found below.

```
Table[{n,alpha[n],beta[n]},{n,1,5}]//TableForm
```

1	1.01321	1.
2	-0.151982	0
3	0.112579	0
4	-0.0379954	0
5	0.0405285	0

The function u defined below represents the nth term in the series expansion. Hence, **unapprox** determines the approximation of order five by summing the first five terms of the expansion.

```
u[x_,t_,n_]:=(alpha[n]Sin[n Pi c t/a]+
        beta[n]Cos[n Pi c t/a])Sin[n Pi x/a];
unapprox[x_,t_]=Sum[u[x,t,k],{k,1,5}]
```

```
x
(1. Cos[Pi t] + 1.01321 Sin[Pi t]) Sin[Pi x] -

   0.151982 Sin[2 Pi t] Sin[2 Pi x] +

   0.112579 Sin[3 Pi t] Sin[3 Pi x] -

   0.0379954 Sin[4 Pi t] Sin[4 Pi x] +

   0.0405285 Sin[5 Pi t] Sin[5 Pi x]
```

In the graphs below, unapprox is graphed over the interval [0,2] (in x) for values of t from t=0 to t=2 using increments of 2/19. This produces a list of 20 plots which is partitioned into groups of four in garray and viewed as a graphics array. These plots can be displayed via a Do command so that the resulting graphs may be animated to see the motion of the string.

```
graphs=Table[Plot[unapprox[x,t],{x,0,1},PlotRange->{-1.5,1.5},
        Ticks->None,DisplayFunction->Identity],{t,0,2,2/19}];
garray=Partition[graphs,4];
Show[GraphicsArray[garray]]
```

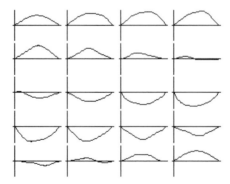

■

Beginning users of Mathematica quickly notice that in order to use results from a previous Mathematica session, they must first be re-calculated. The purpose of the following example is to illustrate how results can be saved for future use.

Application: Zeros of the Bessel Functions

EXAMPLE: Since the zeros of the Bessel functions play an important role in the generalized Fourier series involving Bessel functions, use Mathematica to approximate the first eight zeros of the Bessel functions of the first kind, $J_n(x)$, of order n=0, 1, 2, ... , 5.

SOLUTION: The Bessel function of the first kind of order n, $J_n(x)$, is represented by `BesselJ[n,x]`. Below, we graph the Bessel functions of the first kind of order n for n=0, 1, ... , 5 on the interval [0,33] and display the resulting six graphs as a `GraphicsArray`.

```
graphs=Table[Plot[BesselJ[n,x],{x,0,33},
        DisplayFunction->Identity],{n,0,5}];
array=Partition[graphs,3];
Show[GraphicsArray[array]]
```

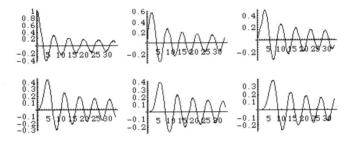

In order to approximate the zeros of the Bessel functions we will use the command `FindRoot`. Recall that `FindRoot[equation,{x,a}]` attempts to locate an approximation of the solution to `equation`, which represents an equation in x, near $x = a$. We use the above graphs to determine initial approximations of the zeros to be approximated. For example, the zeros of the Bessel function of order zero appear to occur at x=2.5, 5.5, 8.7, 11.8, 15.1, 18.1, 21.2, and 24.4. These values are entered in the list `az` which is used with `FindRoot` in `a[0]` to supply the initial guess for each of the first eight zeros. A similar list of approximate zeros is given for each function. In general, `a[i]` is a list of approximations of the first eight zeros of the Bessel function of the first kind of order i.

```
azero={2.5, 5.5, 8.7, 11.8, 15.1, 18.1, 21.2, 24.4};
a[0]=Table[FindRoot[BesselJ[0,x]==0,{x,azero[[i]]}],{i,1,8}];
aone={4, 7, 10, 13.2, 16.4, 19.6, 22.6, 26};
a[1]=Table[FindRoot[BesselJ[1,x]==0,{x,aone[[i]]}],{i,1,8}];
atwo={5.2, 8.4, 11.8, 14.7, 18, 21.1, 24.4, 27.4};
a[2]=Table[FindRoot[BesselJ[2,x]==0,{x,atwo[[i]]}],{i,1,8}];
athree={6.5, 10, 13, 16.2, 19.4, 22.5, 25.8, 29};
a[3]=Table[FindRoot[BesselJ[3,x]==0,{x,athree[[i]]}],{i,1,8}];
afour={7.6, 11.1, 14.5, 17.7, 20.9, 24.1, 27.3, 30.5};
a[4]=Table[FindRoot[BesselJ[4,x]==0,{x,afour[[i]]}],{i,1,8}];
afive={8.9, 12.4, 15.6, 19.1, 22.3, 25.5, 28.7, 31.9};
a[5]=Table[FindRoot[BesselJ[5,x]==0,{x,afive[[i]]}],{i,1,8}];
asix={10, 13.5, 17.2, 20, 23.6, 26.9, 30, 33.3};
a[6]=Table[FindRoot[BesselJ[6,x]==0,{x,asix[[i]]}],{i,1,8}];
```

After these lists are obtained, they are combined to form the single list zeros of which is viewed in TableForm.

```
zeros=Table[a[i][[j,1,2]],{i,0,6},{j,1,8}];
TableForm[zeros]
```

2.40483	5.52008	8.65373	11.7915	14.9309	18.0711
21.2116	24.3525				
3.83171	7.01559	10.1735	13.3237	16.4706	19.6159
22.7601	25.9037				
5.13562	8.41724	11.6198	14.796	17.9598	21.117
24.2701	27.4206				
6.38016	9.76102	13.0152	16.2235	19.4094	22.5827
25.7482	28.9084				
7.58834	11.0647	14.3725	17.616	20.8269	24.019
27.1991	30.371				
8.77148	12.3386	15.7002	18.9801	22.2178	25.4303
28.6266	31.8117				
9.93611	13.5893	17.0038	20.3208	23.5861	26.8202
30.0337	33.233				

We then save this table of numbers, for later use, and name the resulting file **besseltable**. In doing so, these time-consuming calculations may be avoided each time the list of zeros is needed. Instead, the file **besseltable** may be easily read. The symbol >>, representing the built-in function Put, is used to write the table zeros to the file **besseltable**.

```
zeros>>besseltable
```

If the calculations have just been completed, the α_{mn} which are necessary in the calculation of the series coefficients of the eigenfunction expansion are defined in the following way.

```
alpha[i_,j_]:=zeros[[i+1,j]]
```

However, if the zero must first be read in from **besseltable**, the following command must be performed.

```
getzeros=ReadList["besseltable"];
alpha[i_,j_]:=getzeros[[1]][[i+1,j]]
```

■

Application: The Two-Dimensional Wave Equation

One of the more interesting problems involving two spatial dimensions (x and y) is the wave equation. The two-dimensional wave equation in a circular region which is radially symmetric (not depending on θ) with boundary and initial conditions is expressed in polar coordinates as

$$(i) \ \frac{\partial^2 u}{\partial t^2} = c^2 \left(\frac{\partial^2 u}{\partial r^2} + \frac{1}{r} \frac{\partial u}{\partial r} \right), \ 0 < r < R, t > 0;$$

$$(ii) \ u(R,t) = 0, t > 0;$$

$$(iii) \ |u(0,t)| \ bounded, t > 0;$$

$$(iv) \ u(r,0) = f(r), 0 < r < R; \ and$$

$$(iii) \ \frac{\partial u}{\partial t}(r,0) = g(r), 0 < r < R.$$

Notice that with the boundary conditions like those in the wave equation discussed above, this problem is typically solved through separation of variables by assuming a solution of the form u(r,t)=R(r)T(t). Applying separation of variables yields the solution

$$u(r,t) = \sum_{n=1}^{\infty} \left(a_n \cos(\lambda_n t) + b_n \sin(\lambda_n t) \right) J_0(k_n r),$$

where

$$\lambda_n = \frac{c}{R} \alpha_{0n}, \ k_n = \frac{1}{R} \alpha_{0n}, \ a_n = \frac{2n\pi c}{a} \int_0^a g(x) \sin\left(\frac{n\pi x}{a} \right) dx \ and \ b_n = \frac{2}{a} \int_0^a f(x) \sin\left(\frac{n\pi x}{a} \right) dx$$

(α_{0n} represents the nth zero of the Bessel function of the first kind of order zero). As a practical matter, in nearly all cases these formulas are difficult to evaluate.

> **EXAMPLE:** Solve the wave equation with c=1 and R=1 with initial position $f(r) = r(r-1)$ and initial velocity $g(r) = \sin(\pi r)$.

SOLUTION: We, first, read in the table of zeros of the Bessel functions which was created earlier in **besseltable** and call this table getzeros. We then define the function alpha[i,j] which represents the jth zero of the Bessel function of the first kind of order i.

```
getzeros=ReadList["besseltable"];
alpha[i_,j_]:=getzeros[[1]][[i+1,j]]
```

Next, we enter the appropriate radius in capr, parameter c, and initial position and velocity functions, f and g.

```
Clear[a,b,k,lambda,um,unapprox,capr,c,f,g]
capr=1;
c=1;
f[r_]:=r(r-1);
g[r_]=Sin[Pi r];
```

We define the formula for $k_n = \frac{1}{R}\alpha_{0n}$ below. The eigenvalue $\lambda_n = \frac{c}{R}\alpha_{0n} = ck_n$ is defined in lambda. The formulas for the coefficients a_n and b_n, which were derived above, are then defined in a and b so that an approximate solution may be determined. Note that we use NIntegrate in order to avoid the difficulties in integration associated with the presence of the Bessel functions of order zero. In addition, a and b are defined using the forms a[n_]:=a[n]=... and b[n_]:=b[n]=... so that Mathematica "remembers" the values of a[n] and b[n] computed and thus avoids recomputing previously computed values.

```
k[n_]:=alpha[0,n]/capr
lambda[n_]:=c/capr alpha[0,n]
a[n_]:=a[n]=2/(capr^2 BesselJ[1,alpha[0,n]]^2)*
        NIntegrate[r f[r]BesselJ[0,k[n]r],{r,0,capr}];
b[n_]:=b[n]=2/(c capr alpha[0,n]*
        BesselJ[1,alpha[0,n]]^2)*
        NIntegrate[r g[r]BesselJ[0,k[n]r],{r,0,capr}];
```

Below, we compute the first six values of a_n and b_n.

```
Table[{n,a[n],b[n]},{n,1,6}]//TableForm
```

1	−0.323503	0.52118
2	0.208466	−0.145776
3	0.00763767	−0.0134216
4	0.0383536	−0.00832269
5	0.00534454	−0.00250503
6	0.0150378	−0.00208315

The nth term of the series solution is defined in u below.

```
u[n_,r_,t_]:=(a[n]Cos[lambda[n] t]+
        b[n]Sin[lambda[n] t])*BesselJ[0,k[n] r]
```

Thus, an approximate solution is obtained in `uapprox` by summing the first six terms of u given above.

```
unapprox[r_,t_]=Sum[u[m,r,t],{m,1,6}]

    BesselJ[0, 2.40482555769557879 r]
        (-0.323503 Cos[2.40482555769557879 t] +
            0.52118 Sin[2.40482555769557879 t]) +
        BesselJ[0, 5.520078110286310648 r]
        (0.208466 Cos[5.520078110286310648 t] -
            0.145776 Sin[5.520078110286310648 t]) +
        BesselJ[0, 8.653727912911012217 r]
        (0.00763767 Cos[8.653727912911012217 t] -
            0.0134216 Sin[8.653727912911012217 t]) +
        BesselJ[0, 11.79153443901383635 r]
        (0.0383536 Cos[11.79153443901383635 t] -
            0.00832269 Sin[11.79153443901383635 t]) +
        BesselJ[0, 14.93091770848778431 r]
        (0.00534454 Cos[14.93091770848778431 t] -
            0.00250503 Sin[14.93091770848778431 t]) +
        BesselJ[0, 18.07106396791092254 r]
        (0.0150378 Cos[18.07106396791092254 t] -
            0.00208315 Sin[18.07106396791092254 t])
```

Since the function is independent of the angular coordinate θ, we can plot this function over the interval [0,1] to yield a side view of half of the circular region. This is accomplished in `graphs` below by plotting `uapprox` for values of t from t=0 to t=2 using increments of 2/15. The list of graphics which results is then partitioned into groups of four and displayed as a graphics array. A similar list of graphics, can be generated with a Do command by entering

```
Do[Plot[unapprox[r,t],{r,0,1},Ticks->{{0,.5,1},None},
    PlotRange->{-1,1}],{t,0,2,2/15}]
```

so that the resulting list may be animated to show the motion of the waves on the circular region.

```
graphs=Table[Plot[unapprox[r,t],{r,0,1},Ticks->{{0,.5,1},None},
        PlotRange->{-1,1},DisplayFunction->Identity],{t,0,2,2/15}];
array=Partition[graphs,4];
Show[GraphicsArray[array]]
```

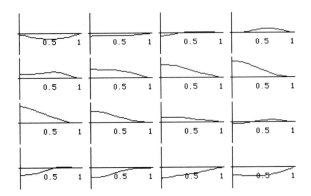

The problem that describes the displacement of a circular membrane in its general case is:

$$(i) \quad \frac{1}{r}\frac{\partial}{\partial r}\left(r\frac{\partial u}{\partial r}\right) + \frac{1}{r^2}\frac{\partial^2 u}{\partial \theta^2} = \frac{1}{c^2}\frac{\partial^2 u}{\partial t^2}, \quad 0 < r < a, \ -\pi < \theta \le \pi;$$

(ii) $u(a,\theta,t) = 0, \ 0 < t, \ -\pi < \theta \le \pi;$

(iii) $\left|u(0,\theta,t)\right|$ bounded, $0 < t, \ -\pi < \theta \le \pi;$

(iv) $u(r,-\pi,t) = u(r,\pi,t), \ 0 < r < a, \ 0 < t;$

(v) $\dfrac{\partial u}{\partial \theta}(r,-\pi,t) = \dfrac{\partial u}{\partial \theta}(r,\pi,t), \ 0 < r < a, \ 0 < t;$

(vi) $u(r,\theta,0) = f(r,\theta), \ 0 < r < a, \ -\pi < \theta \le \pi;$ and

(vii) $\dfrac{\partial u}{\partial t}(r,\theta,0) = g(r,\theta), \ 0 < r < a, \ -\pi < \theta \le \pi.$

Using separation of variables, we obtain that the general solution is given by

$$u(r,\theta,t) = \sum_{n} a_{0n} J_0\left(\lambda_{0n} r\right)\cos\left(\lambda_{0n} ct\right) + \sum_{m,n} a_{mn} J_m\left(\lambda_{mn} r\right)\cos(m\theta)\cos\left(\lambda_{mn} ct\right)$$

$$+ \sum_{m,n} b_{mn} J_m\left(\lambda_{mn} r\right)\sin(m\theta)\cos\left(\lambda_{mn} ct\right) + \sum_{n} A_{0n} J_0\left(\lambda_{0n} r\right)\sin\left(\lambda_{0n} ct\right)$$

$$+ \sum_{m,n} A_{mn} J_m\left(\lambda_{mn} r\right)\cos(m\theta)\sin\left(\lambda_{mn} ct\right) + \sum_{m,n} B_{mn} J_m\left(\lambda_{mn} r\right)\sin(m\theta)\sin\left(\lambda_{mn} ct\right),$$

where J_m represents the mth Bessel function of the first kind, λ_{mn} represents the nth zero of J_m, and the coefficients are given by:

$$a_{0n} = \frac{\int_0^{2\pi}\int_0^a f(r,\theta)J_0(\lambda_{0n}r)r\,dr\,d\theta}{2\pi\int_0^a\left[J_0(\lambda_{0n}r)\right]^2 r\,dr} \; , \quad a_{mn} = \frac{\int_0^{2\pi}\int_0^a f(r,\theta)J_m(\lambda_{mn}r)\cos(m\theta)r\,dr\,d\theta}{\pi\int_0^a\left[J_m(\lambda_{mn}r)\right]^2 r\,dr} \; ,$$

$$b_{mn} = \frac{\int_0^{2\pi}\int_0^a f(r,\theta)J_m(\lambda_{mn}r)\sin(m\theta)r\,dr\,d\theta}{\pi\int_0^a\left[J_m(\lambda_{mn}r)\right]^2 r\,dr} \; , \quad A_{0n} = \frac{\int_0^{2\pi}\int_0^a g(r,\theta)J_0(\lambda_{0n}r)r\,dr\,d\theta}{2\pi\lambda_{0n}c\int_0^a\left[J_0(\lambda_{0n}r)\right]^2 r\,dr} \; ,$$

$$A_{mn} = \frac{\int_0^{2\pi}\int_0^a g(r,\theta)J_m(\lambda_{mn}r)\cos(m\theta)r\,dr\,d\theta}{\pi\lambda_{mn}c\int_0^a\left[J_m(\lambda_{mn}r)\right]^2 r\,dr} \; , \quad \text{and}$$

$$B_{mn} = \frac{\int_0^{2\pi}\int_0^a g(r,\theta)J_m(\lambda_{mn}r)\sin(m\theta)r\,dr\,d\theta}{\pi\lambda_{mn}c\int_0^a\left[J_m(\lambda_{mn}r)\right]^2 r\,dr} \; .$$

We show how Mathematica is used to solve and visualize this problem in the example below.

EXAMPLE: Solve the circular membrane problem with radius a=1, c=10, initial position function

$$f(r,\theta) = f_1(r)f_2(\theta) = \left(\cos\left(\frac{\pi r}{2}\right)\right)\sin(\theta),$$

and initial velocity function

$$g(r,\theta) = g_1(r)g_2(\theta) = (r-1)\cos\left(\frac{\pi\theta}{2}\right).$$

SOLUTION: The table of zeros which were found earlier and saved as **besseltable** are read in and called getzeros. A function alpha is then defined so that these zeros of the Bessel functions of the first kind can be more easily obtained from the list.

```
getzeros=ReadList["besseltable"];
alpha[i_,j_]:=getzeros[[1]][[i+1,j]]
```

The appropriate parameter values as well as the initial condition functions are defined below. Notice that the functions describing the initial position and velocity are defined as the product of functions. This enables the calculations to be carried out in the manner which follows.

```
Clear[a,f,f1,f2,g1,g2,A,c,g,capa,capb,b]
c=10;
A=1;
f1[r_]:=Cos[Pi/(2r)];
f2[theta_]=Sin[theta];
f[r_,theta_]:=f[r,theta]=f1[r]*f2[theta];
g1[r_]:=r-1;
g2[theta_]=Cos[Pi/2 theta];
g[r_,theta_]:=g[r,theta]=g1[r]*g2[theta];
```

The coefficients a_{0n} are determined with the function a below.

```
a[n_]:=a[n]=(NIntegrate[f1[r]*BesselJ[0,alpha[0,n]r]r,{r,0,A}]*
        NIntegrate[f2[t],{t,0,2Pi}])/
        (2Pi NIntegrate[r*BesselJ[0,alpha[0,n]r]^2,{r,0,A}])//N;
```

Hence, as represents a table of the first five values of a_{0n}. Chop is used to round off very small numbers to zero.

```
as=Table[a[n]//Chop,{n,1,5}]

    {0, 0, 0, 0, 0}
```

Because the denominator of each integral formula used to find a_{mn} and b_{mn} is the same, the function bjmn which computes this value is defined below. A table of nine values of this coefficient is then determined.

```
bjmn[m_,n_]:=bjmn[m,n]=NIntegrate[r*BesselJ[m,alpha[m,n]r]^2,{r,0,A}]//N
Table[bjmn[m,n]//Chop,{m,1,3},{n,1,3}]

    {{0.0811076, 0.0450347, 0.0311763},
     {0.0576874, 0.0368243, 0.0270149},
     {0.0444835, 0.0311044, 0.0238229}}
```

Because the initial position function f is defined as the product of a function f1 of r and a function f2 of θ, we determine the value of the integral of the product of f1 and the appropriate Bessel function in fbjmn and create a table of values.

```
Clear[fbjmn]
fbjmn[m_,n_]:=fbjmn[m,n]=NIntegrate[f1[r]*
        BesselJ[m,alpha[m,n]r]r,{r,0,A}]//N
Table[fbjmn[m,n]//Chop,{m,1,3},{n,1,3}]

    {{-0.0959003, 0.0269499, 0.0268211},
     {-0.0866504, 0.000300172, 0.0235597},
     {-0.0755676, -0.0165966, 0.0139515}}
```

The values of fbjmn and bjmn which were found with the Table commands above are used to determine a_{mn} below

```
a[m_,n_]:=a[m,n]=(fbjmn[m,n]*NIntegrate[f2[t]*
        Cos[m t],{t,0,2Pi}])/(Pi bjmn[m,n])//N;
Table[a[m,n]//Chop,{m,1,3},{n,1,3}]
```

```
{{0, 0, 0}, {0, 0, 0}, {0, 0, 0}}
```

as well as the values of b_{mn}. Note that defining the coefficients in this manner

```
(a[m_,n_]:=a[m,n]=... and b[m_,n_]:=b[m,n]=...)
```

cuts down on unnecessary computation time.

```
b[m_,n_]:=b[m,n]=(fbjmn[m,n]*NIntegrate[f2[t]*
        Sin[m t],{t,0,2Pi}])/(Pi bjmn[m,n])//N;
Table[b[m,n]//Chop,{m,1,3},{n,1,3}]
```

```
{{-1.18238, 0.598424, 0.860306}, {0, 0, 0}, {0, 0, 0}}
```

The values of A_{0n} are found similar to those of a_{0n}. After defining the function capa to calculate these coefficients, a table of values is then found.

```
capa[n_]:=capa[n]=(NIntegrate[g1[r]*BesselJ[0,alpha[0,n]r]r,{r,0,A}]*
        NIntegrate[g2[t],{t,0,2Pi}])/(2Pi c alpha[0,n]*
        NIntegrate[r*BesselJ[0,alpha[0,n]r]^2,{r,0,A}])//N;
Table[capa[n]//Chop,{n,1,6}]
```

```
                                                    -6
{0.00142231, 0.0000542518, 0.0000267596, 6.41976 10   ,
              -6              -6
  4.95843 10   , 1.88585 10   }
```

The value of the integral of the component of g, g1, which depends on r and the appropriate Bessel functions, is defined as gbjmn below.

```
gbjmn[m_,n_]:=gbjmn[m,n]=NIntegrate[g1[r]*
        BesselJ[m,alpha[m,n]r]r,{r,0,A}]//N
Table[gbjmn[m,n]//Chop,{m,1,3},{n,1,3}]
```

```
{{-0.0743906, -0.019491, -0.00989293},
 {-0.0554379, -0.0227976, -0.013039},
 {-0.0433614, -0.0226777, -0.0141684}}
```

Then, A_{mn} is found by taking the product of integrals, gbjmn depending on r and one depending on θ. A table of coefficient values is generated in this case as well.

```
capa[m_,n_]:=capa[m,n]=(gbjmn[m,n]*NIntegrate[g2[t]Cos[m t],{t,0,2Pi}])/
        (Pi alpha[m,n] c bjmn[m,n])//N;
Table[capa[m,n]//Chop,{m,1,3},{n,1,3}]
```

```
{{0.0035096, 0.000904517, 0.000457326},
 {-0.00262692, -0.00103252, -0.000583116},
 {-0.000503187, -0.000246002, -0.000150499}}
```

Similarly, the B_{mn} are determined.

```
capb[m_,n_]:=capb[m,n]=(gbjmn[m,n]*NIntegrate[g2[t]Sin[m t],{t,0,2Pi}])/
      (Pi alpha[m,n] c bjmn[m,n])//N;
Table[capb[m,n]//Chop,{m,1,3},{n,1,3}]
```

```
{{0.00987945, 0.00254619, 0.00128736},
 {-0.0147894, -0.00581305, -0.00328291},
 {-0.00424938, -0.00207747, -0.00127095}}
```

Now that the necessary coefficients have been found, we must construct the approximate solution to the wave equation by using our results. Below, `term1` represents those terms of the expansion involving a_{0n}, `term2` those terms involving a_{mn}, `term3` those involving b_{mn}, `term4` those involving A_{0n}, `term5` those involving A_{mn}, and `term6` those involving B_{mn}.

```
Clear[term1,term2,term3,term4,term5,term6]
term1[r_,t_,n_]:=a[n]*BesselJ[0,alpha[0,n]r]*Cos[alpha[0,n] c t];
term2[r_,t_,th_,m_,n_]:=a[m,n]*BesselJ[m,alpha[m,n]r]*
      Cos[m th]*Cos[alpha[m,n] c t];
term3[r_,t_,th_,m_,n_]:=b[m,n]*BesselJ[m,alpha[m,n]r]*
      Sin[m th]*Cos[alpha[m,n] c t];
term4[r_,t_,n_]:=capa[n]*BesselJ[0,alpha[0,n]r]*Sin[alpha[0,n] c t];
term5[r_,t_,th_,m_,n_]:=capa[m,n]*
      BesselJ[m,alpha[m,n]r]*Cos[m th]*Sin[alpha[m,n] c t];
term6[r_,t_,th_,m_,n_]:=capb[m,n]*
      BesselJ[m,alpha[m,n]r]*Sin[m th]*Sin[alpha[m,n] c t];
```

Therefore, the solution is given as the sum of these terms as computed in u below.

```
Clear[u]
u[r_,t_,th_]:=
      Sum[term1[r,t,n],{n,1,5}]+
      Sum[term2[r,t,th,m,n],{m,1,3},{n,1,3}]+
      Sum[term3[r,t,th,m,n],{m,1,3},{n,1,3}]+
      Sum[term4[r,t,n],{n,1,5}]+
      Sum[term5[r,t,th,m,n],{m,1,3},{n,1,3}]+
      Sum[term6[r,t,th,m,n],{m,1,3},{n,1,3}];
```

The solution is compiled below in uc. The command `Compile` is used to compile functions. `Compile` returns a `CompiledFunction` which represents the compiled code. Generally, compiled functions take less time to perform computations than uncompiled functions although compiled functions can only be evaluated for numerical arguments.

```
uc=Compile[{r,t,th},u[r,t,th]]

    CompiledFunction[{r, t, th}, u[r, t, th], -CompiledCode-]
```

and then plotted below with the function `tplot`, which uses `ParametricPlot3D` to produce the graph of the solution for a particular value of t. Note that `th` represents the angle θ and that the x and y coordinates are given in terms of polar coordinates.

```
Clear[tplot]
tplot[t_]:=ParametricPlot3D[{r Cos[th],r Sin[th],uc[r,t,th]},
    {r,0,1},{th,-Pi,Pi},PlotPoints->{20,20},BoxRatios->{1,1,1},
    Shading->False,Axes->False,Boxed->False,
    DisplayFunction->Identity]
```

A table of two plots for t=1/3 and t=2/3 is produced in graphs below. This table of graphs is displayed as a graphics array.

```
graphs=Table[tplot[t],{t,1/3,2/3,1/3}];
Show[GraphicsArray[graphs]]
```

The graphs obtained by modifying the initial condition functions to

```
Clear[a,f,f1,f2,g1,g2,A,c,g,capa,capb,b]
c=10;
A=1;
f1[r_]:=Cos[Pi/2 r];
f2[theta_]=Sin[theta]+theta;
f[r_,theta_]:=f[r,theta]=f1[r]*f2[theta];
g1[r_]:=r-1;
g2[theta_]=Cos[Pi/2 theta];
g[r_,theta_]:=g[r,theta]=g1[r]*g2[theta];
```

are shown below.

```
graphs=Table[tplot[t],{t,1/3,2/3,1/3}];
Show[GraphicsArray[graphs]]
```

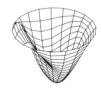

■

Other Partial Differential Equations

A partial differential equation of the form

$$a(x,y,u)\frac{\partial u}{\partial x}+b(x,y,u)\frac{\partial u}{\partial y}=c(x,y,u)$$

is called a **first-order, quasi-linear partial differential equation**. In the case when $c(x,y,u)=0$, the equation is **homogeneous**; when a and b are independent of u, the equation is **almost linear**; and when c(x,y,u) can be written in the form

$$c(x,y,u)=d(x,y)u+s(x,y)$$

the equation is **linear**.

Quasi-linear partial differential equations can frequently be solved using the **Method of Characteristics**. After the package **PDSolve1**, contained in the **Calculus** folder (or directory), is loaded the capabilities of DSolve are enhanced so that DSolve can solve some first-order partial differential equations, as illustrated in the following example.

EXAMPLE: Use the method of characteristics to solve the initial-value problem

$$-3xtu_x+u_t=xt,\, u(x,0)=x.$$

SOLUTION: For this problem, the characteristic system is

$$\frac{\partial x}{\partial r}=-3xt, \qquad x(0,s)=s$$

$$\frac{\partial t}{\partial r}=1, \qquad t(0,s)=0$$

$$\frac{\partial u}{\partial r}=xt, \quad u(0,s)=s.$$

We begin by using DSolve to solve $\dfrac{\partial t}{\partial r} = 1, t(0,s) = 0$

```
d1=DSolve[{D[t[r],r]==1,t[0]==0},t[r],r]
```

```
{{t[r] -> r}}
```

and obtain $t = r$. Thus, $\dfrac{\partial x}{\partial r} = -3xr, x(0,s) = s$ which we solve below and obtain

```
d2=DSolve[{D[x[r],r]==-3 x[r] r,x[0]==s},x[r],r]
```

```
                s
   {{x[r] -> ---------}}
                 2
            (3 r )/2
          E
```

$x = se^{-3r^2/2}$. Substituting $t = r$ and $x = se^{-3r^2/2}$ into $\dfrac{\partial u}{\partial r} = xt, u(0,s) = s$. and using DSolve to solve the resulting equation yields the following result, named d3.

```
d3=DSolve[{D[u[r],r]==Exp[-3/2 r^2] s r,u[0]==s},u[r],r]
```

```
                4 s          s
   {{u[r] -> --- - -----------}}
                3          2
                      (3 r )/2
                   3 E
```

To find u(x,t), we must solve the system of equations

$$\begin{cases} t = r \\ x = se^{-3r^2/2} \end{cases}$$

for r and s. Substituting $r = t$ into $x = se^{-3r^2/2}$ and solving for s yields $s = xe^{3r^2/2}$. Thus, the solution is given by replacing the values obtained above in the solution obtained in d3. We do this below by using /. to replace each occurrence of r and s in d3[[1,1,2]], the solution obtained in d3, by the values $r = t$ and $s = xe^{3r^2/2}$. The resulting output represents the solution to the initial value problem.

```
d3[[1,1,2]] /. {r->t,s->x Exp[3/2 t^2]}
```

```
                  2
              (3 t )/2
   -x    4 E             x
   -- + --------------
    3          3
```

In this example, DSolve can also solve this first-order partial differential equation after the **PDSolve1** package has been loaded. We begin by loading the **PDSolve1** package located in the **Calculus** folder (or directory).

```
<<Calculus'PDSolve1'
```

Next, we use `DSolve` to find a general solution of $-3xtu_x + u_t = xt$ and name the resulting output `gensol`.

```
gensol=DSolve[-3x t D[u[x,t],x]+D[u[x,t],t]==x t,
        u[x,t],{x,t}]
```

```
                          2
               -x      -3 t
  {{u[x, t] -> -- + C[1][----- - Log[x]]}}
               3          2
```

The output

```
            2
        -3 t
   C[1][----- - Log[x]]}}
          2
```

represents an arbitrary function of $-\dfrac{3}{2}t^2 - \ln x$.

The explicit solution is extracted from `gensol` with `gensol[[1,1,2]]`, the same way that results are extracted from the output of `DSolve` commands involving ordinary differential equations.

```
gensol[[1,1,2]]
```

```
                 2
    -x        -3 t
    -- + C[1][----- - Log[x]]
    3           2
```

To find the solution that satisfies $u(x,0) = x$ we replace each occurrence of t in the solution by 0.

```
gensol[[1,1,2]] /. t->0
```

```
   -x
   -- + C[1][-Log[x]]
   3
```

Thus, we must find a function f so that

$$-\frac{x}{2} + f(\ln x) = x$$

$$f(\ln x) = \frac{3x}{2}.$$

Certainly $f(r) = \dfrac{4}{3}e^{-t}$ satisfies the above criteria. Below, we define $f(r) = \dfrac{4}{3}e^{-t}$ and then compute $f(\ln x)$ to verify that $f(\ln x) = \dfrac{3x}{2}$.

```
Clear[f]
f[t_]=4 Exp[-t]/3;
f[-Log[x]]
```

$$\frac{4\ x}{3}$$

Thus, the solution to the initial value problem is given by $-\dfrac{x}{3}+f\left(-\dfrac{3}{2}t^2-\ln x\right)$ which is computed below and named `sol`. Of course, the result returned is the same as that obtained above.

```
sol=-x/3+f[-3t^2/2-Log[x]]//Simplify
```

$$\frac{(-1\ +\ 4\ E^{(3\ t^2)/2}\ )\ x}{3}$$

Last, we use `Plot3D` to graph `sol` on the rectangle $[0,20]\times[-2,2]$. The option

```
                      ClipFill->None
```

is used to indicate that portions of the resulting surface which extend past the bounding box are not shown; nothing is shown where the surface is clipped.

```
Plot3D[sol,{x,0,20},{t,-2,2},PlotRange->{0,30},
       PlotPoints->30,ClipFill->None,Shading->False]
```

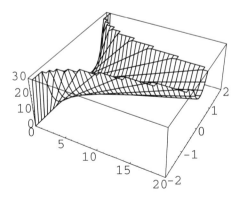

■

CHAPTER 7

Some Graphics Packages

Chapter 7 discusses some of the more frequently used commands contained in various graphics packages available with Mathematica. Most of the packages presented here have not been previously discussed in *Mathematica By Example*. On a computer with a notebook interface, the folder containing the various graphics packages is shown below.

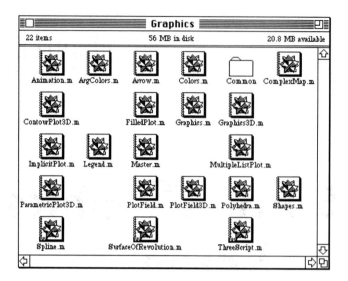

7.1 ComplexMap

A problem of interest in complex analysis is finding the image of a complex-valued function f(z). The package **ComplexMap** provides several commands which are useful in solving problems of this type. The command

```
CartesianMap[f[z],{{x0,x1},{y0,y1}}]
```

gives the image of f[z] using Cartesian coordinate grid lines over the rectangular region $[x_0, x_1] \times [y_0, y_1] = \{x + iy : x_0 \le x \le x_1, y_0 \le y \le y_1\}$.

This is illustrated below with the functions id[z]=z and f[z]=(z-1)/(z+1).

EXAMPLE: Graph the image of the region $R = \{x + iy : 0 \le x \le 2, 0 \le y \le 2\}$ by the mapping $f(z) = \dfrac{z-1}{z+1}$.

SOLUTION: After loading the package **ComplexMap**, we define f. The command

```
CartesianMap[f,{0,2},{0,2},DisplayFunction->Identity]
```

graphs, but does not display, the image of R by the mapping f. Since id[z] is the identity map, each point in the domain is mapped to itself. Hence, the Cartesian grid, called cmid, is unchanged upon application of id[z]. (This region can therefore be viewed as the domain of f[z].) The second graph, cmf, illustrates the effects that f[z] has on the points in cmid. The two graphics objects, cmid and c m f, are viewed in a single graphics cell with Show[GraphicsArray[{cmid,cmf}]. This gives the usual manner in which the domain and image of a function are illustrated.

```
<<Graphics`ComplexMap`

id[z_]=z;
f[z_]=(z-1)/(z+1);

cmid=CartesianMap[id,{0,2},{0,2},DisplayFunction->Identity];
cmf=CartesianMap[f,{0,2},{0,2},DisplayFunction->Identity];
Show[GraphicsArray;[{cmid,cmf}]] Show:GraphicsArray;
```

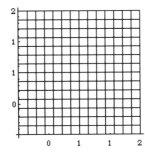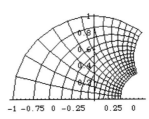

■

In addition to Cartesian coordinates, polar coordinates can also be used. This is done with

```
PolarMap[f[z],{r0,r1},{theta0,theta1}],
```

which produces the image of f[z] over the circular region R bounded by limits placed on the polar coordinates r and θ: $R = \left\{ re^{i\theta} : r_0 \le r \le r_1, \theta_0 \le \theta \le \theta_1 \right\}$.

The following problem is worked in a method similar to that of the previous problem involving Cartesian coordinates.

EXAMPLE: Graph the image of $R = \left\{ re^{i\theta} : 0 \le r \le 2, 0 \le \theta \le 2\pi \right\}$ by the mapping $h(z) = \sin z$.

SOLUTION: The identity map, id[z]=z, is used to produce the polar grid, called pmid, to be viewed as the domain of the function h[z]. The image of h, named pmh, is then determined with PolarMap and two graphs are displayed side-by-side with Show and GraphicsArray.

```
id[z_]=z;
h[z_]=Sin[z];
pmid=PolarMap[id,{0,2},{0,2Pi},Ticks->None,DisplayFunction->Identity];
pmh=PolarMap[h,{0,2},{0,2Pi},Ticks->None,DisplayFunction->Identity];
Show[GraphicsArray[{pmid,pmh}]]
```

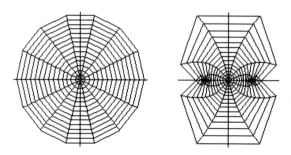

■

The following example illustrates both `CartesianMap` and `PolarMap`.

EXAMPLE: Graph the image of $R_1 = \{x + iy : 0 \le x \le \pi, -2 \le y \le 2\}$ by the mapping $w(z) = \cos 3z - \sin 2z$ and the image of $R_2 = \{re^{i\theta} : 0 \le r \le 1, 0 \le \theta \le 2\pi\}$ by the mapping $m(z) = \dfrac{z-2}{2z-1}$.

SOLUTION: The domain and image of w are called `cmid` and `cmw`, respectively, while those of m are named `pmid` and `pmm`. These graphics objects are shown in the appropriate order with the command

```
Show[GraphicsArray[{{cmid,cmw},{pmid,pmm}},AspectRatio->1].
```

(Notice the grouping of {domain, image} within the `GraphicsArray`.)

```
w[z_]=Cos[3z]-Sin[2z];
m[z_]=(z-2)/(2z-1);
cmid=CartesianMap[id,{0,Pi,Pi/10},{-2,2,2/5},Ticks->None,
        DisplayFunction->Identity];
cmw=CartesianMap[w,{0,Pi,Pi/10},{-2,2,2/5},Ticks->None,
        DisplayFunction->Identity];
pmid=PolarMap[id,{0,1,1/10},{0,2Pi},Ticks->None,
        DisplayFunction->Identity];
pmm=PolarMap[m,{0,1,1/10},{0,2Pi},Ticks->None,
        DisplayFunction->Identity];
Show[GraphicsArray[{{cmid,cmw},{pmid,pmm}}]]
```

$$\dfrac{1}{0}$$

Power::infy: Infinite expression - encountered.

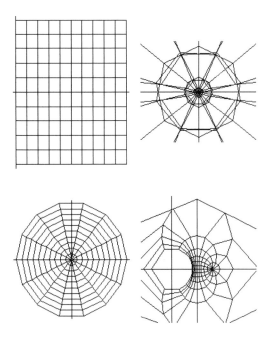

7.2 ContourPlot3D

The package **ContourPlot3D** contains the command `ContourPlot3D` which can be used to graph level curves of functions of three variables and equations in three variables. The command

```
ContourPlot3D[f[x,y,z],{x,xmin,xmax},{y,ymin,ymax},{z,zmin,zmax}]
```

graphs `f[x,y,z]=0` in the parallelepiped $[\text{xmin,xmax}]\times[\text{ymin,ymax}]\times[\text{zmin,zmax}]$; the command

```
ContourPlot3D[f[x,y,z],{x,xmin,xmax},{y,ymin,ymax},{z,zmin,zmax},
    Contours->{c1,c2,...}]
```

graphs `f[x,y,z]=c1, f[x,y,z]=c2`, ... in the parallelepiped $[\text{xmin,xmax}]\times[\text{ymin,ymax}]\times[\text{zmin,zmax}]$.

EXAMPLE: Graph the equation $-x^2 - 2y^2 + z^2 - 4yz = 10$.

SOLUTION: The graph of the equation $-x^2 - 2y^2 + z^2 - 4yz = 10$ is the graph of the level surface of $-x^2 - 2y^2 + z^2 - 4yz - 10$ corresponding to 0. Below we use `ContourPlot3D` to graph this equation in the region $[-6,6] \times [-6,6] \times [-6,6]$.

```
<<Graphics`ContourPlot3D`

ContourPlot3D[-x^2-2y^2+z^2-4y z-10,{x,-6,6},{y,-6,6},{z,-6,6}]
```

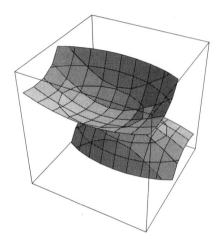

■

In addition to graphing equations, we can graph level surfaces of functions of three variables.

EXAMPLE: Sketch the level curves of $w = x^2 + z^2 - y^2$ corresponding to 0, 1, and −1.

SOLUTION: We use `ContourPlot3D` to graph the level surfaces corresponding to 0, 1, and −1, naming the results `cp1`, `cp2`, and `cp3`, respectively. The resulting three graphs are displayed as a `GraphicsArray`.

```
cp1=ContourPlot3D[x^2+z^2-y^2,{x,-2,2},{y,-2,2},{z,-2,2},
        DisplayFunction->Identity];
cp2=ContourPlot3D[x^2+z^2-y^2,{x,-2,2},{y,-2,2},{z,-2,2},
        Contours->{1.},
        DisplayFunction->Identity];
cp3=ContourPlot3D[x^2+z^2-y^2,{x,-2,2},{y,-2,2},{z,-2,2},
        Contours->{-1.},
        DisplayFunction->Identity];
Show[GraphicsArray[{cp1,cp2,cp3}]]
```

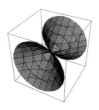 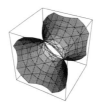 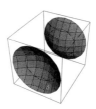

7.3 Graphics

Graphing in Polar Coordinates

Loading the **Graphics** package enables the user to take advantage of several commands which will improve the graphing capabilities previously available. The first command discussed below, `PolarPlot`, allows for the graphing of functions given in polar coordinates (r,θ). This command is entered as

```
PolarPlot[function[var],{var,var1,var2},options],
```

where `var` represents the angular coordinate θ and `var` varies from `var1` to `var2`. This command produces the graph of the function `r=function[var]`.

EXAMPLE: Find the area of the region between the inner and outer loops of the limacon $r = 1 + 2\sin t$.

SOLUTION: We begin by defining $r = 1 + 2\sin t$ and then using the commands `PolarPlot` and `Plot` to graph r in both polar and rectangular coordinates. The polar graph is on the left; the rectangular graph is on the right.

```
r[t_]=1+2Sin[t];
pp1=PolarPlot[1+2Sin[t],{t,0,2Pi},Ticks->{{-1,1},{1,2,3}},
      DisplayFunction->Identity];
p2=Plot[r[t],{t,-Pi/6,2Pi},DisplayFunction->Identity];
Show[GraphicsArray[{pp1,p2}]]
```

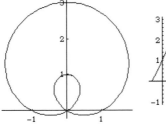 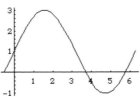

The area of the outer loop of the limacon is given by

$$\frac{1}{2}\int_{-\pi/6}^{7\pi/6}\left(r(t)\right)^2 dt = \frac{1}{2}\int_{-\pi/6}^{7\pi/6}\left(1+2\sin t\right)^2 dt\,,$$

computed below with `Integrate` and named `outer`.

```
outer=1/2Integrate[r[t]^2,{t,-Pi/6,7Pi/6}]

3 Sqrt[3] + 4 Pi
----------------
       2
```

The area of the inner loop of the limacon is given by

$$\frac{1}{2}\int_{7\pi/6}^{11\pi/6}\left(r(t)\right)^2 dt = \frac{1}{2}\int_{7\pi/6}^{11\pi/6}\left(1+2\sin t\right)^2 dt\,,$$

computed below with `Integrate` and named `inner`.

```
inner=1/2Integrate[r[t]^2,{t,7Pi/6,11Pi/6}]

-3 Sqrt[3] + 2 Pi
-----------------
        2
```

Thus, the desired area is given by subtracting `inner` from `outer` as done below.

```
area=outer-inner

3 Sqrt[3] - 2 Pi   3 Sqrt[3] + 4 Pi
---------------- + ----------------
       2                  2

Simplify[area]
area//N

3 Sqrt[3] + Pi
8.33775
```

■

`PolarPlot`, in the same way as commands like `Plot` and `ParametricPlot`, will graph several curves. Entering

```
PolarPlot[{r1[theta],r2[theta],...},{theta,theta0,theta1}]
```

graphs the curves $r_1(\theta), r_2(\theta), \dots$ in polar coordinates for $\theta_0 \le \theta \le \theta_1$.

EXAMPLE: Find the area inside the graph of $r = 1$ and outside the graph of $r = \cos 3t$.

SOLUTION: Below, we use `PolarPlot` and `Plot` to graph the curves $r = 1$ and $r = \cos 3t$ in both polar and rectangular coordinates.

```
Clear[r]
r[t_]=Cos[3t];
pp3=PolarPlot[{1,r[t]},{t,0,2Pi},Ticks->{{-1,1},{-1,1}},
     DisplayFunction->Identity];
p4=Plot[{1,r[t]},{t,-Pi/6,2Pi},Ticks->{Automatic,{-1,1}},
     DisplayFunction->Identity];
Show[GraphicsArray[{pp3,p4}]]
```

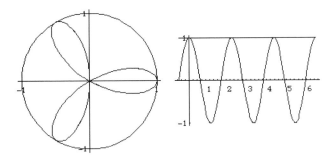

The area of the unit circle is π, while the area of the three-leafed rose is given by

$$\frac{3}{2}\int_{-\pi/6}^{\pi/6}\left(r(t)\right)^2 dt = \frac{3}{2}\int_{-\pi/6}^{\pi/6}\cos^2 3t\, dt$$

because the area of one leaf is given by $\dfrac{1}{2}\displaystyle\int_{-\pi/6}^{\pi/6}\left(r(t)\right)^2 dt = \dfrac{1}{2}\displaystyle\int_{-\pi/6}^{\pi/6}\cos^2 3t\, dt$. These values are computed below in `circle` and `rose`, respectively. The desired area is then given by subtracting the area of the three-leafed rose from the area of the circle.

```
circle=Pi
rose=3/2 Integrate[r[t]^2,{t,-Pi/6,Pi/6}]//Together
area=circle-rose//Together
N[area]

   Pi
   Pi
   --
   4
   3 Pi
   ----
    4
   2.35619
```

■

Creating Charts

Bar graphs can be drawn with BarChart[list]. For each number in list, Mathematica draws a rectangle of that height. These rectangles are drawn in order from left to right. The position of the element is given beneath each rectangle.

EXAMPLE: Energy consumption (in quadrillion Btu) by end-use sector for selected years is shown in the following table. Create a bar chart representing this data.

Year	Residential and Commercial	Industrial	Transportation
1975	24.143	31.528	18.605
1980	25.653	30.609	19.695
1985	26.682	27.200	20.067
1990	28.857	29.904	25.528

Source: *The World Almanac and Book of Facts,* 1993

SOLUTION: We first define the lists res, ind, and tra, representing the energy consumption of residential and commercial users, industrial users, and transportation users, respectively. We then use BarChart to create a bar chart representing the data. The option

```
BarStyle->{GrayLevel[.2],GrayLevel[.4],GrayLevel[.6]}
```

indicates that the bars corresponding to the first set of data, res, are graphed in dark gray, those corresponding the second set, ind, are displayed somewhat lighter, and those corresponding to the third set, tra, are the lightest. The option

```
BarLabels->{"1975","1980","1985","1990"}
```

indicates that the bars are to be labeled 1975, 1980, 1985, and 1990, corresponding to the years given in the table.

```
<<Graphics`Graphics`
res={24.143,25.653,26.682,28.857};
ind={31.528,30.609,27.200,29.904};
tra={18.605,19.695,20.067,25.528};

BarChart[res,ind,tra,
        BarStyle->{GrayLevel[.2],GrayLevel[.4],GrayLevel[.6]},
        BarLabels->{"1975","1980","1985","1990"}]
```

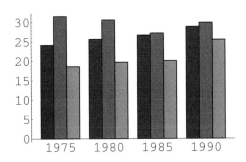

∎

Pie charts are created by making use of the `PieChart[list]` command found in the **Graphics** package.

EXAMPLE: According to the Department of the Treasury, major outlays of Federal expenditures as a percentage of the Federal budget in fiscal year 1990 are shown in the following table. Make a pie chart representing this data.

Purpose	Percent of Budget
Social programs	12%
Law enforcement and general government	2%
Social security, Medicare, and other retirement	31%
Defense, veterans, and foreign affairs	27%
Net interest on the debt	14%
Physical, human, and community development	14%

SOLUTION: We first define `data` to be the list of numbers corresponding to that given in the table. We then use `PieChart` to construct three pie charts representing the data, `pc1`, `pc2`, and `pc3`, and display all three with `Show` and `GraphicsArray`. In `pc2`, the option

```
PieExploded->All
```

indicates that the pie chart be "exploded" while in `pc3` the option

```
PieExploded->{2,.3}
```

indicates that only the second wedge be removed a distance of approximately 0.3 units out of the pie.

```
data={12,2,31,27,14,14};

pc1=PieChart[data,DisplayFunction->Identity];
pc2=PieChart[data,PieExploded->All,DisplayFunction->Identity];
pc3=PieChart[data,PieExploded->{2,.3},DisplayFunction->Identity];
Show[GraphicsArray[{pc1,pc2,pc3}]]
```

7.4 ImplicitPlot

This package includes the command

```
ImplicitPlot[equation,{x,xmin,xmax}]
```

which graphs the implicit equation, `equation`, from x=xmin to x=xmax. The set of y-values displayed may be specified by entering the command

```
ImplicitPlot[equation,{x,xmin,xmax},{y,ymin,ymax}].
```

When graphing relatively simple equations, like those solvable using `Solve`, it is not necessary to specify the y-values in the `ImplicitPlot` command. When `Solve` cannot solve an equation, it is usually necessary to specify both the x- and y-values. In these cases, `ImplicitPlot` uses the same method to produce the graph as `ContourPlot`. However, `ContourPlot` may produce better results.

EXAMPLE: Graph the equation $y^2 - 2x^4 + 2x^6 - x^8 = 0$ for $-1.5 \leq x \leq 1.5$.

SOLUTION: After loading the **ImplicitPlot** package, we define eq to be the equation $y^2 - 2x^4 + 2x^6 - x^8 = 0$ and then use `ImplicitPlot` to graph eq for $-1.5 \leq x \leq 1.5$.

```
<<Graphics`ImplicitPlot`
eq=y^2-x^4+2x^6-x^8==0;
ImplicitPlot[eq,{x,-1.5,1.5},Ticks->{{-1,1},{-1,1}}]
```

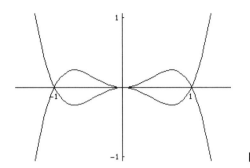

Implicit equations can be plotted simultaneously, as with the command `Plot`, with

```
ImplicitPlot[{eq1,eq2,...,eqn},{x,xmin,xmax}]
```

and

```
ImplicitPlot[{eq1,eq2,...,eqn},{x,xmin,xmax},{ymin,ymax}].
```

This is shown below. Recall that a double equals sign (==) must be used to separate the left and right-hand sides with each equation.

EXAMPLE: Graph the equations $x^2 + y^2 = 1$ and $4x^2 - y^2 = 1$ for $-1.5 \leq x \leq 1.5$.

SOLUTION: Below we use `ImplicitPlot` to graph the equations together on the same axes. The graph of $x^2 + y^2 = 1$ is the circle, while the graph of $4x^2 - y^2 = 1$ is the hyperbola.

```
ImplicitPlot[{x^2+y^2==1,4x^2-y^2==1},{x,-1.5,1.5},
        Ticks->{{-1,1},{-1,1}}]
```

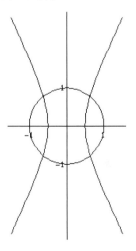

`ImplicitPlot` can be used to graph conic sections.

EXAMPLE: A **conic section** is a graph of the equation

$$Ax^2 + Bxy + Cy^2 + Dx + Ey + F = 0.$$

Except when the conic is degenerate, the conic $Ax^2 + Bxy + Cy^2 + Dx + Ey + F = 0$ is a

(a) **Ellipse** or circle if $B^2 - 4AC < 0$;

(b) **Parabola** if $B^2 - 4AC = 0$; or

(c) **Hyperbola** if $B^2 - 4AC > 0$.

Graph the conic section $ax^2 + bxy + cy^2 = 1$ for $-4 \le x \le 4$ for a, b, and c equal to all possible combinations of -1, 1, and 2.

SOLUTION: We begin by defining `conic` to be the equation $ax^2 + bxy + cy^2 = 1$ and then use `Permutations` to produce all possible orderings of the list of numbers $\{-1,1,2\}$, naming the resulting output `vals`.

```
Clear[a,b,c]
conic=a x^2+b x y+c y^2==1;

vals=Permutations[{-1,1,2}]

    {{-1, 1, 2}, {-1, 2, 1}, {1, -1, 2}, {1, 2, -1},

     {2, -1, 1}, {2, 1, -1}}
```

Next we define the function p. Given a1, b1, and c1, p defines `toplot` to be the equation obtained by replacing a, b, and c in `conic` by a1, b1, and c1, respectively. Then, `toplot` is graphed for $-4 \le x \le 4$. p returns a `Graphics` object, which is not displayed, because the option `DisplayFunction->Identity` is included.

```
p[{a1_,b1_,c1_}]:=Module[{toplot},
       toplot=conic /. {a->a1,b->b1,c->c1};
       ImplicitPlot[toplot,{x,-4,4},Ticks->None,
       DisplayFunction->Identity]
                                              ]
```

We then use `Map` to compute p for each ordered triple in `vals`. The resulting output, named `graphs`, is a set of six graphics objects.

```
graphs=Map[p,vals]

    {-Graphics-, -Graphics-, -Graphics-, -Graphics-,

      -Graphics-, -Graphics-}
```

`Partition` is then used to partition graphs into three element subsets. The resulting 2×3 array of graphics objects named `toshow` is displayed with `Show` and `GraphicsArray`.

```
toshow=Partition[graphs,3];
Show[GraphicsArray[toshow]]
```

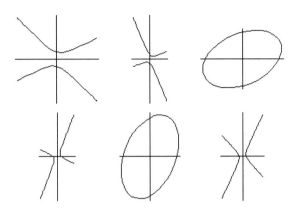

7.5 MultipleListPlot and Graphics3D

The packages **MultipleListPlot** and **Graphics3D** contain several commands for graphing lists and manipulating graphics objects.

In the package **MultipleListPlot**, the function `MultipleListPlot` with syntax

```
MultipleListPlot[list1,list2,...]
```

graphs the lists `list1`, `list2`, ... on the same graph.

In the package **Graphics3D**, the function

```
BarChart3D[{list1,list2, ...}]
```

makes a three-dimensional bar chart using the heights given in `list1`, `list2`, ...

> **EXAMPLE:** In Section 7.2, we defined the lists `res`, `ind`, and `tra`, representing the energy consumption of residential and commercial users, industrial users, and transportation users, respectively, for certain years. Create both a two- and three-dimensional plot representing this data.

SOLUTION: After loading the **MultipleListPlot** package, we redefine the lists `res`, `ind`, and `tra`. We then use `MultipleListPlot` to graph these lists in `m1` and `m2`. In `m2`, the option `PlotJoined->True` causes consecutive points to be connected with line segments.

```
<<Graphics`MultipleListPlot`
```

```
res={24.143,25.653,26.682,28.857};
ind={31.528,30.609,27.200,29.904};
tra={18.605,19.695,20.067,25.528};

m1=MultipleListPlot[res,ind,tra,DisplayFunction->Identity];
m2=MultipleListPlot[res,ind,tra,PlotJoined->True,
        DisplayFunction->Identity];
Show[GraphicsArray[{m1,m2}]]
```

Next, we load the package **Graphics3D** and use `BarChart3D` to construct a three-dimensional bar chart representing the data.

```
<<Graphics`Graphics3D`
```

```
BarChart3D[{res,ind,tra}]
```

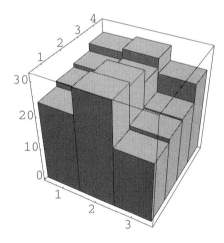

7.6 PlotField and PlotField3D

The package **PlotField** contains the commands `PlotVectorField` and `PlotGradientField,` which are useful in many areas of physics and engineering. The command

```
PlotVectorField[vector[x,y],{x,xmin,xmax},{y,ymin,ymax}]
```

graphs the vector field given by the vector-valued function, `vector[x,y]`. This is illustrated below.

> **EXAMPLE:** Graph the vector field given by the vector-valued function $\langle y, (1-x^2)y - x \rangle$ on the rectangle $[-2,2] \times [-4,4]$.

SOLUTION: After loading the PlotField package, we use `PlotVectorField` to graph the vector field. The option

```
ScaleFunction->(2#&)
```

instructs Mathematica to draw each vector at twice its true magnitude.

```
<<Graphics`PlotField`
PlotVectorField[{y,(1-x^2)y-x},{x,-2,2},{y,-4,4},
      ScaleFunction->(2#&),AspectRatio->1]
```

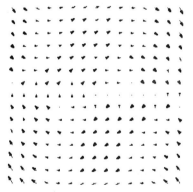

■

The command

```
PlotGradientField[function[x,y],{x,xmin,xmax},{y,ymin,ymax}]
```

graphs the gradient field of the function, `function[x,y]`. This is done by first computing the gradient of `function[x,y]` (which yields a vector field) and then plotting the gradient.

EXAMPLE: Graph the gradient field of $\dfrac{(1-x^2)y-x}{y}$ on the rectangle $[-2,2]\times[-4,4]$.

SOLUTION: In spite of the error messages, which are not all displayed here, generated when Mathematica samples points with the y-coordinate equal to zero, the graph produced with `PlotGradientField` is correct.

```
PlotGradientField[((1-x^2)y-x)/y,{x,-2,2},{y,-4,4},AspectRatio->1]
```

```
                                       1
        Power::infy: Infinite expression - encountered.
                                       0
                                       1
        Power::infy: Infinite expression - encountered.
                                       0
```

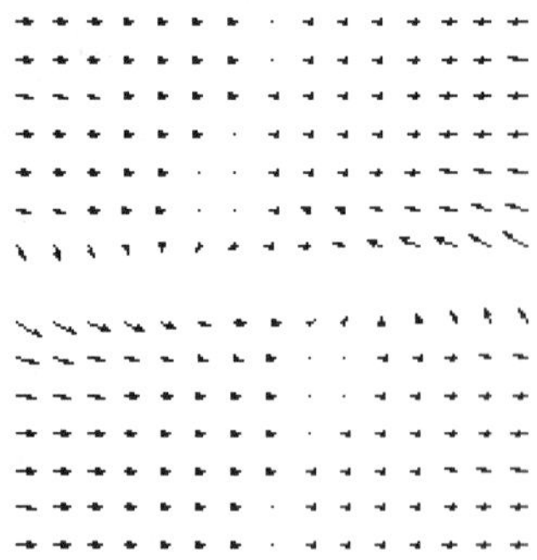

Vector fields can be plotted in three dimensions as well. The commands needed to plot these fields are found in the **PlotField3D** package. The syntax for the `PlotGradientField3D` and `PlotVectorField3D` commands are similar to those used in the two-dimensional cases discussed above with the addition of a z-component.

Vectors with heads are displayed in the final graphics object when the option

```
VectorHeads->True
```

is included.

EXAMPLE: Graph the vector field $\langle -11x+4y+6z,10x-4y+5z,5x+8y-6z\rangle$ on the parallelepiped $[1,3]\times[0,6]\times[1,5]$.

SOLUTION: We use `PlotVectorField3D` to graph the vector field on $[1,3] \times [0,6] \times [1,5]$. The vectors are drawn with arrows since the option

```
VectorHeads->True
```

is included.

```
<<Graphics`PlotField3D`
PlotVectorField3D[{-11x+4y+6z,10x-4y+5z,5x+8y-6z},
      {x,1,3},{y,0,6},{z,1,5},VectorHeads->True]
```

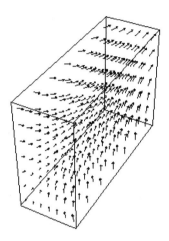

■

Our last example illustrates the use of `PlotGradientField3D`.

EXAMPLE: Graph the gradient field of $x^2 + y^2 + z - 4$ on the cube $[-2,2] \times [-2,2] \times [-2,2]$.

SOLUTION: `PlotGradientField3D` is used to first compute the gradient of $x^2 + y^2 + z - 4$ and then graph the resulting vector field on the cube $[-2,2] \times [-2,2] \times [-2,2]$.

```
PlotGradientField3D[x^2+y^2+z-4,{x,-2,2},{y,-2,2},{z,-2,2},
      VectorHeads->True]
```

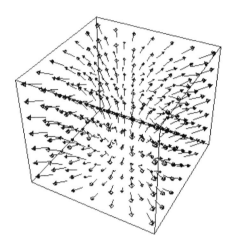

■

7.7 Polyhedra and Shapes

Pictures of polyhedra can be produced with **Polyhedra**. Many geometrical properties of polyhedra are stored in this package, so some pictures can be obtained by specifying a desired polyhedra with Show[Polyhedron[shape]]. Stored polyhedra include the icosahedron, dodecahedron, octahedron, cube, and tetrahedron. shape is one of the following: Icosahedron, Dodecahedron, Octahedron, Cube, or Tetrahedron . If unspecified, the center is taken to be (0,0,0).

EXAMPLE: Display a cube with center (0,0,0).

SOLUTION: A cube centered at the origin in produced below.

```
<<Graphics`Polyhedra`
Show[Polyhedron[Cube]]
```

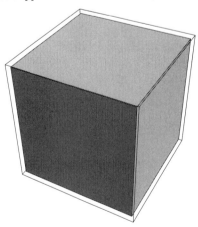

■

Several polyhedra can be shown simultaneously and, thus, complicated three-dimensional objects can be constructed. However, another command which involves more options must first be introduced. Three-dimensional graphics objects are created but not displayed with

```
Graphics3D[shape[{x0,y0,z0},scale]]
```

where **shape** is the desired **shape** from the list of stored polyhedra: **Icosahedron**, **Dodecahedron**, **Octahedron**, **Cube**, and **Tetrahedron**. **{x0,y0,z0}** represents the center, and **scale** adjusts the size. The default value of **scale** is 1, so **scale** >1 produces a larger polyhedron and **scale** <1, a smaller one.

EXAMPLE: Display a dodecahedron, octahedron, and tetrahedron in the same graph.

SOLUTION: The first command below creates and stores (as **fig1**) the graphics of a dodecahedron centered at the origin, using scale = $1/2$. Because **Show** is not used, the picture is not displayed. Next, the graphics of an octahedron centered at **{Cos[Pi/3],Sin[Pi/3],0}** and scale = $1/3$ is created and stored as **fig2**. Also, a tetrahedron with center **{Cos[2Pi/3],Sin[2Pi/3],1/3}** and scale = $1/4$ is stored as **fig3**. Because the graphics of each polyhedra was named, they can be shown simultaneously with **Show[fig1,fig2,fig3,Boxed->False]**.

```
fig1=Graphics3D[Dodecahedron[{0,0,0},1/2]];
fig2=Graphics3D[Octahedron[{Cos[Pi/3],Sin[Pi/3],0},1/3]];
fig3=Graphics3D[Tetrahedron[{Cos[2Pi/3],Sin[2Pi/3],1/3},1/4]];
Show[fig1,fig2,fig3,Boxed->False]
```

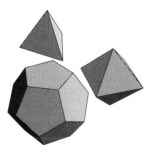

■

Another command available in **Polyhedra** is

```
Stellate[Polyhedron[shape],ratio]
```

where s h a p e is again one of the following: Icosahedron, Dodecahedron, Octahedron, Cube, or Tetrahedron. This takes the symbolic representation of the polyhedron and represents it as a stellated polyhedron. (Each face is replaced by a stellate.)

> **EXAMPLE:** Use Stellate to create a stellated dodecahedron for various ratios.

SOLUTION: We define the function a so that given i, a[i] generates the graphics object Stellate[Polyhedron[Dodecahedron],i], then shows the object without a box. Note that the result of a[i] is a graphics object that is not displayed because the option DisplayFunction->Identity is included. We then use Table to generate a[i] for i-values ranging from 0.25 to 2 in steps of 1.75/8. The resulting set of nine graphics objects, moreshapes, is partitioned into three element subsets with Partition and the resulting 3×3 array of graphics objects is displayed with Show and GraphicsArray. Notice how the pictures change with i. If i <1, the object is concave. If i >1, the object is convex.

The graphics generated by the Do loop

```
Do[Show[a[i],
        DisplayFunction->$DisplayFunction],{i,.25,2,1.75/24}]
```

can be animated to observe the changes which take place as i changes.

```
Clear[a]
a[i_]:=Show[Stellate[Polyhedron[Dodecahedron],i],
        Boxed->False,DisplayFunction->Identity];
moreshapes=Table[a[i],{i,.25,2,1.75/8}];
toshow=Partition[moreshapes,3];
Show[GraphicsArray[toshow]]
```

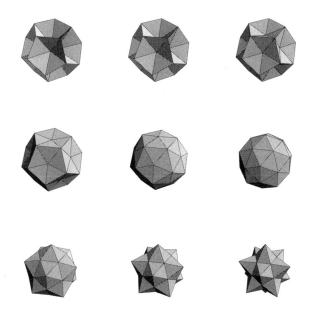

■

Shapes contains commands which produce the graphics of many shapes commonly used in mathematics. As with the all graphics objects, different shapes may be combined and shown simultaneously to create more complicated objects.

Illustrated first below is

```
MoebiusStrip[outerradius,innerradius,n]
```

where `innerradius` and `outerradius` are the inner and outer radii, respectively, and the Moebius strip is approximated using 2n polygons. (`MoebiusStrip` actually produces a list of polygons which are displayed with `Show` and `Graphics3D`.)

EXAMPLE: Generate a Moebius strip with inner radius 2 and outer radius 4.

SOLUTION: We use the command `MoebiusStrip[4,2,30]` to generate the Moebius strip with inner radius 2 and outer radius 4 with 60 polygons. The list of polygons created with `MoebiusStrip` is visualized with `Show` and `Graphics3D`.

```
<<Graphics`Shapes`
Show[Graphics3D[MoebiusStrip[4,2,30]]]
```

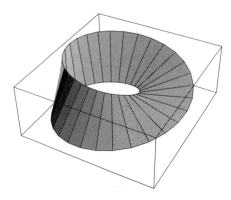

Another shape which can be approximated in this package is that of a torus. This is accomplished with

```
Torus[outerradius,innerradius,m,n]
```

where m times n polygons are used to approximate the shape of the torus.

EXAMPLE: Generate a torus with inner radius 0.5 and outer radius 1.

SOLUTION: A torus of inner radius .5 and outer radius 1 is approximated with 300 polygons and called `torusone`. To show that `torusone` is a list of polygons, we use `Short` to display an abbreviated two-line form of `torusone`. We then display `torusone` with `Show[Graphics3D[torusone]]`.

```
torusone=Torus[1,.5,20,15];
Short[torusone,2]
```

```
{Polygon[{{1.38547, 0.450168, 0.203368}, <<2>>,

    {1.17855, 0.85627, 0.203368}}], <<299>>}
```

```
Show[Graphics3D[torusone]]
```

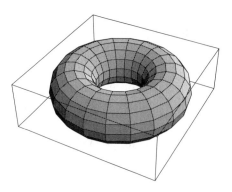

The command `Sphere[r,m,n]` produces an approximation of a sphere of radius r using m times n polygons.

Several other commands are available for visualizing the lists of polygons produced by the commands found in **Shapes**. The command `WireFrame[polygonlist]` replaces each polygon in `polygonlist` by closed lines, so the shape resembles that of a wire frame when visualized.

EXAMPLE: Show a sphere of radius 1 surrounded by a sphere of radius 2.

SOLUTION: The approximation of a sphere of radius 1 is obtained below using 225 polygons; the resulting `Graphics3D` object is named `sphereone`. A list of 144 polygons is used to approximate a sphere of radius 2; the resulting graphics object is named `spheretwo`. `WireFrame` is then applied to the `Graphics3D` object `spheretwo` and the result is named `wiretwo`. The shapes `sphereone` and `wiretwo` are viewed simultaneously using the command `Show`. (The `Show` option, `Boxed->False`, causes no box to be drawn around the sphere.)

```
sphereone=Graphics3D[Sphere[1,15,15]];
spheretwo=Graphics3D[Sphere[2,12,12]];
wiretwo=WireFrame[spheretwo];
Show[sphereone,wiretwo,Boxed->False]
```

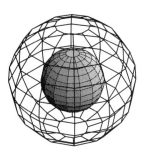

∎

Another shape that can be graphed with **Shapes** is `Helix[r,h,m,n]`, which approximates a helix with half height h and m turns using m * n (where n =20r) polygons.

> **EXAMPLE:** Generate a helix with half height 3 and 5 turns.

SOLUTION: Shown below is a helix of half height 3 with 5 turns. The list of
polygons which approximate the helix is found in `helixtwo`; `Show[helixtwo]`
displays the helix.

```
helixtwo=Graphics3D[Helix[2,3,5,40]];
Show[helixtwo]
```

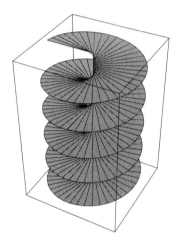

■

Shapes also contains several commands to manipulate shapes. For example,
`RotateShape[shape,xrotate,yrotate,zrotate]` causes `shape` to be rotated
`xrotate` units about the x-axis, `yrotate` units about the y-axis, and `zrotate` units
about the z-axis.

> **EXAMPLE:** Rotate the helix generated in the previous example about the z-axis.

SOLUTION: Below, we redefine `helixtwo` and then use `Table` to generate the
graphics objects

```
RotateShape[helixtwo,0,0,n Pi/6]
```

for n from 0 to 12 in steps of 12/8. The resulting list of nine graphs is named
`graphs` and then partitioned into three-element subsets with `Partition`. The
resulting 3×3 array of graphics cells is displayed with `Show` and
`GraphicsArray`.

```
helixtwo=Graphics3D[Helix[2,3,5,40]];
graphs=Table[RotateShape[helixtwo,0,0,n Pi/6],{n,0,12,12/8}];
toshow=Partition[graphs,3];
Show[GraphicsArray[toshow]]
```

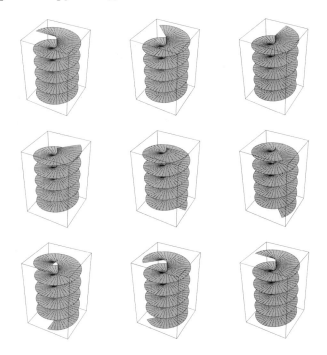

The Do loop

```
Do[Show[RotateShape[helixtwo,0,0,n Pi/6]],{n,0,12}]
```

produces 13 graphics cells which can be animated to view the rotation of the helix about the z-axis. ■

Closely related to RotateShape is the command

```
TranslateShape[shape,{x0,y0,z0}]
```

which translates shape x0 units along the x-axis, y0 units along the y-axis, and z0 units along the z-axis.

> **EXAMPLE:** Generate an animation in which one sphere is revolving about another.

SOLUTION: Below we define sphereone and spheretwo to be spheres of radii 1.5 and 0.5, respectively. For sphereone, we use 144 polygons; since spheretwo is smaller, we use a small number, 64.

```
sphereone=Graphics3D[Sphere[1.5,12,12]];
spheretwo=Graphics3D[Sphere[.5,8,8]];
```

Next we define `tr`. Given `t`, `tr[t]` yields the `Graphics3D` object obtained by translating `spheretwo` 2.5cos*t* units along the x-axis, 2.5sin*t* units along the y-axis, and 0.75+0.25sin*t* units along the z-axis. `m` is defined to show both `sphereone` and `tr[t]`. Note that the result of entering `m[t]` is not displayed since the option `DisplayFunction->Identity` is included.

```
tr[t_]:=TranslateShape[spheretwo,{2.5Cos[t],2.5Sin[t],.75+.25Sin[2t]}]
m[t_]:=Show[{sphereone,tr[t]},Boxed->False,DisplayFunction->Identity]
```

A set of nine graphs is then generated with `Table` and partitioned in the three element subsets with `Partition`. The resulting 3×3 array of graphics cells, `toshow`, is displayed with `Show` and `GraphicsArray`.

```
graphs=Table[m[t],{t,0,2Pi,2Pi/8}];
toshow=Partition[graphs,3];
Show[GraphicsArray[toshow]]
```

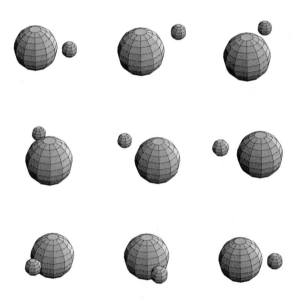

The `Do` loop

```
Do[Show[m[t],
        DisplayFunction->$DisplayFunction],{t,0,2Pi,2Pi/14}]]
```

generates 15 graphics objects which can be animated. ■

Selected References

Abell, Martha L. and Braselton, James P., *Differential Equations with Mathematica*, Academic Press, 1992.

Abell, Martha L. and Braselton, James P., *The Mathematica Handbook*, Academic Press, 1992.

Blachman, Nancy, *Mathematica: A Practical Approach*, Prentice-Hall , 1992.

Blachman, Nancy, *Mathematica: Quick Reference, Version 2*, published by Variable Symbols and distributed by Addison-Wesley, 1992.

Brown, Donald T., Davis, Bill, Porta, Horacio, and Uhl, J. Jerry, *Calculus & Mathematica*, Preliminary Edition, Part I, Addison-Wesley, 1990.

Cheney, Ward and Kincaid, David, *Numerical Mathematics and Computing*, Second Edition, Brooks/Cole Publishing, 1985

Crandall, Richard E., *Mathematica for the Sciences*, Addison-Wesley, 1991.

Crooke, Philip and Ratcliffe, John, *A Guidebook to Calculus with Mathematica*, Wadsworth, 1991.

Ellis, Wade and Lodi, Ed, *A Tutorial Introduction to Mathematica*, Brooks/Cole, 1990.

Gray, Theodore and Glynn, Jerry, *A Beginners Guide to Mathematica, Version 2*, Addison-Wesley, 1992.

Gray, Theodore and Glynn, Jerry, *Exploring Mathematics with Mathematica*, Addison-Wesley, 1991.

Hillier, Frederick S. and Lieberman, Gerald L., *Introduction to Operations Research*, Fifth Edition, McGraw-Hill Publishing, 1990.

Jordan, D. W. and Smith, P., *Nonlinear Ordinary Differential Equations*, Second Edition, Oxford University Press, 1988.

Kreyszig, Erwin, *Advanced Engineering Mathematics*, Seventh Edition, John Wiley & Sons , 1993.

Maeder, Roman, *Programming in Mathematica*, Second Edition, Addison-Wesley Publishing Co, 1991.

Mathematica in Education, (Paul Wellin, Editor, Department of Mathematics, Sonoma State University, 1801 East Cotati Avenue, Rohnert Park, California, 94928, E-Mail: wellin@sonoma.edu).

The Mathematica Journal, (Miller Freeman, Inc., 600 Harrison Street, San Francisco, California, 94107, Telephone: (707) 664-2368).

Powers, David L., *Boundary Value Problems*, Second Edition, Academic Press , 1979.

Skiena, Steven, *Implementing Discrete Mathematics: Combinatorics and Graph Theory with Mathematica*, Addison-Wesley, 1991.

Sparks, Arthur, Davenport, John, and Braselton, James, *Calculus Labs Using Mathematica*, HarperCollins College Publishers, 1993.

Strang, Gilbert, *Linear Algebra and its Applications*, Third Edition, Harcout Brace Jovanovich, 1988.

Vardi, Ilan, *Computational Recreations in Mathematica*, Addison-Wesley, 1991.

Vvedensky, Dimitri, *Partial Differential Equations with Mathematica*, Addison-Wesley,1992.

Wagon, Stan, *Mathematica in Action*, W. H. Freeman and Company, 1991.

Wolfram, Stephen, *Mathematica: A System for Doing Mathematics by Computer*, Second Edition, Addison-Wesley, 1991.

Zwillinger, Daniel, *Handbook of Differential Equations*, Second Edition, Academic Press , 1992.

Wolfram Research, Inc. also publishes the following technical reports:
    Guide to Standard Mathematica Packages;
    Mathematica Warning Messages;
    Installation Manual;
    Release Notes for Mathematica Version 2.2;
    The 3-Script File Format;
    MathLink Reference Guide;
    MathSource;
    PostScript generated by Mathematica;
    The Mathematica Compiler;
    Upgrading Packages to Mathematica 2.0; and
    Major New Features in Mathematica Version 2.2.

For purchasing information, contact Wolfram Research, Inc. at 100 Trade Center Drive, Champaign, IL 61820-7237. Telephone: (217) 398-0700, Fax: (217) 398-0747, E-Mail: info@wri.com.

Index

Palatino denotes topics; **Bold Palatino** denotes packages; `Courier` denotes commands

Palatino denotes topics; **Bold Palatino** denotes packages; Courier denotes commands

Palatino denotes topics; **Bold Palatino** denotes packages; Courier denotes commands

Palatino denotes topics; **Bold Palatino** denotes packages; Courier denotes commands

Palatino denotes topics; **Bold Palatino** denotes packages; `Courier` denotes commands

Palatino denotes topics; **Bold Palatino** denotes packages; `Courier` denotes commands

T...Risk Free!

One of the best ways to explore the power of *Mathematica* is to use it with the book you have just bought and other *Mathematica* books published by AP Professional.

If you don't have *Mathematica* on your computer yet, now is your chance to try it out for yourself, risk free. Order *Mathematica* today and use it to get your work done faster with accuracy you can count on. You will join the several hundred thousand scientists, engineers, educators, students, and other technical professionals around the world who put *Mathematica* to work as they complete projects every day.

To get your copy of *Mathematica* today, in the U.S. call Wolfram Research at **1-800-441-MATH (6284)**.*

If for any reason *Mathematica* does not meet your requirements, just return it to us within 30 days, and you will be issued full credit.

Mathematica is available on over 20 computer platforms, including Macintosh, MS-DOS, Windows, NEXTSTEP, and Unix workstations. Special pricing is available for academic institutions, site licenses, Mathematica teaching labs, and the student version of Mathematica.

*This offer is valid for direct orders through Wolfram Research in the U.S. and Canada only. Outside the U.S. and Canada, evaluation copies of Mathematica are available through your local reseller. For a list of resellers in your area, contact Wolfram Research.

Wolfram Research, Inc., 100 Trade Center Drive, Champaign, Illinois 61820-7237, USA
+1-800-441-MATH (U.S., Canada); +1-217-398-0700; fax: +1-217-398-0747; email: info@wri.com
For European inquiries:
Wolfram Research Europe Ltd., Evenlode Court, Main Road, Long Hanborough, Oxon OX8 2LA, United Kingdom; +44-(0)993-883400; fax: +44-(0)993-883800; email: info-euro@wri.com

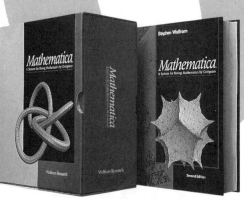

Wolfram Research

P-Code 102